The Green and the Gray

CIVIL WAR AMERICA
Gary W. Gallagher, Peter S. Carmichael, Caroline E. Janney, and Aaron Sheehan-Dean, editors

The Green and the Gray

THE IRISH IN THE

CONFEDERATE STATES

OF AMERICA

David T. Gleeson

THE UNIVERSITY OF NORTH CAROLINA PRESS Chapel Hill

Library of Congress Cataloging-in-Publication Data
Gleeson, David T.
The green and the gray : the Irish in the Confederate States of America / David T. Gleeson.
    pages cm — (Civil War America)
Includes bibliographical references and index.
ISBN 978-1-4696-0756-6 (cloth : alk. paper)
1. Irish American soldiers—Confederate States of America—History.
2. United States—History—Civil War, 1861–1865—Participation, Irish American. 3. Confederate States of America. Army—History. 4. Irish Americans—Southern States—History—19th century. 5. Immigrants—Southern States—History—19th century. 6. Irish Americans—Southern States—Social conditions—19th century. I. Title.
E585.175G56 2013
973.7'420899162—dc23
2013009241

Portions of this work appeared earlier, in somewhat different form, in "Another 'Lost Cause': The Irish in the South Remember the Confederacy," *Southern Cultures* 17 (Spring 2011): 50–74, reprinted by permission; "Irish Rebels, Southern Rebels: The Irish Confederates," in *Civil War Citizens: Race, Ethnicity, and Identity in America's Bloodiest Conflict*, edited by Susannah J. Ural (New York University Press © 2007), reprinted with permission; and "'To Live and Die [for] Dixie': Irish Civilians and the Confederate States of America," *Irish Studies Review* 18 (May 2010): 139–53, reprinted by permission of Taylor & Francis Ltd., www.tandfonline.com.

17 16 15 14 13   5 4 3 2 1

For Amy and Emma

Contents

Tables and Illustrations

Acknowledgments

My first thanks must go to David Perry and Gary Gallagher, who encouraged me to do this project. Since I began, their support and patience have been key to its successful completion. Other folk at the University of North Carolina Press, especially Cait Bell-Butterfield, John K. Wilson, and Ron Maner, have put a lot of work into the production and I am very grateful for that. Gallagher and one anonymous reader provided excellent criticism which helped me greatly improve the final product.

Beyond the Press, numerous people have been helpful with suggestions, sources, and support along the way. Jimmy and Brendan Buttimer have always been supportive and great sounding boards for all things Irish in the South. Their work on Irish Savannah, which I draw on in places in this book, is exemplary scholarship. They are great colleagues as well as great friends. Stephen White from Charleston has been an excellent guide to the Irish element of that city as a very welcoming presence there when I began the project in earnest. David Brown of the University of Manchester has been a long-time fellow researcher in the "plain folk of the Old South" and our numerous conversations at conferences, on research trips, and at football (the real kind!) matches have always aided me in honing my arguments. Other researchers of Irish America and the American South who have provided research leads and analytical insight include, Donald Beagle, Bryan Giemza, Jerry Hackett, Brian Kelly, Frank Towers, Bryan McGovern, Kerby Miller, Randall Miller, Vernon Burton, Malcolm Smith, Mike Thompson, Susannah Ural, Robert Rosen, Christian Keller, David Dangerfield, Miles Smith, Patrick Doyle, Denis Bergin, Bruce Nelson, Matt O'Brien, David Sim, Robert Cook, Mitchell Snay, Andrew Heath, Enrico Dallago, Bernadette Whelan, Úna Bromell, Laura Sandy, Jamie Woods, Jeff Kerr-Ritchie, Fionnghuala Sweeney, Davy Kincaid, Jim Gannon, Donald Williams, and the late David Heisser. My graduate school mentor, E. Stanly Godbold, remains a good friend and a supporter of all my work.

As always, numerous archivists and librarians, the historian's friends as I call them, at all the archives listed in the bibliography have been very helpful. Some went above and beyond their duty to researchers. John Coski and Teresa Roane at the Brockenbrough Library at the Museum of the Confederacy were particularly so, as was Gillian Brown at the Diocese of Savannah.

Paddy Fitzgerald, Christine Johnston, and Brian Lampkin of the Centre for Migration Studies at the Ulster American Folk Park were also very welcoming. Special mention must also be made of Brian Fahey of the Catholic Diocese of Charleston. He has been unfailing in fulfilling my numerous requests both in Charleston and from across the Atlantic Ocean.

Here at Northumbria University my deans, department head, and research leads have always been encouraging of the project. I received ample support and research leave to help me complete this book. Many thanks then must go to Lynn Dobbs, Don MacRaild, David Walker, and Sylvia Ellis. Don and Sylvia as well as other colleagues in my department, especially James McConnel, Tanja Bueltmann, Mike Cullinane, Joe Street, Kyle Hughes, Michael Bibler, Randall Stephens, and Brian Ward, have aided my analysis of all things racial, diasporic, and southern. My Ph.D. students, Brian Langley, Craig McLaughlan, and Peter O'Connor, keep me on my toes and are always good for stimulating discussions of the Civil War. This project began in the United States, and colleagues at my former institutions of work have also played a part in supporting my effort, especially Nancy White and Mike Price at Armstrong Atlantic State University and Simon Lewis, Jason Coy, Marvin Dulaney, Amy McCandless, Lee Drago, Bill Olejniczak, Moore Quinn, Dale Rosengarten, Sam Hines, and Cynthia Lowenthal at the College of Charleston. Graduate assistant at the College, Charles Wexler, did some valuable research on my behalf. Sam Thomas of the T. R. R. Cobb House, Lieutenant Colonel William Bell, USMC, of the Citadel, and Bucky Hoffman of Huntersville, North Carolina, provided some important research on Irish Confederates for me and I thank them for that. Various folk provided accommodation on my travels and I want to recognize especially Catherine Clinton, John Lally, Michael de Nie, Andy Pelland, and Maureen Halliday for doing so. I was also fortunate to receive research fellowships from the Virginia Historical Society and the Filson Historical Club. I am grateful for those and hope this book reflects well on their support.

Finally, I would like to thank my parents, Barry and Freda, and my brothers, Barry and Brian, who have always been very supportive of my scholarly endeavors. My parents provide a haven from the academic world when one needs a break. Barry and his wife Rodica have put me up on my numerous trips to the British Library in London, while Brian has done likewise for my visits to Dublin. Thanks lads!

Since this project began I have begun my own family, and although my wife Amy joined me well into the research and writing of this book, her love and support have been a source of inspiration to me. Our daughter Emma, though too young to understand why I am at the computer all the time, has been fun to watch play around me as I write. Though she doesn't know it yet, her mark is on this book too. For all their love, understanding, and patience I therefore dedicate it to them.

The Green and the Gray

The Fighting Irish

Irish participation in the Confederate experiment represents a complex and imperfectly understood element of the American Civil War. Much less numerous than their countrymen who took part in the Union war effort, Irish Confederates still present serious questions about what it meant to be Irish and American in the mid-nineteenth century. Those Irish who lived in the southern slave states, especially the eleven that seceded from the Union in 1860 and 1861, had to adjust to a third identity, that of Confederate. Though very few had any direct connection with slavery, thousands supported a new republic that had the explicit aim of preserving that "peculiar institution." Their reasons for doing so complicate our view of national identity in this era of the nation-state.

This book then is an attempt not merely to outline the Irish involvement with the Confederacy but to analyze its significance, for both the Irish and the Confederacy. The war experience and its aftermath were crucial to the integration of Irish immigrants into white society in the South. Wars in general, and the commemoration of them, provide great opportunities for scholars to understand better the process of immigrant acculturation. And that process can tell us a lot about the values of the host community. Along with a better understanding of the Irish experience of the South, then, this study will add to our comprehension of the Confederacy and Irish America in general, ultimately challenging popular images of each.

One of the most widely held ethnic stereotypes of the Irish in America is that of the "Fighting Irish," always willing to fight and die for causes domestic and foreign. During the Civil War there were numerous Confederate examples of the insanely brave Irish "Johnny Reb." Dominick Spellman of Charleston, South Carolina, who fought with the "Irish Volunteers," Company K of the 1st South Carolina Infantry Regiment (Gregg's), is a classic example. His Confederate career in some ways personifies the complicated nature of Irish participation in the war. An Irish-born immigrant laborer, the illiterate Spellman never came close to owning any real property, never mind a slave. Nevertheless, he and his fellow Irishmen in the Volunteers joined the Confederate army immediately after Fort Sumter, enlisting "for the [duration of the] war" rather than the typical twelve months. His personal reasons for doing so are unknown, but he seemed to display an amazing ardor for the cause. In the regiment's first serious action in Virginia at the Battle of Gaines's Mill in June 1862, Spellman bravely picked up the battle flag to rally his regiment after three previous bearers had been shot down. His commander, Colonel D. H. Hamilton, mentioned the Irishman's bravery in his report, and Spellman earned the great, if dangerous, honor of becoming the permanent regimental color sergeant.[1]

A few months later Spellman confirmed himself as a fine Confederate soldier. At the Second Battle of Manassas in August, the Volunteers found themselves pinned down by enemy sharpshooters. Spellman had carried the flag with distinction that day, exposing himself to being wounded or killed. Having faced hazardous fire on his feet throughout the battle, he did not take kindly to having to find cover from sharpshooters. After the war, his commander, Edward McCrady Jr., recalled the situation: Spellman apparently grew tired of hiding and gave "the colors to the corporal next to him and seizing his musket quietly walked out in front of the regiment." The Irishman proceeded to aim and shoot at the enemy, casually turning to his fellow Confederates to say, "'dropped that one.'" He then reloaded and shot again, and to "the astonishment of his comrades" hit another Union opponent. Finally, as he reloaded to fire a third time, the stunned Federal soldiers returned fire. One bullet removed "the butt of his musket from his face" and another "felled him." Spellman survived but was severely wounded, and he spent the rest of 1862 and all of 1863 recuperating. He recovered, however, to return to the Volunteers in January 1864.[2]

In this incident at Manassas, Spellman fulfilled the commonly held view of the Irish soldier in nineteenth-century America: the brave, but often foolhardy, fighter. He had also displayed a degree of Confederate loyalty that impressed many natives of the South who might have been skeptical of the commitment of nonslaveholders and immigrants to the southern cause. Company commander McCrady, whose father had signed the South Carolina secession ordinance, certainly thought him the archetypal Irish Confederate and a fine representative of the regular Confederate soldier.[3]

Yet, the reality of Spellman's Confederate identity was more complicated than the reminiscences of McCrady might suggest. After his return to the now much-diminished Irish Volunteers, Spellman was captured at the siege at Petersburg by Union forces on July 29, 1864. Transported to Point Lookout, Maryland, he was eventually sent to the newly established prison camp in Elmira, New York, west of Binghamton. Elmira became notorious as the "death-camp" of the North. Constructed to hold 4,000 to 5,000 prisoners, it eventually held over 12,000, and almost a quarter of those prisoners ultimately died from disease, exposure, and malnutrition. Within a month of arriving there, Spellman had denounced the Confederacy and asked to take the "Oath of Allegiance" to the United States. He explained to his captors that he was merely "an Irish immigrant" who had been "conscripted" into Confederate service in late 1863. According to his interrogators, Spellman stated that upon "refusing to serve in the army, [he] was confined to prison" and agreed to go back to his regiment only to gain his release from incarceration. He also pointed out that he had "surrendered voluntarily" to the Union army and as an Irishman "had lots of friends in the North." The implication was that, if released, Spellman would not return south, but instead go to Irish friends in the North. He was, of course, telling bald-faced lies. He had volunteered in 1861 and served with distinction until his capture. Fortunately, for his future role as the Irish Confederate hero, the Union authorities refused to believe Sergeant Spellman and did not parole him until May 17, 1865, well after his regiment's surrender with General Robert E. Lee at Appomattox.[4]

The representation of the unfailingly brave rebel warrior, however, dominates most of the works published on the Irish Confederates. It's a tough image to challenge because the idea of the Irish as a "martial people" has some basis in reality and very deep roots in Irish and Irish American identity. Irish military tradition has a long pedigree going back to ancient times. The *Táin*, Ireland's version of the *Iliad*, tells stories of legendary battles and the heroes who fought them. One of the most famous of these tales tells of Cúchulainn, Ireland's Achilles and its most famous mythic ancient hero, "the hound of Cullen," who as a young boy killed the favorite dog of Cullen and then offered to take its place. Like "man's best friend," Cúchulainn was loyal and brave to the point of death. He died in battle but retained his honor and remains a hero to the Irish people.[5] From the Middle Ages, when Irish mercenaries were feared throughout Europe, to the early modern era, when thousands of Irish Catholics fled their Protestant-dominated homeland to fight in European wars, Irish military prowess created an international view of the Irish as a martial people.[6] Nineteenth-century Irish nationalists capitalized on this tradition to create a national identity. The founder of this culturally nationalist movement, Thomas Davis, stated unequivocally that "the Irish are a military people—strong, nimble and hardy, fond of adventure, irascible, brotherly and generous—they have all the qualities that tempt men to war and make them good soldiers."[7]

Spellman then was fulfilling the destiny of his heritage, that of the "Fighting Irish" and thus easily became the epitome of the popular contemporary view of the Irish Confederate soldier. It was an image perpetuated by the proponents of the "Lost Cause"—men like Edward McCrady who, after the war, for a variety of reasons, needed an image of gallant and honorable Confederate soldiers who gave their all against superior numbers.[8]

Beyond the South, the Irish aspects of the Confederate story were hardly known at all, because their Civil War participation paled beside the feats of the much larger Irish numbers in the Union army. This emphasis on the Irish in blue is understandable because about 95 percent of the Irish in America in 1860 lived in the North, outside of what became the Confederate states. The 150,000 or so Irishmen in the Union army made it easier for them to form distinct Irish regiments and even a couple of brigades.[9] The most famous was the "Irish Brigade," led by the great national hero and exile Thomas Francis Meagher. It has dominated the popular consciousness of Irish participation in the Civil War.[10] Their famous charge up Marye's Heights at Fredericksburg in 1862 was immortalized by being re-created in the 2003 film *Gods and Generals*. It was the "Pickett's Charge" of the Federal army. Its popular heroic image means that the Irish Brigade is the subject of the most expensive Union prints in the twenty-first-century Civil War art market.[11]

As a result of this fascination with the Irish Brigade, beyond the Lost Cause commemorations in the postwar South, the Irish who fought for the Confederacy received very little attention. The first effort at a comprehensive look at the Irish in the Confederacy came in 1940 with Ella Lonn's *Foreigners in the Confederacy*. While Lonn looked at all kinds of "foreigners," she concentrated on the largest groups in Confederate service, the Irish and the Germans. She did an impressive amount of research, examining both the battle and home fronts, and the book was well-reviewed in the major scholarly journals. The main criticism, however, was that Lonn overstated her case on the ethnic aspects of the Confederate effort. Lonn's aim was to challenge the dominant view, propagated by apologists for the Confederacy, that the white South had been overwhelmed by the immigrant "hirelings" in the Union army. Her book is chock-full of information on foreign participation but limited in its analysis. After providing over 500 pages of solid research, she concluded meekly: "The record is finished. It will probably give offense. Surprises often do not give joy if they overthrow long-cherished conceptions. The descendants of Englishmen who came over during the colonial period may feel that their fathers and grandfathers are being robbed of the distinction of having fought unaided for the great cause to which they devoted their lives."[12] Beyond the listing of foreign contributions, Lonn did not go.

The book's lack of analysis meant that it failed to leave much of an impression with historians, and the focus on nontraditional white southerners quickly shifted to the native-born "yeoman" farmer of the "plain folk of the Old South."[13] Historians examining the broader "plain folk" of the urban South, however, discovered the significance of foreign immigrants in general, and the Irish in particular, in southern towns and cities. The Irish thus began to appear for the first time in the scholarly history of the American South more than thirty years after Lonn's book.[14] Recognition of Irish involvement in the Confederacy grew from this breakthrough and from the explosion of interest in the Civil War created by Ken Burns's hugely popular documentary *The Civil War* (1990). His focus on ordinary soldiers and civilians, along with the usual prominent figures of Lincoln, Lee, Grant, etc., particularly resonated with the millions of Americans who watched the series on Public Television. This enthrallment with the ordinary Civil War soldier coincided with the embrace of the Irish "Diaspora" by the Irish government, when President Mary Robinson, elected in 1990, left a light on in the window of *Áras an Uachtaráin* (the Irish White House) for the Irish and their descendants abroad. She called on the Irish in Ireland to "cherish" their distant and scattered relatives.[15]

The fascination with the common soldiers and common Irish Americans meant that certain prominent Irish Confederates and units began to receive serious attention.[16] All this new interest culminated in some major popular efforts to assess overall Irish participation in the Confederacy.[17] These attempts at a comprehensive description, while providing a lot of new information, have, however, oversimplified the Irish effort for the Confederacy. The narrative in the main remains one of contribution and glory. The bravery, skill, and impact of Irish Confederate soldiers are exaggerated. Irish is also defined too broadly. Anybody with an Irish or Scots-Irish name is included as an Irish Confederate, thereby increasing the numbers of "Irish" in the Confederate army to the hundreds of thousands. Southerners who have some ancestors that may have come over from Ireland in colonial times are put in lists of Irish units alongside companies full of urban Catholic migrants. The Confederate experience of native-born Protestant soldiers who never showed any signs of "Irishness" in their lives beyond their last name was very different from that of a company of Irish famine immigrants who had perhaps been in the South for only a few months, or years at the most, serving in an explicitly Irish ethnic unit.[18]

To be clear, I define Irish here as someone born in Ireland or the descendant of an Irish person who displays an Irish ethnic awareness. Even though not born in Ireland, some Irish Americans did place themselves in the "imagined community" of the Irish abroad. The fresh Irish immigrant, Spellman for instance, who joined a unit such as the Irish Volunteers displayed his ethnicity for everyone to see. But those Irish-born who did not join an ethnic unit could not escape being defined as Irish. For example, Anglican Pat Cleburne was not from a particularly Irish American community (Helena, Arkansas). His military skill and his leadership ability, not his Irishness, made him famous. Nonetheless, many were charmed by his "Irish brogue," and his Irish life definitely influenced his performance for the Confederacy. Cleburne, while not in any way an active leader of Irish immigrants in the South, came to represent the Irish in the Confederacy to many natives. Although he never sought it, he also became a de facto representative of the Irish in the South. During and after the war, Irish immigrants claimed his military success and his memory as their own.[19] He may have been trying to escape Ireland and his Irish past when he came to Arkansas, but others, southern and Irish, would never let him do so.

Beyond the native Irish, those born in the United States of Irish parentage who displayed an ethnic sensibility by joining Irish societies or establishing themselves as spokesmen and leaders of the Irish community are included here. Identity can be chosen and reimagined as one moves through life and from place to place. Changing cultural and political circumstances especially can lead to these reimaginings. Irishness, in its various forms, had to adapt to American circumstances.[20] A. G. (Andrew Gordon) Magrath, for example, was the Charleston-born son of a Presbyterian Irish immigrant. He became a prominent attorney in the city and was elected to the state legislature. A. G. was very involved in the Irish American community. He led a number of organizations such as the St. Patrick's Benevolent Society and captained the Irish Volunteers in the Seminole War of the late 1830s. He also remained very aware of Irish politics and history and took political stances favorable to Irish immigrants. Magrath had no problem retaining an Irish identity with his American one. Despite his American birth and upbringing, he became a community leader and spokesman for the Irish in the city.[21]

On the other hand, the famed southern author, William Gilmore Simms, was also the son of an Irishman, but he became estranged from his immigrant father. Rather than adapting his Irish heritage to his American life, Simms jettisoned it. He completely embraced South Carolina, especially after marrying into a planter family, and emerged as the antebellum South's, but not Irish America's, premier novelist. Unlike Magrath, he was never a member of an ethnic Irish society. Simms did write a Civil War novel called *Paddy McGann* (1863) in which the main protagonist is the descendant of Scots-Irish settlers, but Simms uses McGann as the epitome of Old South rural simplicity, in some ways similar to Wilbur J. Cash's invented Scots-Irish frontiersman, in the classic *The Mind of the South*, the "man at the center" of southern settlement. Simms's vivid descriptions of McGann explore southern issues not Irish ones.[22] Both Magrath and Simms are technically, from a demographic standpoint, Irish Americans, but only Magrath could be described culturally as one. Magrath embraced the Irish side of his heritage but Simms did not. Therefore, Magrath's Confederate experience and image are analyzed in this work but not Simms's.

How many Irish then were in the South before secession? The Eighth Census of the United States, conducted in 1860, did list nativity, but unfortunately not parental heritage, making it impossible to count the first generation of the Americans born to Irish immigrants in the region.[23] Nevertheless, the numbers of Irish born in what would become the Confederate states, as well as the three major border slave states—Missouri, Kentucky, and Maryland, claimed, the former two officially and the latter spiritually, by the Confederate government—is instructive. In 1860, the eleven states that would become the Confederacy contained about 85,000 Irish residents (see table 1). In the three border states lived about 95,000 more Irish, giving a total of about 180,000. This total represented about 11 percent of the 1.6 million Irish living in the United States at this time. The Confederate states total represents just over 5 percent of the Irish in America.

By concentrating in southern cities, however, these small numbers of Irish created vibrant ethnic communities. Over half of the Irish populations in Kentucky and Maryland lived in Louisville and Baltimore, respectively. In South Carolina and Louisiana over 70 percent of the Irish lived in the largest cities, Charleston and New Orleans, respectively. The Irish in the South therefore were very visible minorities in urban areas. More than 20 percent of Savannah's white population, for example, was Irish-born.[24] The Irish exploited this visibility in a political way. They participated actively in the region's politics and maintained a strong loyalty to the Democratic Party. Most supported slavery, but were wary of secession from the Union until after Abraham Lincoln's election.

As reluctant secessionists, would the Irish defend the new Confederate States of America? They were potentially a sizeable pool of recruits in southern towns and cities. Many did, rushing forward to join the Confederate

TABLE 1 Irish in the South, 1860

State	Irish Population
Confederate States	
Alabama	5,664
Arkansas	1,312
Florida	827
Georgia	6,586
Louisiana	28,207
Mississippi	3,893
North Carolina	889
South Carolina	4,906
Tennessee	12,498
Texas	3,480
Virginia	16,501
TOTAL	84,763
Border States	
Kentucky	22, 249
Maryland	28,872
Missouri	43,464
TOTAL	94,585
OVERALL TOTAL	179,348

Source: Kennedy, *Population of the United States*, xxix.

army, but others did not. Confederate recruiters realized that exploiting the fighting traditions of the Irish and the relationship between Ireland and Great Britain encouraged Irish men to sign up. This image of the fighting Irish did transfer to the battlefield, with the Irish gaining a reputation for bravery. Nonetheless, they had a propensity to desert, and this fact, along with the Irish civilian experience of the Confederacy, played a role in undermining the native view of Irish Confederates because it challenged the image of a coherent and united Confederate nation.

The history of the Irish in the Confederacy thus provides some insight into the extent and effectiveness of Confederate nationalism. Irish immigrants had already negotiated their Irishness with an American national identity, and now they faced adapting to a Confederate one. In this adaptation, the Irish displayed clearly the ambiguities within Confederate identity. They vividly portrayed the "serious problems," as one scholar of the subject has assessed it, of the effort "to define a distinctive national identity and a set of expectations about the roles of individual Confederate citizens."[25] As a result, some natives resented them for being so open, for example, in their acceptance of Confederate defeat and Federal occupation. When the Confederacy began to crumble, the only saving grace it retained was the "shared community of sacrifice" where white southerners could unite around "suffering" and "victimhood."[26] Irish deserters, "shirkers," and "collaborators," severely challenged this idea of a shared sacrifice

Yet, in the end, virtually all Confederates accepted defeat and renewed their loyalty to the United States. During the Reconstruction era, however, they turned quickly to commemorating their participation in the Confederacy. The Irish knew their own "lost causes" from Ireland and found it easy to embrace the southern one. The style and paraphernalia of commemorating the Confederacy had strong Catholic overtones with which Irish immigrants were very comfortable. The Irish could banish memories of their ambiguous support for the cause and remember only the "glories."

Dominick Spellman's story reflected this ambiguity toward the Confederacy. Rather than being the ever-loyal Confederate of Lost Cause myth, he had quit his new nation. His desertion, and particularly his seeking to take the oath to gain early release, had they been known, would have been seen by his Confederate colleagues as the ultimate betrayal. His greatest role in life had been his Confederate service, particularly with prominent Carolinians, such as McCrady, pointing him out for public praise and recognition. He did not want to jeopardize his only claim to southern fame. His moment of weakness in Elmira and its subsequent "forgetting," in reality makes Spellman more the typical Irish Confederate than those praising him realized. He is a good personification of the reality for most Irish Confederates, whose relationship with the new nation was often as ambiguous and complex as his, and not just the same old simple tale of the ever brave and true "Fighting Irish."[27]

CHAPTER 1

Reluctant Secessionists

The Irish, Southern Politics, and the Birth of the Confederacy

Irish immigrants were active participants in the politics of southern cities. They generally supported the Democratic Party, attracted to its rhetoric of the common man as well as its pro-immigration platform. The relationship between the Irish and southern Democrats became even closer during outbursts of political nativism. The fact that many southern Democrats were slave owners did not upset the Irish. Indeed, their experience with slavery, albeit, for the most part, second-hand, brought them closer to the proslavery position. Although the vast majority of Irish in the region did not own slaves, they did not object to slavery itself, and when they could afford it, had no compunction about purchasing slaves. With the endorsement of slavery by the likes of Irish patriot John Mitchel and Irish immigrants' own general dislike of "Yankee" and British abolitionists, Irish Catholics became safe on the most important issue to white southerners. Yet, despite this support of slavery, during the tumultuous sectional tensions of the 1850s, the Irish remained steadfast for the Union, declining to support early southern efforts to secede. Even as late as 1860, many remained loyal to the national Democratic Party and its presidential candidate, Stephen Douglas of Illinois. It was only upon Abraham Lincoln's election that the Irish began to heed southern nationalists. They were indeed reluctant secessionists, but ultimately they did abandon the United States for the new Confederate States of America.

When news reached Charleston, South Carolina, of Abraham Lincoln's victory in the 1860 election, many in the city were elated. The election of a "Black Republican" to the presidency of the United States would finally motivate those white southerners who had been reluctant to break from the Union to now do so. There could be no protection now of slavery with the party of "abolition" about to take over the executive branch. Ardent secessionist Robert Barnwell Rhett's newspaper, the *Charleston Mercury*, put a secession flag in the window of his office and stated loudly that "The Tea has been thrown overboard." At last, it continued, "The Revolution of 1860 has been initiated." For almost thirty years Rhett had thought that a slave owning people had to have complete control over their political destiny, and the only sure way to do that was as a separate nation. Long a critic of the national Democratic Party, which he saw as unsafe on the question of slavery, he now felt vindicated and expected a lot of support for his call for "immediate secession." South Carolina could not wait for other southern states to act. It had to lead. Those who thought like him made immediate plans to achieve this secession and fulfill the dream of creating a southern republic.[1]

Rhett had an unlikely ally in this newly charged quest for secession. A. G. Magrath, whose father had come as a political refugee from Ireland, was a federal judge in the Charleston district. When he heard the news of Lincoln's victory while presiding in court, he reportedly took his robes off, folded them on his chair, and announced his immediate resignation from the bench. Now, he argued, South Carolinians had to support their state over the Union. A prominent leader of the Irish American community in Charleston, as an active member of the Hibernian and St. Patrick's Benevolent Societies, as well as a former captain of the Irish Volunteers Militia company, he had been nominated to the bench by President Franklin Pierce for his loyalty to the national Democrats. Magrath had stood by the party in the early 1850s when fire-eaters such as Rhett had tried to pull the South out of the Union in their opposition to the Compromise of 1850. He had forcefully opposed the secessionists then, earning their eternal enmity. Indeed, a vicious article in Rhett's *Mercury* questioning his integrity eventually led to a duel between Magrath's younger brother and Rhett's nephew in which the latter was killed by a bullet to the head on the third exchange of shots.[2]

By 1860, however, Magrath had become disillusioned with the national government and the Democrats. In his Irish politics he had always advocated radical action. An active supporter of every Irish national movement, he was often called upon to make fiery speeches against British rule in Ireland. His father had participated in the 1798 United Irishman rebellion against the British in Ireland that led to the elder man's exile in America. Magrath had a serious "rebel" heritage.[3] Before Lincoln's election, when ruling on the infamous *Wanderer* case, he had hinted at his change of opinion from the bench. The *Wanderer* was a slave ship commissioned by the Georgia adventurer and extremist Charles A. L. Lamar specifically to break the slave trade ban. When its captain was indicted for piracy, Magrath took the case and all but nullified the 1820 law banning the international slave trade in the United States.[4] Some scholars have interpreted this decision as an important element in the growth of the sectional crisis and indeed have even referred to Magrath's action as South Carolina's "second nullification" and as an integral part of the planters' "counter revolution of slavery." The issue with Magrath was, however, that he was not a planter. He was an attorney, the son of an immigrant, a Protestant, though educated in the local Catholic school, but not a member of the elite Episcopal churches in Charleston. He was a slaveholder, but decidedly bourgeois, never owning more than ten slaves (twenty being the usual number for planter status). He saw himself as a friend of the common man and had written a pamphlet in defense of foreign immigrants against the Know-Nothings in the mid-1850s.[5] He had not been a card-carrying original member of the "counter revolution," rather a very late convert.

Magrath's late conversion to secession, though spectacular in some ways, mirrors that of the rest of the Irish in the South. They too had been loyal Democrats. From their earliest presence in the South most had gravitated toward the Democratic Republicans of Thomas Jefferson. Those Irish who had arrived in the South in the 1790s and early 1800s had been politicized by the tumultuous political events in Ireland in the pre- and post-1798 rebellion periods. They displayed acumen for politics. Men like Denis Driscoll of Augusta, Georgia, and John Daly Burk of Petersburg, Virginia, for example, both of whom had left Ireland as political exiles, were very active journalists for the Jeffersonian cause as well as defenders of the South and slavery.[6] Those Irish, usually Catholic, who arrived from the 1820s onward had also been politicized by their Irish and emigration experience.[7]

Any political party willing to reach out to these Irish coming to America in ever larger numbers could profit from this politicization. In the antebellum South, as in the rest of America, that was the Democrats. Among the poorer Irish, as mayor Richard Arnold of Savannah put it in the 1850s, "Democracy, the word is potent with them."[8] There were exceptions who supported the Whigs, such as Irish-born Louisiana planter Alexander Porter and the more plebeian John Prendergast of New Orleans, but they were far from representative of the Irish in the South. Porter merely reflected the prejudices of many Louisiana sugar planters, who favored high protective tariffs for their produce. Prendergast was different. He was editor of the *Orleanian* and saw himself as a friend of the working man. He believed Whig policies in support of national improvements were a boon to immigrants and other poor whites looking for work. Prendergast was correct that Whig policies were more helpful to immigrants than the laissez-faire attitude of the Democrats.[9]

But, for the Irish, as with many other poor whites, cultural issues often trumped economic ones. The Democrats courted the Irish, and the Irish liked these overtures. The rhetoric of the Democrats as the party of the common man also appealed. As early as the 1830s the Democrats in the region boasted of Andrew Jackson as "the son of an Irishman." John C. Calhoun, contemplating a run for the Democratic nomination in 1844, reached out to the Irish by sending his subscription to the Irish Emigrant Aid society. While doing so he remarked how he had always "taken pride in my Irish descent," his father having been born in County Donegal. Louisiana politician and later Confederate ambassador to Great Britain, John Slidell, realized the value of Irish voters by shipping them down the Mississippi River from New Orleans to vote in another parish in the 1844 presidential election.[10]

Irish participation in southern urban politics, both legal and illegal, generated some negative southern reactions. The Louisiana Native Association matched its northern counterparts in its rhetoric, if not in its actions, opposing immigrants' participation in the political process. (Ironically it included a number of Democrats opposed to Alexander Porter's involvement in the state's politics.) Yet, when this opposition reached Congress it was the Democrats, and in particular, a young congressman from Mississippi, who took the lead in attacking nativist demands to curtail the naturalization of foreign immigrants. Freshman representative Jefferson Davis, the future president of the Confederacy, openly defended Irish immigrants and their loyalty to the United States. From the Whig stronghold of Vicksburg, Davis may have been influenced by the fact that a lot of his Democratic colleagues in his home town were Irish. In particular, prominent Irish-born merchant William Porterfield was a strong supporter and friend.[11] It's not surprising then that Irish immigrants, despite the best efforts of John Prendergast, saw the Democrats as their natural allies.

This early nativist threat passed in the 1840s but returned with a new virulence in the 1850s. The death of the Whig Party in the early 1850s over slavery left a vacuum in the American political system. The American or "Know-Nothing" Party was particularly strong in the northeast but also in the mid-Atlantic states, including Maryland. Border state Kentucky also had a powerful Know-Nothing movement. Further south the party was weaker but enjoyed success in former Whig strongholds such as Mobile and Natchez, or where Whigs had always been competitive such as New Orleans and Savannah. The American Party sold itself in the South primarily as the pro-Union party. Anti-immigrant and anti-Catholic rhetoric took a back seat to "saving the Union" from extremists in the North and South, but it did play some role in the southern movement. In the mid-1850s, Mobile Know-Nothings, for example, opposed local Catholic nuns' operation of the city hospital. Anti-immigrant politics was at its strongest in New Orleans, along with the border cities of Baltimore and especially Louisville, which witnessed the incineration of some Irish immigrants, including children, when a nativist mob burned an Irish tenement. Petty, but continuous, violence in New Orleans, particularly around election time, led a local Irish leader to advise against new immigrants coming to the city.[12]

The Irish in the South, however, did not take the attacks lying down. They too could participate in violence and, most famously, supported an attempted coup in New Orleans in 1858 against the Know-Nothing city administration. In Charleston and Savannah, in a more peaceful fashion, they provided the winning margins for anti-Know-Nothing candidates in city elections. Charleston aristocrat William Porcher Miles gained so many votes for mayor, he earned the nickname "Paddy" Miles as a result. In general, the Know-Nothing experience drew the Irish even closer to the Democrats even as the party in the South became more vociferous in its support of slavery. Even John Prendergast came to support the party he had campaigned against for so long.[13]

The fact that many of the most active Democratic opponents of nativism were prosouthern, state-rights Democrats, meant that the Irish were being drawn into cauldron of sectional politics. The "Prince of Fire-eaters," William Lowndes Yancey of Alabama, saw the Know-Nothings as closet abolitionists. Indeed, in the northern states the American Party had antislavery supporters, although it was far from being abolitionist. This reality did not matter to Yancey and other fire-eaters. Even the slightest connection with antislavery was an anathema. Yancey and his fire-eater colleagues also saw anti-immigrant rhetoric as a distraction to defending real southern interests, especially slavery, and were thus, in policy terms, pro-Irish.

The southern Democrat who perhaps played the greatest role in opposing the spread of Know-Nothingism was Henry Wise of Virginia. His victory in that state's 1855 gubernatorial campaign stopped the spread of "the serpent" (abolitionism disguised as Know-Nothingism) southward (from the North and border states) and helped deny the party the successes it had achieved further north. Wise used the usual attack against the Know-Nothings as abolitionists but went further in suggesting that its secret meetings could encourage slave insurrection. More important, from an Irish perspective, he stated that Know-Nothings were merely "the minions of British abolitionists," intent on destroying the peculiar institution and the United States itself. The fact that Wise had been a life-long Democrat and a self-styled representative of the common man only enamored him further to the Irish.[14] When he moved to an extreme state rights position and eventually toward supporting secession, the Irish of Virginia would remember his destruction of the Know-Nothings.

Like Wise, the Irish had long been critics of British abolitionists. The Irish newspaper editor of the pro-Calhoun *Vicksburg Sentinel*, James Hagan, for example, attacked the hypocrisy of the British who condemned, as he put it, the "mote" of American slavery while ignoring the "beam" of their treatment of the poor in Britain and especially Ireland. Hagan held particular ire for the Royal Consort Prince Albert, whom he liked to refer to as the "pensioned German loafer." He often contrasted what he saw as the differences between the treatment of slaves and that of free workers in Europe. Irish-born Richard Elward, who edited the Democratic *Mississippi Free Trader* down the Mississippi River from Vicksburg at Natchez, echoed Hagan's sentiments. Even the more moderate Catholic newspaper of Charleston, South Carolina, the *United States Catholic Miscellany*, edited by various Irish American clerics in the antebellum era, also railed against the "Saints of Great Britain and Ireland" who were "petitioning for NEGRO EMANCIPATION" while simultaneously "straining every nerve to OPPRESS IF NOT EXTIRPATE THE ROMAN CATHOLICS." Beyond the prominent Irish such as Hagan, Elward, and the editors of the *Miscellany*, these sentiments were shared among the less visible Irish. Savannah clerk John McLaughlin, for example, did not like hypocritical Europeans sticking their noses into the issue of American slavery. Neither did railroad worker Pat Kennedy, who wrote to Ireland complaining about abolitionists stirring up "English ladies." Indeed, he added, "The slave in Virginia is better fed and clothed than the poor Irish farmers." For emphasis, he concluded, "Oh it would be well for the Irish labourer if he was half as well fed and taken care of as the slave [whose] master has an interest [in his property]."[15]

Being antiabolitionist did not necessarily mean that one supported slavery wholeheartedly. Some in the South believed that Irish immigrants would undermine slavery. The British actress Fanny Kemble, who had married into a family with major plantations in Georgia, thought that the Irish laborers who dug the ditches in her coastal area would be perhaps, like her, opposed to slavery. She described the Irish as "passionate, impulsive, warm-hearted [and] generous people" who were "pestilent sympathizers." Therefore, they would perhaps recognize a parallel between their poor existence and that of slaves. She believed that "with a sufficient dose of American atmospheric air in their lungs, properly mixed with a right proportion of ardent spirits . . . they might actually take to sympathy with the slaves." Others in the South who, unlike Kemble, supported slavery, also worried about the Irish and poor whites in general when it came to the "peculiar institution." Christopher Memminger of Charleston, for example, despite the fact that he had been born in the German states, worried about poor whites who resented the competition from slave labor becoming "hot abolitionists."[16] Some scholars believe that this fear of nonslaveholders' disloyalty to slavery, including the poor Irish, was the reason for southern secession. This argument is overstated, but if many white leaders were not afraid of the smaller numbers of immigrants in the South, they certainly were of those filling the cities of the North.[17]

The recent scholarship on "whiteness" makes a lot of a potential alliance of Irish immigrants with African Americans against slavery. Native whites feared that Irish immigrants doing "black work" blurred the lines between black and white and undermined the system of racial supremacy behind slavery. This racializing of the Irish as black was something the Irish then had to overcome. To put it succinctly, as one proponent of "whiteness studies" has done, the Irish had to become "white." The reality in the South, and perhaps everywhere else, was that the Irish always were "white" and had no major problems with the dominant racial system in the region.[18] Their endorsement of the Confederacy would indicate that clearly.

Nonetheless, the Irish lived in areas of southern cities with the largest black populations, and as a result they occasionally crossed the color line. This breaking of the racial rules made many native white southerners nervous. There were some spectacular cases of Irish immigrants challenging the definition of the "proper" relationships between blacks and whites in the Old South. Patrick Lynch, originally from Dublin, worked on a Louisiana plantation in the 1840s. While there he fell in love with an enslaved woman and "married" her. White men could have illicit sexual relationships with slaves but they were not to acknowledge these openly and embrace them as "normal" marital relations. Of course Lynch's marriage was not a legal one, and he left the plantation to try to raise the funds to buy his wife's and his baby son's freedom. But he died before he could do so. His son, John Roy, would go on to become Mississippi's first black congressman during Reconstruction.[19]

Across the South in Georgia, James Healy pushed racial mores even further. A small planter near Macon, Healy and one of his slaves lived as man and wife. He freed their children, even sending them north to be educated.

Two of their sons, passing as white, would become important Roman Catholic clerics after the Civil War.[20] Other Irish in less public ways broke racial barriers by illicitly drinking and trading with slaves. Irish lawbreakers were a constant thorn in the side of urban slave owners seeking to control their chattel's access to alcohol.[21] Indeed, one scholar who has examined closely the trading relationships between slaves and poor whites, describes immigrants as "the whites most likely to collaborate and trade clandestinely with slaves."[22] Other Irish were even more dangerous to the slave codes. "Red" Jack McGuigan of Vicksburg, Mississippi, for example, forged and sold passes to slaves on the eve of the Civil War. When discovered, his actions led to a sentence of ten years hard labor.[23]

Active Irish participation in slave ownership countered the actions of race "renegades" like McGuigan. Those immigrants who arrived in the early nineteenth century and were able to take advantage of the "flush times," along with those who inherited wealth from an American family, often became major slave owners. Maunsel White, for example, originally from County Limerick, arrived in Louisiana as a poor immigrant but used his service under Andrew Jackson at the Battle of New Orleans in 1815 to gain prominence and acquire major sugar and cotton plantations. He eventually owned hundreds of slaves. Frederick Stanton from the north of Ireland arrived in Natchez in 1818, got into the cotton business, and eventually earned enough to own six plantations and 333 slaves, making him one of the richest planters in the South at his death in 1859. James Tracy inherited a plantation and a large numbers of slaves from his uncle in Virginia in the 1820s. Other smaller Irish landholders, such as those who settled in "Locust Grove" near Washington, Georgia, in the 1830s and later moved to Sulphur Springs, Mississippi, in search of better cotton lands in the 1840s, owned dozens of slaves. In the towns and cities, businessmen and artisans from the Emerald Isle bought slaves for their homes and businesses. They also, on occasion, speculated in them. Early Scots-Irish migrant James Adger began his American life as a journeyman but ended it as a wealthy shipper and banker in Charleston. Rich enough to move from the northern end of town known as the "neck," where most of his poorer fellow countrymen lived, to a fine mansion in the more salubrious neighborhood "South of Broad," he owned more than a dozen domestic "servants" to cater to his new lifestyle among the Charleston elite.[24]

Even those who arrived later, after the economic boom of the "Era of Good Feelings," still saw slave ownership as the way to success in the South. Drayman Denis Donovan of New Orleans owned six slaves, while journalist

Denis Corcoran owned three in the same city. Clergy such as Father Ignatius Mullen, also of New Orleans, owned "servants."[25] Some Irish even pursued slave trading. John Whelan of Canton, Mississippi, bought and sold slaves for a living, while the Ryan family of Charleston was a major player in one of the hubs of the slave trade. Their property on State and Chalmers Streets near the Cooper River wharves was (and is) known as Ryan's Slave Mart. The Ryans exploited Irish connections for their business, most notably when they went to Lancaster County to settle the estate and sell the more than one hundred slaves of established Irish Catholic planter William McKenna. This large sale prompted an advertising campaign that turned the sale into a major event on the courthouse square. Despite their business, the Ryans remained upright citizens of Irish Charleston.[26]

Famine migrant Patrick Murphy, originally from New Ross, County Wexford, who moved to the Natchez district in the 1850s, has left the most extensive record of a small Irish slave owner. Skilled in construction, Murphy performed services for planters throughout the district but became renowned as a bridge builder. Although successful, he remained homesick and was never fully enamored with his new home in the American South. Despite his lack of assimilation to the region, he still understood and embraced the southern path to prosperity. With the money he earned, he bought slaves to rent out to local businesses and was not afraid to "whip" those he believed needed "punishment." Murphy, however, usually punished with a sense of exasperation, as a parent would when chastising a child. It seems that he had somehow absorbed the paternalist ideal of the southern planters for whom he worked and felt himself to be a substantial citizen. When one planter client made the mistake of attempting to feed Murphy with the slave laborers, Murphy threatened to leave the job for this affront of having to sit at the "second or nigroes' [sic] table." According to Murphy only the planter's sincerest apology made him return to finish the contract. Here was a man sure of his whiteness to the extent of enforcing the strictest racial etiquette.[27]

Thanks to Murphy's extensive papers we get a unique insight into the mind of a rising famine immigrant in the antebellum South. While one cannot be sure that other "middling" Irish slave owners shared his exact sentiments, there is evidence that some, when they could, followed his path to southern prosperity. As a study of the antebellum bourgeoisie in the South highlights, the upwardly mobile southern urbanites often expressed sentiments similar to their northern counterparts, except for slavery, where they saw "no inherent incompatibility" between slavery and economic progress.

Indeed, slavery was a key element that could be "utilized to achieve dreams of a New South," industrialized and modern but still wedded to the "peculiar institution."[28] The Irish seemed to agree with this belief. In one study of slave ownership in five Deep South cities, the Irish were second only to the British, among the foreign population, as the most likely to own slaves.[29] It seems that with time and growing prosperity the Irish became more involved in slavery and even less likely to object to any political maneuvers that sought to defend the institution from "northern attacks."

Indeed, one Irish immigrant in the South actively encouraged participation in slavery and became an avid defender of it. More important, his opinions mattered to the larger Irish community in the region. John Mitchel, the great Irish patriot who hoped to expand opportunities for Irish immigrants, and indeed all southern whites, publicly supported the benefits of slave ownership. Mitchel was a hero to most Irish immigrants, but especially in the South, and he would become one of the most significant supporters of secession and the Confederacy. He was the son of a Unitarian minister from the north of Ireland. As a young man he became an ardent nationalist as a member of the "Young Ireland" group and a stern critic of British rule in Ireland. In particular, he described the Great Famine in Ireland (1845–52) in his newspaper the *United Irishman* (and later in a book) not as a natural disaster, but as a deliberate genocidal policy enacted and encouraged by the British government. His view of the famine remains the dominant one among popular Irish opinion of the calamity to this day.[30] As a result, however, he came to see violence as the only way to respond to British rule in Ireland and political, social, and economic revolution as the only way to save his country. Inspired by the 1848 revolution in France, he called openly for rebellion in Ireland. His incendiary newspaper articles got him preemptively arrested, charged with treason, and sentenced to death (later commuted to transportation to Tasmania). Escaping in 1853, he came to the United States, and Irish and native-born Americans alike welcomed him as a hero and a defender of liberty. He immediately plunged into politics in New York City and founded a newspaper called the *Citizen* to promote his strong Irish nationalism. His advocacy of social as well as political revolution in Ireland through the abolition of the landlord system as well as British rule made him much more popular among the poorer Irish than other Irish nationalists of his generation. He came to define a "Mitchelite" view of revolutionary Irish nationalism that directly inspired future revolutionary efforts.[31]

It seemed surprising then when this great friend of Irish liberty endorsed slavery in 1854.[32] According to Mitchel himself, he arrived at this position because of his dealings with the social reformers of the North. He disliked the "British" style of opposing slavery by these "apostles" of "human progress," a notion he had always opposed in Ireland because it had led to the famine. As an admirer of Scottish conservative historian and theorist Thomas Carlyle, Mitchel had been a consistent critic of laissez-faire capitalism and now an endorser of slavery. He told one abolitionist critic that, "We for our part wish we had a good plantation well stocked with healthy negroes in Alabama."[33]

Mitchel's defense of slavery quickly made him popular throughout the South and reinforced the idea that the Irish in America were safe on slavery. As a result, he became even more enamored with southerners. Invited to speak to legislatures, public meetings, and universities, he came to the conclusion that white southerners had a "peculiar gentleness of demeanor and quiet courtesy," which he believed was "attributable to the institution of slavery." Mitchel eventually moved to the South to near Knoxville, Tennessee, in 1855, and reestablished his newspaper three years later as the *Southern Citizen*.[34]

Mitchel described his new newspaper, "as an Irish American paper," but he considered it primarily "a Southern journal."[35] He saw the Irish and southern causes as similar, indeed as parallel struggles, and set out to explain why they were. The paper's immediate southern purpose, however, was to promote the reopening of the African slave trade. Beginning in the mid-1850s, some southern extremists sought to repeal the 1808 ban on the international slave trade, and Mitchel joined their cause wholeheartedly.[36] As a long-term solution, however, he now favored southern secession, and he hoped to persuade his Irish and native subscribers alike to follow his reasoning.[37]

Mitchel's deep hatred of Britain along with his personal experience of the South and southerners perhaps go a long way to explain his enthusiasm for slavery and secession. But there was something else motivating Mitchel: a sense of Irish racial identity. As a romantic nationalist since the early 1840s, Mitchel believed in the essential nature of a national people. Nationality was not something you invented. It was something innate, with deep historical roots. In his first defense against charges of inconsistency, he played this ethnic/national card. He denied that there was no natural right to liberty: "I am not aware that every human being, or any one has an 'inalienable right to life, liberty, and the pursuit of happiness.' People often forfeit life and liberty; and as to 'happiness' I do not even know what it is. On the whole I fear that this is jargon." The liberty that Mitchel spoke of for

Ireland, he explained, was "the sort of liberty—no better, no worse—[than that] which . . . the slaveholding Corinthians fought for against the Romans, and the slaveholding Americans wrung from the British. It was National Independence."[38]

Mitchel's view of liberty echoed that of most of his nationalist colleagues from Ireland, as well as those who admired him.[39] Nations, not individuals, were entitled to liberty. He thought, however, that only certain races were national in nature and thus fit for independence. In his critiques of British imperialism, for example, he had spoken up for the rights of Indians because they were an ancient race. In vivid terms he criticized British rule and the oppression of "the dominant people of Hindu-stan," who were "of the Caucasian race."[40] Of course the Irish were also from a "distinguished race." He worried that some of his new southern friends, who on the whole he had found not to be nativist, might have absorbed some of the Know-Nothing propaganda. He told them that "the white laborers of Europe are of the highest and choicest breed and blood of men," whose "depressed" condition was due to the "accident of position." Ultimately, the white people of the South might also suffer as the poor whites of Europe, as Ireland suffered under England's rule. "The North is England; the South is Ireland," he said, and "in national character the North is more English, the South more Irish." Mitchel declared: "The actual descent and affinity of the Southern population is by far the greatest part Irish, French, Welsh, Spanish—in any case *Celtic* [his emphasis]." Afraid that southerners might be insulted because they had been bombarded with "Anglo-Saxon" literature, he stated it was "a compliment." It was so because the Celt "was the superior breed; of finer organization, more fiery brain, more a passionate heart—less greedy, grabbing, griping and groveling."[41]

In effect declaring the essential whiteness of the Irish as well as all the "poor whites of Europe," Mitchel therefore explicitly endorsed slaveholding and the white southern way of life for his Irish readership. In fact southerners were the Irish's Gallic cousins, he believed, and the Irish should rally in support of any and all attempts at southern nationhood.[42] His confidence in his own and his countrymen's whiteness implied that the Irish and southerners alike were members of a "superior" branch of the "master" Caucasian race.

As Irish slave ownership indicates, many Irish in the South did not object to Mitchel's logic on their racial supremacy, even if they were not ready to endorse secession from the United States just yet. Some were explicit in their rhetoric. Ulster migrants Robert and William McElderry as well as

John Mitchel (LC-USZ62-103956,
Library of Congress, Washington, D.C.)

Moses Paul, for example, who lived in Virginia in the 1850s, and were open
supporters of Mitchel's views, defended slavery on racial grounds. Robert
McElderry wrote home that "if you ever want to see a happy and contented
lot of creatures, you should see a number of slaves after the day's work in
done and hear them play the banjo and see their dances." His brother William wrote that slaves "go about dressed in the very best . . . and sometimes
make in a week 10 or 12 [dollars] . . . that they have to themselves." Those,
he continued, who he had on occasion seen "whipped . . . deserved it." Another immigrant in Virginia, Moses Paul, was more matter of fact about the
issue, writing that to prosper in the region one was "obliged to own niggers
to make money."[43]

Even the newly arrived Irish could adjust rapidly to the realities of southern slavery. An Irish visitor to his uncle's plantation in Augusta, Georgia,
in 1859, James Hamilton, quickly accepted the nature of the slavery system.
Early in his visit the ugly truth of slave discipline did affect him, as he wrote:
"After Tea & while sitting reading alone heard some loud words & then the
sound of a whip. It did not take much reasoning to find out it was a negro
flogging. I can scarcely write down what were my feelings certain that I felt
my own flesh creep. Was told it was for throwing bad potatoes into the wagon
after being told not to do so." But, quickly his sensibilities came around
to the peculiar institution. Upon seeing some slaves, reportedly imported

illegally from Africa, he remarked that they "were a great deal better looking than the ones around here." He was not bothered by tales of slaves being sold for misbehavior, or when his cousins told him of going on slave patrols where unfortunate slaves found without passes would be chased up a tree and escaped whipping only if they had provided "good sport." He also accepted with ease that although slave trading had been frowned upon, it was now more socially acceptable leading, perhaps, to the official reopening of the African slave trade. The only matters that vexed him, it seems, were the "immorality" of slaves who took too many wives, and the "blasphemous" prayer of a slave preacher. By the end of his visit he could write nonchalantly, upon seeing a slave trader with slaves, of a boy who "had rope fastened to each arm and wrapped around his back" and surmising that the child must have been "addicted to running away."[44]

Those without kin who owned slaves also could absorb the racial mores of the South. Irish immigrants in Richmond, for example, were well aware of the double standards, in whites' favor, prevailing in the city's courts. In Georgia, Fanny Kemble quickly became disillusioned with her belief in the potential of an alliance between the Irish and Africans. Violence between Irish laborers and slaves on the local plantations became so common the work crews had to be segregated. She went from describing the Irish as "pestilent sympathisers" to "despisers of negroes."[45] On a more organized level, Irish workers often resented the competition from slaves and free blacks in the South. In Charleston, Irish artisans joined with native white workingmen in petitioning the South Carolina legislature to enforce the city's strict slave laws. Since the failed Denmark Vesey slave rebellion plot of 1822, slaves in the city were not supposed to hire their own time.[46] In other words, they could be hired out to work only when the contract was negotiated and signed by their masters. The city controlled the hiring out of slaves through the use of badges that were designed to restrict both their movement within the city, but also their economic impact. White workers resented slave laborers showing up at the docks or on construction sites looking for casual work and undercutting the whites' wages. This effort to enforce the laws failed because slave owners found that slave self-hiring was convenient and cost effective. Slaves who earned a little extra cash for themselves were less likely to steal from their masters. Plus the slave owners jealously guarded their control over their own slaves and resented any interference from poorer whites, even those who were looking to enforce the law. Ironically, the Irish and other poor whites who often undermined the dominant racial hegemony were, in this case, the actual upholders of the law. Their opposition to the hiring out of slaves worried men like the aforementioned Memminger, who thought that resentment at slave labor would turn poor white workingmen into abolitionists.[47]

Rather than embracing abolitionism, the Irish workingmen of Charleston accepted their failure to fully enforce the laws on slave hiring. Nonetheless, when Irish policemen received reports of slaves hiring their time without badges, they continued to make arrests. Easing potential proletarian anger perhaps was the fact that slave labor could be more efficiently used in rural pursuits as the price of cotton recovered from the slump of the 1830s and early 1840s and rose steadily through the 1850s. Rice also remained a lucrative crop in the decade and kept many slaves employed on lowcountry plantations. As a result there were 6,000 fewer slaves in the city to compete with white laborers. By 1860, Charleston had become a majority-white city for the first time since the early 1700s as immigrants, mostly Irish, replaced black workers on the docks.[48]

Instead of legislating against slaves, the white workers, Irish included, turned their attention to the sizeable free black population. Free people of color had to pay a capitation tax for the "privilege" of being free. The tax, as with slave hiring laws, had rarely been enforced. In the late 1850s the predominantly Irish police force, which had become more Irish since the Irish community gave its support to William Porcher Miles's mayoral campaign of 1856, began enforcing the tax. Failure to pay could lead to arrest and enslavement through sale to the highest bidder. With encouragement from the workingmen's lobby, the Irish cops seemed to relish the task. This new harassment, along with moves through the legislature to enslave or expel free people of color, made life so intolerable for some that they sought enslavement with friendly whites to protect themselves and their children.[49]

The Irish realized the importance of their skin color in the racial system of the South. An Irish newspaper editor in New Orleans, John Maginnis, recognized the elite economic status of some Louisiana "creoles" of color but also delighted in the fact that they could not vote because of their racial status. The Irish, on the other hand, even though they were foreigners, could. Maginnis, through his paper, the True Delta, encouraged his sizeable Irish readership to exercise this privilege of their race.[50] The Irish were well aware that whatever happened on the margins, laws in the South since the 1820s had created what one scholar has described as more "binary distinction of black and white" than had ever existed before or in the "lived experience of race." As a result "black" or "Negro" became a new "rigid" status for people of color.[51] The Irish, despite occasional negative comments and stereotypes, were definitely outside this category and realized that slavery and the legal structure behind it preserved that reality for them in the South.

This involvement of the Irish in the practice of slavery and their attitude toward the institution and the racial ideology behind it, eased the fears of many native white southerners about the Irish as potential abolitionists. Louisiana fire-eater James D. B. De Bow considered immigration opponents "wrong in political policy and Christian spirit," because restriction of foreign immigration would decrease the South's white population.[52] One proslavery Georgian noted that "the adopted Irish citizens form the strongest pillar of our power in the free states" and he "thanked God" for bringing the Irish to Massachusetts "to overwhelm the abolitionists" there. Preacher James Gardner, also from Georgia, was somewhat frightened of the large numbers of foreigners coming to the United States, but not of the ones acclimatized to southern ways whom he recognized as "valuable citizens." Protestant sectarian though he was, he had to admit that the Catholic Church, unlike many of his codenominationalists in the North, did not preach abolitionist sermons.[53] One Tennessean did not much like Catholicism either but still acknowledged that the Catholic Church was "the most conservative church in the Union on the subject of slavery." While "Popery" was still a "horrid system," the truth was that Catholics "were not as much under the will of the clergy as the [northern] Methodists."[54]

This Tennessee Methodist's brief summation was explored in much greater depth by the great southern apologist for slavery, Virginian George Fitzhugh. Fitzhugh had a great admiration for the Catholic Church. He liked its conservative nature and its support for slavery. This favorable opinion extended to the Irish: "Frenchmen and Germans are generally infidels, agrarians and abolitionists. An Irish Infidel, or an Irish abolitionist, is scarcely to be found." This reality he attributed to Catholicism and its emphasis on family life over the individual. He also actively opposed the Know-Nothings and even dedicated one of his works to its great nemesis, his fellow Virginian, Henry Wise.[55]

Fitzhugh was, to a large extent, correct in his assessment of the Catholic Church and slavery.[56] Irish Catholic clergy had played a role in defending slavery, and the Church itself, unlike the Methodists, Baptists, and Presbyterians, never openly split on the issue.[57] Bishop John England, the first bishop of Charleston, who came to South Carolina from County Cork in 1820, wrote a defense of Catholics and slavery in response to the criticisms of Georgia politician John Forsyth. England argued that the Church did not see slavery as inherently evil, but as part of God's plan. Necessarily, one should be a *Christian* slaveholder and provide proper food, shelter, and Catholic instruction. (An order of nuns that England founded may have continued to educate slaves long after it was banned).[58] He even opened a school for free people of color in Charleston. In 1835, however, after the city rose in anger and paranoia during the abolitionist mail controversy, he had to close it. Abolitionists had been flooding southern post offices with their literature. This mail caused a panic in Charleston, coming as it did just four years after the Nat Turner slave rebellion in Virginia and thirteen years after the failed plot of Denmark Vesey. Vesey, a free person of color, had reportedly planned with slave conspirators to kill large numbers of whites, seize ships in Charleston harbor, and sail to freedom in Haiti.[59] In the wake of these events, it seemed that England's school might be torched by an angry crowd. The mob did not materialize and the school did not suffer that fate, but England had second thoughts about the project and closed it. He, did not, however, blame the local white population for its hysteria or the city authorities for the failure to guarantee the school's protection. Rather, England's newspaper targeted instead northern abolitionists. These "fanatics" had brought about the school's closure because of their "uncalled for and mischievous interference of the *saints* with a state of society which they do not understand, and with which they have no right to interfere."[60]

England saw abolitionism as something inimical, not only to being an Irish Catholic, but a loyal Carolinian and American too. He even criticized Ireland's great political hero, Daniel O'Connell, for his connections with British abolitionists and calls to end slavery. Describing himself as a "Carolinian," England told O'Connell to stay out of American affairs and stop speaking on matters of which he knew little: "I deny your right to interfere, and I pray that you may succeed in raising the status of the ruined population of Ireland to the level of the comforts of a Carolina slave." Other clergy echoed England's criticism of O'Connell. A fellow Kerryman to O'Connell, Father Jeremiah O'Neill of Savannah, who had said Mass in O'Connell's house at Derrynane in Ireland, reportedly scolded the "Liberator" on a trip there for "casting a nettle . . . on the cold grave of the father [George Washington, slaveholder] of my adopted country."[61]

Support for slavery and opposition to O'Connell's stance spread to his cause in America. By the 1840s O'Connell had moved to a new campaign: to repeal the Act of Union (1800) between Ireland and Great Britain. Run along lines similar to his successful campaign for Catholic Emancipation (the removal of the last restrictions on Catholics), it became a mass movement with Repeal Associations forming all over Ireland. On this occasion, however, there was a much larger Irish diaspora than in the 1820s, and Repeal Associations became prominent in the United States. Indeed, with the endorsement of American notables such as Robert Tyler, son of President John Tyler, they provided vital financial support for the movement. O'Connell's open endorsement of abolitionism and explicit condemnation of American slaveholders in 1843 threw the American movement into disarray. The Irish in the South were very embarrassed and reacted negatively. O'Connell went so far as to disavow the patriotism of Irish Americans who supported slavery and opposed abolition, calling them "Irishmen no longer." The disagreement with O'Connell over slavery led Charleston's Repeal Association to disband.[62]

Most of the Irish in the South, however, managed to balance their support for Irish Repeal with support for slavery. The Repeal campaign highlighted the confidence that many Irish in the South felt about their political position: They could balance their Irishness with their Americanness and southernness.

This balance was reflected in the sectional issues that faced the South. Bishop England, for example, had opposed South Carolina's nullification of the tariff in 1832, even though the local Irish militia unit had been called up to respond to the impending conflict with President Andrew Jackson's federal government. His stance on this issue did not, however, ruin his reputation in Charleston. Upon his death in 1842 the Hibernian Society members eulogized him and wore black armbands as mark of respect for a month. They praised him for having "unceasingly and successfully exerted [himself] in behalf of those institutions so peculiar to us as a Southern people, and against which the tide of fanaticism has been so long and wildly beating." Of Bishop England, they declared, "the South [could] boast [of] no one more devoted and unbending."[63]

Yet, supporter of southern slavery and opponent of abolitionism though he was, England still loved the United States and feared any attempt to break it up. His opposition to nullification highlighted this stance. Many of the Irish in Charleston also supported England's position against nullification. The *Irishman and Southern Democrat*, a supporter of the "Irishman's son," Andrew Jackson, took a strong position against the potentially Union-destroying nullification. Of course John C. Calhoun, a proponent of nullification, was also the son of an Irishman, and his followers in Charleston set out assiduously to persuade the Irish to change their minds. The editor of the Calhoun paper in Charleston, Henry Pinckney, was an active member of the Hibernian Society and went to great lengths to attract Irish voters. He had, for example been a prominent supporter of Catholic Emancipation for Ireland and thus had credibility in the Irish community. He and other nullifiers were also more open in their politics, welcoming all white social classes into their associations. Thus, many Irish moved into the extremist camp even though it potentially meant conflict with the federal government. Pinckney's wooing apparently worked, because Charleston elected a nullifier ticket in 1832, and groups such as the Irish Volunteers under A. G. Magrath's father mustered to defend it.[64] Appeals from Irish American friends, who had shown themselves interested in Ireland and Irish immigrants, to support a state cause would work again in the early 1860s and help Irish immigrants overcome their love of Union once more.

All the Irish Volunteers' drilling and marching came to naught, however, as the Irish of South Carolina did not have to fight for their adopted state. When nullification failed to receive the support of other southern states, South Carolina repealed its defiance of the federal government and accepted compromise in early 1833.[65] The next major sectional crisis to threaten the breakup of the Union was a much more widespread one and would affect the Irish across the South. In the aftermath of the popular Mexican War (1846–48), the territory ceded from Mexico came into dispute between northerners and southerners in Congress. Southern opposition to the admission of California as a free state in 1849 and 1850 led to the first serious calls from the fire-eaters for southern secession, but no state wanted to be the first to move. Southern secessionists were dealt another blow when the U.S. Congress cobbled together the Compromise of 1850 to settle the issue of slavery in all the territory ceded from Mexico, including California. The only significant Irish supporter of this early secession movement was Richard Elward of Natchez. As editor of one the state's leading newspapers, the *Mississippi Free Trader*, he did have some political clout. A close supporter of local Democrat, notorious filibusterer, and southern fire-eater John A. Quitman, he was following the lead of his most important subscriber. Yet, even in Natchez, he failed to rouse Irish support for secession in 1850.[66]

In Georgia, Irish voters helped keep Savannah, which had been considered a strong southern rights town, in the Union camp, playing their part in the whole state's rejection of any move toward secession. The Irish voters had taken guidance from the local Hibernian Society and the local Catholic pastor and Gaelic speaker Jeremiah O'Neill. The society contained a number of slaveholders, and O'Neill had shown his southern bona fides on slavery when he had directly challenged Daniel O'Connell. At the Hibernians'

St. Patrick's Day dinner in 1850, many of the toasts to Ireland, America, and Georgia followed the usual pattern. But there was special emphasis on the United States and what it had done for the Irish. Following the playing of "Yankee Doodle," "Hail Columbia," and the "Star-Spangled Banner," the society reminded the revelers, and the local community at large through the copious coverage of the event in the local press, that the "United States of America, Our adopted country" was the "foe of Monarchy, the nurse of Liberty . . . and the asylum of the oppressed." Father O'Neill, who had pastored in Savannah since the early 1830s and was the Irish community leader, rose and stated: "May the general union of Irish hearts, of Irish hands, of Irish sentiment . . . be as perpetual and as divine providence will, I trust, render the confederated Union of our States." O'Neill's calling of God's blessing on the "perpetual" Union of the United States and the other toasts of the meeting sent a clear message to the Savannah Irish that they owed a lot to the United States and needed to support it.

Even in South Carolina, the Irish turned their backs on the radicals calling for immediate secession. Charleston voted for "cooperation" over immediate secession in 1851, and one of the leaders of that cause was A. G. Magrath. After this victory Magrath and other moderates pushed for South Carolinians to return to the fold of the national Democratic Party. This move would be the only way to ensure the preservation of South Carolina's "institutions," but it also led to the charge from the extremists that Magrath and his ilk were not honorable patriots but selfish place-seekers.[67] This charge had traction only in South Carolina and eventually provoked the tragic duel between Magrath's brother and Rhett's nephew in the mid-1850s.[68] Through the rest of the decade, the demise of the Whig Party and the dominance of the Democrats at the national level continued the close connection between the latter and Irish immigrants in the South. As long as a Democrat was president, Irish southerners felt little challenge to their economic, social, and political status. The Know-Nothing effort could have undermined this status, but Democratic opposition to the nativist movement cemented the Irish/Democrat alliance even more than before.

The rise of the Republican Party and its explicit rhetoric criticizing slavery did, however, threaten Democratic dominance of national politics in the mid-1850s. The growing conflict over slavery in the territories, the Dred Scott Supreme Court decision, and John Brown's raid heightened sectional tensions to such an extent that the southern fire-eaters felt confident enough again to make a challenge for secession in 1860. They knew they had to break the white South's allegiance to the Democrats, yet despite the best efforts of John Mitchel, the Irish were among those who retained a strong loyalty to the party of Jackson. At the Democratic national convention in 1860, the fire-eaters succeeded in splitting the party, which led to the national party's nominating Stephen Douglas and the southern rights bolters nominating Kentuckian John C. Breckinridge.[69]

The Breckinridge campaign dominated the South in the fall of 1860. Indeed, Stephen Douglas faced some violent opposition when he came to the region. As the national Democratic candidate, Douglas felt the need to campaign there.[70] Douglas too had fought against the Know-Nothings, and as the representative of the national Democrats he had an automatic appeal to the Irish in the South. Richard Arnold of Savannah, who had previously received major Irish support in that city, had to admit rather dejectedly that the Irish had deserted the southern Democrats. Having become radicalized by John Brown's raid, he had endorsed Breckinridge for the presidency, but his Irish constituents in the city apparently had not. While he did collect some funds for Breckinridge from leading Catholic families in the city, he wrote a friend, "I am sorry to say that there a great many adopted Irish citizens that are inclined to Douglas."[71]

Arnold was correct. Although Breckinridge swept the Deep South in the election, the Irish, for the most part, it seems, stuck with the national Democratic candidate (see table 2). In every southern locality with a large Irish population, Douglas polled above his statewide average.[72]

The only exceptions were Nashville, Tennessee, and Baltimore. Vicksburg and Savannah both were just above the average. In these cases it seems that the Irish connection to strong Breckinridge supporters in the Democratic Party was key. In Nashville, for example, Mayor Randall McGavock had been the leading friend of the Irish, campaigning hard for their vote in mayoral elections. McGavock was also a subscriber to John Mitchel's *Southern Citizen*. As a descendant of Ulster immigrants, he had gained the loyalty of that community, including, it seems, their support for Breckinridge in 1860. The Baltimore Democrats had forged links to the Irish during the Know-Nothing experience, which had driven the Irish into an alliance with large slaveholders in the eastern part of the state in voting for Breckinridge over Douglas. Vicksburg Democrats had always been beholden to Jefferson Davis, who had by 1860 converted fully to the southern rights stand. Naturally, they followed his lead and voted for Breckinridge.[73]

Savannah is the most intriguing case. Despite its large and politically active Irish population, Douglas's percentage of the vote was only 1 percent above his state percentage. Arnold's fears were exaggerated. The figures

TABLE 2 Vote for Stephen Douglas in the 1860 Presidential Election
in Selected Southern Cities

State	State Vote for Douglas (% of Total Vote)	County Vote (% of Total Vote) and Difference from State %
Alabama	13,618 (15.1%)	
Mobile County		1,823 (36.5%) + 21.4%
Georgia	11,618 (10.9%)	
Chatham County (Savannah)		320 (11.9%) + 1%
Richmond County (Augusta)		1,051 (45.7%) + 34.8%
Louisiana	7,625 (15.1%)	
Orleans Parish (New Orleans)		2,998 (27.6%) + 12.5%
Mississippi	3,288 (4.8%)	
Adams County (Natchez)		158 (16.1%) + 11.3%
Warren County (Vicksburg)		83 (5.6%) + .8%
Tennessee	11,384 (7.8%)	
Shelby County (Memphis)		2,959 (43.8%) + 36%
Davidson County (Nashville)		383 (5.7%) - 2.1%
Virginia	16,183 (9.7%)	
Richmond (City)		753 (17.4%) + 7.7%
Ohio County (Wheeling)		757 (36.4%) + 26.7%
Kentucky	25,641 (17.5%)	
Jefferson County (Louisville)		3,441 (36%) + 18.5%
Kenton County (across from Cincinnati, Ohio)		1,312 (36.9%) + 19.4%
Maryland	6,080 (6.6%)	
Baltimore (City)		1,503 (5.0%) - 1.6%

Source: Dubin, *United States Presidential Elections*, 159–88.

suggest that some Irish chose Breckinridge over Douglas. As "the Irishman's friend" in Savannah, his support for the southern candidate had some effect. In contrast, the Irish in Augusta seem to have stuck by Douglas. Indeed, 45 percent of the vote won the election in that city for Douglas, with "Constitutional Unionist" John Bell coming second and Breckinridge a distant third, 32 points below his state percentage. Another Whig town, Richmond, Virginia, did give Douglas almost double his percentage statewide support, but it was the Shenandoah Valley counties and their German farmers who provided his largest votes in the state. Richmond had traditionally been a Whig town and voted for Bell. Breckinridge, however, gained 1,167 votes and Douglas just 753. Undoubtedly, Henry Wise's endorsement helped Breckinridge win the majority of the Democratic vote, in the process pulling some Irish votes that way.

Where Douglas was not an available choice, that is, not on the ballot, such as in Texas, the Irish went wholeheartedly for the Kentuckian over Bell. The two Irish rural settlements in south Texas, Refugio and San Patricio Counties, gave Breckinridge 81.2 percent and 95.5 percent of their votes respectively. The sizeable Irish populations in Galveston and Houston helped provide the southern rights Democrat with just over 72 percent of the votes in each of their counties.[74]

Nonetheless, the fact that Douglas got any support in the areas of strong Breckinridge victories is due to the Irish and other immigrants. In cities such as Mobile, Memphis, and New Orleans, as table 2 highlights, the national Democrat received substantial support. Mobile saw Douglas more than double his statewide percentage, while in Memphis it was almost seven times the percentage of his vote in the state as a whole.[75]

In New Orleans too, the Irish stood by Douglas, thanks in large part to the scourge of the Know-Nothings, newspaper editor John Maginnis. As editor of the *New Orleans True Delta*, he hated the nativists with a passion and loved the Democratic Party with the same intensity. As early as June 1860, he had warned against "disunionists" who intended to break up his beloved party, and ultimately country, and to usher in a Republican victory for Abraham Lincoln. That year he had no doubt who to support: Stephen Douglas for president and Herschel Johnson of Georgia for vice president. His newspaper carried advertisements for all Douglas clubs, meetings, and rallies. These clubs throughout the city showed a strong Irish membership. The Third Ward in the First District was the heart of the established Irish community and included St. Patrick's Church and Hall as well as the offices of the *True Delta*. Irishmen M. J. Kernaghan, H. B. Gilmore, and T. O. Laughlin formed

TABLE 3 1860 Presidential Election in New Orleans

Candidate	First District	Second District	Third District	Fourth District
Bell	2,201 (48%)	1,250 (49%)	773 (45%)	758 (46%)
Breckinridge	1,086 (24%)	627 (25%)	447 (26%)	373 (23%)
Douglas	1,287 (28%)	652 (26%)	505 (29%)	513 (31%)

Source: *New Orleans Daily True Delta*, Nov. 6, 1860.

the club leadership there. Downriver in the poorer Third District, the Eighth Ward club was run by James Boylan while the Ninth Ward "Little Giant" club had John Kelly and Henry Brown as vice presidents. In the Second District (today's French Quarter), the Fifth Ward "Douglas and Johnson Independent Club" had Richard Kelly, Thomas Kavanagh, and Michael Nolan among its top officers. Across the Mississippi River in Gretna the "Douglas and Johnson Guards" included Barney McCabe and Richard Burk as vice presidents. Back in New Orleans, the Douglas and Johnson "Cavalry Club" was run by J. R. Clohecy (or Clohessey) and Michael O'Connor, the latter also being the Marshall of the "Tiger Club" in the Second Ward, First District (home to St. Teresa of Avila Catholic Church founded specifically for Irish Famine migrants). One John Madden coordinated the "Young Douglas Guard."[76] Former friend of the Irish, John Slidell, who supported Breckinridge in 1860, like Richard Arnold in Savannah, became very disillusioned with the Irish, going so far as to claim that they were "at heart abolitionists."[77]

Slidell's comment was hyperbole, but the Irish of New Orleans did reject his southern rights candidate. The political clubs played an important role in motivating Irish voters toward Douglas. Since the rise to power of the Know-Nothings in the city during the 1850s, political participation had declined. There had been nothing really to vote for as the Americans retained a tight grip on the city. While over 6,000 eligible voters failed to vote, almost 11,000 did, which dwarfed some of the turnouts of the late 1850s (only 2,000 voted in the mayoral election of 1857, for example). The support of Maginnis and the other Irish for Douglas seemed to pay dividends. While Bell won the city outright, reflecting the continued strength of the Whig/Know-Nothing element, Douglas beat Breckinridge in every district (see table 3). The centers of Irish settlement in the city were in the First and Fourth districts, with a substantial presence in the Third district too. The biggest defeat for Breckinridge came in the Fourth, formerly the city of Lafayette, and the Irish vote there (in what today is known as the "Irish Channel") played a role in that. Although disappointed that Douglas did not carry the city, Maginnis was glad that the "Little Giant" had at least beaten Breckinridge. Considering that Louisiana's most powerful Democrat, Slidell, and all the machinery of President James Buchanan's administration were behind the Breckinridge campaign, it was a remarkable result for Douglas. Maginnis had no complaints and respected the election results, stating that, "In regard to the police arrangements for the preservation of the peace we cheerfully say that they were admirable."[78] Maginnis never had praise for the Know-Nothing administration so this was a major gesture.

Abraham Lincoln's victory in the presidential election, however, left Maginnis chagrined. Louisiana governor Thomas Moore's call for a special convention to discuss the result angered him even more. He correctly saw this move as one toward secession and opposed the convention and secession with the same passion with which he had opposed nativism. Exacerbating his mood was the fact that "the leading organs of Know-Nothingism formerly, and Bellism latterly" had become "open" secessionists. Their endorsement of taking Louisiana out of the Union made it even easier for him to oppose any moves toward disunion. He railed constantly against abolitionists and secessionists but particularly against the latter. He warned that "this country is not Mexico: its industry, agricultural, mechanical, professional, and commercial cannot afford convulsions every few months as political demagogues or fanatical conspirators may desire or determine." He pointed out to his readers that the move toward secession in South Carolina did "not begin from below and work upwards" but was run by "the men who own three, four, five hundred or more slaves." Maginnis was appealing to the class interests of his downtown commercial readers and the poorer whites, particularly his large Irish readership. He warned that secession and any resulting conflict would mean economic hardship. "How many millions may be deprived of their daily bread; how many thousands, aye tens of thousands, are to be reduced to penury and want: how many now or recently affluent, will find themselves soon in beggary? We don't know," he continued, "and shall never truly ascertain; but enough is understood to enable every citizen to calculate accurately what is likely to be his own share of loss from the revolution and civil war, a fanatical faction in the free states, and the machinations of political demagogues in the slave states have initiated."[79] Secession and war would cost the Irish jobs.

South Carolina's secession on 20 December 1860 did not change his opinion. Indeed, it hardened his Unionism. Maginnis was perplexed by the strange alliance of "two swarms of insatiable office hunters—one the Slidell faction [Breckinridge Democrats], and the other the debris of Know-Nothingism." He took particular joy in pointing out the inconsistencies of the former Know-Nothings/Bell faction who, just weeks before, had put themselves forward as the defenders of the Union but were now endorsing immediate secession. Maginnis promoted his appeal to his large Irish readership by reprinting a section from the Constitutional Union Party platform that stated: "To our naturalized fellow citizens, we feel confident but a word is necessary—Everything they have gained in this land of freedom is at stake—those inestimable boons of liberty and republicanism for which they left their native land, which they sought as a heritage for their children, will be as dust and ashes in their grasp should vandalism [disunionism] destroy our fair republic." While highlighting the irony of this statement emanating from the "debris" of the Know-Nothings, Maginnis endorsed the sentiment wholeheartedly, and encouraged his fellow Irish men to stand by "this land of freedom."[80]

Maginnis realized quickly however that the sole viable alternative to immediate secession was the "cooperationist" ticket, which advocated that Louisiana secede only with the full cooperation of the other southern states. Maginnis, knowing that many Upper South states had sizeable unionist populations, argued that these be included in this cooperation because they were vital to New Orleans's prosperity. He dismissed prosecession Mississippi and Florida, which had followed the Palmetto State out of the Union in early 1861, as "unimportant" to Louisiana's economic well-being. Missouri and Kentucky were far more vital. Again, he hoped to influence the poorer folk, including the Irish, by emphasizing the disastrous economic results secession would bring. In this appeal, however, he conspicuously failed to acknowledge that one of the leading cooperationists opposed to immediate secession was the Honorable John T. Monroe, the Know-Nothing mayor of New Orleans.[81]

Maginnis's position and influence among the Irish were a threat to the secessionists' plans. They were indeed worried about the poorer whites' interest in their movement. In cities like St. Louis and Baltimore there was serious working-class opposition to precipitous moves toward leaving the Union.[82] Secessionists sought therefore to keep poorer whites, including the Irish, onside.

Even South Carolina radicals had to deal with this reality and encouraged poor whites to support their cause. Barnwell Rhett's *Charleston Mercury* went out of its way to praise the efforts of the Irish in late 1860 and early 1861. It sought to defend the Irish against charges they might be against secession. In one article it pointed out that the greatest critics of the South in England were also the greatest condemners of the Irish. The *Mercury* explained this congruence thus: "The first and obvious [reason] is that the Irish, whether living in the North or the South, are, to a man, on the side of the constitution, and will always be found there, in peace or war." Also: "The spectacle of an Irish Abolitionist is a phenomenon not often beheld in this part of the world. The Irish have seen so much of real slavery in Ireland, that when an Englishman affects to sympathise with the woes of 'nagurs,' Patrick, who knows by his own sad experience the hypocrisy and heartlessness of John Bull, only feels the most intense disgust and contempt." Contrary to English criticisms, the paper concluded, the Irish were not "indolent" but "industrious" and "their contributions to the labor of this country have given an irresistible impetus to all its great works of public improvement," the implication being that they would continue to do for the new republic of South Carolina.[83]

In Memphis those in favor of secession were more nervous, especially with the size of the Irish population in the city and their large vote for Douglas. The Democratic *Memphis Appeal* was not rabidly secessionist, but was sympathetic to moves in that direction. Its editor John M'Clanahan had been a stalwart friend of the Irish in the city, opposing the Know-Nothings and running for office on the Democratic ticket. Like Maginnis in New Orleans he had wholeheartedly supported Douglas in 1860, accounting in no small part for Douglas's sizeable vote there (see table 2). After Lincoln's victory, M'Clanahan endorsed secession as the only solution for Tennessee, especially after Mississippi seceded in January and more especially when the first seven seceded states formed the Confederate States of America in February and March 1861. Aware that his unionist arguments in the election campaign had persuaded many working-class Memphians, of whom the Irish were at the core, to vote for Douglas, he now felt the need to prod them gently toward secession. He published articles such as "The Advantages and Disadvantages of Trading with the Southern Confederacy— Important Considerations," to "The True Question—White slavery or black—the Non-Slaveholders' Interest," and articles on Irish struggles for freedom. In a direct appeal, "To the Non-Slaveholders of Tennessee," borrowing from the work of polemicist J. D. B. De Bow, he proposed "to demonstrate that the non-slaveholder of the South is directly interested in the institution of slavery as it now exists, and that the abolition of slavery in the South would be as detrimental to the prosperity of non-slaveholder, both pecuniarily and socially, as to the slaveholder."[84]

M'Clanahan began by describing how tough free laborers had it in the North, having to do the "menial" work that was reserved for slaves. They could not afford to send their children to school and thus had to send them to "free schools, where the child of the free negro is admitted to the same seat, the same rights and privileges, the same social position." In these schools children were instilled with the values of that "hydra-headed monster, abolition," which opened "Pandora's box" and all of the radical ideas such as "Mormonism, spiritualism, Fourierism, Millerism, freeloveism agrarianism, socialism and many other ideas of iniquity." Christianity was impossible in such a situation. In the South things were much better for the worker. First, pay for laborers and artisans was much better ("almost double"). Slave owners generated lots of business for carpenters, blacksmiths, and so on, as they used their slave labor in the fields. In the drayage business, one in which the Irish had a large presence, "nine out of ten" hacks owned their own horse and cart. He reminded non-slave-owning merchants that the planter was their greatest customer and thus "you have a direct interest in slavery even if you do not own one." All of this prosperity was jeopardized by one thing, abolition. The freed slave would "underbid you" if able to leave the plantation. As it currently stood, "not one in five hundred" competed with free labor, the implication here being that 499 more would be on their way to compete if the Republicans had their way. M'Clanahan was playing an explicit race card. Freed slaves would challenge non-slaveholders' livelihoods and their families.[85]

In another article he challenged some Memphis unionists who had used their own class arguments against secession. They had declared that as secession had begun in South Carolina, policies there did not come "from the masses" but from "the small minority who have wealth and political influence." In fact, they argued, South Carolina's government was of a "despotic form" and had to be treated with a severe skepticism. M'Clanahan countered that South Carolina, indeed all the slaveholding South, believed in the "'levelling up' principle," according to which "the social equality of the white race . . . [was] secured by the presence of a class who should perform menial services, and this was [one of] the most beneficial results of slavery." As South Carolina had the highest number of slaves to whites "in the Union," the only "aristocracy" it personified was "the aristocracy of race."[86] The Irish were a part of that race and thus had access to this "levelling up."

Whose argument would win the day among the Irish in the South? Some still retained a lot of affection for the Union. An unlikely reluctant secessionist to the end was sugar planter, international slave trade advocate, and sponsor of John Mitchel (he subsidized Mitchel's paper) Maunsel White. Despite his extreme position on slavery, White was still grateful to the United States for the success he had achieved after leaving County Limerick as a young man. He had fought with Andrew Jackson at the Battle of New Orleans during the War of 1812 and had supported Old Hickory and his party throughout his life, when most of his fellow sugar planters had supported the Whigs. Although a strong supporter of "southern rights," he had openly endorsed Stephen Douglas in 1860. Lincoln's victory in that election scared him immensely, but he was still nostalgic for the Union. At the height of the secession debate in early January 1861 he woke up on the morning of the eighth and wrote, "Very foggy misty morning now 46 years gone by since we defeated the British on the plains of Chalmette 6 miles below New Orleans. I am now an old man. I fear our Southern country have worse foes in the 'Yankees.'" In February he returned from New Orleans having celebrated George Washington's birthday and complained in his journal about the "machinations of corrupt and unprincipled politicians" who had broken up the Union and were condemning America to civil war.[87]

In Charleston the young Irish American attorney Michael Patrick (M. P.) O'Connor was also nervous about immediate secession after Lincoln's victory. Elected to the General Assembly in Columbia in 1858, O'Connor was a national Democrat. He had made his name warning against hysteria after John Brown's attempt to encourage slave insurrection at Harpers Ferry. He defended the Union by appealing to the patriotic spirit of the Mexican war and warning that, "If this Union should ever go down, which God forfend, it will go down in blood. The steps of the capitol will drip with the blood of its partisans." By March 1860, however, he had become more skeptical of this Union. In a St. Patrick's Day address to the St. Patrick's Benevolent Society, of which A. G. Magrath was a prominent member, O'Connor, mentioned how loyal the Irish in America, as political refugees, were to the "stars and stripes." However, he continued, "when the government ceases to perform the Constitutional functions, betrays its high and solemn trusts, and commits treason against the people, the adopted sons of South Carolina will be the first to trample it into the dust." Their first allegiance was to "the State that gives you protection." Thus "the Irishman beneath the shade of the Palmetto, can contemplate with surer hope the future if his native land, while he adheres to the preservation of liberty and of law, under the aegis of the ancient Commonwealth of South Carolina." As a result of this change of heart, O'Connor appeared on a large number of state-rights tickets for the 1860 election. But after Lincoln's victory, with the timing ripe for secession, he balked at the chance to secede immediately. Instead, he joined the cooperationist forces in the state assembly, much to the chagrin of Rhett and the fire-eaters in Charleston. O'Connor seems to have been out of step with his constituents too as he failed to get elected to the secession convention.[88]

John Mitchel had no such cold feet. He had left the United States in 1859 to pursue an opportunity to help the recently established Fenian Brotherhood raise funds in France. From Paris, though, he kept in touch with the United States, becoming a foreign correspondent for the *Charleston Mercury*. His articles focused on European matters, but he had been a secessionist well before Lincoln's election. To reluctant Irishmen he reminded them again that the only solution to America's sectional conflict was the same as Ireland's—"*Repeal of the Union*."[89]

While the vast majority of Irish in the South had ignored Mitchel's extreme "solution" in the late 1850s and through 1860, they were ready to embrace it after Lincoln's victory. In South Carolina Magrath had led the way with his flamboyant resignation. His action was endorsed by Irish supporters who helped elect him to the secession convention ahead even of Robert Barnwell Rhett. His former unit, the Irish Volunteers, mustered and drilled in the weeks following Lincoln's victory, saluted the "Liberty Pole at Hayne Street," and marched to the offices of the *Mercury* to cheer it and the "Palmetto Flag" hanging in its window. In Savannah, the Irish attended the massive secession rally in Johnson Square held just days after Lincoln's election. Savannah's immediate secessionists faced no opposition in their election to state convention from the Irish.[90] Richmond's Irish followed the already very "pro-Southern" Democratic Party and Henry S. Wise toward secession. In Memphis, Irish militiamen also participated in welcoming recently seceded Mississippi's troops into the town, months before their own state of Tennessee seceded. Even in rural communities such as the Irish settlement near Paulding in Jasper County, Mississippi, came out for secession.[91]

Every county with sizeable Irish settlement, except Adams (Natchez) and Warren (Vicksburg) Counties in Mississippi and Richmond County (Augusta) Georgia, endorsed immediate secession. (The three exceptions had always been strong Whig/Unionist areas). Of the six Irish-born members of secession conventions, four in Louisiana, one each in Florida and North Carolina, all supported secession. In North Carolina, County Tipperary–born attorney William Lander represented Lincoln County from the central part of the state. Although not a major planter, he was a slaveholder and an immediate secessionist. In Florida, Amelia Island planter Joseph Finegan represented his county and was also an immediate secessionist. Thanks to his close relationship with secessionist U.S. Senator David Yulee, he played a prominent role in the convention, chairing an important committee and actually calling for the vote to secede.[92]

In Louisiana, two of the Irish delegates came from rural areas. John Elgee represented Rapides Parish incorporating Alexandria on the Red River. Elgee was a forty-seven year-old attorney in this plantation district and owned extensive property, including sixteen slaves. To the northeast, Edward Sparrow, though trained as an attorney, was a major planter in the cotton-producing Mississippi River plantation area on the border with Arkansas. He owned two plantations and 226 slaves. In New Orleans, however, the two Irish representatives were of more modest circumstances. Thomas Kennedy was an attorney from the Second Ward while James McCloskey was a coal merchant in the adjacent Third Ward. Both wards were in the First District, the center of the Irish settlement in the city. Kennedy owned three slaves but McCloskey none. Although the vote was close in the first district, the two Irishmen and their fellow immediate secessionists swept the election to the secession convention. There were no Irish among the cooperationist candidates opposing them. In Baton Rouge, Kennedy and McCloskey followed a strict secessionist line, as did Elgee and Sparrow. The Irish delegates were a solid part of the secession majority and Louisiana became the sixth state to secede on 26 January 1861.[93] Despite the best efforts of John Maginnis then, the Irish, across class and geographical lines, had, in the aftermath of Lincoln's victory, endorsed the breakup of the Union.

Ultimately, the Irish accepted that Lincoln's election had changed everything. By early March 1861 seven states with about 50,000 Irish residents had seceded and formed a new political entity, the Confederate States of America (CSA). The secessionists had created a new nation and a state apparatus around it. The CSA's founders hoped to attract other slave states and become a powerful rival to their former nation.[94] Although never simply the "despisers of niggers," as Fanny Kemble had described them, the Irish acknowledged that the region's "peculiar institution" was valuable to them, even if they would never have the opportunity to participate in it directly. Their confidence in their own membership of the white race assured that they opposed the Republicans and embraced racial supremacy, even if they often bent the racial rules surrounding it.[95] But their support for secession had come late and reflected certain ambiguities toward the breakup of the nation. The question arose: would they be willing to fight for the new republic that had racial slavery as its "cornerstone"?

CHAPTER 2

Irish Rebels, Southern Rebels

The Irish Join the Confederate Army

The secession of southern states and the creation of the Confederate States of America compelled the Irish who wished to remain in those states to switch their allegiance to the new nation. Many also responded to calls to defend it, often forming their own ethnic units. About 20,000 Irishmen would serve in the Confederate armed forces. Rhetoric and images comparing the South's struggle with the North to that of Ireland with Great Britain were powerful motivators for joining up, more so than defense of slavery or the dire economic need of steady work in tough economic times. Feelings of manliness associated with going to war and getting caught up in the excitement at the beginning of conflict, as well as defense of home and family, played roles in encouraging the Irish to enlist. Nonetheless, some Irish remained reluctant to serve, and Confederate authorities would try to force them to do so. Those claiming "foreign exemption" from service as "British subjects" who had "never acquired domicile" in the South, and others who took money as draft "substitutes" drew particular attention and damaged the overall reputation of the Irish as Confederate patriots among the native-born community. Ultimately, then, the Irish would have to go beyond merely signing up and take their share of suffering on the battlefront to prove their loyalty to the Confederacy.

As John Maginnis kept up his harangue against secession in early 1861, his newspaper hinted at alternative Irish opinions in the city. On January 9, more than two weeks before Louisiana seceded, the paper reported that "New Orleans was alive with strange gatherings." These gatherings were the organizing of a task force, which the prosecession governor of Louisiana, Thomas Moore, had ordered to gather near the Mississippi River docks at the foot of Canal Street. Maginnis saw troops marching down St. Charles Avenue, close to the office of the *True Delta*, and turning right on Canal Street toward the River. Governor Moore had tasked them to take a steamer to Baton Rouge to aid the militia units there in the seizure of the Federal arsenal. The Washington Artillery, made up of the city's great and good, led the procession followed by the Louisiana Grays and the Louisiana Guards. Bringing up the rear, however, was the Sarsfield Rifle Guards, named for the famed Irish seventeenth-century cavalryman, Patrick Sarsfield. They were commanded by Captain James O'Hara and were the Irish militia company of "uptown" New Orleans, based in the heart of the community around St. Patrick's Church on Camp Street. O'Hara ran a boarding house and had a personal estate worth $500, but he was not a slave owner. Nonetheless, he led his Irish unit in the confrontation with Federal authorities, obeying the orders of his adopted state and ignoring his oath to his adopted country. He and his fellow Irishmen had rejected John Maginnis's calls for opposition to the convention trying to take Louisiana out of the Union.[1] The Sarsfield Rifles were thus among the earliest to defend the nascent southern revolution in Louisiana.

But it was across the South, in Charleston, where the Irish had been the first to participate in the seizure of Federal property. The Irish Volunteers may have serenaded the city's secession newspaper in the run-up to the state's secession, but it was the Meagher Guards, named in 1853 for Thomas Francis Meagher, who were involved in the "thrilling [military] activities" after South Carolina left the Union on December 20, 1860. They had already declared their motto as "Independence or Death" and exhibited themselves well as "citizen soldiers, the pride of Carolina, and the hope of the young Republic."[2]

These "activities" took place when the city woke up on the morning of December 27 to see smoke rising from Fort Moultrie on Sullivans Island near the mouth of Charleston harbor. The previous night, Major Robert Anderson of the United States Army had moved his command from Moultrie to the far more defendable Fort Sumter in the harbor and had been destroying some guns he could not carry with him. Charlestonians were outraged, and almost immediately military units mustered in the city. Under the command of Colonel J. J. Pettigrew, various units, including the Meagher Guards, now led by Captain Edward McCrady Jr., prepared for conflict. Organized as the "Rifle Battalion" the militiamen "advanced in double-quick time without music toward the Cooper River." There they boarded the *Nina* and sailed to another Federal fort, Castle Pinckney, on a spit of land in the Cooper close to the city. They stealthily landed and using scaling ladders entered the fort at its rear, opened the gate, and forced its one Federal officer, and a gang of civilian laborers, to surrender. In an act of open defiance of the Federal government, to great cheers they hoisted the flag of the *Nina*, a white star on a red background, over the "Castle." The Meagher Guards had participated in the first military action of what would become the Confederate States of America. Given the honor of stationing Pinckney, the Guards were now part of the siege of Fort Sumter.[3]

The eventual firing on Fort Sumter on April 12, 1861, by Confederate forces, and President Lincoln's call for 75,000 volunteers to put down the "rebellion," brought even John Maginnis around to the Confederate cause. He was the most reluctant of Irish secessionists, but he, and many other die-hard Unionists like him, embraced the new Confederacy once war began.

One of Maginnis's Douglas campaign colleagues, Captain Michael Nolan of the Montgomery Guards, was another classic example of that transition. The Montgomery Guards, oldest Irish militia unit in the city, founded in 1830, were drilling weekly in New Orleans after Louisiana's secession. Born in County Tipperary, Ireland, Nolan owned a coffee house, although not the property in which it was located, in the Fifth Ward in what today is known as the French Quarter, and had been treasurer of that ward's "Douglas Independent Club" in 1860. Indeed, this group supporting the national Democratic candidate for the presidency had been founded in his establishment. Thus, he had agreed with Maginnis's stand on the presidential election. But, as with most Irish, he had moved to the secession camp after Lincoln's victory, and, like many, he was prepared to fight for it.[4]

So ready was Nolan and his unit, they were among the first mustered into full Confederate service. Armed with guns seized from the armory in Baton Rouge, in part provided by their compatriots in the Sarsfield Guard, they were mustered in as Company E of the 1st Louisiana Infantry at the St. Charles Armory in late April 1861. Captain Nolan was presented with a sword by some of his sergeants and they all then participated in a parade of Confederate units around the city. The Irishmen were in line just behind the Wigfall Guards from Galveston, who had the honor of leading the procession because they had captured the Federal ship *Star of the West* off the coast of Texas just a week earlier. The Texans thus carried the Confederate flag at the head of the parade. The pole on which they carried it, though, had been supplied by Irish New Orleanians. It was "six feet of wood, more or less" and "borne sixty-three years ago in a more desperate War than the south is now engaged in—in the 'Irish rebellion' of '98, when it bore upon its top an Irish pike . . . a glorious weapon that saw good service on Vinegar and Oulart hills [important clashes in the 1798 rebellion], and on many a country road in the Old Land."[5]

The Montgomery Guards' lending of their historic staff to the Wigfall Guards was of huge symbolic significance. The anticavalry pike with its spear point and curved blade to tear at tackle was the iconic symbol of Irish nationalism and the Irish "revolutionary weapon" from 1798 until well into the nineteenth century.[6] Its ceremonial use meant that the Confederate and Irish causes were similar. The Irish military tradition of resisting Britain and its union with Ireland would, the pike staff implied, stand the South in good stead during the upcoming war.

This idea of the South's and Ireland's parallel struggles had resonance with natives because some of their leaders had already endorsed the comparison. As early as 1847 a prominent supporter of John C. Calhoun had warned that northern control of the Federal government meant it would dominate the South like Britain dominated Ireland, placing the South in a position similar to "the condition of Ireland." Calhoun agreed and claimed hyperbolically that year, as Ireland suffered through its Great Famine, that "the position of Ireland would be one of bliss compared to ours [within the Union]."[7] Jefferson Davis, too, found the Irish analogy compelling when motivating his fellow southerners to resist northern influence: "Shall we [southerners] stand with folded arms until a sectional party with the unchecked power of a three-fourths majority holds sway over us? Shall we sink in the United States Congress to the helpless condition which Ireland occupies in the British Parliament?"[8] By 1860, with the "Black" Republicans poised for electoral victory, many came to agree with Davis's view that the South's relationship to the North was as dysfunctional as that of Ireland's to Britain, and the only solution was, as John Mitchel had put it, "Repeal of the Union."[9]

For the Irish in the South, their own history proved inspiring for the upcoming Confederate struggle. It was the prime recruiting tool. In an attempt to raise a militia unit in Charleston in late 1861, in the aftermath of the Federal seizure of sea islands to the south of the city, slave dealer Thomas Ryan, for example, sought to, as he put it, "Raise a company of IRISH REBELS to enter into Confederate service for the defense of South Carolina." Ryan believed that the Irish soldier embraced "the name Rebel because his ancestors have been so called for more than six hundred years." The Confederate cause was the same as Ireland's, he said, because "the fanatical Puritans have landed on our soil. Oliver Cromwell lives again in the person of Abraham Lincoln. Should they succeed in capturing Charleston the butcheries of Drogheda will be repeated in our streets. Come forward then, my countrymen," he concluded, "and unite with the Cavalier and the Huguenot to expel them from our beloved State, and ensure to ourselves and posterity peace and happiness for ages to come."[10] The images of the "fanatical" Puritans and Cromwell in Ireland were powerful ones. Cromwell's place in the history of Ireland is a controversial one for scholars, but to most Irish he has the lowest place as the bringer of dispossession, destruction, and death. Ryan also made sure to mention the town of Drogheda in County Louth, the scene of the Cromwellian army's most notorious massacre in Ireland.[11]

Ryan knew his intended audience well. He opened his ad for Irish soldiers with an appeal to their Irishness but ended it by reminding them of their connection to their new home. Other recruiters also used examples of combined Irish and American patriotism to get the Irish to sign up even before the war. New Orleans, Richmond, Memphis, Mobile, Augusta, Savannah, and Charleston all had "Montgomery" Irish companies formed in the antebellum era, with a number of them mustering into the Confederate army in 1861. General Richard Montgomery was an Irish American patriot who had died fighting the British at Quebec in 1775. His death made him the first American martyr of the Revolution, and he seemed to epitomize the Irish willingness to fight to the death against a larger and better equipped foe.[12]

Savannah also had a unit called the "Irish Jasper Greens," named for the revolutionary war hero Sergeant William Jasper, who, like Montgomery, died fighting the British. Jasper had also been a hero at the British naval attack on Charleston in 1776, rallying the troops by waving the flag over the parapet despite the hazard of artillery fire. Similarly, he was leading a charge against the British lines during the "siege of Savannah" in 1779 when he was killed. Irish Savannahians claimed him as their local Irish American example when they founded their own ethnic militia unit in 1842.[13]

These American heroes could now be co-opted into the Confederate cause. Just as the Confederacy itself had seized George Washington for its own cause by placing him on its official seal, so too, could the Irish transfer their American loyalties to the new nation. Jefferson Davis had shown the way in his inaugural address claiming the memory of "our fathers" their "Constitution," and the "inalienable" rights of the Declaration of Independence. Davis's emphasis on the American and conservative nature of secession was in the main an appeal to other slave-state residents who still had affection for the Union and had not yet endorsed the Confederacy, but it would also have appealed to the reluctant secessionists among the Irish.[14]

Some Irish units embraced the new southern cause more openly. In Houston, Texas, local bar owner Dick Dowling, originally from County

Galway, led a company of Irish artillerymen named for the new president. The Jeff Davis Guards would form part of the 1st Texas Artillery, defending their state's coast against potential Federal invasion.[15] Similarly, in New Orleans, the Calhoun Guards were organized and named for the great southern hero and defender of slavery John C. Calhoun. Recruited and led by Henry Strong, an Irish-born coffee house operator in the Third Ward in uptown New Orleans and a slave owner (the census indicates he owned three), the company was overwhelmingly Irish.[16] Strong's choice of the late Calhoun for the company's name signaled that he and his soldiers were Confederate patriots, but he must have also been aware of Calhoun's Irish ancestry.[17]

Confederate patriotism for the Irish then was closely tied to their experience of Ireland and America. The organizing and naming of Irish Confederate units clearly indicates this connection and tells us much about the motivations of Irish volunteers. Irish heroes and themes dominated the specifically Irish ethnic units that served in the Confederate army (see table 4). Emmet was the most popular name, with six units using it and at least two others in 1861—one in Columbia, South Carolina, and another in Natchez, Mississippi—that apparently later merged into other units.[18] These units were named for Robert Emmet, who had led an abortive revolt against British rule in Ireland in 1803. He was tried and executed, but on his condemnation, made a speech from the dock advocating the rights of Ireland as a nation. Most famously, he insisted that "no man write [his] epitaph" until Ireland "[took] its place among the nations of the Earth." It seemed appropriate then to use his name for defenders of a new nation that had yet to be recognized. Though not as important perhaps as other United Irish leaders such as Wolfe Tone, Emmet's failed but romantic attempt at insurrection, his eloquent words, and the fact that his brother, Thomas Addis Emmet, kept his memory alive in America made him a hero to Irish Americans throughout the nineteenth century.[19]

Emmet inspired native-born Confederates too. For nations seeking their place among "those of the Earth," his rhetoric of sacrifice and unapologetic defense of the rights of national peoples was useful. As early as 1858 the "Prince of the Fire-Eaters," William Lowndes Yancey, had told northerners that he accepted the title of "rebel [and] traitor" in his desire to "dissolve the Union," and he embraced any price to be paid and would "appeal to . . . posterity, to the judgment of the world, to vindicate my name and memory, when as Emmett [sic] said, my country shall have taken her place once more as an equal among the nations of the earth."[20] The commencement exercises at the University of North Carolina in 1862 included a recitation on

TABLE 4 Irish Units in the Confederate Army

Unit (by state and city)	Confederate Designation
Alabama	
Emerald Guards, Mobile	Co. I, 8th Alabama Infantry
Emmet Guards, Mobile	Co. B, 24th Alabama Infantry
Georgia	
Jackson Guards, Atlanta	Co. B, 19th Georgia Infantry
Irish Volunteers, Augusta	Co. C, 5th Georgia Infantry
Montgomery Guards, Augusta	Co. K, 20th Georgia Infantry
Lochrane Guards, Macon	Co. F, Phillips Legion
Emmet Rifles (1), Savannah	Co. B, 1st Georgia (Regulars) Infantry
Emmet Rifles (2), Savannah	Co. F, 22nd Georgia Artillery Battalion
Irish Jasper Greens, Savannah	Cos. A (2nd) and B, 1st Georgia Volunteers (Mercer-Olmstead's)
Irish Volunteers, Savannah	Co. E, 1st Georgia Volunteers (Mercer-Olmstead's)
Montgomery Guards, Savannah	Co. E, 22nd Georgia Artillery Battalion
Telfair Irish Grays, Savannah	Co. H/A, 25th Georgia Infantry
Louisiana	
Moore Guards, Alexandria	Co. B, 2nd Louisiana Infantry
Irish Volunteers, Donaldsonville	Co. F, 7th Louisiana Infantry
Emerald Guards/Milliken's Bend Guards, Milliken's Bend	Co. E, 9th Louisiana Infantry
Madison "Tipperarys," New Carthage	Madison Light Artillery (Capt. Moody's Battery) (more than 160 Irish members out of 450)
Calhoun Guards, New Orleans	Co. B., 6th Louisiana Infantry
Emmet Guards, New Orleans	Co. D., 1st Louisiana (Nelligan's) Infantry
Irish Brigade (Co. A), New Orleans	Co. I, 6th Louisiana Infantry
Irish Brigade (Co. B), New Orleans	Co. F, 6th Louisiana Infantry
Louisiana Irish Regiment, New Orleans	Louisiana Militia (about 350 members)
Montgomery Guards, New Orleans	Co. E, 1st Louisiana (Nelligan's) Infantry
Sarsfield Rangers, New Orleans	Co. C, 7th Louisiana Infantry
Southern Celts, New Orleans	Co. A, 13th/20th Consolidated Louisiana Infantry
Mississippi	
Sarsfield Southrons, Vicksburg	Co. C, 22nd Mississippi Infantry
Shamrock Guards, Vicksburg	Co. C, 3rd Confederate Infantry
Missouri	
"Fighting Irish," St. Louis	Co. F, 5th Missouri Infantry
South Carolina	
Irish Volunteers, Charleston	Co. C, Charleston Battalion (later Co. H, 27th South Carolina Infantry)

Irish Volunteers "for the War" (originally Meagher Guards), Charleston	Co. K, 1st South Carolina (Gregg's) Infantry
Tennessee	
"The Irish Regiment," Memphis	2nd Tennessee (Walker's) Infantry/ 5th Confederate Infantry (about 700 men out 1,100 were Irish)
Jackson Guards, Memphis	Co. C, 154th Tennessee Infantry
"Sons of Erin," Nashville	10th Tennessee Infantry (about 800 Irishmen from central Tennessee)
Texas	
Jeff Davis Guards, Houston/Galveston	Co. F, 1st Texas Heavy Artillery
Virginia	
Emmet Guards, Alexandria	Co. G, 17th Virginia Infantry
Irish Volunteers, Alexandria	Co. C, 19th Virginia Heavy Artillery Battalion
O'Connell Guards, Alexandria	Co. I, 17th Virginia Infantry
Virginia Hibernians, Covington	Co. B, 27th Virginia Infantry
Montgomery Guard, Charlottesville	Co. F, 19th Virginia Infantry
Jeff Davis Guards, Lynchburg	Co. H, 11th Virginia Infantry
Emerald Guard, New Market	Co. E, 33rd Virginia Infantry
Emmet Guards, Richmond	Co. F, 15th Virginia
"Irish Battalion," Richmond and Covington	1st Virginia Infantry Battalion (about 320 Irish, approximately half of the original enrollment)
Montgomery Guards, Richmond	Co. C, 1st Virginia Infantry Regiment

Sources: Compiled Service Records of Confederate Soldiers, NARA; Lonn, *Foreigners in the Confederacy*, 496–502; Rogers, *Irish-American Units*, 18–42; Gannon, *Irish Rebels, Confederate Tigers*, 335–43; 362–68, 380–86; O'Brien, *Irish Americans in the Confederate Army*, 215–25; *Savannah Morning News*, Oct. 9, 1862; WPA, "Sources on Mississippi History: Warren County, MS," NARA; E. Gleeson, *Rebel Sons of Erin*, 341–54; Driver and Ruffner, *1st Battalion Virginia Infantry*, 91–129.

Emmet's life. Jefferson Davis's daughter Winnie, "the Confederacy's daughter," was so enamored with the Irish Rebel that she eventually published an essay about him in the 1880s.[21] Emmet fit well with the parallel struggle idea.

The next most popular choice of Irish names for Confederate units was the aforementioned Richard Montgomery. Montgomery would have also been familiar to most native-born Confederates as an early American hero. After Montgomery came Patrick Sarsfield. Sarsfield had been a great Irish cavalry hero in the Jacobite/Williamite wars against King William III (of Orange) in the late 1680s and early 1690s. Defeated, he and thousands of other Irish soldiers moved to mainland Europe, where they formed Irish regiments and brigades in the Catholic armies of the Continent. Sarsfield joined the French army, in which he died fighting in 1693, reportedly exclaiming at his death that he wished it had "been for Ireland." Other "Wild Geese," as they became known, followed the initial exodus to fight in European armies throughout the eighteenth century. The most famous unit was the Irish Brigade in the French army, which avenged numerous Irish defeats with its significant role in the defeat of British forces at the Battle of Fontenoy in 1745 during the War of Austrian Succession.[22]

The Irish Brigade's fame encouraged Irish Americans of both the North and the South in the Civil War to try to form their own version. Thomas Francis Meagher succeeded in the North because of its much larger Irish population, eventually filling the unit with three regiments from New York and one each from Massachusetts and Pennsylvania. Its name helped it become the most famous Irish unit of the Civil War, and one of its core regiments, the 69th New York Volunteers, recognized its origins by including banners that read "Remember Fontenoy" in its parades.[23] New Orleans with over 25,000 Irish residents in 1860 offered the best chance of an Irish brigade in the Confederacy, but eventually only two companies, mustered into the 6th Louisiana Infantry, took that title. Even regiments with "Irish" in their name, such as the 1st Virginia Battalion, the 2nd Tennessee (Walker's, reorganized in 1862 as the 5th Confederate), and the 6th Louisiana had large numbers of non-Irish members. Nonetheless, the Irish managed to keep and maintain an image of their units as "Irish." The closest to a totally Irish regiment in the Confederate army was the "Sons of Erin" 10th Tennessee Infantry recruited for the most part in Nashville and Clarksville, but it was undersized with just over 700 members.[24]

Units with the names Irish Volunteers, Emerald Guards, Hibernians, and Shamrock Guards indicate the influence of the Society of United Irishmen and their 1798 rebellion on the imaginations of Irish Confederates.

The original Irish Volunteers in Ireland had been founded in 1778, ostensibly to protect Ireland from French invasion during the War of American Independence, but they quickly developed into a force that pushed for Irish autonomy and legislative independence. Its leadership was Protestant and many of its members became United Irishmen. The most famous Confederate "Irish Volunteers" came from Charleston, where the original unit was founded in 1794, mostly by Protestants favorable to Irish independence. It was a United Irishman, William Drennan, a Presbyterian from County Down, who coined the term "Emerald Isle" in his poem "When Erin first Rose." The United Irishmen used the wreath of Shamrock and Harp as their main icons. These symbols spoke to an ancient Irish past before the religious divisions of the Reformation and various wars of the sixteenth and seventeenth centuries. (The Roman Saint Patrick had in legend used the Shamrock while the Celtic harp had long been the instrument of choice for the Irish bard.) Using the Roman classical name for Ireland, adopted by various "Hibernian" societies, was also an attempt to connect Ireland to an ancient past. It is not surprising that mid-nineteenth century Irishmen would use these terms to designate their ethnicity in, and connection to, the Confederate cause. The harp and shamrock were also incorporated in a lot of Irish Confederate flags. The Sarsfield Southrons of Vicksburg, for example, reflecting the dual nature of their identity, incorporated both in their flag. They chose the first national Confederate flag the "Stars and Bars" but with wreaths of shamrock as well as a Gaelic inscription on it. The Montgomery Guards of Savannah included a harp and Confederate stars on their banner. The Irish Volunteers of Charleston also included a harp on their flag.[25]

The most intriguing unit name would have to be the Southern Celts, who served in the 13th/20th Louisiana Infantry. Led by former New Orleans police chief Stephen O'Leary, who had lost his position and almost his life during the Know-Nothing conflicts of the mid-1850s, the unit's name hinted at the growing racial awareness among the Irish. O'Leary and his company, organized after secession in the Fourth District and headquartered on Tchoupitoulas Street underneath the Mississippi River levee, seem to have absorbed some of John Mitchel and other ethnic Irish nationalist theories on the "scientific" basis of the "Irish Race."[26]

The only surprising title for an Irish Confederate unit is the O'Connell Guards of Alexandria, Virginia. Presumably named for Daniel O'Connell, the Liberator had indeed been a great hero to the Irish, but his opposition to slavery and the American annexation of Texas and made him persona non

grata to most white southerners and to many early Irish immigrants. The unit probably contained more recent immigrants and perhaps the furor over O'Connell's positions taken in the early to mid-1840s had faded somewhat from memory.[27]

The striking absence in unit names is "Saint Patrick," which Irish volunteers, for example, had embraced in the Irish unit that went to Rome in 1860 to defend Pope Pius IX against Italian nationalists.[28] The name might have been tainted in the United States because it had been used by the "traitors" from the U.S. Army who went over to the Mexicans and fought alongside them as the "San Patricios" during the Mexican-American War.[29] The San Patricios had definitely been an embarrassment to the Irish in America. One Whig national correspondent in Mexico admitted when reporting on the "scoundrels" of the "St. Patrick's Battalion," that "to their credit, it must be said, the Irish in our army are loudest in denouncing the miserable wretches who fought and killed so many under this flag."[30] Nonetheless, the Irish were still ashamed. Democrats in the South started a rumor that the infamous ringleader John Riley, whom they called "Ryley," was not an Irishman at all but "a Londoner or Englishman" and his name was "really Ryder."

"Ryder," they added, had served in the British army in Canada before he came to the United States. The fact that the San Patricio flag had a harp and St. Patrick on it as well as *Érin go Bragh* (Ireland for Ever) emblazoned under the harp was ignored. This effort to turn "Ryley" into an Englishman failed to remove completely the odium of military units named for Saint Patrick and may explain its absence among the Confederate Irish.[31]

Other company names highlight local influences rather than Irish ones. The Jackson Guards of Memphis, led by the son of the first prominent Irish Catholic Memphian, was an old unit in the city named for the state's most famous son, Andrew Jackson. The Moore Guards of Alexandria, Louisiana, were named for the secessionist governor of that state and the Lochrane Guards of Macon for their sponsor, local Irish immigrant and prominent Georgia jurist, Osborne Lochrane. The Telfair Irish Greys seem to have been a spin-off from the Irish Jasper Greens named for Edward Telfair, a Scottish-born member of the Continental Congress and a major Georgia slaveholder. The Madison Tipperarys, or sometimes "Tipps," reportedly reflected that this group of Irish laborers working on the canals and ditches of the Mississippi River in northern Louisiana came from that county in Ireland. "The Fighting Irish" company F of the 5th Missouri only gained that title during the war. It contained numerous former Irish St. Louis militiamen who had been in units such as the Washington Blues.[32]

While ethnic units displayed Irish participation in the Confederate military effort most prominently, many Irish could be found in other units. Virtually every New Orleans company, unless designated as German, had a sizeable Irish presence. The Violet Guards of the 6th Louisiana, for example, raised in New Orleans, was largely Irish. Major Roberdeau Wheat's infamous Louisiana "Tiger" Battalion (1st Special Battalion Louisiana Infantry) recruited on the docks of New Orleans was almost half Irish. The 7th Louisiana Infantry had a number of Irish-dominated companies, again from New Orleans, especially the Virginia Blues and Virginia Guards. Similarly "Lee's Foreign Legion," the 10th Louisiana Infantry, had Irish scattered throughout the regiment but particularly in the Sheperd and Derbigny Guards. Even units made up of soldiers from the upper classes such as the Washington Artillery had Irish members.[33] Confederate units from other southern towns and cities usually had Irish members too. Companies such as the Republican Blues from Savannah and the Charleston Light Infantry, for example, who served alongside the Irish Jasper Greens and the Irish Volunteers in the 1st Georgia Volunteers and the Charleston Battalion respectively, had at least twenty Irish members.[34]

Smaller towns without specifically Irish units could have a sizeable Irish presence in their companies. The small Irish community in Natchez, Mississippi, made serious efforts to raise an Irish company but failed to do so for financial reasons. Irishmen instead joined units such as the Natchez Fencibles and the Adams Light Guard. Irish rural settlers often joined local companies as well. A small group of Irish immigrants farmed and founded their own Catholic church near Paulding, Mississippi. Many of the young men there supported secession and about thirty joined the Jasper Grays. Led by the Catholic Irish American newspaper editor J. J. Shannon, they mustered into the 16th Mississippi. Some of the immigrants in the well-established Irish settlements in South Texas at San Patricio and Refugio also joined the Confederate army.[35]

Specifically Irish ethnic units formed in rural areas were made up largely of labor gangs. The Hibernian Guards of the 27th Virginia and the Emerald Guards of the 33rd Virginia were recruited among Irish laborers in the Shenandoah Valley who worked on various public works projects. Similarly, the Irish Jeff Davis Guards of Lynchburg contained a number of Irish railroad workers. Laborers, usually ditch diggers and dock workers, who worked in the booming plantation counties of 1850s along the Mississippi River, signed up for the Madison Tipperarys, originally an infantry company that became an artillery one in Virginia, as well as the Emerald/Milliken Bend Guards. The sugar parishes of south Louisiana produced the Emmet Guards of the 7th Louisiana Infantry made up primarily of Irish ditch diggers.[36] One recruiter of Irish laborers in the Mississippi Delta stated that groups he met "confessed a willingness to fight for the Confederacy," which may explain why Vicksburg, with a relatively small Irish population numbering only in the hundreds, was able to produce two distinctly Irish companies.[37]

Urban areas, however, remained the main producer of Irish soldiers. The nascent Confederate marine corps, for example, had a large number of Irish members because it recruited primarily in southern port cities. The first marine company was raised in Montgomery, Alabama, but attention quickly shifted to the South's largest maritime city, New Orleans. A company was organized there by June 1861. The fall of that city in April 1862 meant that the marines had to move to Mobile, and it was in this city, along with Savannah and Charleston, that the majority of Irish marines were recruited. The Confederate capital and Wilmington, North Carolina, also had contingents of Irish marines. The marine corps proved attractive to the Irish because being stationed in the port cities meant the enlisted would not have to leave the cities in which their families, if they had any, resided marines usually served in coastal or river forts or on ironclads in the rivers such as the James or the coastal channels near Charleston. Some Irish transferred from army units into the marines in order to stay close to the city in which they lived. The Confederate marines never reached their allowed quota under navy regulations, but by 1863 there were about 560. Of these, about 150 were Irish or Irish American.[38]

The Confederate navy too attracted Irish immigrants because of its recruiting in southern port cities. The navy had a much tougher time organizing than the army had, because although the region had a strong military tradition, it did not have much of a maritime one. Most American ships and sailors had been based in the North. The South thus found itself at a disadvantage at the beginning of the war. In addition, the region had a history of mistreating foreign sailors of mixed racial heritage. For example, South Carolina's notorious Negro Seamen Act (1822), passed in response to the Denmark Vesey slave plot in Charleston, required free black sailors to be "quarantined" in the city's jails until their ship left port. Those "unclaimed" could be sold into slavery. Similarly, laws targeting ship captains with large fines for, wittingly or unwittingly, hiring runaway slaves discouraged mariners from settling in the South. Native-born slaves picked up the slack, playing a major role in the maritime business, especially in the intracoastal trade. But slaves could not be official military sailors.[39] As a result, the Confederate navy needed outsiders for its nascent force. While the Irish, like white southerners, did not have a particularly strong maritime tradition in the nineteenth century, many in the South had experience with harbor or river work.[40] One study found there were more than 600 Irish or Irish Americans in the Confederate navy, in a service that had only about 4,000 members (excluding marines). Irishmen could be found on virtually every ship doing all sorts of tasks. Most were regular sailors, but some were engineers, pilots, or gunners. As with the marines, some transferred from the army to the navy. Two members of the Irish Volunteers from Charleston, for example, left the army to serve in the navy.[41]

On the face of it, the Irish turnout for the Confederate armed forces seems impressive, with over thirty ethnic companies and a sizeable presence in the navy and the marines. The total number of Irish Confederates remains difficult to ascertain though. Very few of the existing muster rolls listed place of birth, and the Confederacy did not keep track of the ethnicity of their army. John Mitchel estimated that 40,000 Irish served in the Confederate army. In the 1860 census, there were about 84,000 Irish people listed for the entire Confederate States. Among the Irish population of three major southern cities, the percentage of males age fifteen and older (i.e., old enough to fight) was as follows: Richmond, 50 percent; Mobile, 46 percent; and New Orleans 42 percent, for an average of 46 percent. Applying this statistic across the South suggests a potential recruiting population of just over 39,000 Irishmen. This is something of an overestimate in that the Confederacy initially required only men age eighteen to thirty-five to serve, then later extended it to ages eighteen to forty-five, and eventually, near the war's end, ages seventeen to fifty.[42]

Even allowing for the inaccuracies of the census data, accepting Mitchel's number would mean a 100 percent Irish recruitment rate for the Confederacy. Of course, he may have been including soldiers from the border slave states such as Maryland, Kentucky, and Missouri in his estimate. Baltimore had an Irish population of more than 25,000, many of whom were in sympathy with the Confederacy, and thus a potential recruitment of around 12,000 Confederates.[43] Many Irish Baltimoreans had reacted negatively to Abraham Lincoln's election and participated in the infamous riot against Massachusetts and Pennsylvania troops traveling through the city on their way to Washington in April 1861. The harassing, blockading, and assaulting of the soldiers as they marched through the city finally caused them to retaliate by opening fire. Among those killed were several with Irish names, including Patrick and William Maloney, Francis X. Ward, James Carr, Patrick Griffith, Michael Murphy, and John McMahon.[44] Despite their prosecession sympathies, however, the vast majority of Irish Marylanders did not move south to join the Confederate army. Very few Irish names appear in the "Maryland Line," which consisted of the 1st Maryland Infantry Regiment, one other infantry battalion, two cavalry battalions, and four artillery battalions, and company B of the 21st Virginia Infantry (the "Line" was organized in Richmond and Harpers Ferry). For example, of the 4th Maryland Artillery's (Chesapeake Battery) 136 members, organized from among the militia of Baltimore and St. Marys County (on Maryland's western shore) who made it south to Richmond, only 10 had Irish surnames. In another unit, reportedly recruited from the Baltimore area, the 2nd Artillery (Baltimore Light Artillery) had only 33 Irish names out of 330 members listed. Ultimately, Irish Marylanders in the Confederate army probably totaled somewhere around 200.[45]

Similarly, in another border state, Kentucky, which had over 22,000 Irish residents, very few Irish joined the Confederate army. Unlike Maryland, Kentucky did not have a large pro-Confederate population, its only strong support being in the Bluegrass region around Lexington, along the mid-Tennessee border, and in the extreme western part of the state. Even though it was the border state with the largest investment in slavery, it had voted for Constitutional Unionist candidate and former Know-Nothing John Bell in the 1860 presidential election. It also elected a strongly pro-Union legislature in 1861 and 9 of its 10 congressmen were opposed to secession.[46]

The Irish, however, had had a traumatic relationship with Kentucky Unionists. The Know-Nothings had taken control of the state in 1855 and were particularly strong in Louisville, where the largest concentration of Irish lived. It was here, on the election day and night of August 6, 1855, that the greatest atrocity of the Know-Nothing troubles occurred. Organized violence against Irish and German immigrants led to over twenty-two deaths, attacks on a number of Catholic churches including St. Patrick's, and the firing of an Irish tenement known as Quinn's Row in which two children burned to death. Nobody was convicted of the crimes. Many immigrants left the city, leaving only 6,000 in the city in 1860.[47] Despite this atrocity committed by the Unionist Know-Nothings, it seems there was little Irish sentiment for secession in Kentucky. Native Kentuckian John Breckinridge came in a distant third in Louisville in the 1860 presidential election, and the Louisville Courier blamed Irish support for Douglas and German support for Bell as the reason for his poor showing.[48]

The location of Irish settlement in the state also worked against Confederate recruitment. The majority of the Irish lived in Louisville and Covington, the state's two largest cities. Both are on the Ohio River and had strong economic connections to the North (Covington is directly across the river from Cincinnati, Ohio, and Louisville had important railroad links with Chicago). Louisville, in particular, was vital to Federal interests, and Kentucky Unionists as well as the Lincoln administration made sure to secure the city. By September 1861 open support for secession had been quashed there. The city would become a major supply depot for the Union armies in the western theater. Louisville actually did very well economically during the war.[49]

A few Irish from Louisville did join the 9th Kentucky Confederate Infantry as part of the famous Orphan's Brigade but Irish names numbered only about 65 in the whole regiment. In contrast, just Company G of the 15th Kentucky Federal Infantry, recruited in Covington, had more Irishmen in it than all of the Confederate 9th.[50] Most Irish Kentuckians, however, followed their native neighbors and "sat out this fight." Only about 75,000 white Kentuckians, 25,000 Confederate and 50,000 Union, out of a potential recruitment population of 262,000, fought in the war, making an enlistment rate of only 29 percent. If that rate is applied to a potential Irish fighting population of 10,000, it means that only about 3,000 Irish from Kentucky joined up in total. Applying the statewide ratio of 2:1 Federal to Confederate recruitment, which may be too high on the Confederate side because most Irish lived under Federal control in Kentucky, would mean at most 1,000 Irish Kentucky Confederate recruits. The actual number is probably closer to 500.[51]

Missouri had the largest potential Irish population for Confederate recruitment in the border states. The 1860 census listed almost 30,000 Irish residents of St. Louis and 43,000 for the whole state. St. Louis, at the confluence of the Mississippi and Missouri Rivers, had strong connections to the state's plantation belts along both rivers as well as to the slave states down the Mississippi.[52] Indeed, it was the 50,000 strong German population in the city that provided the backbone of pro-Union support there. Missouri, unlike Kentucky and Maryland, also had an explicitly prosecession governor in Claiborne Fox Jackson. The Democrat Jackson had been elected in August 1860 and took office in early 1861. He called for a state convention to respond to Lincoln's election and the founding of the Confederacy, but to his chagrin, the convention meeting in March 1861 refused to endorse secession.[53]

There was, however, a major confrontation between Missouri Confederates and Unionists in St. Louis, and the Irish were involved in it. Governor Jackson tried again to stir his fellow Missourians after President Lincoln's call for volunteers, writing a stern letter to Secretary of War Simon Cameron refusing Missouri's cooperation with Lincoln's policy. Worried about Jackson's belligerence, U.S. Army officer Nathaniel Lyon took matters into his own hands and organized two pro-Union regiments of Germans with the aid of local Republican politician Frank Blair Jr. In response, Jackson called out the militia in St. Louis under the command of Brigadier General Daniel M. Frost. Frost gathered his soldiers in Lindell Grove in early May just west of the city, renaming the area Camp Jackson in honor of their supreme commander. Among the companies in the 1st Missouri Militia Regiment were the Sarsfield and Emmet Guards under the command of Captains Charles Rogers and Phillip Coyne as well as the St. Louis Grays, Washington Blues, and Washington Guards, commanded by Captains Martin Burke, Joseph Kelly, and Patrick Gorman, respectively. Just a few days after mustering, however, Captain Lyon marched his troops from the St. Louis Arsenal to Camp Jackson, surrounded the militia, and ordered their surrender. General Frost complied and surrendered his men and their weapons. As Lyon's soldiers escorted the militia to prison, a raucous crowd gathered to jeer and insult the "Dutch" (German) Union soldiers. Eventually a shot rang out, and the soldiers commenced to open fire on the crowd. In the resulting violence at least thirty-six people died, including twenty-seven civilians, among them a boy and a girl, both fourteen years old, and Irishmen Thomas Ahearn, Patrick Enright, and Francis Whelan. The militia men were released over the next few days, but there was much bitterness in the city against the German soldiers. Nevertheless, the city stayed firmly in Union hands and those wishing to join the Confederates gathering at the centrally located state capital, Jefferson City, would have to do so clandestinely.[54]

There were some Irish who did. One unit, the Washington Blues under Captain Joseph Kelly, was already in the Confederate headquarters near the capital. They had left Camp Jackson just before Lyon's move, and Kelly and his men now took part in the organizing of the Missouri State Guard to oppose the "occupying" Union forces in the state. Along with the state guard, some of whom had been organized into the 1st Missouri (Confederate) Infantry as early as June, a number of new regiments were organized in January 1862 and all became the 1st Missouri Brigade. There were a number of Irish in the 1st and 5th Infantry Regiments and others in the various artillery units organized from St. Louis militia. Prominent Irishmen included Captains James Kelly, Martin Burke, and Patrick Caniff, the latter becoming commander of the famous "Fighting Irish" company of the 5th.[55] Irish numbers grew so large that Father John Bannon, originally from County Roscommon, snuck out of St. Louis to join the Confederate Missourians in mid-December. It took him five weeks to make it to the newly organized brigade. He would serve as their unofficial chaplain until the siege of Vicksburg in the summer of 1863 (see chapter 5). Bannon estimated that he catered to the spiritual needs of about a thousand Catholics. The majority of these would have been Irish or Irish American, although some of these Irish "Missourians" were recruited from Memphis and New Orleans. Two companies of the 1st Missouri, for example, had Irish members from these cities. After the Battle of Pea Ridge, Arkansas, in March 1862, the Confederates lost their foothold in southern Missouri and "organized" Confederate recruiting in the state was limited to guerillas and Sterling Price's "raid" in 1864. Nonetheless, it can be assumed that there were about 800 Irish in the brigade.[56]

Some Irish Missourians, however, joined other states' units. Patrick Ahearn (also spelled Ahern), for example, had come to St. Louis in 1854 from County Tipperary. He was a member of the Washington Blues captured at Camp Jackson, but after his release he decided "to find a way to get to the South." He and a couple of colleagues "went to work and raised

40 men." To avoid the suspicion of the Federal authorities, Ahearn organized his group as a laboring gang and they "went to work as Railroad hands at Evansville, Indiana." From there they managed to travel to Cairo, Illinois, and then took a steam boat to Paducah, Kentucky. Once "the boat landed" the relieved Irishmen "walked out and raised the Confederate flag on the wharf." They eventually made it to Memphis, where they met a Captain George Hunt from Greenville, Mississippi, who had 60 men ready to enlist. The two forces combined and enlisted as a company (Ahearn claimed the name Erin Guards for it after the war) in the 13th Arkansas Infantry in Belmont, Missouri, in July.[57]

With these Irish like Ahearn scattered through other units, overall there were about a thousand Irish Missourians in Confederate service. Ahearn and his cohorts' extreme effort to join the Confederate army was the exception rather than the rule, however. As in Kentucky, far more Missourians served in the Union army than in the Confederate one, and the same is probably true for the Irish who lived in the state.[58] Ultimately, some 1,800 Irishmen served the Confederacy from the border states.

The vast majority of Irish who served were therefore from the eleven Confederate states. How then to measure the Irish enlistment when estimates vary for the total number of Confederates in general? Counting Irish soldiers is complicated. Some original company rosters, such as those for the 6th Louisiana Infantry and the Emerald Guards, Company I, 8th Alabama Infantry, list nativity, but not for every soldier.[59] Problematic though it is when working with a definition of "Irish" as one of birth or active Irish ethnicity, one is left with surname analysis as the only practical way to assess total Irish numbers.[60]

This name analysis works best with a list of Mobile, Alabama, companies compiled by the United Daughters of the Confederacy in the late nineteenth century. The official compiled service records in the National Archives are more difficult to deal with because they are organized by regiment and then by surname, not by geographical location. Company names are listed, but usually only by letter, often giving no hint of the geographical origin of the company. Having 38 infantry and artillery companies (and 2 cavalry companies) listed for the same city with a sizeable Irish population makes Mobile an ideal sample for an attempt to assess overall Irish recruitment. The 38 companies compiled include the names of just over 3,300 soldiers. There were 532 Irish names listed, making up 16 percent of the total number of soldiers.[61] The 1860 census listed a potential Irish recruitment of 1,530 adult males. If these two numbers are correct, that means that 35 percent of Irish males age fifteen and above joined up in 1861 and early 1862.[62] If this recruitment rate of 35 percent for the Irish was repeated across the Confederacy, it would mean an Irish enlistment of 13,560. Adding the 1,800 from the border states, and those in the marines and the navy, brings the total number of Irish in the Confederate armed forces to more than 16,200.

Of course, this number would have been supplemented as the war continued. These numbers do not include those Irish who joined state militias or home guards, particularly in locations such as Montgomery, Mobile, and New Orleans. When cities faced immediate Union attack, Irish men and other foreigners could be called into local defense units. There were at least 350, for example, in the Louisiana Irish Regiment from New Orleans.[63]

Some number of Irish were also conscripted once the Confederacy was created or took the place of others as paid substitutes after the enactment of the Confederate draft in April 1862. A study of "reluctant rebels," those who did not volunteer during the first outburst of Confederate enthusiasm in the spring and summer of 1861, estimates that 24 percent of Confederate soldiers who served were either drafted or took money to become substitutes. Using this Confederate rate of 24 percent of recruits as conscripts means that another 5,000 or so Irish should have been drafted. This number brings the total Irish recruitment to somewhere around 21,350, although this may again be too high, because New Orleans had fallen before full implementation of the draft.[64] If one accepts, say, 20,000 as a reasonable compromise, it would mean an enlistment rate just over 50 percent among the eligible Irish in the South, which is still fairly remarkable. Many Irish laborers in the South were very transient, and the fact that the Confederacy managed to recruit that many, either voluntarily or involuntarily, speaks well of its enlistment structure. A similar enlistment rate among the Irish in the northern states would have provided close to 300,000 recruits for the Union army rather than the 150,000 or so there were.[65]

There is also evidence, however, of a number of Irish in the South avoiding military service. In May 1861 they were given an excellent opportunity to do so legally when Queen Victoria, on behalf of her government, declared that all her subjects had to remain neutral in the Civil War. The British authorities did not recognize foreign naturalization, so even those Irish who had become American could claim British citizenship as a valid excuse for not signing up.[66] Thomas Hagan of Augusta, for example, decided to take advantage of this fact in July 1863 when he wrote to the British consul in Savannah to inform him that he and other British subjects were to be forced into the militia, even though the city was not under threat of Federal attack. He felt this action would violate his "oath not to take up arms" and he would rather go to prison "than to join any of their military companies." It's not known if Hagan's appeal worked, but it is unlikely it did. Governor Joe Brown of Georgia refused to intervene in the case, and the Confederacy withdrew recognition of British consuls in October of that year.[67]

The Confederate conscription legislation did initially acknowledge this exemption for non-domicile, but only for those who had not naturalized or declared an intention to do so. Some Irish claimed the exception to avoid conscription well before Hagan did. They sought certificates from British consuls as proof of their British citizenship. John Mangan of Charleston, for example, received one from the consul there in September 1862 stating that "after careful examination" the consul had "good reason to believe" that Mangan was "a native of Ireland" and "a Subject of Her Britannick Majesty, who never forfeited his claim to the protection of the Queen, by becoming a Subject or a Citizen of any Foreign State."[68]

These certificates seem to have numbered, at most, in the hundreds, though. Some Irish may not have needed them to avoid service. Many types of skilled workers would have been exempt under the April 1862 draft law. Records indicate, however, that even with British consuls working hard to support those who wished to remove themselves from the draft, the Confederate Conscription Bureau granted only 371 foreign exemptions in those areas east of the Mississippi River under their control in the summer of 1862 (officially listed as Virginia, North Carolina, South Carolina, Georgia, Alabama, Mississippi, Florida, East Tennessee, and East Louisiana).[69] Of the 371, some 167 were given in North Carolina alone, a state with a minuscule Irish population. Like North Carolina, Alabama also had 167 exemptions and, with its larger foreign population, some Irish must have benefited here. Virginia gave only a measly 25 exemptions, which means that the Irish in this state would have found it very difficult to avoid the draft on account of their British citizenship. Georgia granted only 12, and South Carolina none, even though both states conscripted approximately 9,000 men. Both had tough enlistment policies, in Georgia's case, much to Thomas Hagan's chagrin, for the militia too. By the end of 1863, Georgia, Mississippi, South Carolina, and North Carolina had made service in their respective militia compulsory for all adult males between the ages of eighteen and fifty (extended to fifty-five in Georgia in 1864). Many of those Irish who had occupational exemptions may have lost them in 1864 and 1865.[70]

These low totals of foreign exemptions, however, perhaps do not reflect the numbers who applied. Some Irish were undoubtedly forced into service. As early as the summer of 1861, Irish in New Orleans and other cities complained to the British consuls of their treatment. John Kilday, for example, was seized from outside his house in New Orleans in May 1861 and press-ganged into the "Tiger Rifles." His friends interceded on his behalf but failed to win his release. At least a half dozen more cases occurred in June and July. Michael Martin was "seized on the levee, whilst carrying a bunk from a steamer" and forced into the Ripley Guards. According to his wife, James Gorman was seized by soldiers of the Carroll Guards and forced to sign up after being "severely cut and bruised, and his clothes torn off his back." A common tactic was to have men arrested for "desertion." Michael McCann was "seized at his boarding house, 29 Girod Street, by a soldier from the Ripley Rifles assisted by police officer Duncan, upon the false pretext of his being a deserter, but three respectable witnesses swear that he had only arrived in the city day previous, he being employed on the [Mississippi] River."[71]

British consuls seem to have taken care of these egregious early cases, and some Confederate authorities ordered that respect be paid to consular certificates of exemption. The 1862 conscription legislation was supposed to bring a consistency to the process, but it made things worse for Irishmen reluctant to serve, particularly those far away from any sort of consular protection. The massive casualties taken by Confederate forces in the spring, summer, and fall of 1862, for example, created an acute need for manpower. One young Irishman, Charles Haley, just seventeen, found himself caught up in this desperate climate. He was drafted in Chattanooga, Tennessee, in September 1862. Before being shipped to the front, Haley escaped to Knoxville but was arrested there and returned to the army. Fortunately, the young man made his plight known to the British consul in Charleston, South Carolina. The consul lobbied the Confederate War Department, and the Irishman was eventually discharged in February 1863. At least Haley could write and inform someone within the Confederate lines of his predicament. The British consul in Mobile worried that, in more rural regions of his jurisdiction with poor communications, those Irish faced with an aggressive "Enrolling officer," who "defies all British protection," could easily be forced into the army.[72]

Confederate conscription officials definitely forced some reluctant Irishmen into the military, but the draft provided financial opportunity for others. The first conscription act of April 1862 allowed the traditional practice of hiring a substitute. Those with the means could hire another to take their place in the draft. Over 70,000 draftees purchased substitutes for the

Confederate army. The men hired were usually "desperately poor" and thus the Irish were among them.[73] There was serious money to be made. One Virginia native-born soldier complained to the press in October 1862, when the age for conscription had been extended to forty-five, that his brigade was "besieged by swarms of citizens between the ages of thirty-five and forty-five each of them bringing with him a substitute for himself and several for his friends at home." These substitutes were "all Irishmen" who were "taken with the least ceremony."[74]

The most remarkable record that exists for Irish substitutes is the one kept by Bishop John Quinlan from Mobile, who acted as a banker for substitutes, looking after their fee while they served in the army, and also guaranteeing to the payer that the substitute did not abscond. Some "professional" substitutes, numbers of whom were Irish, did just that. One Daniel Dwyer, for example, from Lynchburg, Virginia, who had a tattoo of the crucifixion on his arm, enlisted in the 23rd Georgia as a substitute in 1863 and deserted just one day later.[75] In Quinlan's ledger there is evidence of at least forty Mobile Irishmen between 1862 and 1863 receiving between $1,000 and $3,000 for replacing a draftee. The fee increased in the latter year because of the increasingly bloody nature of the war and rampant inflation in the domestic Confederate economy. Even $1,000 represented at least two year's wages for most laborers. It's no wonder many jumped at the chance to sign up instead of leaving the Confederacy to avoid service. Some of these Irish substitutes could indeed have left because they had connections up north. On depositing their money with Bishop Quinlan, a number named beneficiaries outside the Confederacy, to whom their money should be sent in the event of their death in service. Substitute Edward Kennedy, for example, left instructions for any legacy to be sent to his brother and sister, Patrick and Eliza, in Boston, while John Keating wanted any surplus funds sent to his wife and three children in St. Louis. Others wanted money sent to relatives in New York, Ohio, and Illinois, and/or, if possible, to family in Ireland.[76]

Why did these men choose to stay in Mobile rather than join their friends and family in the northern states where they were less likely to be drafted into service? Most Irish, apart from most of those in New Orleans, who had come to the South in the antebellum era, had not come there directly because of the lack of direct shipping links between southern ports and the United Kingdom. Even those who had come directly may have had friends and/or relatives in the North. By 1862, however, it was very difficult to travel around the South without a "passport," and crossing military lines without one was illegal. The whole country was littered with Provost Marshals checking on people's movements. Transportation itself was also difficult because the Confederacy's rail network creaked under the pressures of transporting men and supplies for the war effort.[77]

Later in the war, even if one had the means and the inclination, some Confederate authorities did not like foreigners who had lived under the Confederacy's "protection," leaving just as their adopted state needed them. Thomas Hagan, who had complained to the British consul in Savannah about being drafted into the militia, had tried to go from Augusta to Virginia to travel across the lines "under a flag of truce" into a Federal controlled area. He had, as he put it, attempted "to leave this unhappy country and had my clothes packed up and my passport for Richmond procured . . . when they published in the city papers that they shut down the passport window office and refused to give any passports to foreigners." He "and a great many others who [were] ready [were] disappointed for the present," although he "hoped" it would reopen soon.[78]

Irishmen who worried about having to serve in the Confederate armed forces could, however, have left during the period of secession. The Philadelphia artisans working on a Natchez planter's dream mansion, for example, put down their tools and left immediately for the North on the war's outbreak. Why did large numbers of Irishmen, skilled and unskilled, stay?[79] Many Irish were perhaps too poor to leave at such short notice. The economic situation in New Orleans declined immediately after the outbreak of war, when a rapid fall off in trade, the city's lifeblood, halted business activity. Tax receipts dropped precipitously, and the city faced bankruptcy in early 1862. The Confederacy's self-imposed embargo on cotton exports to pressure European governments into recognition only exacerbated the situation. Public and private works projects halted, leaving many Irish laborers out of work.[80] The situation seemed so grievous to the British consul in the city that he "found it impossible to assist everyone" who applied for aid and, as a result, "some of them in order to save themselves from starvation, enlisted in military companies to serve in the present war."[81]

For some it may have been the only option. Those Irish laborers up the Mississippi River, for example, whom a Confederate recruiter had declared "confessed a willingness to fight," may have done so just to earn a living.[82] Assessing the socioeconomic status of Irish Confederate soldiers is difficult, because original muster rolls that recorded occupational status are rare. There are, however, five Irish ethnic companies that can be analyzed. Table 5 examines the occupations listed for Irish soldiers in these companies. The occupational status of these five companies generally mirrors the

TABLE 5 Occupational Status of Irish Confederate Soldiers in
Selected Companies

Company	White-Collar	Skilled/ Artisan	Semi-skilled/ Unskilled	N (100%)
Co. I, 8th Alabama (Emerald Guards, Mobile)	24%	34%	42%	101
Co. B, 6th Louisiana (Calhoun Guards, New Orleans)	9%	38%	53%	138
Co. F. 6th Louisiana (Irish Brigade Co. B, New Orleans)	11%	13%	76%	107
Co. I, 6th Louisiana (Irish Brigade Co. A, New Orleans)	5%	15%	80%	93
Co. C, 1st Virginia (Montgomery Guards, Richmond)	12%	18%	70%	92
Combined companies	12%	25%	63%	531

Sources: Compiled Service Records of Confederate Soldiers, NARA; Gannon, *Irish Rebels, Confederate Tigers*, 335–43, 362–68, 380–86.

Irish male population in the South as a whole, in that those in semi-skilled and unskilled positions dominated. These percentages virtually match the overall occupational statistics recorded for Irishmen in Mobile, New Orleans, and Richmond in the 1860 census. There is not much real sign of a major overrepresentation of the very poor. Looking at the units individually, the Montgomery Guards of Richmond and the two companies of the "Irish Brigade" from New Orleans had about 10 percent more members in the lowest socioeconomic scale than the general Irish male working population of their respective cities. Richmond, with its industrial base, had the highest proportion of Irish skilled workers in the South in 1860, and many of these artisans probably found work in the booming war industries in the town and did not have to join up to earn a living.[83] In Richmond, too, all Irish, skilled or unskilled, would have, because of geographical proximity, found it easier to move North immediately after secession. It seems surprising that so many laborers decided to stay and enter Confederate service when they had more opportunity to move "back" to the United States. Leaving New Orleans may have been easier from a logistical, if not financial, standpoint with the large number of ships and river boats in the city. The British consul quoted above may have exaggerated some, but it does seem that the economic downturn after the war's beginning left military service as the only option for some of the poorest Irish. This factor may explain the larger numbers of laborers in the Irish Brigade companies compared to the others.

The Calhoun and Emerald Guards, however, highlight that other forces beyond steady pay were incentives for the Irish to sign up. Personal connections and appeals to friendship and acquaintance could be more powerful than soldier's pay. Both units were led by prominent Irish businessmen, Henry Strong and P. N. Loughrey, respectively. The former operated his coffeehouse in the heart of Irish New Orleans and owned substantial property, including slaves. He seems to have used his business connections to recruit a number of clerks and skilled men, who perhaps frequented his establishment, to serve with him in Confederate service. He certainly was popular in the 6th Louisiana as a whole, because in May 1862, under the reorganization required and elections granted when Confederate soldiers had to reenlist "for the War," he was elected lieutenant colonel of the regiment.[84]

Loughrey did an even more impressive job of recruiting among the white-collar Irish. A prominent merchant, he owned three slaves in 1850 (the 1860 census taker seems to have missed him). He had a large number of clerks and fellow merchants in his company, making up almost 25 percent of his company. The Mechanics' Fire Company also seems to have enlisted into the company, giving it an overall much higher socioeconomic status than other Irish companies.[85] Most companies on both sides during the war were recruited locally and thus knew well the men they served with. Harry Hays, a prominent lawyer in antebellum New Orleans, who would later become commander of the 1st Louisiana Brigade in the Army of Northern Virginia, for example, recruited among the law offices in New Orleans to create the Crescent Rifles, Company H of the 7th Louisiana, one of the most white-collar companies in the Confederate army.[86] Strong and Loughery seem to have used similar tactics in their recruiting.

The Irish had an added an incentive for signing up: national pride, and not the Confederate kind. As highlighted earlier, Confederate recruiters found Irish nationalism very useful in their recruiting appeals. The parallel-struggles concept was a powerful one. Confederate organizers would not have used it so much if it did not work. Organizer Thomas Ryan, who appealed to Irish awareness of the dreaded Cromwell, had already been in the

Irish Volunteers (Company K [Gregg's], 1st South Carolina Infantry) before returning to Charleston to raise his own company. Having served with a large number of poor Irishmen, he knew what could motivate them to sign up.[87]

Irish history could encourage American-born Irish southerners too. Lying in his hospital bed after being wounded and captured at Gettysburg, the young John Dooley Jr. of Richmond consoled himself with Ireland's history in continuing the fight against the Union army. With time on his hands he was reading about the United Irish rebellion against British rule and wrote in his diary: "Read today of the fearful cruelties perpetuated by the English soldiers in '98 [1798] upon the Irish. Their fiendish acts upon defenseless people we find sometimes paralleled by the infamous brutalities of the Yankee mercenaries of the present day." Dooley never took the oath of allegiance and was not exchanged until February 1865, after two and a half years in Union prisons.[88]

Connections to the Irish past could be instilled by family members too. Ulster immigrant and Charleston-based Presbyterian minister Thomas Smyth told his son, who wanted to join a South Carolina unit, to "remember that your blood is of that richest patriotic character—Scotch Irish—combining the mingled elements of English, Scotch, and North Irish." Smyth then personalized it for his son: "Your grandfather Smyth was in early life a soldier; and in middle life a captain of the Irish rebels in the Irish rebellion of 1798, and a prisoner of war who narrowly escaped the same gallows upon which was executed the noble patriot, William Orr."[89] Orr was another example of the brave Irish rebel who had died in a righteous cause. The older Smyth continued that this history accounted for "the genuine hatred of British intolerance and cruel injustice toward Ireland which every member of our family seemed to be imbued [with]" and which he was now transmitting to his son for inspiration in the new struggle against the "Yankees."[90]

Smyth was also appealing to the manly as well as Irish example of his ancestors. Grandfather Smyth had displayed his manhood by joining a dangerous but righteous cause and refusing to betray it. Masculinity played a major role in military enlistment for both sides in the war, but it may have been even stronger in the South. The region's love of military academies highlights this extra importance. In these academies and through regular military service southern men could form "their [own] vision of manhood," which "moderated traditional southern manhood" based on "mastery and independence" and create a new conception that included "self-discipline, education, and industry." Military activity could also provide the same for immigrants. It was a way to counter the image of the drunken and violent

Irishman. The "displayed physicality" and "military spectacle" of Irishmen in uniform parading through their adopted cities on their way to defend their new country proposed a more honorable violence, one of discipline and control.[91]

Their predecessors in southern cities who had founded and joined antebellum Irish militias had shown the way to manly respectability. The Irish Volunteers of Charleston, for example, when led by A. G. Magrath when he was just a young attorney, had left the city in 1837 to fight in the Seminole War in Florida. Most of his soldiers were poor laborers, some of whose families had to depend on charity from the Hibernian Society to survive the loss of their main breadwinner to military service. Although there was no auspicious service in that "war," the Volunteers still received heroes' welcomes when they returned to the city. Charleston's other militia companies formed a guard of honor for their parade, and one local newspaper reported, "A civil feast awaits those brave and generous men and their gallant officers, in further testimonial of the high and grateful esteem in which their fellow citizens hold their gallantry, humanity and patriotism." Almost twenty-five years later another Charleston newspaper would again commend the performance and display of the Irish soldiers, but this time for their state and not their United States service.[92]

Military service was inseparable from "manliness" but also from citizenship. Jefferson Davis's opposition to the effort to recruit slaves into the Confederate army toward the war's end, for example, highlighted that "the nexus of manhood, military service, and citizenship, was so tight in the nineteenth century, even in a pro-slavery republic . . . [that] Davis balked at violating it" and held out until the bitter end before granting African Americans the "privilege" to take up arms.[93] Davis and other Confederates did not "balk" at the Irish expressing their masculinity in the armed forces, and neither did the Irish themselves.

The same adulation then from their "fellow citizens" was available to the Irish volunteers of 1861. The excitement around secession and the firing on Fort Sumter created a rush to join up throughout the Confederacy that was echoed by Irish immigrants like Michael Nolan of New Orleans and the Irish drilling on the streets of Charleston.[94] Flag ceremonies and parades did generate an atmosphere conducive to joining up. The most thorough study of these public military events, however, notes that the initial ceremonies emphasized secession and southern rights. They were very "political" in tone, getting into the detail of southern justifications for secession rather than trying to create a new sense of cultural nationalism.[95]

Even if it was not explicitly recognized, this secession was of course to protect slavery, because the institution was the "cement that held Confederates together even under almost impossibly trying circumstances."[96] Most Confederate soldiers did not own slaves, but most did have a connection to it, particularly through family. An examination of soldiers in the Army of Northern Virginia found that "Southerners who resided in slaveholding families turned out in disproportionate numbers to fight . . . comprising four of every nine men." Also, however, among those who "rented land from slaveholders, or whose principal clients were slaveholders and whose livelihood depended on slave labor, the figure soars well above half the soldiers." A study of Virginia soldiers indicates that the richer the county and the stronger its connection to slavery, the more likely it was to provide Confederate units for the war.[97]

Foreigners in the Confederate army were, however, the least likely to own slaves. Was defense of slavery then a motivation for Irish soldiers? The evidence is thin, but there are some hints of Irish opinion on the matter. Many Irish and Irish American unit commanders owned slaves or had connections to slavery. Henry Strong and William Monaghan of the 6th Louisiana, Randall McGavock (colonel of the 10th Tennessee), Patrick Loughery and Bernard O'Connell (Emmet Guards, Co. B. 24th Alabama) of Mobile, John Dooley Sr. of the 1st Virginia, and the captains of the two Irish Volunteer companies of Charleston, Edward McCrady Jr. and Edward Magrath, all owned slaves or were members of slave-owning families. First Lieutenant Thomas Ryan of McCrady's company actually came from a slave-trading family.[98]

These men, though exceptional in some ways, were role models to their Irish soldiery and respected enough to be elected leaders of their units. The Irish support for secession after Lincoln's election suggests that Irishmen in the South knew what the fight was about and in some way bought into the rhetoric of the various "appeals to the non-slaveholding classes." They understood the competition of free black labor and resented it. One Irish private of the 12th Georgia Infantry hinted at what most knew to be what the war "was about," when he half-jokingly told his native comrades that "he [had] bought a negro . . . to have something to fight for."[99] The reality, nonetheless, was that whatever their connection to slavery, the Irish were *less* connected to it than native white southerners. While they did not object to slavery or fighting for its preservation, it could not have been a primary motive for the vast majority of them.

Ultimately, perhaps, those who signed up felt some kind of bond with the South and its new nation in the sense that it was home. Thomas Ryan's advertisement for Irish soldiers to defend against the new "Cromwell" did not advocate protecting Ireland from the "Roundheads," but saving Charleston from Drogheda's fate. Irishmen did sign up to prevent what they believed could be another "Drogheda" occurring in their new homes. Indeed, for some native Confederate soldiers, the harder the Union war effort became, the more patriotic they became. They might have been critical of the Confederate government, but word of Union atrocities and deprivations inflicted on southern soil against fellow citizens only increased their ardor for the cause.[100]

It grew particularly so for the first American-born Irish generation. John Dooley Jr. of Richmond, for example, had not joined his father and brother in the 1st Virginia when war broke out in 1861, as "his health was considered too delicate to endure the rigors of active army life." He did, however, enlist in the home guard when the Confederate capital came under direct threat in the summer of 1862. Ultimately though, he "tired of remaining in the City catching deserters & Conscripts" and "resolved at once to enter the field where I considered it the imperative duty of every young man to serve." He became a boon companion of John Mitchel's son James, serving with distinction until wounded and captured at the Battle of Gettysburg.[101] Young Catholic and Virginia-born John O. Farrell of Harpers Ferry also felt the call of service to his new nation as it suffered Federal invasion and he endured its "occupation." Escaping the attentions of the Union forces in his home town and the vicinity around it, he managed to make it to Richmond in early 1862 and joined the "Richmond Howitzers." So excited at getting his uniform, he immediately went and had his photograph taken. He too would serve through the war with distinction.[102]

A southern home under threat could also be a serious motivator for Irish immigrants to join the Confederate army. "Reluctant rebel" John Patten of Yazoo City, Mississippi, for example, may have signed up just to protect his new home. He did not volunteer until late April 1862, right after the draft had been introduced but also as Mississippi faced Union invasion. He rose to the call only when his new home in Yazoo City was threatened.[103]

John Logan Power of Jackson, Mississippi, was another. He had come to America as a printer and in 1860 became the editor and publisher of the *Jackson Mississippian*. The *Mississippian* was a staunchly Democratic and secessionist paper. Power reputedly published the lines of the patriotic hymn, the "Bonnie Blue Flag," written by fellow "Irishman" Harry McCarthy. He had been an inaugural member of the "Minutemen" who had formed to protect the state against the "Black Republicans" just after Lincoln's election.

John O. Farrell (Museum of the
Confederacy, Richmond, Virginia)

Yet, he too was a reluctant rebel when it came to fighting, enlisting only in April 1862. Despite their tardiness in joining up, Patten and Power would serve until the end of the conflict. Both were captured at Vicksburg and paroled, with Patton rising from private to lieutenant by war's end and Power promoted to the field staff of his regiment until 1864, when the governor appointed him the keeper of military records for the state of Mississippi. Using his journalism skills, he acted as a public relations officer for Mississippi regiments. Patten and Power felt motivated to defend their new home and stayed loyal and patriotic to the end. Power remained a Confederate propagandist, and Patten continued to hope for "peace with honor" while still in service in 1865.[104]

Just because a man signed up late did not mean he was not patriotic, and defense of home, more so than manliness, slavery, or memories of Ireland, could bind Irish men to the Confederacy. Another Irish Mississippian, who has left us his personal thoughts on the matter of Confederates' motivations, summed up this feeling of home best. Patrick Murphy was a Famine migrant and bridge builder in Natchez who had earned enough money to buy slaves in the 1850s. Despite the success he had participating in the South's "peculiar institution," he was a reluctant secessionist and Confederate. But, when word reached him that the "cursed Yankees" were approaching on the Mississippi River, he felt it his duty to defend his new home and "go" where he was "needed." He signed up for a Louisiana artillery battery, rose to the rank of corporal, and was captured in Natchez in the mop up of Confederate units along the river after the fall of Vicksburg on July 4, 1863. He was a prisoner of war for nearly two years, but never took the oath of allegiance, and was exchanged only in March 1865.[105]

Actual military service then, rather than merely signing up, was what really counted in terms of Irish Confederate patriotism. Despite those Irish who had conspicuously volunteered in the spring of 1861, the impression remained among some natives that the Irish were not doing enough for their adopted country. Even though the Irish had enlisted in large numbers, native reluctance to acknowledge the overall shortcomings of the Confederate war effort could provoke negative coverage of the Irish. Southern newspaper editors attacked in general all those who shirked their duty to defend the Confederacy, but often reserved particular ire for foreigners living among them. The *Charleston Courier*, for example, which had reported copiously on an Irish Volunteers' flag ceremony and the Confederate patriotism on display there in September 1861, was, by May 1862, complaining that the Irish had formed only "two companies, and one of them is said to be partly made up of substitutes." The editor was responding to a charge from a Columbia newspaper that Charleston had not "furnished her quota" of enlistees. In defense of his city, he blamed the "alien" Irish for any shortfall: "Rumor says that large numbers of Irishmen have sold themselves as substitutes—it may or may not be true, but this does not alter the figures," the "figures" showing that the Irish, he believed, were seriously underrepresented in the Confederate army.[106] The two Irish volunteer companies were not made up of substitutes, but rumors about the lack of Irish patriotism seemed useful to print when the city of Charleston's Confederate reputation was on the line. The memories of the flag ceremonies had faded quickly to the realities of having to win an increasingly harsh and bitter conflict. The Irish would have to prove their loyalty to the Confederacy, not just in parades through southern towns and cities, but also on the battlefield.

CHAPTER 3

Faugh a Ballagh! (Clear the Way!)

The Irish in the Confederate Army

Fulfilling in part the stereotype of the "Fighting Irish," Irish soldiers earned a reputation for bravery in the Confederate army as well as one for being difficult to manage. One of their commanders observed, for example, that with the "strong hand" of good officers, they could be great soldiers.[1] Unfortunately for Confederate authorities, even "strong hands" could not stop Irish men from deserting the cause. The story of the Irish Confederate soldier is filled with contrasting examples of bravery and treachery. Their nationalism, at times, seemed very shallow. Even if slavery was, as Confederate Vice President Alexander Stephen put it, "the cornerstone" of the Confederacy, most Irish would need a different motivation to fight.[2] For a combination of Irish, southern, and purely military reasons, Irish Confederate soldiers often did fight well, and their example became a key element in defining Irish loyalty to the Confederacy. Bravery and sacrifice on the battlefield was the greatest measure of national spirit, and southerners expected all their soldiers, native and foreign, to maintain this patriotic standard. Supporters of the Irish in the Confederacy knew this only too clearly and sought every opportunity to highlight the fighting Irish Confederates' contribution to the war effort.

The Montgomery Guards were Richmond, Virginia's elite Irish unit. Founded in 1849 they looked very smart in their green militia uniforms. Led by Captain P. T. Moore from County Galway and Lieutenant John Dooley Sr. from County Limerick, both prominent merchants and minor slaveholders (Moore owned six, Dooley five), the unit had mobilized in 1859 in response to John Brown's raid at Harpers Ferry in October. They would witness his execution as a unit at Charlestown, Virginia, the following December. It was natural then that they would be among the first companies to respond to Virginia's joining the Confederacy. They mustered into Confederate service as Company C of the First Virginia Infantry (called the "Old First" to distinguish it from newer "first" regiments) on April 21, 1861, the day after Virginia's secession. The regiment included other prominent militia units from the state. The Guards received their blessing in the local Catholic church (St. Peter's Cathedral just a few blocks from what was about to become the Confederacy's capitol) and, like Michael Nolan's Montgomery Guards of New Orleans, they too had their "pikes" to display their Irish heritage.[3]

Having organized so quickly and being so close to Irvin McDowell's Union army preparing to invade Virginia meant that they became part of the Confederate army whose task it was to halt the first major Union attack on the state. On the morning of July 18, 1861, the Irishmen found themselves near Manassas Junction, an important railroad intersection in northern Virginia, aligned along the southern bank of a creek named Bull Run as part of General James Longstreet's brigade. The morning passed peacefully enough with the men eating breakfast of "crackers and raw bacon" having been under orders not to light fires. Longstreet knew that Federal forces were just a few miles north at Centreville and did not want to signal his presence along Bull Run. As the heat of the day rose some of the Confederates dozed in the summer sun. The Guards' peace was shattered just around noon, when Union artillery fired on their positions. Their brigade was directly in the path of the left wing of the Union army, which had orders to reconnoiter the Confederate forces near Manassas. The Union commander was aggressive, though, and sought to push on to the strategic junction at Manassas.[4]

A young Irish immigrant, Private Frank Potts, was one of the Montgomery Guards facing the Union attack. Just four days before, jaded with camp life, he began a diary to record his army career. He was not bored on the 18th. After absorbing the Union artillery barrage, the 1st Virginia, now under command of the Montgomery Guards' old captain, P. T. Moore (Moore had been promoted to Colonel of the regiment when it had organized back in April) helped drive back the first lines of Union soldiers to approach the creek. Potts was so full of nervous energy that he "fired twice at random while in the woods." He calmed himself, however, and "loaded my piece at 'a ready' for a sure shot." When he saw "a fellow creeping forward . . . I came to aim, steadied my piece, and aiming at his breast I fired." Potts "saw him no more. God have mercy on him" he continued, "the distance was about 70 yards and I could not miss him." Potts also saw men on his own side go down. He witnessed "[Michael] Redmond," a young Irish-born coppersmith from Portsmouth, Virginia, being "shot right through the knee." Redmond was "suffering great pain," and Potts remembered that. "'All for my country,' was all [Redmond] could say." Potts also noted that Redmond was taken from the field "after amputation" and said, "[I] gave him all the smoking tobacco I had." Redmond would die from his wound and leave a young Irish widow behind.[5]

Potts's commanders recognized that their soldiers were "green" and needed encouragement in this, their first fight. Colonel Moore led from the front and, after the first Union assault had been driven back, moved his regiment across Bull Run and up the bluff on the other side. Waving his sword in the air he encouraged his men up the hill and could be seen through the smoke rallying the troops. His bravery gained him a serious wound, which led to him being removed from the field. It also earned him, however, a mention for courage in the dispatches of his superiors, Generals Longstreet and P. G. T. Beauregard.[6]

Command of the regiment fell to Major Frank Skinner, who, according to Potts, saw the Montgomery Guards as the vanguard. "He took a particular fancy to our company, was all the time calling for Captain Dooley and seemed to think that we Irish were the very boys to fight." Skinner encouraged the Irishmen to rise up and go after the enemy. "In we went," Potts wrote, "with a 'Faugh a Ballagh,' which means 'clear the way.'" "Faugh a Ballagh" was an Anglicization of the term *Fág an Ballach*, and was the famous war cry Irish troops in various European armies had used for generations. The Guards chased for a while, but for Potts and his countrymen, "tho the spirit was willing, the flesh was weak." Having driven off the Federal forces they retreated to the creek and protected the ford over it. Recently promoted Captain Dooley walked among the men and "told us 'to keep cool' and fire should they attempt to cross, jump over the ditch and give the bayonet." As a prominent supporter of the Catholic church back home in Richmond, Dooley told his men: "'Let each of us commend ourselves to God and pray to him for courage and our hopes and confidences in Him, we cannot be beaten.'"[7]

The Guards and the other men of Longstreet's Brigade took a stand on Bull Run that forced General McDowell to shift his focus to the Confederate left, where he would launch the main assault three days later. The Irish Richmonders had played an important role in protecting the vital Confederate railroad junction. As part of the 1st Virginia they and their native-born colleagues had performed "with particular distinction in crossing the stream and routing the enemy." Captain Dooley and Colonel Moore, once the latter had recovered from his wound, managed to recruit five more Irish soldiers in the aftermath of the battle.[8] Their company suffered two men killed that day and seven severely wounded, one of whom, the company sergeant, would die of his wounds. They had seen the "elephant" and not flinched. Alongside them was the 17th Virginia Infantry, which included two Irish companies from Alexandria that had been among the first troops assigned to defend Manassas. They, too, had held up well under fire in this first skirmish of the first major battle. Their commander, speaking of the regiment as a whole, reported that "officers and men displayed a good deal of coolness and bravery" despite "the shot and shell poured incessantly over their heads." The Irish Jeff Davis Guards from Lynchburg of the 11th Virginia were beside the 17th in the fight, although they had not crossed Bull Run in pursuit of the Union attackers.[9]

Later, on July 21, Irishmen from the New Orleans docks in Wheat's Battalion faced serious combat and took serious casualties, while men of the Virginia Hibernians and the Emerald Guards were part of the 27th and 33rd Virginia Infantry regiments, respectively. Some of the reinforcements under the command of General Thomas J. Jackson helped turn the tide of the main battle: the Emerald Guards, in their blue uniforms, were part of the specific turning point, the famous charge that took the artillery pieces near the Hill House. One Private Owen McLaughlin, for example, a thirty-five-year-old laborer in the Hibernians, was "slightly wounded" while capturing "a prisoner by himself from one of the enemy's guns."[10]

In this first major battle of the war, Irish soldiers had quickly displayed their willingness not just to sign up for the Confederacy, but also to fight for it. The Montgomery Guards had led the way on the first day of serious action. They fought for their new nation, and a few, like Private Redmond, had given "'all for [their] country.'" Yet, according to Potts, it was the Irish cry of "'Faugh a Ballagh,'" as well as praise of Irish fighting ability, and not appeals to Confederate nationalism, that had helped the inexperienced Irish Confederates to overcome their initial fear of being in combat.

Less than a year later, however, a large element of this Irish company that had displayed such courage, turned their backs on the Confederacy and the unit ceased to be, in a meaningful way, Irish. Many of the men who had fought at Bull Run would face combat again at the Battle of Yorktown in May 1862, as Confederate forces attempted to halt General George McClellan's Union army on its march up the Peninsula below Richmond. More Montgomery Guards would die in that battle, but that was not the reason for the decimation of the unit. Instead, a large number of them sought to claim the foreign exemption offered under the first Confederate draft of April 1862. The Montgomery Guards had signed up for twelve months and under the new law would have had to re-sign up "for the War." Many balked at that change and sought a discharge from the Confederate army because they had, as the law described, "never acquired domicile." At least twenty-eight seem to have left the front without permission, applied for the exemption, and provided "evidence" of never having been naturalized or having intended to do so. Another four or five seem to have just disappeared. This loss of men reduced the company's effective strength by over a third. Private William Buckley, a twenty-six-year-old laborer originally from County Limerick, for example, had a friend back in Richmond testify that Buckley had never intended staying in Virginia, but had always planned to return to Ireland as soon as possible. Private Matthew Bresnahan of County Kerry had the British Consul in Richmond write him a letter claiming that he had come to America only for "a visit" and had always intended on returning to Ireland. This "visit" had, however, lasted three and a half years! Indeed, in overall terms, the Irish were the least likely group of European immigrants to leave America for their homeland. Nonetheless, the Confederate secretary of war eventually granted Bresnahan, as well as Buckley and the others, discharges based on not having established domicile. The company survived but only as a shell of its former self. Later desertions reduced the "Irishness" of the company even further. It stayed alive only as Company C with the addition of conscripts, most of whom were not Irish.[11]

Another Richmond unit, the Emmet Guards, Company F of the 15th Virginia Infantry, lost so many members during the same period, it had to be disbanded and the few remaining soldiers distributed through the rest of the regiment. Information is sketchy on the incident as the whole regiment's records had "been destroyed." What can be ascertained, from the one extant officer's report, written sometime in July 1862, is that the Emmet Guards and a predominantly German company, also from Richmond, had claimed "exemption from service under the clause of the conscript act approved April 1862 discharging from service 'non-domiciled residents.'" They had apparently "refused to reenlist." In his letter of resignation from the company, Second Lieutenant James Collins, an Irish American hatter from Richmond, wrote that his company had been made up of "aliens" and "since the 1st of May—when the term of their original enlistment expired" most had "left." That meant that "there remains fit for service not more than 10 or 12 men." Collins felt that such a small number of men did not need "4 officers" to command them.[12]

Despite Irish Richmonders' mass exodus from Confederate service in the spring of 1862, there was still a sense among many natives that the Irish remained good fighters, and thus, good Confederates. The history of the predominantly Irish 6th Louisiana Infantry highlights the case for this impression. The 6th included three explicitly Irish companies (see table 4) and three others with large Irish numbers. There was also a German company in the regiment and three native-born companies. Despite these other elements in the unit, the 6th's "Irishness" shined through in combat and even obscured the valor of the non-Irish. The 6th was part of the 1st Louisiana brigade in what would become the Confederate Army of Northern Virginia.[13] The Irish of the regiment particularly impressed their brigade commander, General Richard Taylor. This affection that Taylor had for his Irish troops is somewhat surprising, because this wealthy Louisiana sugar planter had been a Know-Nothing in the 1850s and was elected to the state senate on its ticket in 1855. Taylor had blamed the influx of foreign immigrants for the increasing sectional tensions because their "numbers were too great to absorb" into native society and were detrimental to American politics.[14]

In his memoirs though, published fourteen years after the war, he was effusive in his praise of the Irish soldiers in his ranks. Commanding Irish Confederate troops changed his opinion of Irish immigrants. He described them as "stout and hardy fellows" who could be turbulent in camp but with a "strong hand" he believed the Irish became excellent soldiers. Indeed, he believed that, if treated with "kindness and justice," they would be "ready to follow their officers to the death."[15] The 6th first faced combat in the Shenandoah Valley in the late spring of 1862, and, unlike the Montgomery and Emmet Guards of Richmond, they had not tried to take advantage of the new conscription legislation to get out of service. From the beginning, they showed their mettle in battle. As part of General Thomas "Stonewall" Jackson's so-called foot cavalry they had to move rapidly up and down and in and out of the Shenandoah to avoid encirclement by Union forces. There were many long and tiring marches and sleep was rare. The Irishmen in the 6th, in their first actual skirmish with the enemy at Front Royal in late May 1862, though they did not have a major role in the battle, performed well. A day later, at General Jackson's order, they and the rest of the brigade, which included more Irishmen, attacked a rearguard Union column near Middletown, and Captain Henry Strong's Calhoun Guards captured a battle flag from the Federals.[16]

On Sunday, May 25, however, they had their finest hour of the campaign at the First Battle of Winchester. In pursuit of General Nathaniel Banks's Union forces at Winchester, the Louisiana brigade was part of General Jackson's column marching north down the valley along the Winchester

Pike toward the right flank of the Union forces on Bower's Hill. Jackson ordered Taylor and the Louisianians to take the Union right at all costs. It was a daunting task as there were trees, rocks, and fences to cross. Using the shelter of a creek bottom at the bottom of the hill and the morning fog, the Louisiana troops marched around the hill, and although under artillery and musket fire, managed to get up the hill, flank the Union troops, and descend on their position. The commander of a Pennsylvania regiment opposing this movement on the extreme right of the Union line stated, "We received their fire for some minutes and promptly returned it. For a moment the enemy seemed to stagger, but it was only for a moment; for, feeling confident in their great strength, they charged down the hill upon us, with deafening cheers." The Louisiana soldiers forced the Pennsylvanians back initially in "good order" but commanders eventually found it "impossible to preserve our ranks" in the retreat. An Indiana regiment beside this unit also retreated in the face of a "superior attack" and the "whole regiment retir[ed] over the hill in much confusion."[17]

The 1st Louisiana Brigade, with the Irish 6th leading the attack, had turned the tide of the First Battle of Winchester. The Union line collapsed across the whole front and retreated in disorder through the town. Although this was a Louisiana victory, the 6th took the most casualties, with fifty-one dead, wounded, or missing. They and their commander, "the aging Colonel [Isaac] Seymour," led the charge that broke the Union line.[18] The Irish soldiers of the whole brigade came out of the battle with great credit. Even the "Rebel Yell" of their magnificent charge, reportedly the first time it was heard in the Shenandoah Valley, was given to them. One Alabama soldier, William Calvin Oates, saw the charge and wondered who it was leading the attack. One of his fellow soldiers beside him, "one of the Irishmen from Captain Hart's company," exclaimed, "Ah me boys that's Taylor [and the Louisiana Brigade]." How did he know? He knew because the charge cheer was the "jenewine [sic] Irish yell."[19] Irish performance, it seemed, had overpowered the Louisiana nature of the brigade.

After the victory at Winchester, when Jackson moved south through the valley to help the Confederate forces facing General George McClellan around Richmond, the Irishmen of the 6th provided the rearguard, which calmed the rest of the brigade. They refused relief from this duty despite thunderous weather that produced "hailstones as large as hen eggs." According to Taylor, the Irishmen exclaimed to him: "We are the boys to see it out." This cry, as Taylor put it, "from half a hundred Tipperary throats" clinched his transition from Know-Nothing to Irish advocate. "My heart has warmed to an Irishman since that night" he concluded. The unit would go on to fight later that year at the battles of Malvern Hill, Second Manassas, and Antietam.[20] Another native officer was, in 1863, still describing the Irish soldiers as "noble fellows" who "caused many a Yankee to bite the dust." As late as the summer of 1864 the Irish 6th was still providing vital service halting a Federal attack at the Battle of the Wilderness.[21]

The Irish Louisianians solidly established their reputation as good soldiers and thus good Confederates. Yet, just as these men from the docks of New Orleans and the ditching crews of the lower Mississippi River valley were gaining this standing in the Shenandoah Valley, their compatriots who remained in New Orleans undermined the Irish Confederate reputation. The Irishmen, stationed at Fort Jackson near the mouth of the Mississippi River, defending their adopted city of New Orleans, performed poorly against a U.S. naval assault in late April 1862. In fact, they were eager participants in "the largest mutiny in the Civil War."[22] They, along with many non-Irish soldiers, rebelled against their Confederate commanders trying to rally them for a defense of the fort against a Union infantry assault. In the initial naval attack, the soldiers manning the cannons of Fort Jackson, although receiving the praise of their commander, General Johnson K. Duncan, had failed to hit any of the Union ships. A few days later on the night of April 27, around 300 soldiers, under the command of their noncommissioned officers, assembled with arms loaded and told their commanders that they no longer cared to fight and wanted to leave the fort. If the officers resisted, they promised violence. Some of the mutineers mounted the parapets and spiked the cannons. Faced with this major rebellion, which even the pleas of a Catholic chaplain could not quell, General Duncan allowed the mutineers to leave the fort. On the afternoon of the next day (April 28) he sent a surrender note to the Union commander, leaving the city open to Federal occupation.[23]

Duncan placed the blame for the mutiny squarely on the fact that "they were mostly foreign enlistments [Irish, German, and northern], without any great interests at stake in the ultimate success of the revolution [i.e., the Confederacy]." He still praised their initial demeanor under fire but blamed their move to rebellion on the "reaction that set in among them during the lull of the 25th, 26th, and 27th, when there was no other excitement to arouse them than the fatigue duty of repairing our damages," along with "the rumor . . . that the city had surrendered and was then in the hands of the enemy." He had attempted to rally the immigrant soldiers with a nationalist oration: "The safety of New Orleans and the cause of the

Southern Confederacy, our homes, our families, and everything dear to man yet depend on our exertions." This appeal for the "cause of the Southern Confederacy" failed, as that same day, the mutiny occurred. Those few foreigners who did not leave "were completely demoralized" and Duncan had "no faith or reliance" on them to withstand any further Union attacks. A couple of weeks later, having been paroled into the new Union-controlled New Orleans, Duncan became ever more despondent about his "foreign enlistments" when even those few who had not mutinied and had received their Confederate back pay, thanks in large part to his efforts, had by the "scores . . . been daily going over to the enemy and enlisting." Rather dejectedly, Duncan continued: "Although I really did think at the time of the surrender that some few of the men were loyal . . . nearly every man in both forts was thoroughly implicated and concerned in the revolt on the night of April 27th with the exception of the St. Mary Cannoneers, composed mostly of planters."[24]

Thus, foreign soldiers, including the Irish, were not to be trusted in their dedication to the Confederacy. One member of the St. Mary's unit was more blunt than Duncan. It was "Democracy + Foreign voters" who were responsible for the fall of New Orleans. "So fell the Great and Proud city of the South . . . betrayed by the foreign population" and their sponsors, the Democrats.[25] The New Orleans press, including John Maginnis's *True Delta*, does not seem to have commented publicly on this version of the mutiny, perhaps because of embarrassment at the performance of Irish/German "Democrats." His more likely reason, however, was the rapid Federal takeover of the city. Condemning treason against the Confederacy would have drawn unwelcome attention from Union commanders in the city. Nonetheless, the ease with which the forts fell must have shocked pro-Confederate residents who had been told that both were "abundantly sufficient" to defend the city, especially as numbers of these "sufficient" defenders were now wearing blue uniforms or working for the occupiers in a civil capacity.[26]

With these contradictory performances of Irishmen from the same southern city, how then does one assess the overall actions of Irish Confederate soldiers? Some from New Orleans mutinied and/or joined the Union army at first opportunity, while others, from the same socioeconomic background, were charging up and down mountains in Virginia in the teeth of enemy cannon and musket fire. Similarly, what changed so many Montgomery Guards from brave soldiers to non-domiciled foreigners in under a year? Table 6 tries to examine this mixed record of Irish Confederates in a more systematic way.[27]

TABLE 6 Irish Confederate Casualty and Desertion Rates in Selected Units

Unit	Killed in Action	Wounded in Action	Deserted	Deserted/Oath to U.S. Taken	POW	POW/Oath to U.S. Taken	Discharged for Non-Domicile	N (100%)
Emerald Guards, Co. I, 8th Alabama	33%	44%	5%	1%	28%	4%	0%	102
Emmet Guards, Co. B, 24th Alabama	11%	8%	5%	8%	22%	11%	1%	90
Emmet Guards, Co. D, 1st Louisiana	21%	30%	11%	0	16%	5%	4%	57
"Fighting Irish," Co. F, 5th Missouri	17%	34%	10%	2%	56%	10%	0	41[a]
Irish Volunteers, Co. K, 1st South Carolina	15%	32%	16%	2%	15%	5%	2%	117
Jeff Davis Guards, Co. F, 1st Texas Heavy Artillery	0	3%	12%	0	0	0	0	112
Montgomery Guards, Co. E, 1st Louisiana	17%	31%	16%	2%	12%	6%	6%	101
Montgomery Guards, Co. C, 1st Virginia	9%	18%	17%	2%	9%	3%	26%	106
Shamrock Guards, Co. C, 3rd Confederate Infantry	9%	27%	9%	2%	20%	11%	0	45[a]
Southern Celts, Co. A, 13/20th Louisiana	10%	23%	8%	0	25%	8%	0	147[a,b]

Virginia Hibernians, Co. B, 27th Virginia	15%	24%	27%	1%	30%	6%	4%	71
Mean, Army of Northern Virginia	18%	30%	15%	2%	18%	5%	7%	561
Mean, Army of Tennessee	12%	23%	8%	3%	31%	10%	1%	326
TOTAL (including *Jeff Davis Guards*)	14%	25%	12%	2%	21%	6%	4%	1,002

Source: Compiled Service Records of Confederate Soldiers, NARA.
Note: Units in italics are those belonging to the Army of Northern Virginia.
a. The compiled service records of these units are incomplete.
b. The Southern Celts had a large number of Irish transfers from the 11th Louisiana Infantry who came from the Baton Rouge area.

The statistics for these eleven units display quite a variance. Some units show unusual rates for killed in action (KIA). The Emerald Guards had an astronomical combat death rate, one more than double that for the Army of Northern Virginia as a whole.[28] Adding those who were wounded at least once (44 percent) but survived means that 77 percent of the unit took at least one bullet or piece of shell for the Confederacy. No other unit comes close to this KIA rate, with the Emmet Guards of the 1st Louisiana (Nelligan's) Infantry next at 21 percent. In terms of combined killed and wounded, these Louisiana Emmet Guards again and the Missouri "Fighting Irish" come in at 51 percent each and the Montgomery Guards, also of Nelligan's Infantry, and the Irish Volunteers of Charleston, with 48 and 47 percent, respectively. At the other end of the scale, the lowest KIA rates were for the Jeff Davis Guards from Texas, who had no one killed in action, the Montgomery Guards of the 1st Virginia, and the Vicksburg-based Shamrock Guards of the 3rd Confederate Infantry both at 9 percent. The Virginia Montgomery Guards' rate was especially low for a company in the Army of Northern Virginia, mostly because it was the only unit that had large numbers of exemptions for non-domicile and thus many of its members were not around to fight after the Spring of 1862. For combined killed and wounded, the Jeff Davis Guards again lead the lower end with just 3 percent, followed by the Emmet Guards from Mobile in the 24th Alabama with 18 percent.

The large anomaly of the Jeff Davis Guards is easy to explain because they served in their home state of Texas, which just did not see the degree of action of other theaters. They were also stationed as heavy artillery in fortified coastal defense positions such as forts and avoided participation in major moving campaigns.[29] Death, however, was not unknown to the unit, with a number of men succumbing to disease. Duty in fortifications along the Sabine River in Texas was not the healthiest of posts. Beyond this Texas unit, the casualty rates for those companies that served primarily in the western theater were lower than those in the eastern theater, where all the units listed in italics in table 6 served in what would become the Army of Northern Virginia. Although they would be on the winning side more often than the Confederates in the West, they took part in the bloodiest campaigns and battles of the war. The concentrated geographical area of the eastern theater, basically between Petersburg, Virginia, and Gettysburg, Pennsylvania, meant less time travelling to fights and thus more time fighting. The Irishmen of the 6th Louisiana, for example, fought almost constantly from their first experience of combat in the Shenandoah Valley in April 1862 until the Battle of Fredericksburg in December of that year. Between those dates the unit saw serious action at Malvern Hill, Ox Hill, Second Manassas, and the bloodiest single day of the war, Antietam.

The fact then that the Emerald Guards served in the East played a part in their high casualty rate. Their regiment, the 8th Alabama Infantry, was among the first to see action in the defense of Richmond at the Battle of Williamsburg in early May 1862. Just a few days after the Irish 6th had their first hour of glory in the hills above Winchester, Virginia, the Guards were involved in the Battle of Seven Pines. The company lost men in both battles, including commander P. N. Loughrey, killed in action at Seven Pines. The fact that the company, and indeed the regiment, took a lot of casualties at what would turn out to be some of the more minor battles in the East meant that the Emerald Guards had already suffered more than most Confederate units even before the major casualty-inflicting battles of the Seven Days, Antietam, Gettysburg, and so on.[30]

Another factor explaining the high casualty total of the Emerald Guards was that they had "enlisted for the War." Most of the early volunteers responding to the firing on Fort Sumter signed up for just twelve months. The Irishmen of the Emerald Guards seemed more eager for the Confederacy than many of their compatriots in the South. Yet, one other unit listed in table 6 also signed up "for the War" in the late spring of 1861. The Irish Volunteers of Charleston, which included Dominick Spellman, had done the same as Loughrey's Mobilians. The strongly ideological atmosphere of Charleston undoubtedly played a role in this commitment. Their casualty rate was slightly above the average for the Army of Northern Virginia, and as a part of A. P. Hill's "light division," this fact is not surprising. Hill's command was often at the forefront of General Lee's various offensives. Company K was also the official color company of its regiment and thus often the target of Federal sharpshooters.[31]

Nevertheless, there is still a large difference between its casualty rate and that of the Emerald Guards. Ultimately, this discrepancy might be accounted for by the fact that the Emerald Guards had a very high socioeconomic status (see table 5 in chapter 2). About 58 percent of its volunteers were in skilled or white-collar occupations, which made them, by far, the most elite, in an economic sense, Irish Confederate unit. They had more of an economic and social stake in the South and the survival of its peculiar institution. Detailed statistical studies of the Confederate war effort highlight that it was far more than just a case of "Rich man's war, poor man's fight." On the contrary, those with the most invested in the southern economic system were the most likely to volunteer and stay in service.[32] It seems that the Emerald Guards' record is another piece of evidence sustaining this fact.

Similarly, socioeconomic differences might explain the variance in desertion rates among the Irish companies. Table 6 again highlights that the Emerald Guards had the lowest desertion rate, 6 percent, followed by four units from the western theater: the Southern Celts, 8 percent; the Shamrock Guards, 11 percent; the Fighting Irish and the Jeff Davis Guards, both 12 percent. These western units' percentages are indeed quite low, compared to the 14 percent average, for example, for all infantry units in the Army of Northern Virginia.[33] The Irish units with rates of desertion closest to the Emerald Guards is, as with the casualty rate, the Emmet Guards of the 1st Louisiana, which had a desertion rate of 11 percent followed by the Louisiana Montgomery Guards and the Irish Volunteers of Charleston, both at 18 percent.

This discrepancy in desertion rates between the Irish units in each theater could be misleading, however. The lower casualty rates in units in the western theater do not necessarily mean those units were less committed to the cause than units in the East. The Army of Tennessee lost more battles than it won and thus had much higher prisoner-of-war totals than those in the East. The four companies from that army listed in table 6 show that 31 percent of their number were taken prisoner at least once, while it was only 18 percent for the Irish companies in the Army of Northern Virginia. The Irish captured in the West were also less likely to return to their units either, with almost twice as many taking or seeking to take the oath to the United States than those in the East. These western Irish Confederates had the option of joining the "Galvanized" Yankee units organized from western prison camps such as Camps Douglas (Illinois), Morton (Indiana), and Chase (Ohio) rather than returning to Confederate service.[34] Or, in many cases they could refuse to be exchanged. John O'Brien of the Emmet Guards from Mobile, for example, was captured at the Battle of Chickamauga in September 1863 and took the oath of allegiance and promised to "stay north of the Ohio [River]" in return for his release.[35]

Despite the higher number of prisoners captured in the West, the 66 percent POW figure of Company F of the 5th Missouri needs explaining. In this sample in table 6, they were the only unit to participate in the siege of Vicksburg in the summer of 1863. They, like all the other Confederate defenders of this city, surrendered to General U. S. Grant's forces on July 4, 1863, thus inflating their POW numbers.[36]

All units, Irish included, in Lee's army were less likely to fall into the enemy's hands as their counterparts further west. Apart from the Battle of

Gettysburg and the major battles of the summer above Richmond in the 1864 "Overland" campaign, Army of Northern Virginia soldiers were not falling into Federal hands in large numbers. Therefore, if seriously disillusioned with the war and/or Confederate service and looking to get out, the quickest way was to desert. The Virginia Hibernians (Company B, 27th Virginia), for example, had a desertion rate of 28 percent, double the average rate for the army as a whole, and much larger than Irish units based in the West.

Some Army of Northern Virginia "deserters" did, however, return to Confederate service. While this changing of units without permission was disruptive to Confederate organization, for the purposes of this study, only Irish commitment to the cause as a whole, and not necessarily one particular unit, is important. About a half dozen men from the Montgomery Guards of the 1st Louisiana, for example, decided to abandon their unit during a hospital furlough in early 1864 and join instead John Hunt Morgan's cavalry. One Private Peter Keating was among them. He had been wounded at Gettysburg. While convalescing in Richmond he must have decided that his odds of survival or opportunity for more glamorous service were better in Morgan's famous unit.[37]

Keating and his colleagues' reenlistments were unusual though. Most deserters stayed gone. With the Virginia Hibernians, for example, none of those listed as deserters enlisted elsewhere. The Hibernians had been recruited in the western part of the state in May 1861 and were primarily railroad workers. They came from the lower end of the economic scale, had lived a nomadic lifestyle, and probably had connections in the North. Such circumstances made these Irish less likely to stay "with the army." One Michael Harrington, age seventeen, went absent without leave twice, once in 1861 and again in early 1862. On the first occasion he lost his corporal's stripes and was reduced to the ranks, and on the second occasion, when, having reenlisted for the war, he failed to return from furlough, he was put under arrest. He lost all of his pay for the remainder of 1862 and was sentenced to one month's "hard labor" in early 1863. Back in the company for the Battle of Chancellorsville, he deserted for good on the march to Pennsylvania before the Battle of Gettysburg, only to be picked up by the Union authorities in that state nearly three weeks after the battle.[38]

Overall, the Irish units had more deserters than the average unit in the Army of Northern Virginia. In the 6th Louisiana (see table 7), those Irish companies with the lowest socioeconomic profile (Companies F and I, see table 5) had extremely high desertion rates in comparison to some native

TABLE 7 Company Casualty and Desertion Analysis of the 6th Louisiana
Infantry

Company	Killed in Action	Deserted	Oath to U.S. Taken	N (100%)
Co. A, Union and Sabine Rifles, Union and Sabine Parishes	13%	13%	18%	120
Co. B, Calhoun Guards (Irish), Orleans Parish	14%	19%	14%	162
Co. C, St. Landry Guards, St. Landry Parish	14%	12%	6%	147
Co. D, Tensas Rifles, Tensas Parish	10%	20%	5%	104
Co. E, Mercer Guards (mixed but mostly native, >10% Irish), Orleans Parish	8%	41%	3%	90
Co. F, Irish Brigade Co. B, Orleans Parish	17%	28%	4%	115
Co. G, Pemberton Rifles (German), Orleans Parish	18%	24%	19%	109
Co. H, Orleans Rifles (c. 30% Irish), Orleans Parish	17%	22%	12%	109
Co. I, Irish Brigade Co. B, Orleans Parish	17%	25%	12%	106
Co. K, Violet Guards (c. 50% Irish), Orleans Parish	18%	30%	2%	125
TOTAL, 6th Louisiana Infantry Regiment	15%	23%	10%	1,168

Source: Gannon, *Irish Rebels, Confederate Tigers*, 394.

companies (Companies A and C). Even Henry Strong's Calhoun Guards, with its higher socioeconomic status, shows a rate substantially higher than the average for the Army of Northern Virginia as a whole. Indeed, Irish Louisianians generally showed a higher propensity to desert Confederate service.[39]

Worse than desertion was taking the oath of allegiance to the United States, and the Irish were more likely to do this than most native-born soldiers. For them, taking the oath was easier to do from a practical standpoint, because many had lived in the North before coming South and/or had relatives there. Those, like Dominick Spellman, who wanted to take the oath late in the war often had their request denied, their long service to the Confederacy highlighting perhaps their less-than-patriotic reasons for reestablishing loyalty to the United States. Those who left earlier in the war and sought the oath often got the opportunity to take it and get out of prison. They usually had to show some connection with the North to secure passage there and promise not to return to the Confederacy. A few of the men in the "Fighting Irish" company of the 5th Missouri, for example, were willing to take the oath after capture at the siege of Vicksburg. Private Phillip Purcell, an Irish-born laborer, had fought with the company from 1861 when it was still part of the Confederate Missouri State Guard, had served through all of its skirmishes and battles from then until the summer of 1863, but had had enough by Vicksburg. A few days after the city's surrender his captors offered him parole, which would have returned him to Confederate service. He refused. By the end of the month he was still incarcerated in the Graciot Street Prison in St. Louis but from which, after taking the oath to the United States, he returned to his pre-Confederate life.[40] Similarly, Thomas O'Neil (sometimes O'Neal), a twenty-five-year-old Irish laborer from New Orleans, joined James Nelligan's Emmet Guards (Company D, 1st Louisiana) in April 1861. In April 1862, he tried to claim non-domicile status but changed his mind and signed up for another two years. Although wounded in the right arm at Malvern Hill in July, he continued to serve through the rest of that year and well into the next, until captured at the Battle of Chancellorsville in May 1863. While in Union custody in Washington, D.C., he changed his mind again, immediately took the oath, and upon release went to St. Louis.[41]

Desertion and absence without leave were destructive to unit and army efficiency, even if the soldier later returned to service. But taking an oath of allegiance to the enemy removed a Confederate soldier from service permanently. As was the case with desertion, oath-taking rates were generally higher among Irish companies than native-born ones. In the 6th Louisiana (see table 7) the one German and six Irish companies had higher oath rates than most of the native ones. Similarly, in table 6 the average rate of oath-taking, among deserters and POWs combined, was about 8 percent, although it was closer to 18 percent for units in the West, surpassing the rate of some of the companies in the 6th Louisiana. The opportunity to take the oath was higher in the western army because, again, combatants were more likely to be captured there.

Some who took the oath did more than just leave the Confederate service for good, actively joining the other side. Six regiments, numbering around six thousand former Confederate prisoners, were organized as U.S. Volunteer infantry to serve on the western frontier, so as to avoid fighting their former Confederate colleagues down south. Irish and Germans were prominent in the units, but so too were Confederate prisoners who came from the hill countries of Tennessee, Virginia, and North Carolina. Among the Irish, Michael Shea of the Vicksburg Shamrock Guards, for example, fell into Union hands in September 1864, and he eventually decided to take the oath at Camp Douglas and join the 5th U.S. Volunteers on April 6, 1865, ironically just as the Civil War was ending. Sergeant James Daily (Daly) of the New Orleans Southern Celts, after becoming a prisoner in the run up to the Battle of Chickamauga, transferred from Camp Chase to Rock Island, but he joined the U.S. Navy rather than the army. In the process, however, men like Shea were freeing up regular Union forces to leave the western frontier to fight the Confederates.[42]

Records also indicate a few Irishmen joining eastern units to get out of prison and thus potentially fighting against their former comrades. Dennis O'Leary, for example, of the 5th Missouri Fighting Irish, escaped Camp Morton in Indiana by joining the newly formed 7th Indiana Cavalry in 1863 which fought in Tennessee, Mississippi, and Arkansas. Thanks to his new Federal unit moving further west rather than east, O'Leary avoided coming up against his former comrades, but it could easily have been different. Similarly, Corporal James Powers of the 1st Louisiana (Company E) spent eight months in Fort Delaware after being captured at Gettysburg before taking the oath and joining the newly formed 3rd Maryland Federal Cavalry. Fortunately for him, his new unit was shipped to Louisiana for the Red River campaign and eventually served in Alabama at the war's end, and he too avoided fighting directly against his old regiment.[43]

One member of the Calhoun Guards of the 6th Louisiana was less fortunate. He had "deserted to the Yanks" in May 1862 and subsequently joined a Federal unit. In late 1863 he was captured by his old unit and sentenced to death. One of his officers described him as "a sullen, cross, ugly, fellow, who seemed to be entirely devoid of pride and sensibility." The former Confederate was paraded in front of the unit, given the last rites by a priest, a crucifix to kiss, and an opportunity for some last words. He apologized to his fellow Irishmen and Louisianians and accepted that they were only doing their duty in executing him. He swore that he had not "pulled a trigger against his old comrades." We do not have information on the impact of the apology beyond the officer who ran the execution. He found it a terrible sight as the firing squad put nine bullets in the traitor's head.[44] Deserting and taking the oath to save one's skin was one thing to the Irish Confederates who stayed in service, but joining the enemy was quite another.

The Irish were not the only ones to take the oath and/or join the other side before war's end. As mentioned earlier, the majority of those in "Galvanized" Federal units were native southerners. The same was true for oaths. Tennessee produced by far the largest number of oath takers, followed by Virginia, Alabama, and North Carolina. It is estimated that between 1863 and war's end more than 10,000 Tennesseans and almost 5,000 Virginians took the oath. Using an average Irish oath rate of 8 percent (see table 6), would mean that something over 1,500 Irish Confederates of the 20,000 or so who served might have taken or tried to take this option.[45]

Many of the Irish companies listed in tables 6 and 7 do, however, show very high oath rates. Does this imply a disbelief in the Confederate national project? Were many oath takers in the Confederate army only because, as they often claimed to their captors, the Confederates had forced them into service? Understanding the deeper reasons for Irish oath taking would help explain the discrepancy outlined in this chapter, for example, between the performance of Irish New Orleans during 1862 in Fort Jackson and in the Shenandoah Valley. One historian who has examined the Fort Jackson mutiny in great detail believes that the event was not just peculiar to the circumstances of the fort in the wet spring of 1862, but intimates a deeper reluctance to serve among immigrants and a hidden dislike of the Confederacy that manifested itself only when the proper opportunity arose.[46]

The mutineers' motives are hard to ascertain directly, because none of them left a record of their thoughts. When one looks at those seeking to take the oath, the same problem arises in terms of sources. One must therefore surmise motive. As life in a Union prisoner of war camp was usually not comfortable and indeed quite dangerous to health and life, attributing oath-taking to a secret love of the Union and/or a hatred of the Confederacy is problematic.

The case of Thomas O'Neil (O'Neal) from the 1st Louisiana mentioned above should make one cautious in such an ascription. While in service, for which he had volunteered, he had been wounded at the Battle of Malvern Hill in July 1862. He returned to his unit and served through Gettysburg, and, only in late 1863, deserted to Union forces. He claimed to have been in the militia before hostilities broke out and of having been "forced" into the "Rebel army." O'Neill took the oath of allegiance to the United States of America at Fort Delaware and left prison. Despite his desertion and oath of loyalty, he had apparently not abandoned the southern opinions that had encouraged him to volunteer for the Confederacy in 1861. Upon release he moved to St. Louis, where he found work in his trade as a carpenter. In October 1864, however, O'Neil was arrested on the basis of testimony from witnesses who heard him say at the dinner table in their boarding house that, "Bill Anderson did right in killing Union soldiers at Centralia," because "a Federal officer had suffered his men to kill and scalp rebels in the state of [Missouri]." ("Bloody" Bill Anderson was a notorious Confederate partisan who had executed Union soldiers he captured on a train near Centralia, Missouri, in September.)[47] O'Neil's pro-Confederate stance made one witness describe him as "a rebel and a dangerous man to be at large." The provost marshal of St. Louis took the charge seriously, arrested O'Neil, and there is no record of his release before the war's end.[48] He, it seems, had not left his colleagues in the Confederate army for ideological reasons but practical ones.

Still, O'Neil had deserted, and he and the many other Irish who did indicated the shallowness of their Confederate nationalism. The ease with which Irishmen, many of whom had fought with distinction, took the oath, shows that they did not completely see the United States as the enemy "other." Confederate recruiters' reminding potential enlistees that the Yankees were Puritan Cromwellians had some appeal. But, when the hardness of war became real, either early on in the boredom and poor conditions of camp life, or later in the reality of the sheer human destruction of this conflict, the appeal to national pride wore off. Yet, while still in service, Irish units retained a reputation for bravery. Even when they acted poorly, as when the 1st Virginia "Irish" Battalion ran from a cavalry charge and refused to regroup at the Battle of Cedar Mountain in August 1862, their reputation was not totally destroyed. Indeed, General Stonewall Jackson made the battalion the provost guard for his division.[49]

Irish companies did have high killed-in-action rates. Nine of the ten predominantly Irish companies from the Army of Northern Virginia surveyed in tables 6 and 7, for example, had KIA rates that were higher than the army had as a whole, the only exception being the Richmond Montgomery Guards, which had virtually ceased to be an Irish company after May 1862. Getting killed may not have been the most effective method of winning a conflict, but in the Confederate war, paying the "death sacrifice" was the highest form of patriotism.[50]

One is left then with a paradox. Irish men fought hard but also deserted and took the oath in larger numbers than native southerners. Also, not every Irish unit had higher than average desertion/oath rates. While the Emerald Guards' low desertion/oath rates can be explained by its high socioeconomic status, the performance of Nolan's Montgomery Guards is less easy to explain. Nolan himself had been a Douglas Democrat, a reluctant secessionist, and his men from New Orleans probably fit or were close to the socioeconomic profile of the Irish companies in the 6th Louisiana (see table 5). Unit cohesion played a major role, and Nolan's seems to have been cohesive under his leadership.

One of the contemporary historians of the Army of Northern Virginia explains that this cohesion between officers and enlisted, rich and poor, slaveholder and nonslaveholder was built on the bond of their common belief in "Confederate liberty." He defines it thus: "The foundation for [Confederate] group motivation was support of slavery and a vision of Confederate liberty. Whether they owned slaves or not, Confederate soldiers understood and embraced the ideas that Africans were inferior beings who were ideally suited for slavery; that slavery was a right inherited from their ancestors; that the Founding Fathers had secured that right in the Constitution; and that if Southern whites allowed Northerners to strip them of those liberties, then they were no better than slaves themselves."[51] Racial superiority and a belief in the right to own slaves made the Army of Northern Virginia a coherent and often devastating fighting force.

Another study of "Why Confederates Fought" indicates that defending slavery became even more of a motivator as the war dragged on. Indeed, "instead of discouraging Confederates, the Emancipation Proclamation promoted a stronger and more public defense of slavery" and "the most egregious aspect of the North's hard war, from the perspective of white southerners, was emancipation."[52]

Did racism account for the successful performance of Irish units such as Nolan's company? Irish Confederates in general saw blacks as "inferior beings" (see chapter 1), but there is very little evidence of this being a strong motive for hard fighting. Nolan, for example, had no direct link to slavery.

Those Irish Americans actually born in the South, however, may have been more inclined to see an explicit defense of slavery as a strong motivator. Irish American volunteer Anthony M. Keiley was, like most Irish southerners, an active Douglas Democrat. American-born to an Irish father and mother, Keiley was young when the family moved to Petersburg, Virginia, where they became one of the most prominent Catholic families. He was a member of the Petersburg Riflemen and was among the first to enlist "for the War" on April 19, 1861, with Company E of the 12th Virginia Infantry.[53] He was elected sergeant and eventually commissioned as first lieutenant in late 1861. He led the company on a charge up Malvern Hill and was shot in the instep. It was an awkward if not severe wound and thus he returned to the regiment in late 1862. His injury made marching difficult, however, and he wrote to his political connections to find a new, noncombat post either as a judge advocate or as a clerk. In his letters Keiley became most effusive in proclaiming the war as a racial contest between the gallant "knighthood" of the South against "the howling clamorous rabble" of "whining Roundhead[s], corrupted by two generations of attendance upon spindles from Puritanism."[54]

Keiley never saw mere ownership of slaves as the motivation for fighting the "Yankees." He proclaimed that his strong loyalty to the Confederacy was based on the zeal of "*nonslaveholders*" to the cause. Indeed, "none were so tardy in enlisting [in] the service" he believed, "as slaveholders and none so eager to avail themselves of legal exemptions." This was so because "property always timid followed its instincts then and since." The rich, in the Confederate case the planters, had too much to lose and therefore were less inclined to fight and die for the cause.[55] Keiley was not, however, an opponent of slavery itself, just resentful of the idea that to defend the institution and the South's "honor," required one to own slaves. African Americans, he believed, were still inferior and fit only for slavery. Back home in Petersburg, he was captured while trying to defend his city during the Bermuda Hundred campaign of May 1864. On being brought before the Union commander, General Benjamin Butler, Keiley noticed immediately "the presence and prominence of *the negro*." In fact, under Butler, "Abyssinia ruled the roost. It was a nigger everywhere." When sent to his prison quarters, Keiley became even more virulent in his racism. On his way he walked past, as he put it, "rows of grinning Ethiops, dirty, oleaginous, and idle." These black soldiers were to be his guards and he resented it highly. They were "sable patriots" who were "insolent" and whose "conduct is as black as their skin." Ultimately the "Yankees" had "in liberating four millions of blacks, enslaved eight millions of whites."[56] Keiley then was clearly an exponent of this "Confederate liberty." White freedom depended on black slavery and, although he was an early critic of slaveholders, when the reality of black freedom hit him, he regained his ardor for the Confederacy.

Keiley was, of course, not an immigrant but the son of one. The only major explication on race and the war from a native Irish soldier came from General Patrick Cleburne. Cleburne was from County Cork and had emigrated to America in the late 1840s, having served for a time in the British army. Eventually settling in Helena, Arkansas, Cleburne became a prominent citizen of the town but not a slaveholder. Nonetheless, he was an enthusiastic Confederate, joining a local company as a private but eventually rising through the ranks to become a major general in late 1862 and commander of a division in the Army of Tennessee. He was an excellent solider and leader of men. By early 1864, however, he had become skeptical about the chances of Confederate victory. In particular, he was concerned about the lack of manpower in the Confederate army and, speaking to his colleagues and staff subordinates, he made public a plan to recruit slaves into the military. In return for their service, these slaves would be given their freedom. With a major incentive to fight, Cleburne believed, slaves would, as in antiquity, make good soldiers.[57] Their enlistment would also increase the likelihood of European recognition of the Confederacy by shifting the focus from defending slavery to "independence," something he cherished above "every other earthly consideration," which included property in slavery.[58]

Cleburne's proposal was met with skepticism by many of his subordinates and colleagues. No other division commander and only one of his own brigade commanders signed it, and only some of his regimental commanders did. He nevertheless brought it forward to his commander, General Braxton Bragg, who in turn forwarded it to President Davis. Davis immediately ordered the subject dropped, and even bringing it up perhaps cost Cleburne further promotion. Cleburne's "evident enthusiasm" for his proposal could indicate that Irish Confederates, even in their most ardent form as Cleburne undoubtedly was, were not that committed to slavery. His move, in part, exhibits a certain naiveté toward the "cornerstone" of the Confederacy or at least the ideology behind it. Prominent Confederate general and politician Howell Cobb expressed this belief best in a letter to the secretary of war: "The day you make soldiers of them [slaves] is the beginning of the end of the revolution. If slaves make good soldiers, then our whole theory of slavery is wrong." Cobb wrote this letter in the dire days, from the Confederacy's viewpoint, of January 1865, thus highlighting how radical Cleburne's stance was in early 1864. Indeed, the Irish general had been contemplating his plan as early as 1863.[59]

Cleburne may have been naïve about the possibility of emancipation, but not in the importance of slave labor to the Confederacy. Cleburne's vision was for black soldiers, not black citizens in the Confederacy. On the contrary, their "emancipation" was to be a limited one. While family relationships would be legalized, "wise legislation" would be needed to "compel [former slaves] . . . to labor for a living."[60] Somewhat ironically, Cleburne drew on the Irish experience he had fled from, concluding in one letter that "writing a man 'free' does not make him so, as the history of the Irish laborer shows." Cleburne understood clearly then that the subordination of blacks would be a key element of the independent Confederacy that he continued to fight for with such gusto. Through his proposal, he believed that "we can control the negroes . . . and they will still be our laborers as much as they now are; and, to all intents and purposes will be our servants, at less cost than now." To let the North win and the Confederacy be destroyed would, instead, lead to the dreaded racial "equality and amalgamation."[61]

By including himself as part of these southern views of "Confederate Emancipation" with the use of "we" and "our," Cleburne explicitly agreed with the dominant southern view of the "inferiority" of blacks and his fear of full "equality" and racial "amalgamation," underscoring that racial motives inspired some of his Confederate patriotism. In his division, he had hundreds of Irish soldiers from Mississippi and Tennessee in the 3rd and 5th Confederate Infantry regiments (which had consolidated into one regiment by early 1864), and their regimental commander, Colonel Richard Person, had signed Cleburne's proposal. There is no direct evidence that his Irish and native soldiers knew of his proposal, but it became so well known among the officers of his division, it is likely that some version of it did filter down the ranks. The Irishmen in his division would have easily recognized the vision of Confederate defeat he outlined in his proposal. The Confederate nightmare he portrayed was not just racial amalgamation but also a land where "Northern school teachers" and "Northern school books" would portray "their version of the war" and "regard our gallant dead as traitors." In Ireland it was British schoolbooks in Irish schools and it was Irish heroes who were seen by the ruling classes as "traitors." The victorious Yankees would also set up of a "spy system" and a "secret police" force familiar to them from their homeland across the Atlantic. But whether they believed in his racial rhetoric and/or his project for emancipation is impossible to discern. Some may have actually opposed the overall plan because of their fear of black competition for menial jobs following emancipation or may have disliked the potential presence of black soldiers in their ranks, something highlighted by Cobb in his 1865 letter. He believed that recruiting blacks would mean that "your white soldiers [would] be lost to you" because you could not "keep black and white troops together."[62]

What is clear, however, is that most Irish Confederates did not object to his views. Cleburne's division was the best in the Army of Tennessee, a "model of discipline, cleanliness and competence under fire," and he "was the idol of his division and perhaps the entire army as well."[63] The Irish soldiers under him were among this elite.[64] Whatever his views on slavery and race, it was his example and coolness in command that inspired them to become some of the best soldiers in the Confederate armed forces.

Perhaps the key then to Irish Confederate performance was leadership. Organized and brave officers (Cleburne died leading his men into the Battle of Franklin in late November 1864) could motivate fighting men, especially those filled with the notion of being "a fighting race." Poor leaders could have the opposite effect. For all the speculation about closet Unionism among the Irish troops at Fort Jackson on the Mississippi, "Poor officers no doubt also hurt morale." Therefore, good officers could increase morale and be Confederate role models for their troops.

The Louisiana Montgomery Guards' record of high casualty and low desertion rates, for example, was in large part due to Michael Nolan's example. He displayed his qualities as a commander from the very beginning. During his company's first confrontation with the enemy at King's School House (just outside Richmond) on June 25, 1862, Nolan showed great military aptitude. His company and regiment came under severe fire as they marched along the Williamsburg Road. Nolan eventually found himself in command of the regiment and "drove the Yankees back." In the process "Captain Nolan's Louisianians took the battle flag of General Daniel Sickles famed 'Excelsior Brigade.'" Nolan received quick promotion and, later in the summer 1862, was made a lieutenant colonel.[65]

Nolan increased his reputation further on August 30, 1862, at the Second Battle of Manassas, where in command of his much-depleted regiment in the center of the Confederate line, not far from where Dominick Spellman had performed his crazy act of bravery, Nolan's regiment was attacked by Union troops. With the defenders lined up along the top of the railroad cut, the fight became desperate as "'the flags of the opposing regiments . . . [were] almost flapping together.'" The Louisianians were running out of ammunition when one man named "O'Keefe" (probably Private Michael

O'Keefe of Nolan's Montgomery Guards) reportedly shouted: "Boys, give them rocks."[66] Nolan ordered his men to rain rocks down on the northerners in the railway cut, catching them by surprise. The Confederates had the advantage of high ground, and the men in blue retreated. Despite the fact that the battle was almost over and the Union attack had run out of steam, the rock throwing incident became famous and the "fierce defense of the railroad grade became well known throughout the South and made Starke's brigade something of a legend. As the heroic episode was retold over the years, the Louisianians' stand on the bloody embankment was seen as the epitome of southern bravado." Nolan had been in command of this successful defense, a moment of glory that many of his comrades from the Montgomery Guards shared with him.[67] Nolan would add his name to the roll of honor when he led the regiment and the remnants of his old Irish company up Cemetery Hill on July 2, 1863. He and his unit came under "murderous fire" from the well-positioned Union defenders and he was "one of the first to fall" to an enemy bullet, dying instantly.[68] The Douglas Democrat from County Tipperary and New Orleans had died at the head of his men at the most famous battle of the Civil War.

Was Nolan reenacting something from the Irish past or did his bravery stem from his love for the Confederacy? Like his unit's namesake, Richard Montgomery, he had died in an attack on a strong enemy position. The Guards did have a flag of "green silk with gold fringe" with "'Montgomery Guards, organized Jan'y 8 1861' surrounded by a wreath of shamrock" on one side. But on the front of the flag were "the words 'Louisiana Our Home, Her Cause is Ours,' surrounded by a wreath painted in gold, as was the declaration of fidelity to the state, representing the sugar cane and cotton boll."[69] Nolan's Confederate career embodied the notion of the parallel struggle. Irish causes inspired him to join and to fight as the "Fighting Irish" had done for generations, but so too, it seems, had a desire to defend his new country, the Confederate States of America. His example rubbed off on his Irish comrades.[70]

Irish commanders could get the fighting spirit from their soldiers too. Lieutenant Dick Dowling found himself in command of his company of 40 artillerymen in late September 1863 in Fort Griffin along the west bank of the Sabine River, near where it entered the Gulf of Mexico, as 5,000 Union soldiers prepared to invade Texas. Dowling sought orders from his commander, General John Bankhead Magruder, who assessed the situation as hopeless and told Dowling to spike his guns, abandon his fort, and withdraw. But Dowling, finding the spirits of his men high, with them expressing a strong

Richard (Dick) Dowling (Museum of the Confederacy, Richmond, Virginia)

desire for combat, even against overwhelming odds, decided to stay and fight. His artillerymen halted the invasion with some rapid and accurate fire on the Union gunboats in the river, disabling two of the major boats leading the invasion. As a result, the Union forces withdrew, leaving behind 400 prisoners and two gunboats.[71] Dowling made "particular mention" of Private Michael McKernan for "his shot" which had disabled one of the gunboats. Dowling noted that he had chosen McKernan to operate the cannon trained on the main Union vessel because of "his well-known capacity as a gunner." He also knew the rest of his men well, and they withstood fire from the gunboats during their firing of 107 shots from five artillery pieces in just thirty-five minutes. "All my men behaved like heroes; not a man flinched from his post" he wrote in his official report. He concluded dramatically: "Our motto was 'victory or death.'"[72]

This kind of Irish bravado was not unique to Dowling and his men. The Charleston-born son of Irish merchants, William Ryan, led the original Irish Volunteers (Company C of the Charleston Battalion) in defense of the city in June 1862. Union forces based on Folly Island, just southeast of the city, intended to attack it from that direction. Standing in their way were Confederate forces on James Island. The invaders sent a reconnaissance force to Sol Legare Island on June 2. The Irish Volunteers were among the first to respond with Ryan in command. Leading a charge against a group of Pennsylvania soldiers, he eventually jumped into the Union position and grabbed the commander by the throat, ordering his men to surrender. Another Union soldier tried to run Ryan through with a bayonet but he did not flinch. Instead he depended on one of his Irish Confederate colleagues, Private Rody Whelan, to intercept the attacker. Whelan's and the Union soldier's "bayonets locked" and "twisted like wire" before Whelan subdued the would-be assailant. Less than two weeks later, Ryan led the Irish Volunteers at the Battle of Secessionville, where he and they, through the effective manning of cannons, halted an advance by the 79th New York Highlanders. Ryan would again perform with valor at the attack on Battery Wagner on Morris Island in July 1863 (made famous by the participation of the African

American 54th Massachusetts and immortalized in the movie Glory), when he left the bombproof shelter to drive out some Union soldiers who had made their way into the fort. Leading from the front, he was killed in the action.[73]

Like Ryan, William Monaghan was just a clerk in New Orleans, but he actually organized the Patrick Sarsfield–inspired "Irish Brigade" (which became Company F of the Irish 6th) in New Orleans. He had lived in the city at least eleven years with his Irish wife Sarah and was middle class but not wealthy or a slaveholder. As a company organizer he enlisted with the rank of captain in 1861. He proved his command mettle early on and was promoted to a staff position (major) in June 1862, despite being a prisoner of war at the time, and was promoted to colonel in charge of the Irish 6th and command of the 1st Louisiana Brigade in late 1863. He provided vital leadership at the Battle of Spotsylvania, in Virginia, on May 12, 1864, when he found himself in charge of the Consolidated 1st and 2nd Louisiana Brigades in the "Muleshoe" (a salient of Confederate breastworks that jutted beyond the regular lines in the shape of a mule's shoe). This horrendously bloody battle was almost a disaster for the Confederates as Union "brutal assaults" overwhelmed the Confederate forces in the breastworks to his right. Rather than retreating or surrendering, which many did, he moved his men 150 yards away and had them "realign perpendicular to the breastworks." With the new alignment Monaghan's men were in good position to shoot into the advancing Union troops, and when they appeared he roared "'Fire!' and the Louisianians obliterated the first line." Monaghan's quick thinking under fire helped slow the Union advance and allowed time for a second set of defense works to be created to the south. After the action, only 60 men of the 6th Louisiana were fit for duty. Monaghan survived this battle but would be killed in action near Sheperdstown (Virginia) in August 1864.[74] The nonslaveholding merchant and former commander of the "Irish Brigade" company, had, like Sarsfield, died on a foreign field.

The greatest example of Irish command and bravery was Patrick Cleburne. His sobriquet as "Stonewall of the West" was well-earned. Cleburne's experience in the British army during the 1840s certainly gave him some military training but it was his disillusioning experience of policing the Irish Famine (1845–52) that truly marked him as a potentially good Confederate. He had hoped to escape Ireland for an exotic part of the British Empire with opportunities for glory, but instead found himself stuck at home guarding food convoys from starving peasants. This soul-destroying service made him choose emigration, and he found opportunities in Arkansas unavailable to him in Ireland. He was a Protestant, but not a leading landowning member of the Anglo-Irish "Ascendancy," which one of his biographers puts forward as a reason for his strong Confederate sympathies. The disappointing experience of British rule in Ireland, not his desire to re-create it in America, made him a Confederate. His description of a conquered South came from his Irish experience and his disdain for it.

Men like Nolan, Dowling, Ryan, Monaghan, and Cleburne certainly enhanced the reputation of Irish Confederates. Other prominent Irish officers who supported the Confederacy did so as well, although their military reputations sometimes came from luck rather than skill. Even though Florida secessionist Joseph Finegan had served in the U.S. Army early in his American life, he gained a commission as a brigadier general because of his connection to Senator David Yulee. Stationed in his home state, Finegan happened to be in command when Confederate forces won the Battle of Olustee in 1864. The battle was won, in spite of, rather than because of, his leadership. Nonetheless, he received the credit for it. Similarly, when his brigade of Floridians transferred to Virginia, they provided vital service at the Battle of Cold Harbor, receiving the praise of Confederate commanders including Robert E. Lee. Unlike Cleburne, Finegan was no military genius, but he still had a reputation as a good Irish general. Like Cleburne, too, he would be feted by the Irish community as an example of their loyalty to the Confederacy and, in the process erase sectarian divisions within the Irish community in the South.[75]

Even a Protestant commander of Irishmen who was not as explicitly Irish as Cleburne and Finegan could be claimed by Irish Confederates as one of their own to enhance their overall reputation. Colonel Randall McGavock of the 10th Tennessee "Fighting Irish" Infantry was born into a prominent middle Tennessee family, his great-grandfather having emigrated from County Antrim to America in the 1750s. The fact that his Scots-Irish roots went back that far meant that McGavock did not grow up like the Magraths and Smyths of Charleston, regaled with stories of "the men of '98." He did, however, visit Ireland on a European tour after his graduation from Harvard University in the 1850s. McGavock was aware of his Irish ancestry but had never embraced it like the Protestant Irish of Charleston.[76]

McGavock was, nonetheless, a member of his class first. Upon arrival at Dublin in "auld Ireland" his first remark was that he was in "the land of potatoes and poverty." He complained that "The streets are narrow and dirty and filled with swarms of human beggars, who are not only annoying to strangers but disagreeable to look at."[77] It was relief to McGavock when he got to the home of his ancestors, Ulster. He described the industrial Belfast (Ireland's Manchester), as "by far the most attractive place in Ireland. The streets are wide and well built and the place looks clean and decent." "Londonderry" he described as the most "interesting place" he had been in Ireland. McGavock was equally impressed with Scotland.[78] His trip to the British Isles highlights that he distinguished his Ulster lineage from that of the "real Irish." Unlike Magrath of Charleston, he did not wish to claim Irishness beyond distant ancestors. He saw no commonality between himself the "filthy" Irish of the south of Ireland.

His involvement in Democratic politics back in Nashville, however, gave him a new connection with these other Irish. As an attorney he had represented many Irish residents in various law suits and as a follower of politics he had subscribed to John Mitchel's *Southern Citizen*. McGavock later purchased a copy of Mitchel's edition of Irish nationalist's James Clarence Mangan's poetry in which he found "several interesting pieces."[79]

McGavock's newfound interest in romantic Irish nationalism was undoubtedly influenced by his growing sense of southern nationalism, which increased through the sectional conflicts of the 1850s. He also undoubtedly found it useful, however, in speaking to his Irish constituents. The nativist Know-Nothingism of the decade and its ties to the dreaded, newly formed Republican Party scared McGavock. In 1856 he rejoiced at the Democratic victory in the presidential race because "The Principles of the Constitution have been upheld by the voice of the people, notwithstanding the wild cry of the fanatic and the demon spirit of the K N who sympathized with those who were fighting against every principle of right, honor, and justice." Know-Nothingism remained strong, however, in his native city. Thus, McGavock decided to run for mayor in 1858. The growing Irish population of Nashville, which had exploded since the Irish Great Famine, welcomed the man who had defended their legal rights in court and on at least one occasion had escorted a recently naturalized Irishman to the polls and ensured that he could cast his ballot. On another, he helped naturalize a number of Irishmen, despite the loud protests of local Know-Nothings. In his campaign for mayor he rediscovered the immigrant networks that he had never had to use. He attended St. Patrick's Club dinners, Irish funerals, and even went to the Irish boarding houses including one "Mrs. O'Sullivan's . . . on Front Street" which after visiting he declared in his journal: "I am confident of every vote in that house." He won with ninety-three votes to spare over his closest rival in a four-way race. His "fellow" Irishmen did not forget their role in his victory, often coming to the office of Nashville's youngest-ever mayor for financial help. McGavock for the first time went to St. Patrick's Day celebrations.[80] The great-grandson of Ulster migrants was rediscovering a certain sense of Irishness that seemed to go beyond the seeking of votes.

This newfound connection with the Irish was cemented in the Confederacy. Like his Irish constituents, McGavock was not a fire-eater, but did embrace his state's secession in June 1861. He volunteered for Confederate service and helped organize a number of Irish companies for the 10th Tennessee Infantry—"the Bloody 'Tinth.'" For forming this predominantly Irish regiment, McGavock was rewarded with a commission as lieutenant colonel. His troops liked him, particularly because he was often lenient with their love of whiskey. While completing the monotonous and dirty work of building Fort Henry on the Tennessee River in late 1861 and early 1862, McGavock realized that alcohol could be an important distraction from the morale-sapping digging.[81] After the fall of Fort Henry and nearby Fort Donelson in February 1862, and their subsequent capture, McGavock did not return to his unit until September of that year. He noticed that the unit was indeed smaller, but those who were there "were all exceedingly glad to see me, which was very gratifying." McGavock was gratified even more when the Irish men of his regiment ignored the recommendations of the commanding general (Lloyd Tilghman of Kentucky) and unanimously re-elected him lieutenant colonel as well reelecting all his choices, including his brother "Ed," for lower positions. Tilghman "expressed great dissatisfaction because my regiment did not elect any of his K[entuck]y friends."[82] The Irish of his regiment liked their Scots-Irish commander.

Sent into Mississippi to help protect Vicksburg, the newly reelected McGavock led the regiment (consolidated with another from Tennessee) at the Battle of Raymond on May 12, 1863. Leading a charge he was killed almost instantly. Despite McGavock's death, the Irish of the 10th fought well for the rest of the battle, pulling a small piece of victory out of what was ultimately a Confederate defeat.[83] They did not, however, forget their red-haired commander. One Pat Griffin, a poor Catholic and a private in the regiment, recalled that McGavock was "God's own gentleman" and was pleased to play a role in the dead colonel's recovery from the battlefield. Captured by the victorious Union soldiers at Raymond, he persuaded one Captain Maguire, an "Irish Yankee," to remove Colonel McGavock for burial. Maguire "came from the same county in Ireland my parents came from" and inquired about the dead officer. When Griffin replied "that it was my own colonel, McGavock— an Irish name—he took it for granted that Colonel was a 'townie' of mine and he ordered his men to place the body in one of the army wagons." A couple of days later Maguire gave Griffin and some other prisoners permission to bury McGavock. Griffin's reflections of his Civil War experience are very self-serving, extolling in particular his own record.[84] But the other hero who emerges is his Scots-Irish commander, even though Griffin served under Catholic commanders as well. Of course, the circumstances of McGavock's death automatically made him a hero, but hardly "God's Own Gentleman." It is a remarkable acknowledgment that Griffin remembered his Protestant commander so fondly fifty years after his death and continued to recognize him as a fellow Irishman, especially since that man had only recently openly recognized his own "Irishness" and formed a relationship with his own poorer countrymen in America.

Not all meetings between Irish Confederate and Irish Union soldiers were so positive. Despite the strong ethnic connections between themselves and Irish Union soldiers, Irish Confederates seem to have felt no compunction about fighting their compatriots in this American conflict. A British army officer who visited the Confederacy as an unofficial observer in the summer of 1863 and met some Irish Confederates in Virginia agreed "that Southern Irishmen make excellent 'Rebs' and have no sort of scruple in killing as many of their northern brethren as they can." On asking one Irish veteran if he had killed "lots" of his compatriots on the other side, the Irishman replied rather fatefully, "Oh yes, but . . . they must all take it as they come."[85]

Irish units on both sides did face each other on the battlefield, yet there is very little record that these meetings left much of an impression on Irish Confederates. The Southern Celts as part of the 13th/20th Louisiana and the Irish Memphians of the 2nd Tennessee/5th Confederate Infantry faced off against the 15th Kentucky Federal Infantry made up mostly of Irishmen at the Battle of Perryville, Kentucky, in October 1862.[86] Similarly the two companies of Irishmen in the 1st Louisiana and the Irishmen scattered throughout Lee's "Foreign Legion" in the 10th Louisiana charged up Malvern Hill outside Richmond on July 1, 1862 against the 88th New York of Meagher's Irish Brigade, but the only note of this encounter was an Irish Union soldier's (incorrect) claim that they had fought off Roberdeau Wheat's "desperados" of the 1st Louisiana Special Battalion.[87]

The most famous Irish clash, however, occurred at the Battle of Fredericksburg in December 1862, when Thomas Francis Meagher's Irish Brigade charged up Marye's Heights toward certain death as Confederates ensconced behind a stone wall poured fire into the charging Irishmen.[88] Some claim that the 24th Georgia, which opposed the Irish Brigade at the stone wall, was an Irish regiment, and the belief in it has become so widespread that it is portrayed as fact in the movie *Gods and Generals*. It was not, nor indeed were the Irish-commanded McMillan Guards (Company E) of the regiment from Habersham County in North Georgia. The regiment's colonel, Robert Emmet McMillan, was an Irish immigrant from Ulster, and had organized the company with his name on it. A Protestant, he had prospered in Georgia in the thirty years he had spent there before the war, becoming a very wealthy attorney and the owner of at least twelve slaves. Unlike most of his Irish compatriots in Georgia, he had been a secessionist from as early as 1851, running as an unsuccessful Southern Rights candidate for Congress that year. His son, also named Robert Emmet, reflecting his sympathy for Irish rebels, was in his company, as were four other Irishmen. The rest of company was decidedly American, which is not surprising considering the mountainous parts of North Georgia had very few Irish residents.[89]

McMillan did indeed play an important role in halting the Irish Brigade's charge when command of the whole Georgia brigade fell to him upon the death of General Thomas R. R. Cobb. McMillan had no problem in ordering his soldiers to fire on his fellow Irishmen, shouting out, "Give it to them Boys!" Considering his given name, "Robert Emmet," perhaps he had some sympathy for them as they wore green sprigs in their kepis and coats to highlight their ethnicity.[90] McMillan's Irish background, however, has been imposed incorrectly on to his company and regiment.

There was, however, an Irish company present behind the wall at Fredericksburg as a part of the Georgia-organized Phillips Legion. The Lochrane Guards from Macon, under the command of Captain Patrick McGovern, were stationed just to the left of the 24th Georgia and did fire upon the Irish Brigade. By December 1862 the company had been reduced to about forty-seven men but apparently none of these left evidence of their experience. McGovern, for example, returned to Georgia and lived until 1895 but does not seem to have recorded a reminiscence of the battle. To them, and McMillan, it seems it was just another fight against the Union army. The Irishmen opposite were just part of the general Federal assault on their position.[91]

Another Irish Georgian gives us some perspective on what the attitude toward Irish Union soldiers might have been. Captain John Keely of Atlanta was the commander of the Irish Jackson Guards, the color company of the 19th Georgia. He served at Fredericksburg but not, as he later claimed, directly opposite Meagher's Irish Brigade. He did, however, encounter an Irish Union soldier at the Battle of Chancellorsville in May 1863. The battle took place in an area of Virginia known as the Wilderness, covered with trees and thick underbrush. During the fighting the brush caught fire, leaving wounded men who were unable to move vulnerable to burning to death. In the battle, Keely came upon an Irish soldier with a broken leg. He halted to help the stricken man in blue even though, as he put it "As we tore through the flame our hair, our eyebrows, our mustaches were burned off." He did it, he later surmised, "not because he was an enemy, nor did I assist him because he was an Irishman—I knew only that he was helpless, and in imminent danger, and that I could assist him—and I did."[92] Keely had come, as perhaps the Irish Union officer who helped Patrick Griffin with Randal McGavock had, to the conclusion that there was a certain bond between combatants that at times transcended the ideologies of the conflict. By 1863, that may well have been true even as ideologies hardened with the introduction of total war. For many Irish Confederates the war was becoming more about "comrades" than about "cause." Indeed, as historian Gerald Linderman puts it, "ideological forces" were not the major influence on soldiers, but instead for them "the war reduced itself to other men, comrades and adversaries, whose actions were informed by familiar moral values, to courage pitted against courage."[93]

This sense of courage in combat, seems to have been a serious motivator for Irish troops. In some ways they bought into the "Fighting Irish" legend, especially in battle, and did try to live up to that mantle. The story of Henry Strong of the New Orleans Calhoun Guards, 6th Louisiana, is illustrative. Strong was an ideological supporter of the Confederacy from the beginning of the war, organizing the company and naming it for that great defender of the South and slavery, John C. Calhoun. He was popular with the men of the 6th, eventually rising to the rank of lieutenant colonel and command of the regiment. In the Battle of Second Manassas, as the ranking officer, he found himself in command of the brigade, a task that seemed above him. At Ox Hill, Virginia, unable to move his troops correctly, he placed them in such a way that they did not face the enemy. As a result, when attacked, they had to retreat in "confusion." General Jubal Early placed the blame squarely on Strong's "want of sufficient skill in the command of the brigade."[94]

There is no direct evidence of Strong's reaction to this criticism, but he was obviously stung by it and sought to make up for his mistake. To restore his honor, he decided to lead his Irish 6th while riding a white horse into the Union positions across the cornfield near the Dunker Church at the beginning of the Battle of Antietam on September 17, 1862. On his white steed he never stood a chance and was killed in the cornfield, his horse too, which was hauntingly captured by a photographer after the battle. Strong had, however, restored his reputation, even if Early mentioned his death in the official report only as an excuse for not discussing the full role of the Louisiana brigade in the battle. His own troops noticed though. Native Louisianian Lieutenant George Ring wrote in his diary that Strong "was killed while bravely leading his men in battle."[95] Strong had maintained the fighting reputation of the Irish Confederate and his soldiers, and some in the Confederate press noted his bravery at Antietam. His passing was mentioned in his adopted hometown of New Orleans, picked up from a Confederate newspaper in Grenada, Mississippi, but considering its circumstances under Federal occupation, his bravery was not extolled publicly.[96]

Other Irish officers kept the reputation up too and were recognized publicly for it. William Ryan's charge at the Federals on Legare Island in June 1862 was described in the local press as "a gallant charge of the Irish volunteers led by Captain Ryan," and the account went on to say that his service was "approved and commended by all who had opportunities of seeing his conduct in action." Some local citizens presented him with a sword for his courage under fire. His death at Battery Wagner the following year made headline news in the *Charleston Mercury*, which declared that "no nobler soldier fell" in that battle.[97] Robert McMillan's bravery at Fredericksburg was described by the *Richmond Whig*, never a pro-Irish newspaper, with the headline "A Gallant Irishman at Fredericksburg." The story was picked up by other southern newspapers from all political persuasions and reprinted as an example of Irish Confederate patriotism.[98]

Even Confederates skeptical of the Irish, such as William Calvin Oates of Alabama, who thought the few Irish laborers and artisans in his company, to put it kindly, were not too bright, could acknowledge Irish bravery. As part of the 15th Alabama, Oates and the Irishmen in his unit were at the extreme right of the Confederate line on the second day at Gettysburg, charging up Little Round Top at, among others, Colonel Joshua Chamberlain's 20th Maine. Oates remembered years afterward that Sergeant Pat O'Connor on the charge up the hill "stove his bayonet through the head of a Yankee, who fell dead." O'Connor, Oates agreed, could be relied on too to transform reluctant Confederates into patriotic ones. One John Nelson, a native southerner from the regiment, had claimed that he would "fight anybody" and was eager to get into battle. Once the bullets started flying, however, his performance left something to be desired. O'Connor was put in charge of him to make him a more effective soldier. Thanks to O'Connor, Nelson's actions matched his rhetoric at Gettysburg, where he died charging a Union position. O'Connor's work with the men made him officer material, and he was promoted in late 1863. He was killed in action at Ashland, Virginia, in June of the next year.[99]

With praise from skeptics such as Oates, Irishmen like O'Connor knew that military service was the key to proving loyalty to the Confederacy. All the rhetoric about parallel struggles between Ireland and the South or fighting for the "southern way of life" did not matter if men did not sign up and then fight when in battle. When the *Charleston Courier* criticized the "British subjects" of the city for trying to avail themselves of consular certificates, Sergeant Alexander O'Donnell of the Irish Volunteers wrote from Virginia back to Charleston, asking the Irishmen still there not to shirk their duty to the Confederacy. He warned them: "As we unfortunately come under the heading of British subjects I hope there are none of us so forgetful of our relations with England as to accept the protection of their government after forcing us to lose sight of the cherished hearth stones of our forefathers by the galling hand of oppression and tyranny." To those who had already done so he stated: "Shame on the Irishmen who will be so degraded. Would Robert Emmett, would Wolfe Tone, would Lord Edward Fitzgerald!" All three of these Irish heroes, leaders of the United Irishmen, had given their lives to their yet-to-exist nation, or as O'Donnell put it, "They failed in their undertaking [to overthrow British rule in Ireland], and cheerfully died martyrs for their Country's Cause, in preference to living a life of thralldom and slavery." He then made the connection to the Confederacy: "And in every sense of the word, the Southern people are now engaged in the same cause, but more fortunately in shaking off that form of government that was disgustful to them. If we are heeding to the teachings of the idols of our country why not take up the cause of freedom and justice and proclaim to the world by our acts that we are alive to the privileges and blessings of a free people."[100]

Up to this point O'Donnell had been addressing his fellow countrymen, but his conclusion was as much a statement to native Confederates as to any potential Irish ones. "I am a member of the Irish Volunteers from Charleston in Colonel Gregg's Regiment, now stationed at Camp Huger, near Suffolk, Va," he began, and when the company formed under Captain McCrady just after secession, "I took my stand in an address to my Countrymen to rally to the standard of the Southern Cause, to identify themselves with the infant Republic, and aid in propping it up by our own arms until it would be able to stand on its own bases." As a result the Irish of Charleston would "occupy a position on the grand program that was being enacted thereby securing to our future generations an envious legacy," that is, a free and independent Confederacy.[101]

For Irish Confederates then, fighting for the new republic would create an "envious legacy" for their "future generations." All Irishmen therefore had to "assist in hurling into the Sea the imbecile fanatics who yet persevere in attempting to coerce these great, glorious and free people." O'Donnell would make sure that native Confederates "knew of the sacrifices the Irish were making on their behalf." After the Battle of Gaines's Mill in June 1862, where the Volunteers first saw action and Dominick Spellman had picked up the flag, O'Donnell had a letter to his brother reported to the *Charleston Courier*, the newspaper that only a few months before had questioned Irish commitment to the Confederacy. He wanted to tell all Charlestonians of the brave deeds of the city's Irish soldiers against the Yankees. Under the headline, "The Irish Volunteers in the Great Battle," He noted the bravery of the men in their first facing of the enemy and praised the bravery and skill of Spellman. He also mentioned the three "martyrs" from the company killed in action. These three "met their deaths gloriously and nobly defending the sacred trust reposed in their keeping, the emblem of our adopted state."[102] These Irishmen had not died fighting for Ireland but for South Carolina and the Confederacy.

Again, for all the national feelings and the pageantry surrounding the birth of the Confederacy, it was soldiers like O'Donnell and his comrades who would have to maintain southern independence.[103] Supporters of the Irish immigrants in the South knew this very well. Walter Phelan was the son of Irish American Confederate Senator James Phelan of Alabama (see chapter 4) and served in a non-Irish unit during the war. He, nonetheless, took to heart any attacks on Irish loyalty toward the Confederacy. In the dark days after Gettysburg and Vicksburg in 1863, Phelan wrote from the field to a newspaper in Mobile reminding southerners that they "must not forget or suffer . . . to overlook the many noble, free-hearted, thorough going Irishmen who, through pride and patriotism rallied around the Confederate banner at the beginning of the war, and upon a hundred battlefields have fought with that undaunted courage and desperation so characteristic of their native land." In camp, but particularly in battle, "when naught is heard but the rattle of musketry or the roar of artillery, the Irishmen are the same steady and resolute patriots." Phelan then highlighted the specific examples of the "*Bloody Tinth* [10th]" Tennessee "being composed of Erin's sons," which was "one of the first to come forward and meet the dastardly foe and so well have they performed their part that mankind will reverence them through all coming time." He claimed the 7th and 8th Louisiana in Virginia for the Irish too, saying that they, like the 10th Tennessee, had also "verified the glorious reputation" of the Irish Confederates and the "fifty odd thousand" Irishmen who were in the Confederate army. Therefore, he concluded, with a little false modesty, that he was "writing no idle scroll or fulsome eulogy, no fancied sketch or high flowing phrases, but simply a paragraph in honor of those to whom honor is due—*our Irish Soldiers* [his emphasis]."[104]

Getting Irish Confederate soldiers "their due" was an Irish concern. Phelan was not alone in trying to correct, and overcorrect, the record. One writer to an Augusta, Georgia, newspaper complained that Irish service was hidden. "Shamrock" was upset that the Irish of the city were not getting enough "credit" for signing up, and the way to do so was to join the "Banner Company of the 5th Georgia, the Irish Volunteers." He hoped that any Irish left in the city before suffering the ignominy of being "conscripted and sent among strangers" where the Irish bravery would be lost to most native Confederate eyes, would do so. Being a Confederate patriot was not enough, one had to be a visibly Irish Confederate patriot. In November 1863, Anthony Keiley, in his new capacity as a state legislator, encountered some anti-Irish feeling in Virginia over the purported lack of service to the Confederacy. To "repel imputations upon the loyalty of our fellow citizens of Irish birth" he hoped to "fortify" himself for the propaganda battle with "information of Irish troops in the service." He believed that the only way to counter these "imputations" was through the military stories of Irish soldiers in Irish units.[105]

Soldiers' brave deeds were the way to prove Irish loyalty to the Confederate nation. And, for the Irish, the positive stories could on occasion mitigate the negative ones. The only eyewitness account of the mutiny at Fort Jackson is from an aide to General Duncan, William J. Seymour. Seymour gives us much of the detail of the event when the soldiers, despite their officers' orders and pleas, vacated the fort. He never, however, mentions the obvious ethnicity of many of the mutineers. His traumatic experience in Fort Jackson, it appears, did not turn him against foreign soldiers, or make him mistrust their loyalty to the Confederacy. On the contrary, he joined the staff of the 1st Louisiana Brigade in which his father, Colonel Isaac Seymour, commanded the Irish 6th. The younger Seymour also often found these Irish soldiers difficult to control in camp and on marches, but in battle he found them excellent. In action along the Rappahannock River in April in 1863 he admired the performance of the 6th under Federal fire. He wrote in his diary that his men were "noble fellows [who] strove manfully to maintain their position." He also expressed admiration for Irish commanders such as William Monaghan.[106] He apparently retained no ill will toward the Irish from the Fort Jackson debacle.

But if the Irish Confederate soldier had on many battlefields proved brave and true to men such as Seymour, who had, in his case, every right to be skeptical of Irish loyalty, why then did Anthony Keiley need to collect information on their deeds and Phelan need to write in their defense to a newspaper? They may have had to because of the actions of the Irish still on the home front and the effect that they were having on native views of the Irish as Confederates. One of the key elements of the mutiny at Fort Jackson was the presence of family members nearby who reportedly undermined the morale of the soldiers in the fort. William Seymour certainly thought it the major reason for the insurrection of his troops. Post commander Duncan had refused to let civilian family members live with their loved ones, and Seymour blamed a woman who came to the fort from a nearby quarantine station for bringing the false news that the city had surrendered. Later, a Memphis newspaper claimed that "Irish women" had been given money by Union officers to spread this false rumor and to tell their men to surrender.[107]

Whether this story of bribes is true or not, Irish family members could have a major influence on their men in uniform. While Confederate nationalism depended on the performance and success of its military, its cultural development was away from the battlefield. Most citizens of the Confederacy, native or Irish, were not soldiers. For an Irish soldier, going to the front, while physically challenging in the sense of putting one's life on the line, was, in an ideological sense, a manifest and public way of displaying loyalty to the new republic. Irish civilians would have to find different ways to display Confederate nationalism, a difficult task with an ideology so much wrapped up in the idea of military service and sacrifice.

CHAPTER 4

Hard Times

The Irish on the Home Front

Support for Irish Confederate soldiers from home was vital both for encouraging them to stay in the army and to highlight to native white southerners that the entire Irish community was behind the Confederacy. Civilian leaders of the Irish in the South did embrace the Confederate national project and most became advocates of a "hard-war" policy. They accepted that state and individual rights could not stand in the way of victory over the enemy. Prominent Irish spokesmen, such as John Mitchel, were ardent Confederate nationalists, having learned the bitter lessons of defeat in Ireland. Even the most reluctant Irish Confederate of them all, John Maginnis, eventually rallied to the war effort. Nevertheless, as the war became increasingly costly, and Irish civilians began to suffer directly the deprivations and hardships of conflict, Irish support for the Confederacy waned. It declined to the point that many accepted with ease the occupation of the victorious Federal forces, clearly indicating the equivocal nature of their new Confederate identity.

It was different, however, at the beginning of the conflict. In July 1861 the students and faculty of St. Vincent's Academy in Savannah, Georgia, changed their graduation festivities. That year the graduates from the city's Catholic secondary school for girls, operated by the Sisters of Our Lady of Mercy, enacted a "Secession Conference" pageant as a part of their commencement ceremony. The event began with the local Irish Catholic pastor, the Reverend Jeremiah O'Neill, crowning a girl representing South Carolina with a garland of flowers. She then in turn crowned Mississippi and so on and so forth until every state in the Confederacy had been recognized. In 1862 they repeated the exercise and sang the pro-Confederate anthem "Maryland, My Maryland," and in Catholic wishful thinking crowned Maryland a Confederate state as well. They also included speeches on "Southern Patriotism" and "Sewing for the soldiers."[1] In Charleston the young, mostly Irish, students of the local Catholic schools, made the flag of the Irish

Volunteers. Their sewing of it was to remind the Irish soldiers of what they were fighting for, not just for the Irish tradition and the Confederate cause but also for their community at home. Young Ellen Lynch and her sisters of Cheraw, South Carolina, made a flag for the Emmet Guards of Columbia at the suggestion of the Volunteers' local, but native-born, commander. The Irish women of New Orleans gathered to collect clothes for one of their units heading for the front in Virginia.[2]

All of these examples of support for the Irish Confederate soldiers indicate how the Civil War also provided civilian immigrants a chance to "prove" their loyalty to their new home.[3] Most Irish in the South were not soldiers but were still important to the Confederate effort. The fact that the majority of Irish civilians lived in towns and cities, which often were strategic railroad junctions, ports, and/or centers of Confederate industrial production, made their support more important than their relative numbers might suggest. These civilians, however, could not perform the ultimate overt act of patriotism, fighting and dying for the Confederacy. Their loyalty would have to be expressed in other ways.[4]

Confederate leaders knew that civilian support, native and foreign, was vital to the military effort. Authorities thus took the new national project seriously. They quickly sought to construct a national identity for their new country. Most scholars agree that the Confederates did create a nation-state, but whether this state had a coherent national ideology is debated. Despite all the trappings of a functioning government, was the Confederacy a nation without a nationalism?[5] Others interested in understanding "why the South lost the Civil War," believe that the lack of a strong cultural nationalism "made the Confederacy more vulnerable to the demoralizing effect of heavy casualties and hardships." Soldiers at the front and civilians, women especially, on the home front faced these "demoralizing effects." Ultimately, whether through a crisis in confidence at the battle front, or a "crisis in gender" on the home front, the Confederacy's "lack of will constituted the decisive deficiency in the Confederate arsenal."[6]

Some historians have recently made a renewed case for Confederate nationalism. They point out that the traditional debate has focused too much on the politicians and the generals and not enough on the ordinary Confederates. "Confederates sustained their nationalism in the face of challenges not through a centralized propaganda apparatus, but through countless personal exchanges." In fact, the Confederate war effort was remarkable and it could not have lasted without Confederates using a strong "common vocabulary" based on "nationalist and patriotic rhetoric."[7]

Most of the Irish were "ordinary" folk, but whether wealthy or poor, did they adopt this "common vocabulary" of "nationalist and patriotic rhetoric"? As immigrants they were already attuned to issues of identity. After secession they had to become Irish Confederates just as they had previously tried to become Irish Americans in the antebellum era. This adaptation to the realities of southern society, as highlighted in chapter 1, had been an imperfect, arduous, and unfinished process. They now faced the reality of living in a new nation that almost immediately entered a war for its very survival. Irish civilians and their lives in the Confederacy thus have an importance beyond their own story, telling us not just about immigrant life in the mid-nineteenth century, but also about their host society and the success of its attempts at cultural and political independence.

Early Irish endorsement of the Confederacy, as that displayed by the students and women of Savannah, Charleston, and New Orleans, was exactly what the new southern government wanted. Support from the young was particularly gratifying. They were the future of the new southern nation.[8] Irish community leaders echoed these initial efforts. The members of the Savannah Hibernian Society celebrated St. Patrick's Day 1861 with toasts to Jefferson Davis and the Confederate constitution, as well as Irish patriot and Confederate sympathizer, John Mitchel. They also toasted their fellow countrymen, many of whom at the celebration were preparing to fight for the cause. President D. A. O'Byrne, whose father was from County Mayo, toasted "Irishmen—Ever ready to meet a foreign foe." In this case the "Yankees" and not the Irish were the "foreigners."[9]

The Charleston Hibernians unanimously withdrew the honorary membership it had given to Thomas Francis Meagher when he came out for the Union and began recruiting his Irish Brigade. T. W. MacMahon of Richmond wrote a scathing attack on Meagher and other Irish supporters of the northern cause, pointing out what he saw as the glaring contradiction of advocating the repeal of the Union between Ireland and Great Britain but opposing the Confederate repeal of the American Union. John McFarland, a cotton factor from New Orleans and Yazoo City, who had arrived, as he put it, "a penniless youth" in the South, gave money to a local volunteer company that changed its name to the McFarland Rifles in his honor. An anonymous "Irish druggist" offered $500 at a public meeting in Richmond to build an ironclad and $1,000 for it if it was built in one month.[10] These public displays were noted and highlighted in the press as examples of Irish Confederate patriotism. The fact that Irish community leaders had stood so early and firmly for the Confederacy had made a positive impression on native Confederates.

Two men in particular, though, took Irish Confederate patriotism further: T. W. MacMahon and John Mitchel. MacMahon published a dense and elaborate defense of the Confederacy and slavery in 1862 that garnered acclaim throughout the South. He had come to the United States in 1849, settling in New York, where he became active in Democratic politics. He seems to have moved to Virginia only in 1860. Nonetheless, he quickly embraced the South. He first appeared as a spokesman for Irish Confederates with his attack on Thomas Francis Meagher. He explained his support for the new nation further in his extended pamphlet *Cause and Contrast: An Essay on the American Crisis*, published in Richmond in 1862. He dedicated this work, in long-winded fashion, to "His Excellency Jefferson Davis, First President of the Confederate States: Soldier, Orator, Statesman, and Chosen Chief of United Southern Patriotism; who, in Violation of No Constitutional Obligation and Usurping No Principle of Special or Universal Liberty, Stands Forth, A True Representative of Pure Americanism; A Guardian of Individual Rights; and Upholder of State Sovereignty." He then outlined a racial and cultural defense of the Confederacy.[11]

MacMahon was a firm believer in "Confederate liberty" and therefore the core of his Confederate nationalism was racism. He believed strongly in the rightness of black servitude in the South, insisting that "with the dawn of history and civilization there existed antecedent to all written codes, showing that the subordination of the negro to the Caucasian is not slavery but that of physical and intellectual organism. . . his normal condition." Echoing the rhetoric of John Mitchel's campaign to reopen the transatlantic slave trade, he wrote that enslavement had "elevated the negro to a standard of civilization which he never attained before." MacMahon delved into ancient history showing the "universal" nature of slavery in ancient civilizations but he also in obscene terms dismissed Africans as mere "cannibals." Quoting the new pseudo scientists of race, MacMahon asserted that there were "forty six instances wherein the anatomy of the negro differs from that of the Caucasian" and ultimately "the skull of the negro, [was] approximated to its situation in that of the Chimpanzee and Ourang-Outang." Intermarriage between "noble Caucasians" and other "lesser" races led to a loss of virility, an increase in sterility, and in Mexico, for example, "the half-Aztec, half-monkey physiognomies of those regions."[12]

Here, MacMahon repeated some of the usual arguments of the proslavery position, familiar to most white southerners. His embrace of "scientific" racism, however, put him on the very extreme of the proslavery side.[13] The problem, from an Irish Confederate perspective, with endorsing this racial defense of slavery, was that these same scientists often saw the "Celt" as inferior to the mighty Anglo-Saxon. Alabama scientist and racial theorist Josiah Nott, for example, had described the "Celtic" Scots Irish of the southern backcountry as "stupid and debased in the extreme," because of their "racial mixing."[14] MacMahon dealt with this issue by highlighting the strong cultural traditions of the Celts. Even if many had been the slaves of the Greeks and the Romans, they were still part of the "creative branches of the great Arian family." Ireland had thus produced such "illustrious statesmen" as Edmund Burke and writers such as Jonathan Swift and of course the fact that "in the great drama of military skill and undoubted heroism surely the Irish Celt has had his share." MacMahon concluded his defense of the Irish race bluntly: "What analogy, then can be made between the Celt and Gladiator, and the African negroes of Virginia? None."[15] The Irish could be full members of the master race.

Northerners, however, were not. White southerners had begun during the sectional crises of the antebellum era contrasting the elite "Southern Cavalier" with the dour "Yankee Puritan." This contrast grew to racial proportions during the Civil War, and the Confederacy exaggerated "racial" differences in a quest to create a distinct Confederate identity. Thus men, whose ancestors, according to MacMahon, "had Roman Catholics sent to the gibbet" were currently engaged in "a systematic assault upon the institutions of the States which retained [slavery]."[16] Misguided philanthropy that had ignored the plight of "white slaves [in] Scotland, Lancashire, Worcestershire, and Ireland" was now interfering unjustly in the South.[17] With Lincoln's election, compromise was impossible, and the South had to secede and found its own nation. Though new and smaller, the Confederacy, MacMahon concluded, much as "David taught Goliath," would defeat "the tyrant" of the North with its "soldiers of Justice." Of course Irish Confederate soldiers would also mete out this justice. In good propaganda fashion, he described the great Confederate victories of First Manassas, but ignored or dismissed the setbacks. Focusing on the good news of the "important victories and [an] unexpected chain of successes" the citizens "of our Confederacy have reason to rejoice." If they "buckle on the armor of fortitude, be patient under difficulties, and unflinchingly resolute and determined in the hour of danger," then the God who had tested the "fidelity and soothed the sorrows of Job" and "delivered His people from Egyptian bondage" would not let the South down.[18]

Jefferson Davis could not have written it better. MacMahon's work aimed to boost Confederate morale. It was well received throughout the

Confederacy. The *Richmond Dispatch* described it as an "able and brilliant vindication of the Southern Cause." In the same city the *Examiner* was sure that this "graceful exposition of Southern political philosophy" guaranteed MacMahon "a place in the standard literature of the South." The reviewer for the *Richmond Whig* left the book with "a more enlightened, a warmer and more genial love for our Southern brothers, their happy homes, their sunny climes, and their wise institutions." The wisest institution was of course slavery, and it was so because MacMahon had shown vividly "the peculiar traits of the negro race, physical, moral, and mental, and makes apparent the impassable gap that God has placed between him and the white man; forever preventing the equality of the races—the negro doomed to inferiority for all ages, past, present, and future." Down the road in Petersburg, the *Express* found MacMahon's defense of slavery and description of the sectional crisis as "a valuable service not only to the cause of Southern Literature but [also] to the cause of truth and justice." In Charleston, a reviewer recognized MacMahon for his 1861 skewering of Meagher and described his work as "one of the most remarkable books contributed to Southern Literature." The Irishman had played a role in creating a Confederate national literature, key to any national ideology. It was one, however, based strongly on white supremacy and the inferiority of African Americans. All the quotes listed here came from an advertisement placed to encourage purchase of the book. Headlining the book as "True Southern Literature," the publisher claimed that it had sold over 3,000 copies in a week.[19] MacMahon had shown quite vividly that it was compatible to be Irish and Confederate. The Irish "Celt" understood just as well as the southern "Cavalier" the superiority of the white race and the dangers of "Puritan" abolitionism.

Whatever the sales success of his work, the book did not make MacMahon the most famous Irish propagandist for the Confederate cause. More prominent was John Mitchel. His proslavery and prosecession rhetoric had impressed many leading southerners. Renowned Louisiana propagandist J. D. B. De Bow was a major booster, seeing Mitchel's support of the South as "bold" and "fearless." Mitchel had left the South in 1860, however, to help the cause of the Irish national movement in France. He was a fund-raiser for the recently founded (1858) Irish Republican Brotherhood, or Fenian Brotherhood, as it was called in America. The Fenians aimed to overthrow the Union between Ireland and Britain by any means necessary. Mitchel also hoped the tensions in Europe would lead to war between France and Britain, something he wanted to encourage further. He stayed in touch, however, with issues in the United States, having become a citizen just before he left in May 1860. Ironically, when he became an American, he was already a strong advocate of southern secession. While in France he kept well abreast of the sectional crisis and the outbreak of war. Two of his sons had remained in the South and joined the Confederate army. He was working as the European correspondent of the *Charleston Mercury* but by the middle of 1862, he became disillusioned with the Fenians and skeptical of any European war that Ireland could take advantage of. He decided to return to the United States, or more correctly, in his opinion, the Confederate States.[20]

With his youngest son Willy, but leaving his wife and daughters behind, he sailed to New York and then ran the blockade from Maryland into Virginia, crossing the Potomac from the Eastern shore on a fishing boat. He arrived in Richmond late in the year but in time to observe the Battle of Fredericksburg that December. At the age of forty-seven, Mitchel did not join the army, but he did serve in the ambulance corps. Beyond this service, Mitchel felt he could best help the Confederacy as a journalist. (He also needed to earn a living in one of the most expensive cities in the country). An ardent and well-known "foreign" Confederate, Mitchel acquired a position at the strongly pro-Jefferson Davis *Richmond Enquirer*. He became its editor, and with his publishers serving in the Confederate army, Mitchel was in charge of its operation. As a proadministration paper, the *Enquirer*, and thus Mitchel, were part of what scholar George Rable has called the "National" faction of Confederate politics. At its founding, most Confederate politicians had rejected, at least in a rhetorical sense, the old antebellum party politics of Whig versus Democrat. They believed that their new republic would be virtuous and rise above factionalism. Confederate politics did not develop a party system, though some clear splits emerged, particularly as the war dragged on. The major divide was between supporters and opponents of Jefferson Davis.[21]

As a part of the pro-Davis faction, Mitchel supported a vigorous prosecution of the war. It endorsed the ideals of the president's inaugural speech that the Confederacy meant sacrifice. In defense of "our inherent right to freedom, independence and self-government," Davis stated, Confederates "united and resolved cannot shrink from any sacrifice . . . however long and severe may be the test of their determination."[22] Mitchel understood this rhetoric. It was the view of his early association with the nationalist Young Ireland movement, that a nation united could not be defeated. It also echoed his personal story of sacrifice for Irish independence. He had been a fairly prosperous, Protestant, middle-class attorney and could have lived a quiet life of family and business in Ireland.

But he chose a different route and gave his all for his country. He now transferred this loyalty and self-sacrifice to the "civilization" he admired against the one he despised. No wonder then that Mitchel accepted the harsh measures such as conscription and the suspension of habeas corpus in the pursuit of Confederate victory. The Enquirer, under his guidance, had no time for political bickering and constitutional nit-picking in the mortal situation the Confederacy found itself in. He understood the strength of northern military might, having opposed the power of the British Empire. So virulent were he and his colleagues on the paper that in 1863 they actually called for a temporary "military monarchy" to prosecute the war, because the Confederate Congress did not seem to be up to the job. Mitchel's strong support for any and all means necessary to win the war drew the ire of those more skeptical of the whole process. As a prominent Irish rebel and now the effective mouthpiece of the Davis administration, he was attacked by enemies of the policy who questioned his validity as a Confederate. William Holden of North Carolina, editor of the Raleigh Standard and perhaps the strongest critic of the war and the Confederacy itself, openly attacked Mitchel's Irish background as incompatible with southern patriotism. Holden implied that the firebrand's Irish roots meant that this proadministration man could be safely ignored.[23]

Mitchel could hardly be ignored, and no one could question his Confederate bona fides, with three sons in the service and his voluntarily returning through the blockade to support a nation he had been calling for since the late 1850s. So strong was his love of the Confederacy that he eventually became a critic of the Davis administration, especially after the losses at Gettysburg and Vicksburg in the summer of 1863. With the defeat at Chattanooga in November of that year, which he put down to the "slackness . . . in the whole of our military operations," he had to leave the pro-Davis Enquirer. His publishers remained supporters of the president and could not accept Mitchel's change of position.[24]

As such a prominent Confederate nationalist, Mitchel was not unemployed for long. He was too valuable an advocate of the war to be kept silent. He quickly found a position at the Richmond Examiner, owned and operated by John Daniel, who was already a severe critic of Davis and the running of the war. Daniel, like Mitchel, believed that the Confederate government had not gone far enough in its prosecution of the conflict and that the Davis administration was incompetent. The Examiner suited Mitchel for other reasons too. First, it "extolled a Southern ideal of social order based on chattel slavery and dedicated to freedom of whites." Second, it was sensationalist in tone and full of "atrocity" stories. Mitchel had had a lot of training in this genre in his writing on the Great Famine and general British rule in Ireland. He embraced the style wholeheartedly, remarking: "I point out diligently and conscientiously what is the condition of a nation which suffers itself to be conquered, draw pictures of disarming, and disfranchisements, and civil disabilities such as we have experienced in Ireland, and endeavor to keep our good Confederate people up to the fighting point."[25]

Mitchel would keep at the forefront the idea of the parallels between Ireland and the Confederacy. Irish Confederates could force native Confederates to understand the realities of a defeated national cause and thus keep them dedicated to its success. He was just the assistant editor at the *Examiner*. Nonetheless, he dominated its editorial writing. One scholar estimates that Mitchel wrote 80 percent of the opinion pieces.[26]

Whatever Mitchel's percentage of the writing, it is often difficult to discern who was writing the scathing censures of the Davis administration. Undoubtedly though, Mitchel's belief in the cause continued. Although severe critics of Davis, both Mitchel and Daniel had no truck with "libertarian" critics of Confederate war policies, that is, those who opposed to conscription, suspension of habeas corpus, etc., some of whom, by 1864, were calling for peace negotiations with the Federal government. One of the leaders of this movement was a former United States senator from Mississippi, Henry S. Foote. Foote, a prewar Unionist, represented Tennessee in the Confederate Congress. Having been a bitter rival of Jefferson Davis in the early 1850s, Foote became the president's strongest critic in the Confederate House of Representatives. This opposition might have made him and Mitchel tactical allies. But when Foote introduced resolutions in the Senate in favor of peace negotiations with the Lincoln administration, Mitchel opposed him vehemently. Foote had also apparently attacked the other leading Irish Confederate propagandist, T. W. MacMahon, for being a "favorite" of the president and attributed his exemption from Confederate service to this favor. It was now time, Mitchel believed, to challenge Foote's Confederate patriotism.[27]

Mitchel, as the most prominent Irish civilian Confederate in the capital, felt confident enough in his own position to appoint himself as an arbiter of Confederate loyalty. He attacked Foote directly for not supporting all the hard-war measures. The dispute quickly became an affair of honor. Foote was a noted duelist, and should have felt the aggrieved party, but it was Mitchel who apparently issued the demand "for satisfaction." Mitchel's second, William G. Swann, his former partner from the *Southern Citizen*, tried to deliver the challenge, but got into a fray with Foote and struck him on the head. Foote drew a pistol, but neighboring guests intervened and prevented further bloodshed. Mitchel and Foote were called before city court and bound to the peace, with Foote required to deposit a $5,000 surety. Mitchel had to deposit only $2,000. Foote inquired of the judge the geographical "limit" of the injunction, to which the judge replied "the Commonwealth of Virginia." It seems that Foote wanted to continue the affair outside of the jurisdiction. The duel never happened, but Mitchel's action was one of madness. By this stage he had lost two sons in combat: Young Willy, who had accompanied Mitchel on the 1862 blockade run, joined the 1st Virginia Infantry and was killed at Gettysburg. Meanwhile John Jr. died while in command of Fort Sumter in July 1864. Moreover, Mitchel had a wife and two daughters to take care of. (His surviving son was still in service). He had risked all for his support of the Confederacy and his opposition to all its enemies, both real and perceived. Mitchel must have felt vindicated when Confederate forces caught Foote trying to cross the lines without a pass in early 1865 to begin his own unilateral talks with the Federal government. The Confederate House censured the Tennessee congressman for this action, although it failed to reach the two-thirds majority to remove him from office. Disgraced anyway, Foote left for Europe and the House on this occasion unanimously expelled him.[28]

Mitchel had gotten his satisfaction, but he had taken his Confederate patriotism almost to the point of death. With the loss of his two sons, he was a full participant in the culture of "sacrifice" so central to Confederate nationalism. Mitchel had the credentials to explain to other southerners why all the suffering was worth it. He reminded them of the realities of "subjugation" to northern rule if they lost the war. "In short, if this Confederacy should be defeated or should consent on any conditions, to lay down her arms, before having assured and established complete separation and independence, all the evils that ever lay heavily on a conquered nation would be hers. Being weary of the 'Horrours [sic] of War,' she would find that she had rushed into the far more horrible horrours [sic] of peace." What were these "horrours"? Well, overall they were the fate of the conquered peoples of Europe, "the Poles, or the Venetians, or the Irish." There "would be a reign of 'Commissioners of Forfeited Estates' to seize property of "rebels" and give it to new "settlers, just as the English had done in Ireland. There would also be a series of coercive laws to trample on the rights of southern whites. Union authorities would appoint a "Viceroy" to rule. The franchise would be withdrawn. To keep the disfranchised in line "it will be found necessary to copy pretty closely the code of 'arms acts' and 'insurrectionary acts' in Ireland," which would empower the "Viceroy" on a whim "to proclaim . . . martial law and pour into [the defeated South] large numbers of police, with orders to search houses of suspected persons at any hour of the day or night." Mitchel, drawing on personal experience from Ireland, became more specific. He claimed that he was not "speculating upon what might be done in this country, but relating what is actual and frequent practice in another country, held in subjection by military force." Thus, the reality for defeated white southerners would be: "A house is entered at midnight by a police guard; the inmates are ordered to rise out of bed in order that the beds and mattresses be searched for gun-locks, or barrels, or stocks, or else bayonets, pikes or other weapons. If any part of any such weapon is found, the father is carried off in handcuffs to answer for his offense."[29]

Mitchel's missive was effective propaganda. The white male southerner's house, whether he be rich or poor, slaveholder or not, was his castle. His mastery began at the fence line.[30] It was what most Confederate soldiers were fighting for. Defeat then, according to Mitchel, would lead to the invasion of the household, the harassment of women and children, and the destruction of the family. Who or what would replace the southern family? "Yankee claimants" would, and they would become "*our* masters." Union armies were using the precedent of the British in Ireland for their military policy, where "the English army occupied Ireland . . . the inhabitants [were] driven into foreign lands and actually dispossessed of the property and new population introduced." In another article, warning of how "degenerate" the Yankee had become, Mitchel's racial ideology shone through. Since the Republican takeover of government, "White House and Black House are synonymous, 'Yellow colonels,' gingerbread surgeons, and 'black Anglo-Saxons' are the pets of every social occasion." Mitchel then raised the specter of miscegenation, that "monstrous word of Yankee coinage." But keeping with the views he had expressed since he first arrived in the South, he stated that "The manners of the Southern dining-room servant are better than those of his Northern patrons." Ultimately, he told native Confederates that the avaricious "Yankee," kith and kin to Puritan Englishmen, was far more dangerous than the slave. "Sambo may take to his sooty bosom their daughters and their sisters; Sambo may eat at their tables; Sambo may lord it over the Irish and the Dutch; Sambo may even buy, as at Beaufort [South Carolina], his old master's deserted mansion and hold it until Confederate armies come again; but as for a substantial share in any present or future profits of the Great National Speculation, Sambo may indulge his native genius in whistling for it." British speculators, on the other hand, would gain handsomely from Confederate defeat.[31]

Mitchel had lost none of his hatred of the speculative "spirit of the age" or his jaundiced view of British philanthropy. These beliefs made him an excellent propagandist. He became so successful at it that he felt he could support his wife, Jenny, and two of his daughters who longed to be reunited with him. Their running of the blockade in early 1864 was traumatic. Aboard the *Vesta*, Jenny and the girls stopped in Bermuda to refuel. Chased and fired upon by the blockading squadron off Wilmington, North Carolina, the drunken captain ran the ship aground near the South Carolina border, removed the crew and passengers, and set fire to the ship. The Mitchels escaped, but lost all their possessions and eventually, after walking cross country, made it to Wilmington and took the train to Richmond. They now had to face the hardships of war life in Richmond. Mitchel understood these well and spoke up for the common soldier and "mean whites" in his journalism. One of the major reasons he turned against Davis was the lack of support for poor soldiers. He was particularly worried about the lack of food for civilians and knew how dangerous it was for morale.[32]

In his concern for the poorer classes, he had particular interest in the Irish. Mitchel could not understand why Irish would fight to preserve the Union in America, while opposing the one in Ireland. Nonetheless, he remained sympathetic to the Irish wherever they were. Writing on the Battle of Fredericksburg, he expressed admiration for the Irish Brigade's efforts, but lamented that they "fought against people who never harmed them." Aware of the potential danger of negative Confederate impressions of the Irish, Mitchel reminded Richmond readers that the Irish in the North were impoverished and used merely as "cannon fodder" by the Union forces. Lincoln used these poor folk to feed the "profits" of New England businessmen by continuing the hard and brutal war. Another reason was, claimed Mitchel, "Peace destroys the wealth New England has horded and returns her soldiers back upon her barren soil to be supported at home instead of being fed and shot at national expense."[33]

As the northern Irish developed a more jaundiced view of the Union cause in 1863, Mitchel sought to encourage this growing attitude by reminding Irish northerners, and southern readers, that the "Know-Nothing" northern troops had burned Catholic churches in Florida and Mississippi. Therefore, "One of the essential differences, on which the Confederacy may pride itself, as making us a distinct people from the Yankee nation, is the complete absence of religious intolerance; while the prevailing Puritan element which dominates in the country to the North of us, constantly, necessarily, impels it to persecution of Catholics." This northern anti-Catholicism was now being transferred to all southerners, driven from their homes in a manner akin to the "doom executed upon the many thousands of Irish the last century when they were forced to remove into the moors and wilderness beyond the Shannon, under the terrible sentence, To Hell or to Connaught!"[34] Both Irish and Southrons needed to acknowledge the parallels of their cause against intolerant English and "Yankee" Puritanism.

By 1864 Mitchel was comfortable promoting a more positive view of the Catholic Irish up north in the *Examiner*. It was they, he highlighted to Confederate readers, who were most opposed to Lincoln and gave the Confederacy its best hope, the defeat of the Republican president in the November election. Mitchel also tried to deflect criticism of the Irish by focusing on British foreign policy as the real culprit for Confederate setbacks. He accused the British government of being so beholden to commercial interests that their foreign policy was one of de facto support for the North. British access to northern markets was far more important than recognition of the Confederacy or the halting Union recruitment in Ireland.[35]

Despite criticism of his Irishness, the fact that he had put himself in harm's way for the Confederacy, had encouraged his wife and daughters to join him when it looked bleak for Confederate success, and had lost two sons in Confederate service ensured his reputation as the civilian Irish Confederate. Along with putting himself forward as the classic example of the Irish Confederate, he promoted the Irish Confederate effort. He came up with the exaggerated number of 40,000 as an estimate of the Irish in the Confederate army to counter the anti-immigrant rhetoric of some native Confederates, thereby highlighting that large numbers of Irish were on the "right" side too. He stayed in Richmond until the bitter end in April 1865, evacuating only with Lee's army, leaving his wife and daughters behind in the now former capital. After the surrender, he managed to get to New York City, where he wrote for a New York newspaper. The loss of two of his sons made him remark ruefully that he had "suffered heavily indeed, one way and another, by that Confederate business, and although it was a good cause, I must admit I grudge it what it cost us."[36]

Irish American Confederate leaders also demonstrated prominent support for a strong war effort. The man who, in one way, began the whole process of secession, A. G. Magrath, became an ardent Confederate. He commenced his Confederate career as secretary of state for South Carolina but became a Confederate district judge for Charleston in 1862. In this position he upheld the constitutionality of the Confederate Sequestration Act, which gave authorities broad powers to seize "alien enemy" (i.e., northern) property in the state, including, controversially, the debts owed by northerners to southern creditors.[37] More important, in terms of the status of the Irish in the Confederacy, Magrath upheld the alien clauses of the Confederate conscription act. In a case brought by some members of the German Artillery from Charleston, who claimed that as they had signed up for only twelve months, the section of the Confederate Conscription Act of April 1862 extending all twelve-month sign-ups to "for the War" did not apply to them. As citizens of Hanover who had never intended to become naturalized, they argued, they should be discharged and exempted from Confederate service. Magrath dismissed their argument, stating that as they had lived under the State's protection they were obliged to defend it through service in the local militia. His decision opened up the forcible recruitment of foreigners who had thus far, for whatever reason, avoided military service or did not want to continue providing it. It was a landmark decision and a boon to the military effort, even if it created problems for some Irish residents of the Confederacy.[38] Confederate success was more important to him than defending the "alien rights" of Irishmen who had not served.

His strong national jurisprudence, balancing state rights with Confederate rights, impressed many of his colleagues, and in December 1864 the South Carolina legislature elected him governor. In his inaugural address, which according to a newspaper account attracted huge crowds to the capitol in Columbia, Magrath promised to provide a balance between upholding the Confederate and South Carolina constitutions. He valued personal liberty, he told the crowd, and wanted to have some state supervision of military seizures and impressments. Nonetheless, he promised vigorous government action against the Federal armies and reminded his listeners of what would happen to "private property" and "private security" if the North won. Echoing the rhetoric he had used in many antebellum speeches describing English rule in Ireland, he told of the "wanton, cruel violence which has marked the conduct of the enemy . . . the destruction of property, the violence to persons, the disregard of sex, the torture of the helpless [and] the desecrations even of the temples we have raised for the worship of our God." Mitchel would have liked his style. Inaugurated on the day before the fourth anniversary of his signing the secession ordinance, he restated what they were fighting for. "Regarding that domestic institution, which had been so long instituted among us, it has become the corner stone on which our social economy and political institutions depends, as the cause of this War, has already been doomed by our foes, and its extinction decreed." Ending this "domestic institution" would lead to "the disruption of ties by which society has been held; the overthrow of restraints by which its elements have been kept in harmonious operation; the cessation of labor; the confusion of caste; developing the worst passions of our race." This scenario would eventually lead to "anarchy." This anarchy then would affect all white people, not just those who owned slaves. As a result, he thought that "if ever there was an appeal to a people which would now summon forth all their energy, demand all their power, make willing every sacrifice, it is now made to the people of these Confederated States."[39]

In office, Magrath maintained his enthusiasm for the cause, even as the situation became dire. Savannah fell to Sherman at Christmas, less than a week after his inauguration. Nonetheless, he wrote generals, congressmen, militia commanders, other governors, and the president himself, in his effort to defend South Carolina from federal invasion.[40] In particular, he was adamant that Charleston be protected from falling into enemy hands, advocating that the Confederacy could not survive without it. His family, friends, and many of his fellow Hibernian and St. Patrick Benevolent society members, as well as his property, were there. When Union forces crossed the Savannah River into his state in early January, he issued a proclamation, reminding his fellow Carolinians that "You first fired the gun at the flag of the United States, and caused that flag to be lowered at your command. As yet you have suffered less than any other people. You have spoken words of defiance—let your acts be equally significant." Those acts were to "suspend business," "remove your property," and "destroy what you cannot carry." Magrath called for every man to offer "resistance onto death." "Rise, then," he concluded, "with the truth before you that the cause in which you are to arm is the cause of Justice and of Right!"[41] In this case, unlike what happened to the rebels of Ireland, Magrath hoped that "Right" would triumph over "Might."

He also, however, included a special message for the Irish (and other foreigners) whose rights he had long supported in his legal and political careers. "It is said there are some who think they are not bound to fight with us; who affect a desire not to forfeit what they call their allegiance to some foreign Power. It may be that there are some who have been misled." Misled or not, Magrath continued, "I will not believe that there lives in South Carolina now, any man who having been under the protection of the State and as that State treats its own citizens, will at this time, attempt to find in this affected zeal for an allegiance he has practically abjured, an excuse, for the succor he is bound to render." As a leader of the Irish community he had helped immigrants stay and prosper in Charleston, but now, "If there are such [who will not fight], let them depart."[42]

Despite all the Carolina bravado displayed by Irish and native alike in the exciting days of 1860 and '61, then, Magrath knew that many could not be trusted to fight until "death." In the Marion district along the Pee Dee River, he had to deal with roaming bands of southern deserters and draft dodgers. He complained to one state politician that "all our men are in Virginia or Tennessee," and to Robert E. Lee that he had to face "50,000 to 60,000 men flushed with triumph, [and] experienced in War" with "scarcely 16,000 men, a large proportion of whom were militia, composed of boys of 16 years of age." (Magrath had extended the eligibility for conscription to ages sixteen to sixty.) He made plans for military coordination between himself and the governors of Georgia and North Carolina, saying that if "the necessities of the Confederation compel the [central] Government [to come to] the defense of a state and if it is the duty of that state to remain loyal to the compact of that Confederation, it is evidently also its duty to provide for its own safety." But any such plans also came to naught.[43]

Sherman's forces marched through the state in about a month, Columbia falling on February 17 and Charleston on the 18th.[44] Magrath had escaped upstate and reestablished his executive office in Spartanburg. There, he tried to muster as many militiamen as he could to protect this last corner of Confederate South Carolina. Even after Generals Robert E. Lee and Joseph Johnston surrendered the major Confederate armies in April, he stayed in his position, even returning to Columbia. As late as May 14 he was still writing letters as governor, fretting about the end of slavery and its impact on the South's economy and social relations. By then, however, he had admitted that the Confederacy was lost, and he opposed any continued fight in the "Trans Mississippi District." "Guerilla warfare" would be worse and "the mischief it [would] produce must be tenfold more than any we have yet known." Though he felt his days as governor were numbered, he believed that it was his "duty to carry on to the end." This end came with Magrath's arrest and incarceration in Fort Pulaski near Savannah.[45]

Other prominent Irish American politicians of the Confederacy also showed strong nationalist tendencies. Irish-born immediate secessionists William Lander of North Carolina and Edward Sparrow of Louisiana were both rewarded with successful elections to the first Confederate Congress, the former to the House and the latter to the Senate. Both favored strong war policies, but only Lander supported the Davis administration wholeheartedly. The Louisiana legislature elected Sparrow twice to the Confederate Senate. He kept his state colleagues happy by standing up for their fellow Louisianian, General P. G. T. Beauregard. Davis had relieved Beauregard from command of the western army in 1862 because of Beauregard's retreat to Tupelo, Mississippi, and his extended absences from the front. Sparrow had petitioned Davis to restore Beauregard to military favor, but not only did Davis turn him down, he also publicly ridiculed Sparrow's request. The Irishman had been a prewar Whig and was one of the largest slaveholders in the South. He did not take too kindly to Davis's public attack and became an implacable enemy of the administration. He nonetheless, like John Mitchel, remained a nationalist critic of the administration.[46]

Irish American attorney James Phelan of Mississippi was also a strong war supporter in the Confederate Senate, but unlike Sparrow, was also a close confidant of Jefferson Davis. (His son Walter had defended Irish Confederate soldiers in print.) As the Sparrow petition highlights, the president was touchy about any sort of criticism of his judgment, real or implied. Phelan it seems, however, could give him bad news. It came in part from Phelan's strong defense of Davis in the Confederate Senate. Blessed as a good orator and a zealot for the rebel cause, which one commentator attributed to his acknowledged Irish heritage, he defended the president with gusto. On one occasion Phelan, drawing from his interest in his Irish ancestry, went as far as to imply that one of the president's military critics was a "Cromwell in embryo!," seeking to overthrow the constitutionally appointed president.[47]

Davis appreciated loyalty above everything else, and Phelan became his eyes and ears in the Senate and in the country at large. Davis took Phelan's correspondence seriously and forwarded his military suggestions and queries to the relevant officials. Having built this trust, Phelan could tell Davis honestly how unpopular legislation, such as the draft, was among common Confederates. The exemption for supervision of slaves particularly irked many. Like most Irish Americans, Phelan had been a loyal Democrat before the war, representing the interests of the common man for his constituency in northeastern Mississippi. A strong believer in the need for conscription, he nonetheless commented privately on the slaveholding exception that exempted those supervising twenty slaves or more from service: "Never did a law meet with more odium. . . . Its influence upon the poor is calamitous. . . . It [has] aroused a spirit of rebellion in some places." Another issue was substitutions, which again increased the idea of the Confederate effort being a "Rich Man's War," but a "Poor Man's Fight." Phelan led the charge in the Confederate Senate to abolish the substitute policy. His negative views of the Confederate national spirit continued to the end of the war, when he warned President Davis that he was still the "bearer of ill tidings."[48]

Phelan's support for Davis and his honesty did not help him politically. Proadministration votes cost him his seat, as they did County Tipperary–born William Lander as well, in the 1863 elections. Phelan was replaced by a cooperationist Whig who had been opposed to immediate secession and Lander by an avowed "Unionist" who wanted immediate peace negotiations. Lander, had supported the various administration-initiated war measures, though he too had protested "unjust [draft] exemptions." These complaints did not save him with the electorate in his district because many saw him as a "last man, last dollar" Confederate, that is, someone like John Mitchel, willing to sacrifice all in the struggle against the Federal forces.[49]

Mitchel, Phelan, and Lander, however, had some unlikely allies in their hard-war stance. The two Irishmen in the South who had been critical of immediate secession, M. P. O'Connor and John Maginnis, did rally to the Confederacy and endorsed strong measures to ensure victory. O'Connor's foot dragging on secession after Lincoln's presidential victory did not endear him to many Charlestonians. He failed, for example, to gain a nomination to the secession convention, something fellow Irish American A. G. Magrath did easily. Nevertheless, he did retain his seat representing St. Michaels and St. Phillips Parish (Charleston) in the state legislature throughout the war. O'Connor was keen to display his patriotism. In November 1862, for example, he introduced a resolution: "That in the engagements of the past year, in this contest for the liberty and independence of the South, it has been the proud privilege and distinction of South Carolina to have witnessed on the part of her troops, a heroic display of constancy and endurance under privation which never bent in the camp of valor—which never broke in the field." O'Connor had no objection, it seems, to the fact that most South Carolina troops were not serving in the state. On the contrary, South Carolina soldiers had spilt their "patriotic blood" answering "their country's call" at the "Walls of Richmond," "the Northern banks of the Potomac," "Manassas twice," indeed on "every battle field from Sharpsburg [Maryland] to Mobile." For this sacrifice in the fight for the Confederate nation and against "tyranny," they had "bequeathed to their State, the richest legacy a nation can inherit, an immortality of fame; and to their children they have left the eternal memory of their worth." For this, he concluded: "The State honors them, The State mourns them." His resolution passed unanimously.[50]

O'Connor went beyond fine patriotic words, advocating better provisions for both soldiers and their dependants. In the same session he introduced another resolution, which was "considered immediately" and "agreed to," on the "inadequate and insufficient . . . supply of clothing" supplied "by the Confederate Government" and that the State government should come up with "a plan" for acquiring "such clothing as may be needed for her soldiers." O'Connor could also be counted on for votes to increase civilian support—that is, taxes—for the war effort. In this task he was supported by fellow Charlestonian Edward Magrath, younger brother of A. G. and former captain of the Irish Volunteers (Company C, Charleston Battalion), who was elected for the 1862/63 session. Aware perhaps of the situation in his Irish company, Magrath worried about soldiers' dependents and asked the legislature "to devise and report some scheme of legislation having for its object reasonable aid and assistance to indigent families of soldiers in active service." Both O'Connor and Magrath seem to have been rewarded for their efforts as both, but especially O'Connor, did well among the soldiers' vote in Charleston. A local newspaper recognized "'The O'Connor'" for "his well earned reputation for ability and eloquence . . . full of ardor and love of liberty, characteristic of his Irish descent."[51] O'Connor was thus popular among soldiers and in the press not just as an ardent Confederate but as an ardent Irish Confederate.

John Maginnis did not come to Confederate patriotism until after the firing on Forth Sumter. Although resigned to secession after Louisiana left the Union in January 1861, he had continued to snipe at the way it had been done. He praised the moderates in the border slave states and Virginia for their refusal to join the new Confederacy, which he still referred to as the "Anti-Democratic Revolution."[52] After Sumter, finally acknowledging "the Union For ever Dissolved," Maginnis wrote that despite his "devotedness" to the "reconstruction" of the United States, he would now "use every talent and power we possess or are endowed with, to assure for our country the independence she has thrown down the gauge of battle to achieve."[53] True to this word, Maginnis endorsed a strong war policy. In particular he was critical of the poor economic preparations for war and advocated "patriotic" sacrifice from all. He supported without reservation, for example, the interference of the Confederate government in the market economy when it called for an export ban on cotton to put pressure on European powers to recognize the new Confederacy, and he thought it a key element in "checkmating the North." Despite his avowed love of "Democracy" he called for "governors now in the individual states of the Confederacy, who are unfamiliar with military affairs to retire from their posts, to allow them to be replaced by citizen soldiers of experience in military matters." These "citizen soldiers" would know how "to make available every man for offensive and defensive purposes." No fear of Napoleons for Maginnis. Indeed, his call for a type of military rule in 1861, came long before that of others, putting him well ahead of hard-war policy men like Mitchel.[54]

Part of this hard-war stance for Maginnis included maintaining his newspaper's (self-appointed) role as the "Organ of the People." To be fair, Maginnis realized, as James Phelan had, that civilian support for the war effort was crucial. He quickly attacked, for example, "speculators," who were driving the price of food "up to famine rates." Hinting at righteous violence, he warned these speculators that "if hunger becomes desperate, brick walls will be no impediment between [the hungry] and bread." Maginnis also hoped to "distrain" the property of landlords who evicted soldiers' wives for nonpayment of rent. He advocated that the well-to-do ladies committees formed to help soldiers could also give some charity to their poorer "sisters."[55] Part of this purview on behalf of the poorer Confederates was to highlight the Irish support for the cause. Maginnis's newspaper gave copious coverage to Irish units, their drilling, flag presentations, and their journey to the front in Virginia. On the way to his office one day, for example, Maginnis remarked how he had to move through "[a] perfect jam of the sons of Erin" on St. Charles Avenue as they queued to sign up for "Capt. Monahan's [Monaghan]" Company B of the "Irish Brigade."[56]

John Maginnis and John Mitchel had been miles apart on secession, but on support for the Irish in the Confederacy, they were in total agreement. Other Irish American leaders in the region showed similar concerns. M. P. O'Connor continued to look after his Irish American constituents. In 1862, for example, he introduced a resolution to gain back pay for one P. O'Connell, "a state constable." On another, he promised to introduce legislation with another Catholic member of the legislature to ensure the incorporation of the Ursuline community (convent and school) in Columbia at the behest of the Irish-born bishop of Charleston, Patrick Lynch. In late 1863, he also worked hard to counter poor publicity generated by, as he put it, "the bad behavior of some of my constituents among the Irish Volunteers" who, according to O'Connor, had tried "to escape," (from service presumably). Nonetheless, he was "not astonished" at the attempted desertion as "the war everyday is becoming so hopeless of an early termination."[57]

In Virginia, Anthony Keiley had left the service in 1863 after being elected to serve in the Virginia legislature. Already a friend of the common soldier, and critical of the rich southerners who avoided service, he was fearful that some of his rich colleagues in the legislature might begin to deflect negative attention from all weak-willed Confederates toward the Irish civilian population of Richmond. He therefore collected information on Irish soldiers in the Confederate armed forces to assuage any doubts of Irish loyalty. He sought, for example, the help of an Irish friend, Bishop Lynch of Charleston, asking him for information on the Irish units from Charleston.[58] The Irish Confederate soldier could perhaps save the reputation of the Irish civilian.

These efforts of O'Connor and Keiley indicate, however, that for all the prominently displayed patriotism from leaders such as themselves, or spokesmen such as Mitchel and Maginnis, there was still a disconnect between the official rhetoric of Confederate sacrifice and the reality of civilian life in the wartime Confederacy. How effective then were the pro-Confederate speeches and articles of both native and Irish Confederates? Initially, it seems, very effective. Although poor Irish civilians did not leave written records of their feelings, as Irish units sprang up all over the Confederacy, they packed the various churches and lined the streets to cheer their boys off. Occasionally, to make the support more personal, they followed them to camp. Captain William J. Seymour, on one occasion met an Irish female cook/washerwoman who had followed her compatriots to Virginia. Seymour seemed pleased to meet her as she knew his father and had flattering things to say about him. Other support for the Irish soldier at the front was temporary, but more personal. Catherine Culhane, for example, an Irish tavern keeper from Natchez, Mississippi, went to visit her surviving son (two others having died in service) in Virginia in June 1863, just before he too was killed in July at the Battle of Gettysburg.[59] Irish civilians could show their support in less direct ways too. The secession conference at St. Vincent's, for example, was not just a display of Irish Confederate patriotism for the local native-born population but also a message of kinship with their relatives at the front. A number of the students and the nuns had brothers in the Confederate army. Young Ellen McGowan had one brother in the Irish Jasper Greens and another in a different unit serving in the army. Her participation in the secession pageant marked not only her graduation and her Confederate patriotism but also her support for her brothers.[60]

Other Irish tried to indicate their Confederate patriotism more publicly. Harry Macarthy (sometimes McCarthy), the "Arkansas comedian," was born of Irish stock in England. Emigrating to America in 1849, he performed in the theater and was particularly known for his Irish comedy. Eventually settling in Arkansas, after a move to New Orleans, he developed a solo show there. He happened to be in Jackson, Mississippi, when that state seceded.

He became so caught up in the excitement and celebrations of secession that he felt moved to compose the first three verses of "The Bonnie Blue Flag." He performed it for soldiers in New Orleans, including some Irish troops, about to travel to Virginia, and it became a rallying song for all Confederates. Put to the famous tune of the "Irish Jaunting Car," Macarthy wrote the song for "sons of the native soil" but expressed sentiments that other Irish southerners could adhere to too. In verse two he wrote: "As long as the Union was faithful to her trust—Like friends and like brethren, kind were we, and just—But now when Northern treachery, attempts our rights to mar—We hoist on high, the Bonnie Blue Flag that Bears the Single Star." Macarthy eventually, after escaping from occupied New Orleans, toured the Confederacy performing his Confederate, Irish, and blackface minstrelsy songs for soldiers and civilians alike. The "genial Irishman," as a New Orleans obituarist called him, also played numerous benefits throughout the Confederacy for both soldiers and their dependents, and in the process again publicly displayed the Confederate patriotism of a nonfighting Irish immigrant.[61]

Also in New Orleans, the late Joseph Brenan, a protégé of John Mitchel's in the Young Ireland movement, could also inspire Confederates. Like his mentor, he too ended up in America and became a journalist and advocate of the southern cause in New Orleans.[62] Something of a poet, as a lot of Young Irelanders were, he penned "A Ballad for the Young South" sometime in mid-1856 in a New Orleans newspaper as the battle for Kansas between proslavery and antislavery forces became very violent. Again, like Mitchel, Brenan was more advanced in southern nationalism than many of his fellow Irishmen in New Orleans. The fact that his work drew the ire of the Republican *New York Tribune* and the abolitionist *Boston Liberator* in an article cleverly titled "The Pat-riot-ism of an Irishman at the South" only increased his standing among native white southerners though. "Men of the South, Our foes are up in fierce and grim array" he began. "The Saints of Cromwell will rise again in sanctimonious hordes—Hiding beneath the garbs of peace, a million ruthless swords." Brenan hoped the South would wake up and face the threat, reminding them of the example of two Irish American southerners: "And by the fame of John Calhoun—To honest truth be true—And by Old Jackson's will—Now do what ye can do!" Brenan's poem was reprinted in other parts of the South, where the young John D. Keiley of Petersburg (Anthony's brother), felt so inspired he clipped and pasted it to the inside of his letter book. When war broke out he immediately joined the Montgomery Guards of Richmond.[63]

Some anonymous writer also tried to inspire Irish troops with an original version of the song "The Irish Brigade," which spoke of the actions of Irish Missouri Confederates who took on Irish Union soldiers from Illinois at the Battle of Lexington in September 1861. The song made it to Richmond, where another anonymous songster amended it. It was probably written by an Irishman or Irish American because the lyrics reminded Irish Confederates of the connections between their cause and Ireland's: "They have called us Rebels and Traitors—But Themselves have thrown that off of late—They were called it by English invaders—At home in the year of '98." Here the lyric expressed that Irish Confederates were the true Irish patriots. Indeed, in the mid-nineteenth century, song lyrics became the most important element of Irish-Americans' culture and their way of portraying themselves to Americans. Thus, the song was also aimed at native Confederates to remind them of the fighting prowess of the Irish in their army. The original chorus had been: "Three Cheers for the Irish Brigade—Three Cheers for the Irish Brigade—All true-hearted Hibernians—In the ranks of Kelly's Irish Brigade." In Richmond it changed to: "When they met the Irish Brigade—When they met the Irish Brigade—Didn't those cowardly Lincolnites tremble—When they met with the Irish Brigade."[64] Here then this "Irish Brigade" was not a threat to the South, but to the invading "Lincolnites," intent on the destruction of the Confederacy and the slave system that underpinned it. The irony of "Kelly's Irish Brigade" was that those Irish Federals whom they defeated were hardly "Lincolnites." Most would have been supporters of the Democrats and opposed to ending slavery.[65]

Nonetheless, support for the local Irish boys could also lead some Irish civilians to dislike the northern Irish. In Charleston a crowd of local Irish turned on a bunch of Irish Union prisoners in 1861 and showered them with rocks and other missiles. The recorder of the event, a native Confederate guarding the prisoners, was forced to fix bayonet to keep the Irish Charlestonians from doing even more violence to their northern compatriots. Of course many of their family and friends in the Confederate army agreed. The company that had become the core of the Irish Volunteers for the war in that city had originally been the Meagher Guards but they had quickly discarded the name of their former hero, when he chose to raise troops for the United States Army.[66]

Others also explicitly promoted the patriotism of the Irish to counter the view that the Irish were Yankee "hirelings." An Irish friend of Edward McCrady collected money and clothes for the Irish volunteers and lost no opportunity to promote the effort of his fellow "countrymen." Another, who identified himself only as "Garryowen" (a famous Irish marching tune and neighborhood in Limerick), wrote to the *True Delta* chastising a "native of the soil" recently heard asking why would the Irish not "fight at the front?" As an example of Irish patriotism, he used the family of Eugene Sullivan from the Third District (i.e., the poorer section of town downriver) "which at one time, consisted of five members, father, mother, three sons. How many prythee [sic], now remain 'at home at ease?' The mother, solus." The three boys were at the front in Virginia or Tennessee and the father was away on duty with the militia. Indeed, "the last of the race the *ould* [old] woman were it not for her sex, would assuredly follow, to the red field of slaughter, her gallant family, shouting the inspiring Irish slogan *Faugh a Ballagh* 'clear the way' for her brave boys." The Sullivans were not alone among the Irish in sacrificing for the cause: "Hundreds, aye tens of hundreds from the chivalrous little 'isle of the ocean' . . . have, in the day of Southern need and the Confederacy's extremity, nobly forgotten the brass knuckle era and chased from their memory the gloomy period of thuggery and prejudice [Know-Nothingism]." Having thus "forgotten," they would "[d]epend upon it, in the moment of emergency they will faithfully realize their proverbial trait, and be 'first in the field and last in the fight.'"[67] "Garryowen" made it very clear to all Confederates that the Irish of New Orleans were, despite the attacks on them in the "brass-knuckle" Know-Nothing times, just as patriotic, if not more so, than natives.

Irish civilians could help the war effort in more practical ways than public defenses of Irish loyalty to the Confederacy. They were an integral part of the Confederate military complex. In one month in 1862 William Ahern of Georgia offered to make a bayonet for double barrel shotguns. M. J. Doyle of Savannah, describing himself as "a strenuous supporter" of the state governor, offered his services as a commissary in the city or "to some other position I am competent to fill no matter what." John H. Flynn of the Western and Atlantic Railroad in Atlanta helped turn his company's machine shop toward military purposes.[68] Anthony Murphy of the same company assembled men to make guns for the Confederate State of Georgia. He also famously played an important role in chasing, by handcar, foot, and backward-steaming train, the Union raiders and spies of Andrews' Raid, the so-call "Great Locomotive Chase," who stole the steam engine *General* near Atlanta in April 1862 and tried to destroy the railroad leading to Chattanooga. Another railroad worker, Irish immigrant master mechanic William Rushton, designed and supervised the construction of cannon for the defense of Atlanta.[69]

At an even more substantial level, Thomas (T. J.) Coghlan of Sumter, South Carolina, turned his iron foundry over to military purposes. In Nashville, mechanical engineer and locomotive maker Thomas Brennan, made cannons and shells for the state. When the city fell to Union forces, he reestablished his munitions work in Jefferson County, Alabama, near what would become the industrial giant Birmingham after the war. Another Trinity graduate, John Irwin, helped produce future military leaders as the principal of St. John's Military Academy in Spartanburg, South Carolina. Nonspecialists such as Richmond merchant Mark Downey, originally from County Cork, could participate in the war effort too. He provided various military accoutrements to military companies in the city and continued to pay the salaries of three of his clerks who had joined the army. He also served in the reserve defense corps for the city. Irish-born Mary Hill of New Orleans could not serve in the army but did try to help the cause by smuggling messages through the lines. She earned some time in a Union jail for her efforts and was released only on the intervention of the British Consul, who used her Irish birth to secure her release. She became a military nurse in Richmond, and her trojan work in this effort earned her the title "The Florence Nightingale of the Army of Northern Virginia."[70] John Knox, an Ulster emigrant who lived in Charleston, was an investor in blockade running and played an important part in bringing vital supplies into that port city.[71]

General laborers contributed too. In Charleston, for example, skilled and unskilled Irish found work in the Charleston Arsenal.[72] The numerous factories in the Confederate capital also provided work for the Irish, although usually in unskilled positions. Most of the skilled workers in the Tredegar Iron Works, for example, were British or German. The Irish, however, did work as laborers and "puddlers" (feeding the hot molten iron and furnaces turning pig iron into wrought iron) for which they commanded higher wages in a time when so many were at the front. Some skilled Irish metalworkers found jobs at the Richmond arsenal assembling locks and forging butt plates for muskets. Others could be hired on a contract basis. In November 1862, for example, one John Driscoll was hired for twelve days at $2.50 per day to work at forging bayonets. Irish women also found work in the semi-skilled but vital work of making ammunition. Dozens of Irish women worked at the Richmond Arsenal in 1863 and 1864 making cartridges for the army. It provided steady work almost to the war's end.[73]

Despite these opportunities for patriotic work, many Irish and other poor white Confederates faced a desperate economic situation in the cities of the Confederacy. Confederate authorities responded to the needs of the patriotic urban poor through the establishment of "free markets." These markets would collect food, and money to buy food, to distribute to the destitute families, whose major breadwinners had gone to the front to defend the new nation. Considering the economic status of many Irish soldiers (see table 5), large numbers of their loved ones stood to benefit from these markets. Historian Emory Thomas acknowledges that while these free markets were an added burden to city authorities in the South, and achieved only partial success, they were still "indications of heightened social and economic conscience." Indeed, being poor and desperate may have been a sign of Confederate patriotism over those who hoarded and exploited through the black market.[74] Even before the war, southern leaders were aware of the power of charity in binding poor whites to their section's cause, but the "free markets" were unprecedented. Prewar charity had been mainly for schools and orphanages with very little movement toward spending tax dollars to support institutions in this area. The free markets were unprecedented too in that they interfered in the sacrosanct area of market forces. For all their talk of "avaricious Yankees," most southern leaders had been opposed to state interference in the economy and any meddling with, not just their chattel work force, but also the products of that labor.[75]

Why had they changed their minds? It seems to have been a combination of the reality of destitute soldiers' families filling the streets of southern towns and cities and the pressure put on them by soldiers' wives and widows. In response to poverty, native-born soldiers' wives exploited Confederate patriotism to get a governmental response. At least one Irish woman used the same tactic. In October 1863 one Mary O'Donnell was charged with being drunk and disorderly and "disturbing the neighborhood" when she became too intoxicated and boisterous at an Irish wake. Witnesses saw her attack another woman. The only defense she put forward was that "she was a soldier's wife and all the Irish at the wake were British subjects," that is, claiming foreign exemption. Like them she was Irish, but unlike them, she was a loyal Confederate. Nonetheless, despite this appeal to Confederate patriotism, the court convicted her and confined her to jail because she could not pay a bond "to keep the peace." O'Donnell's play of the "soldier's wife" card failed, but, by 1863, these soldier wives throughout the Confederacy had helped make that year, as one scholar puts it, "the formative moment in Confederate welfare policy."[76]

There was also an element of ethnic awareness among native Confederate leaders. They had to on occasion show their respect to the Irish community. Governor Francis Pickens of South Carolina, for example, felt the need to proclaim his general pro-Irish sympathies after he refused to commute the sentence of an Irish convict. He denied that there was any anti-Irish aspect in his decision: "As to the difference between an adopted citizen and native born citizen; I shall never know any difference in any course." He continued: "I know full well the courage and patriotism of the Irish and return them my sincere thanks and gratitude for their noble conduct." As proof of this belief, Pickens emphasized that "I appointed the son of Mr. [John] Mitchell [sic], the Irish patriot, Lieutenant, expressly on account of his noble service, and his heroic race."[77] Loyal Irish Confederates would be recognized and rewarded and treated no differently than natives. A New York politician seeking the votes of Irish residents of that city could not have made a better statement of his respect for Irish patriotism.

Even former critics of poor whites came around when they saw Irish civilian patriotism. Confederate secretary of the treasury, Christopher Memminger had before the war, distrusted the South's nonslaveholders and only reluctantly welcomed them to the "peerage of white men" when war broke out. He was more encouraged, however, when he received a substantial donation from the predominantly Irish congregants of the Cathedral of St. John the Baptist in Savannah. He wrote their County Kerry–born priest to thank them for their generosity to the cause and noted it as "evidence of the earnest and settled community" to support the new nation's war effort.[78] The Irish, rather than symbolizing crippling division, had come to symbolize national unity and "purpose."

These initial recognitions of Irish patriotism encouraged positive welfare responses in southern cities. New Orleans had its free market up and running by August 1861. There, according to one newspaper, following the "appeals of the press and the people," a free market in food was established to help "Volunteers and their Families," thanks to support from "Ladies Aid Societies," a "handsome sum" appropriated by the city council, and "individual efforts performed by our citizens, of both sexes." Tickets were issued "to all registered parties" by the Free Market committee, which they could then redeem for free food. Established in the market at the end of Canal Street, only three or four customers were admitted at a time to maintain "order." The eligible beneficiary presented "her [my emphasis] ticket," and was then supplied with meat and vegetables by the committee members behind the counter, most of whom were wealthy men wearing "aprons" and with their "sleeves rolled up," working harder apparently than "grocery clerks half an hour before dinner time." It was clear that women were the intended beneficiaries. "Hundreds" were helped on the first day of its official opening. The observer of this meeting was pleased not just with the aid provided but also with the way "the members of the subcommittee . . . were as polite, and as kind, and attentive toward every woman, as a refined dry goods clerk is to the ladies when he shows the last Parisian fashions." Class and ethnic unity was on display here. By early 1862 over 1,300 families were receiving aid.[79]

Mobile was also operating its market by late 1861 and plans were already afoot for similar systems in Augusta and Savannah. Charleston, Natchez, and Memphis had established ones in 1862, the Mississippi town helping more than 100 families, and the Tennessee city over 1,100.[80] Although late to the effort, by 1862 the Charleston market was well established and had the Irish-born bishop of Charleston, Patrick Lynch, as one of its committee members and the chair of its appeal to the public for donations. Food transported from the upstate for the market was done so gratis by the railroad companies.[81] That first year it received $45,000 from the city to dispense food to 558 families. Despite a cut in city funding, much criticized by the committee, they continued to manage with private donations, some small, some large, the latter coming from some of the blockade-running companies in the city.[82]

Even this noblesse oblige from prosperous Confederates for the good of the nation's Irish poor could not halt the realities of invasion and shortage. Some Irish wealthy enough to do so did evacuate areas in the path of Union invasion and/or the focus of Union blockade, and lived the lives of "refugees." One Mrs. Barry, for example, had fled western Virginia for Confederate lines, because her husband and son were in the Confederate army. Staying with Irish friends in McPhersonville, South Carolina, by late 1862 she was in financial dire straits and needing desperately to find work for her two daughters because "every article is such fabulous price," she wrote to Bishop Lynch of Charleston. As members of the middle class she, of course, wanted them to "to [teach] small children or [work] in the Confederate note department in Columbia."[83] When Charleston itself came under attack, large numbers of other middle-class Irish there seeking to leave also contacted the Bishop to help them out. Many were anxious to make contact with his brother in Cheraw, South Carolina, about 150 miles inland, to inquire about availability of accommodation. Some did make it out as the priest based in Augusta spoke of the "Catholics scattered up and down the railroad between here and Charleston." Sumter, in particular, attracted Irish families such as the Doughertys and O'Neills, because it had a good railroad link and an established Irish Catholic community.[84]

Having to leave homes affected Confederates' morale. It made vivid to many, Irish and native alike, the military failures of their new nation. It increased class tensions too. To the formerly well-off refugees, having to live among poorer folk was often disdainful. On the other hand, many poorer whites resented the fact that the rich could leave and avoid the worst effects of the war.[85] Most Irish women in Charleston, for example, could not leave the city when it came under invasion threat and siege. One priest, who catered to a mostly middle-class congregation, admitted that the loss of his parishioners inland had made his duties "light enough" except, he added, for "issuing certificates of marriage for women to avail themselves of the free market." The poor soldiers' wives were not ashamed to claim for their sacrifice to the Confederate cause.[86]

The Free Market may have actually been an incentive for some civilians to stay in the city. Unfortunately, it may have also kept them there through the Union bombardment that began in August 1863 and continued, with varying intensity, into 1864. Assessing casualties is impossible because the Charleston newspapers, to sustain morale, did not report them, but shells did fall on one traditional Irish area of the city, in the Third Ward near the docks on East Bay Street. On one occasion a major fire started there because of the shelling. Fortunately by then, most of the Irish in the city had moved to other Irish neighborhoods north of Calhoun Street, which was just about beyond the effective range of the shelling.[87] The only other city with a sizeable Irish population to come under severe bombardment was Vicksburg, Mississippi, and here there were Irish civilian casualties. Worse for the vast majority who did not fall victim to enemy shells in the besieged city were the horrible living conditions, which made one soldier feel, despite his own tough life in the trenches, "heartsick to see the condition of the women and children in Vicksburg."[88]

The hardships of civilian life in Vicksburg were unique, but the Union blockade of the Confederacy as a whole caused much more widespread distress. Prices for the necessities of life just continued to go up and up until only the richest could afford the inflated prices. As early as the winter of 1862, the British consul in New Orleans had complained about commodity costs and of how close many "British subjects" were to "starvation." Some were so poor that they had applied to him for the money to travel north or back to Europe. He did not have the funds but recommended that the British government commission a ship for that purpose.[89] In Mobile, after the fall of Vicksburg, the activities of Union forces disrupted transportation of foodstuffs to the city causing "all the necessaries of life to advance to the most unheard of prices." The price of clothes was "beyond belief" while "what would formerly be enough for the daily support of a family will now hardly purchase one pound of meat."[90]

As many Irish sought to just survive, the supplies at the free markets began to dry up. Mobile's British consul wrote that the "entire efforts of the authorities" were not on feeding poor dependants but "are directed towards the obtaining of persons for military service to the exclusion of all other subjects." In Charleston the city cut off funds for the market in 1863 and by 1864 it seems to have disappeared. Between September and December 1863, desperate circulars appeared in inland newspapers appealing "especially" to the "farmers and Planters from the Mountains to the Seaboard" for provisions to be sent to Charleston. In early 1864 the market could not meet its "$14,000" monthly cost and was "sorely in need of help." The publisher of this article hoped that he did "not appeal in vain," but it seems that he did as that was the last mention of the market in the Charleston newspapers.[91]

Along with supply issues affecting government support, negative opinions of Irish immigrants could also cause problems for the poor Irish on the home front. Richmond, for example, had some of the greatest logistical problems as refugees and soldiers flooding the city put pressure on housing and food supplies, but native ire over Irish use of the foreign exemption clause to get out of the army made the situation worse.[92] This was the ultimate disloyalty and called into question all Irish support for the Confederacy. Many citizens especially resented those Irishmen who refused to join militias when the city came under attack in the summers of 1862 and, even more so, 1864. Some foreign workers at the Tredegar iron works, for example, among whom were numbers of Irish, left the foundry as early as 1862 to avoid military duty. They even refused to join the Tredegar Battalion, which was used only in extreme emergencies and usually just served in the trenches around Richmond. Native white southerners had to make up the bulk of the battalion.[93]

Some native Confederates also took exception to Irish who, they believed, sought to take advantage of the economic shortages. One James Healy, who worked eleven hours a day at the Charleston Arsenal, refused to continue working unless he received higher wages. His employer sent immediate word to the provost marshal in the city, who arrested Healy and conscripted him into the army. Unlike many speculators and blockade runners, Healy was not trying to profit but, according to his advocate, only to get enough pay as a laborer "to meet the enormous rise in the price of food."[94] No matter, the Irishman had openly opposed the national demand for civilian self-sacrifice and now found himself subject to military justice. As in Richmond, anger against Irish civilians intensified in Charleston when the city faced Federal attack. During these crisis periods in 1863 and 1864 numbers of Irishmen who refused to serve in the defense forces were thrown in the city jail, which was within range of the Union guns besieging the city. One James Gorman, a laborer, for example, complained that he was locked up for not serving, even though he was a British subject and had never been naturalized. When the British consul got him released and he returned to his place of work, his employers refused to reinstate him in his old position or give him back pay worth almost $150.[95]

Beyond Gorman's story, unless one was vital to the military effort in munitions, mining, etc., refusing to serve could exacerbate your economic situation. In 1863 Virginia passed a law that denied any and all business licenses to foreigners not enlisted in the militia. But those who wanted to leave faced the obstacle of getting passes to cross to the Union lines. The Confederate government recommended that they could go only to "neutral" ports, something impossible to do with the Union blockade. The British consul in Richmond, George Moore, felt so exasperated by the situation that he asked that the Foreign Office "have steamers sent to City Point on the James River [near Richmond] for their [British subjects'] conveyance to Baltimore or New York." In the Confederate Congress the following year, one senator wanted to expel all foreigners who had not signed up within sixty days. He remarked callously, considering how difficult life in the Confederacy was in 1864: "The time has come we can entertain you no longer."[96]

Along with Irish shirkers, the actions of Irish women also annoyed native Confederates. Following city news in Richmond, for example, especially from the courts, one finds a lot of Irish women involved in illicit activities. In the coverage, they were often, it seems, drunk, fighting, or thieving. Some ran illegal grog shops and a few "Houses of ill-fame."[97] Mary Broderick and Mary Gleeson, for example, were charged with "selling ardent spirits without a license" to soldiers. They denied the charge, but the mayor fined them twenty dollars and warned Broderick that he might require her to provide a bond to keep the peace.[98] In 1863 a group of Irishwomen were attacked in the press for buying up all the fruit from the Second Street market to retail later (or perhaps turn into alcohol) in their homes. In general, however, the one charge the Irish usually avoided was speculating. They were usually too poor to hoard supplies. This charge was usually reserved for the "Dutch" (i.e., Germans), and often "Jews." Some of the anti-Semitic outbursts against "Jewish Shylocks," "greasy Jews," and "Jew extortioners" were far more virulent than anything expressed against Irish residents. (The town of Thomasville, Georgia, actually tried to ban "German Jews" from its city limits.)[99]

The Richmond "Bread Riot" of April 1863 brought Irish women's disloyalty into sharper focus, when one Richmond paper referred to the riot as the work of "prostitutes, professional thieves, [and] Irish and Yankee hags, gallows birds from all lands but our own." One police officer did observe a "chuckle headed Irish woman assail a store door with an axe." While most of the rioters were not foreigners but had names such as Bell, Hampton, Johnson, Pomfrey, Radford, Smith, and Taliaferro, the stigma still stuck.[100] Other bread riots also showed a preponderance of native-born southerners at the forefront.[101]

No matter. In June 1864 the *Richmond Examiner*, at which John Mitchel remained a prominent writer, railed against the city for supporting the "families (Yankee, English, Irish, Scotch, Dutch) whose heads never felt the misfortune of war, but who only enriched themselves by speculation and extortion, and betook themselves to the enemy on the very first sight of danger. First," the paper continued, "give to the deserving poor," that is, soldiers' wives and widows. The irony here was that there were numbers of Irish soldiers' wives and widows in the city, which John Mitchel knew very well, implying that his boss John Daniel wrote this piece. Whether Mitchel tried to tone down this rhetoric is not known. It would have been useless anyway, because when word reached the *Examiner* that a number of foreign women had sought to go North, as the Union forces tightened their grip around Richmond, the paper hoped, and Mitchel would have agreed with this sentiment, that "the Council of this city, at their next meeting, adopt measures which will ensure than none of them who wish to depart shall not be compelled to remain from lack of funds to pay their passage." Despite the serious shortage of funds, city authorities could not "spend one hundred thousand dollars so advantageously as in getting rid of this entire class of our population." After all "they in no way contribute to the public weal. The nearest approach to work they ever make," the article continued, "is the keeping of little dram shops and buying stolen goods from negroes." Anyway, the paper concluded, there would be more food for "our soldiers and their wives and children" and reduce the numbers of "vicious and unproductive consumers."[102] Even one of the Irish Confederates' great advocates could not mitigate the actions of some Irish civilians.

Again, as with the Bread Riot, the reality was that Irish women were not the main culprits in the city's troubles. The arrest records of the Richmond provost marshal show that the vast majority of problems were created by off-duty soldiers. Even among the civilian arrests, the Irish were a distinct minority. Of the approximately 300 white civilians arrested between February 1863 and the end of January 1864, only 34 had Irish names. Most of the reasons are unstated, although there were a few like John Fitzpatrick, who was arrested "trying to cross the Potomac without a pass." (Ironically, he was arrested by one William Flaherty of the First Virginia "Irish" Battalion, a major element of the provost guard of the Army of Northern Virginia.) The vast majority, however, of those arrested for trying to "cross over to the enemy" had non-Irish names and many seem to have been northerners trying to return home.[103]

Nonetheless, as the Confederacy tottered toward defeat, any Irish who accepted the coming reality faced harsh treatment. In 1864 three Irishmen, two of whom had worked at the Tredegar Iron Works, were found wandering the Virginia countryside close to the Union lines, having abandoned the threatened capital. They told their arrestors that they were searching "for work on Virginia farms" and not trying to cross to the enemy. Confederate authorities wanted to charge them with "treason," punishable by death. Cooler heads prevailed as the Irishmen's labor was needed back at the foundry and, over the protests of the provost marshal, who still wanted to proceed with a trial, they returned to work.[104]

Why did some Confederates react so violently in such an aggravated fashion against Irish and other foreign residents as the war dragged on? They did so because some of these foreigners had expressed the ultimate lack of faith in the Confederate national cause. By refusing to serve in the military and/or seeking to leave the besieged Confederacy, these Irish civilians were literally voting with their feet. They, vividly and publicly, highlighted the limits of Confederate nationalism. Of course, they could be dismissed as "Yankee, Dutch, and Irish hags" etc., but the reality was that most of the women and men rioting, buying stolen goods, and gouging were native. The Confederate boosters could not face this reality. Some tried to make the foreigners the scapegoat, but the problem was they were not a perfect fit. The papers that complained about foreigners also expressed admiration and gave good coverage to foreign units in service. The *Charleston Courier*, for example, which had been supportive of the Know-Nothings in the 1850s, could complain one day about the lack of Irish participation in the Confederate effort in one column and then express admiration for the Irish in the next. In one issue, for example, it covered the brave actions of the Irish Jasper Greens at the siege of Fort Pulaski near Savannah, but just two months earlier it had published a poem entitled "Yankee Doodle's ride to Richmond" with a line declaring that the northern army included "thieving Yankees, filthy Dutch and Irish from the Bogs." The Irish of Charleston and Savannah, apparently, were not "from the Bogs" but instead were one of Savannah's "favorite companies" whose commander, one Major Foley, was "an officer of much experience and undoubted gallantry." This contradiction existed beyond the newspaper columns too. Sergeant W. M. Andrews of the First Georgia Infantry (Regulars), who served with and enjoyed the company of Irish soldiers in his own unit, could state when remembering the Union Irish Brigade's bloody fight at the Battle of Fredericksburg in 1862, that "The Confederates are now fighting the World, Burnside having German, Irish, and Italian brigades . . . Every foreigner who puts his foot on American soil joins the Northern Army, for the sake of the bounty paid, if anything." He never noticed the contradiction between his anti-foreign rhetoric and the fact that he served with Irish Confederate soldiers.[105]

Of course the Confederate national focus was mostly on soldiers. The true route to patriotism was service in the armed forces. Your national spirit was tied closely to your willingness to arm and defend well your new country. This masculine military paradigm of nationalism did not leave much room for civilians to prove themselves. Yes, they could wave flags, collect money, and suffer the deprivations in silence, but this would never measure up to fighting bravely at the front. Also, you could present the flag only once. These ceremonies, mostly in 1861, faded quickly in memory, as the harsh realities of war began to bite. The growing blockade and prioritizing of resources for the soldiers dissipated the collecting of money and ended the "silent suffering." For nationalist inspiration, Confederates had to look to their armies and generals in the field.[106]

Ultimately, service in the army was the best way of proving one's Confederate loyalty. Civilians, Irish and non-Irish alike, could show patriotism through public support for the cause, but as shortages increased and the war progressed badly, many were too busy trying to survive to think about secession pageants or other forms of Confederate display.[107] One scholar believes that "plain folk" women ultimately became not just antiwar but anti-Confederate too. She contrasts their more open opposition to the cause with that of the private disillusionment of richer planter wives and daughters to the point that these poorer women developed a certain class consciousness, declaring "fighting anymore is fighting against God." Some others, female and male, took opposition to the extent of actively and openly seeking the overthrow of local Confederate authorities.[108] In Texas,

Germans with abolitionist sympathies openly opposed Confederate recruitment and paid a high price for it, while in Atlanta a secret Unionist circle actively tried to undermine the Confederate cause. In the mountainous regions of east Tennessee tens of thousands of native southerners joined the Union army. In Jones County, Mississippi, anti-Confederate guerilla bands fought against draft enforcers.[109] In general, Confederate authorities had always seen the greatest potential for internal opposition from native-born southerners and those who had been born in the North. Indeed, the Confederate Alien Enemies Act, passed in August 1861, was focused on internal dissenters not "real foreigners."[110] Irish men and women on the home front did not have this strong Unionist consciousness as those in the hills of Tennessee or the "Free State of Jones."

But, neither were many willing to sacrifice everything on the altar of the new nation as it disintegrated before their eyes. They were ambiguous Confederates, supporting the cause in the early days, excited by the sight of their fellow countrymen in gray, but as the fight for its survival grew tougher, ready to drop their support when the opportunity arose. When the "Yankees" finally "came," most Irish were ready to rejoin the United States. John Maginnis, for example, had eventually supported the Confederacy, but when New Orleans fell, he thought the new Union commander of the city, Benjamin Butler, deserved a chance to succeed in reviving the city's moribund economy. Butler also, Maginnis reminded his Irish readers, had been a prewar Democrat and had played a prominent role in fighting the nativist Know-Nothings as well as the abolitionist Republicans.[111] This tolerance of "Beast" Butler made Maginnis, and his copublisher, Irishman Hugh Kennedy, no friends among those still fighting for the Confederacy. One Irish soldier in the Confederate army, recognizing their late endorsement of the cause, had referred to their paper as the "False Delta" as early as 1861, and wished Louisianans would pay no attention to it. Those newspaper editors whom soldiers perceived as undermining the cause often felt the wrath of the boys in uniform well beyond pleading letters to relatives.[112]

Nonetheless, Butler found many other Irish in the city who were conducive to his rule. One John Hughes immediately offered his and a number of his staff's shipbuilding services. Another, John Murphy, "a loyal citizen of Louisiana," desired to "strike a blow for the cause of the Union" by raising a company of soldiers for the United States. Jeremiah Hurly, informed Butler that the some Union associations had been infiltrated by spies who were encouraging men to leave New Orleans and return to Confederate service. "Master machinist" Francis McDermott turned in a New Orleans doctor and his wife who he told Butler were "consummate secessionists" and whose sons were "blockade runners." As a result of these Irish and other offers, Butler felt confident that he could raise a number of Union companies in the city.[113] Numbers of Irish received jobs on the docks and on public works while others found employment, according to one Union officer, with the nearby "planters . . . in place of the negroes who have run away." As a result, the same officer had difficulty recruiting Irish soldiers into the Union army.[114]

So many former Confederate Irish received jobs that those who had remained loyal to the Union resented it. Annie Grace wrote to Butler to complain that her husband had "opposed taking up arms against the [U.S.] government that had offered him shelter what the British denied him of." Because of his refusal to serve, he had "not worked three months" since June 1861, had been "threatened with imprisonment," and all "who had loved him . . . soon considered him an enemy." What really galled Grace was that her husband had not yet received work while "the United States government has employed men who fought at Fort Jackson and Shilo[h] and expresses their anxiety in fighting agin [sic] when the Confederates return to drive out the invader as they call them." She insisted that "union men" should get preference.[115] Much to Grace's distress, former Irish Confederates seemed to have no compunction in dropping their support for the southern state, and working for the new administration, to the detriment of true loyal men like her husband. She implied also that they would be ready to shift back to the Confederacy again if its forces managed to retake the city.

Irish Confederates in other cities could quickly adjust to occupation too. In Memphis the Irish played the key role in reestablishing city government under Federal control in 1862 by collaborating with commanding General William T. Sherman. In Savannah, at Christmas 1864, the Irish there were not too upset to think about holding their first St. Patrick's Day parade since the beginning of the war the following March, even though some of their fellow countrymen from the city were still fighting in Virginia and North Carolina.[116] Some in the Confederacy observed with horror and disgust the ease with which the Irish seemed to accept and even embrace Union occupation. One commentator, for example, complained of "Irish and Dutch" renegades from Louisiana now serving in the Union army. The True Delta's endorsement of Ben Butler was also noticed and condemned. Another Confederate published without comment an article from a New York newspaper titled "Savannah under Sherman," which mentioned that "none of the better class of citizens" turned out, only the "poor classes were represented . . . composed of Irish and Dutch women, [and] negroes." The article also mentioned that these poor folk assembled into a mob and with the aid of "thievish soldiers" had "broke open stores and sacked them."[117]

Irish dealings with Federal occupiers countered the carefully constructed narrative of what brutes the Yankees were, challenging even the view of General Butler as the "Beast of New Orleans." Confederate nationalism required southerners under Federal occupation to act with "honor" and if "unwilling to confront and revile the enemy" at least "still affirm their patriotism through noncooperation or passive resistance." Irish Confederates seemed to have abandoned any concept of this southern honor and did not care what the community, the bestower and remover of said honor, thought of their actions. They did not endorse this call for noncooperation and passive resistance.[118] Worse was the valuable ammunition Irish cooperation provided to northerners who had always propagated the idea that the slave society of the South was degrading to poor whites. Now, with this flocking of the Irish to the Union occupiers, northern propagandists could speak of Confederate leaders as that "abominable set of men" who had tried to achieve "the total enslavement and the subversion of the rights of the great mass of the laboring white population." Lincoln's government was bringing "Emancipation" to the Irish as well as to the enslaved African Americans.[119]

The Irish home-front experience highlights the divided nature of the Confederacy. It also shows that wars do not always easily give immigrant civilians a chance to "prove" their loyalty to their new home. Indeed, the Civil War provided opportunities for the Irish to show their disloyalty too.[120] Influenced by the hardships his family experienced while he was away from them, one Irish Confederate soldier serving in Savannah believed that the war had brought only misery to him and his. He decided to act on his feelings and collaborate with the enemy. While on guard duty at a prison in the city, he told some Union prisoners that he could not wait for General Sherman to capture the city, so he could return to his loved ones in Atlanta. In the meantime he did all he could to help the officers under his supervision plan their escape. In Charleston, too, Irish prisoners in the city jail disillusioned with the Confederacy expressed similar feelings of desire for a Union victory to a northern officer incarcerated there. They, apparently, could not wait for Union victory.[121]

This unwillingness of a lot of Irish civilians to give all to the Confederacy, in spite of all the exhortations to do so, undermined the careful narrative of the patriotic Irish Confederate constructed by the likes of John Mitchel and Anthony Keiley. Irish loyalty to the new nation was shallow.

In the Confederacy as a whole, the failure to build a solid secular cultural nationalism that people could rely on in times of trouble meant that religion became the only consolation for many seeking a justification for the cause and the sacrifices they had made for it.[122] In this aspect of the Confederate experience, the Irish like their white southern neighbors also sought solace from their religious faith. In practical terms, for the vast majority of Irish Confederates, this meant the Roman Catholic Church. The opinions of their bishops, priests, and nuns counted on virtually all matters, and that included the Confederacy.

CHAPTER 5

For God, Erin, and Carolina

Irish Catholics in the Confederacy

Although Irish religious leaders of all denominations supported the Confederacy, it was Catholic clergy and sisters who natives saw as the leaders and role models of the Irish community. Thomas Smyth from Second Presbyterian Church in Charleston, for example, was a prominent cleric and Irish immigrant, but it was his Catholic counterpart and fellow Irish immigrant across the city at the Cathedral of Saint Finbar and Saint John the Baptist, Bishop Patrick Lynch, who came to represent the larger Irish Confederate population. Indeed, the vast majority of Irish Confederates whether in military service or on the home front, were Roman Catholics. The position of the Catholic Church on the Confederacy was fundamental then in determining significant Irish support for the new nation. Beyond the confines of the Confederate States, the fact that Irish Catholics had connections to their co-religionist countrymen in the North and across the Atlantic Ocean gave them significance beyond their rallying of Irish southerners to the cause. In the patriotic effort, they ultimately failed, as most Irish Confederates accepted defeat with relative ease. The example of Irish Catholic bishops, priests, and nuns, as well as some prominent lay spokesmen, left an impression of Irish loyalty to the cause greater than it actually was.

From the beginning of the conflict, native Confederates welcomed Catholic leaders' encouragement of Irish congregants to join the armed forces. On September 17, 1861, at his cathedral in Charleston, for example, Bishop Lynch spoke publicly to the Irish Volunteers who were just about to muster into Confederate service. On this day, in front of their bishop and their friends and families, they were to receive their company flag, which had been made by the students of the local Sisters of Mercy. He told the Irish soldiers that "The banner I present today is the work of fair hands of innocence. It gives to the breeze and the light of the sun the emblems of Erin—the Shamrock and the Harp—with the Palmetto of Carolina and Stars of our Southern Confederacy. You will recollect all those lessons of religion and innocence that have been taught you." He reminded the Volunteers of the company's history of service in every American war since its foundation in 1797. He concluded: "Receive it then [the flag]—rally around it. Let it teach you of God—of Erin—of Carolina. Let it teach you your duty in this life as soldiers and as Christians, so that fighting the good fight of Christians you may receive the reward of eternal victory from the King of Kings." Captain Edward Magrath thanked the bishop and the "young ladies of the Institution of the Sisters of Our Lady of Mercy for this beautiful present at their hands." Magrath vowed to protect the flag's honor and that of the ladies who had made it. He then lined his soldiers in front of the altar before the packed cathedral and reminded them of the pledge they had made to the cause of their "adopted State" and the symbolism of the flag under which they would fight. "Dear Harp of their Country!" he exclaimed "what associations does the sight not give rise to in the bosoms of Irishmen . . . True, the sons of Ireland are scattered everywhere. Yes, like the children of Israel, they had sent forth a prayer for a blessing on the land of their birth." Magrath then spoke that this quest for Irish freedom matched that of Carolina's. Led by their color sergeant the Volunteers marched out of the packed cathedral and through the streets with their new flag.[1]

The Volunteers' Confederate service had been blessed by their spiritual leader. This religious endorsement of the cause was vital to Irish Confederates, as indeed it was for all Confederates. Soldiers, in particular, found comfort in religion. It provided a motivator for upcoming fights and assurance of salvation if one died in the struggle for a righteous cause. With God on your side, as Bishop Lynch had assured the Irish Volunteers, you could fight with honor and receive the "eternal victory from the King of Kings."[2]

For life in general, clerical leadership was very important to Irish immigrants in America. In turn, the Irish were very important to the Catholic Church, providing the majority of its congregants, clerics, and sisters. The roots of clerical leadership of Irish Catholic communities in America lay in the fact that Catholic clergy had been the most prominent supporters of their interests in Ireland often organizing and leading opposition to impositions from landlords, the government, and the established Anglican Church of Ireland.[3] Catholic revanchism had begun in the 1820s with Daniel O'Connell's Catholic Association and the influence of triumphal predictions such as the "Pastorini prophesies," which had proclaimed the ultimate victory of Roman Catholicism over Protestantism. O'Connell's achievement of Catholic Emancipation in 1829 opened up politics to many Catholics and increased the influence of their church. The Catholic Church in Ireland thus

Bishop Patrick N. Lynch *(Courtesy of the Archives of the Catholic Diocese of Charleston)*

played a prominent role in politics using Mass on Sunday to propagate various positions and collect "rents" from parishioners for causes such as Emancipation and Repeal of the Union. Along with this increased presence in public life, the devastation of the Great Famine in the late 1840s created a "devotional revolution" as thousands sought solace and explanation for the devastating mortality that came with the potato blight. Astute bishops used this increased devotion to organize the Catholic Church in Ireland into the country's dominant cultural force and one of its most important political ones.[4] This heightened Catholic observance was part of the cultural baggage most Irish immigrants brought with them from Ireland to the South.

The Church, therefore, was a major part of the Irish American milieu. By the 1861 there were three archdioceses (Baltimore, New Orleans, and St. Louis), and twelve dioceses in what would become the Confederate States. Every southern state, except Florida and North Carolina, had resident bishops.[5] Despite this institutional growth, outside of south Louisiana, Catholics remained a distinct minority and the Church underfunded in the region. Where it was strong, however, was in southern towns and cities. Charleston, for example, had four Catholic churches and numerous other Catholic institutions on the eve of the Civil War. For the Irish, who mostly lived in towns and cities, the Catholic Church was a vibrant presence and a very important part of their immigrant lives.[6]

Clerical leadership was important too, especially in times of crisis. Priests and bishops had rallied the Irish community during the Know-Nothing challenge of the 1850s. It was natural then that as sectional tensions increased, the Irish in the South looked to clergy for guidance.[7] Father Jeremiah O'Neill Sr., who had defended the Union with such gusto during the near secession of Georgia in 1850 and 1851, was still the main leader of the Irish community in Savannah. After Lincoln's election in 1860 local secessionists, keen to get Irish support for Georgia's secession, invited O'Neill to speak at a rally in Johnson Square, right in the heart of the city. O'Neill's speech pleased the secessionists when in a still discernible Kerry accent, he reportedly told the crowd, that he was a "*sacessionist*."[8] He continued to express public support for secession and the Confederacy, and when war broke out, he endorsed it too. He said Masses of praise for the Confederate armies and raised money for the government among his predominantly Irish parishioners at the Cathedral of St. John the Baptist.[9] He was apparently not alone among the Irish clergy in Savannah. One Irish priest who visited Savannah in early 1861 stated that "Fr. [Peter] Whelan with all the priests tried to make me a secessionist." The visitor had expressed some regret at the breakup of the Union but Father Whelan chastised him for his doubts and warned the skeptical priest of "tars and feathers" if he continued in his view of the new reality.[10]

These priests, and others, could not have been as steadfast for the Confederacy as they were without the approval of their bishop. O'Neill and Whelan had received strong support from their own, who had embraced the Confederacy from the very start. Augustin Verot had been born in Le Puy, France, but he quickly came to appreciate the area in which he did missionary work for most of his American life. Appointed bishop of Savannah in 1860 with responsibility for Georgia and Florida, after Georgia's secession and the foundation of the Confederacy he took it upon himself to write "a tract for the times on abolition of slavery." In it he claimed that he had "proved the legitimacy of slavery." He would later write a Catechism "for the use of Catholics in the Confederate States of America." Apparently, the one that that had sufficed for the Church when Georgia was part of the United States was no longer useful. In the section on the fourth commandment ("Honor thy father and mother") he added "*Q. Is it forbidden to hold slaves? A. No, both the Old and New Testaments bear witness to the lawfulness of that institution. Gen. XVI, 9; 1 Tim VI, 1, 2, 8.*"[11] Of course during the antebellum era the Church in all of America had supported the existence of slavery. The American bishops in general, while advocating the amelioration of the conditions of slaves and opposing the breaking up of slave families, did not deny the legitimacy of the institution itself.[12]

Verot, however, did more than just affirm slavery; he also advocated the Confederate war. His cathedral church observed official "public day[s] of humiliation and prayer." In September 1862 he wrote "we had a grand Te Deum for the victories of the Confederate Armies." He longed to use his influence in Europe in the cause of Confederate victory. Again, in 1862 he wrote to a colleague: "Sometimes I wish I was in France to represent things there in their true light and cause perhaps an intervention from the Emperor." As late as 1864 he supported the scheme of an Irish Catholic layman to establish an explicitly Catholic and Confederate newspaper. All his efforts on behalf of the Confederacy earned him the title "Rebel Bishop."[13]

Thus, thanks to Verot's Catholic catechism, any Irish immigrants in Savannah or other parts of the South worried about the morality of the new nation and its explicit endorsement of slavery could be assured of the justice of the southern cause. They need have no qualms about fighting for the Confederacy. Indeed, as Lynch had highlighted in his sermon to the Irish Volunteers in Charleston, they were obliged to take up arms and defend their new nation.[14]

Verot's catechism was important to Catholic Confederates, but Lynch was the most important public defender of the Confederate cause. His state was the first to secede and, within days of the secession ordinance passing in Charleston, he allowed his diocesan newspaper, the oldest in the country, to change its name from the *United States Catholic Miscellany* to the *Charleston Catholic Miscellany*.[15] Indeed, even before South Carolina had seceded, the *Miscellany* was already defending the morality and "right of secession, and [to] maintain it, if need be by force of arms against aggression from any quarter."[16] The final step of changing the banner was taken by the newspaper's editor and close confidant of Bishop Lynch, noted Irish American theologian Father James Corcoran. It was a major symbolic step. The paper had been founded in 1822 by John England and he had deliberately chosen to include "United States" in the title not just because it was the first Catholic paper in the country, but because he wanted to recognize explicitly the compatibility between Roman Catholicism and the American republic. He included under the banner, not lines from the Bible or a Papal encyclical, or indeed any religious text, but the separation of church and state clause from the First Amendment to the United States Constitution. England appreciated the freedom and equality given the Catholic Church in America but denied it back home in Ireland. He was naturalized in 1826 and advocated his flock's active participation in American politics. Even though a supporter of slavery, he remained pro-Union during South Carolina's nullification crisis.[17] Thus, Lynch's change of title was a massive one. He also replaced the text of the Constitution's First Amendment on separation of church and state with the similar clause from the South Carolina state constitution.[18] It was very clear then to native and immigrant Catholic alike; the diocese of Charleston had also seceded from the United States of America.

Lynch went beyond merely falling in line with his state when he challenged one of his fellow bishops who supported the United States government's war policy. As leader of the largest Catholic population in the United States, Archbishop John Hughes of New York was the most powerful cleric in the country. An Irish native, he had come to America as a penniless immigrant. He entered Mount St. Mary's Seminary in Emmitsburg, Maryland, and, after serving in the diocese of Philadelphia, was promoted to the bishopric of New York in 1842. He had in 1844 most famously threatened to turn New York City, referring to the Russian burning of their leading city in the face of Napoleon's 1812 invasion, into "the Moscow on the Hudson" if Catholic institutions were attacked by nativists as they had been in the Kensington riots in Philadelphia. No churches or schools were harmed.[19] Although personally opposed to slavery, Hughes was no friend of abolition or abolitionists. He had always opposed immediate abolition on American grounds, declaring it unconstitutional and detrimental to the Constitution. Nonetheless, when war broke out in 1861 the new Republican administration courted his support.[20] After secession and the firing on Fort Sumter, he could discard his fears of disrupting the Union and he wholeheartedly came out in support of the Republican-driven war effort. Describing the United States as "an indestructible whole," he endorsed his flock's joining the Union army and flew the Stars and Stripes over his cathedral.[21]

Lynch, as a patriotic Confederate, felt obliged to explain to Hughes why the South had seceded and respond to Hughes's endorsement of the Union cause. Initially, the Charleston bishop did so privately through letters to Hughes, but eventually publicly, after Hughes's diocesan newspaper published their correspondence. Lynch began by defending Father Corcoran and the Miscellany's explicit recognition of South Carolina's leaving the Union. He acknowledged that he was "not a Union man" but that he and South Carolina had been driven to secede because those who were "inimical to its interests" were now in charge of the Federal government. Therefore, "the sooner" his state was out of its "clutches" the "better." In the meantime, Lynch hoped northern Catholics would not be encouraged to take up arms against the South. Hughes responded that most northerners did not want to "conquer" or "subjugate," just return the South to the Union and preserve that region's "ante-bellum" [his emphasis] rights. He hoped that southerners would form a convention to put their grievances before the Federal government as part of a process to reenter the United States. In the meantime, Catholics, especially the Irish, should feel obliged to fight for the "country" that had welcomed them. Lynch in reply emphasized that this was a misguided and ultimately disastrous policy because "The separation of the South is un fait accompli. The Federal government has no power to [reverse it]." Any attempt to do so, however, would lead to "bloody" and "needless" war. This war would be purely the fault of the "Black Republicans," and not, as Hughes had implied, the seceding states.[22]

Through his public row with Hughes, Lynch established himself as the leading Catholic exponent of the Confederacy. Throughout the Confederate States people thanked him for his response and newspaper editors published his defense of secession.[23] Although Irish-born, as a substantial slaveholder Lynch's strong Confederate stance is perhaps not surprising. Catholic bishops in the South who also had connections to slaveholding such as Bishop of Natchez William Henry Elder, who hailed from a prosperous old Maryland family, were also ardent Confederates.[24]

Others with less connection to the peculiar institution, however, also displayed a Confederate patriotism that impressed Irish and native alike. Bishop John Quinlan of Mobile had been born and educated in County Cork. He had come to America in 1844 at the age of eighteen and entered Mount St. Mary's to become a priest for the archdiocese of Cincinnati. He first served as priest in a small town in Ohio and eventually at St. Patrick's Church in Cincinnati itself. Although only in his early thirties, with the support of his influential archbishop, John Purcell, a fellow Cork man who, like Quinlan, had come to America in his late teens and attended seminary in Emmitsburg, Quinlan was elevated to the See at Mobile in late 1859. In the summer of 1860 he traveled to Rome and Ireland to raise money and recruit priests and nuns for his underdeveloped diocese. When he returned to the United States in November, Lincoln had been elected and moves toward secession were already under way in Alabama.[25]

Despite his very recent arrival in the state along with the fact that his mentor, Archbishop Purcell, was the most outspoken Catholic supporter of President Lincoln, Quinlan had no qualms in telling his flock that while the breakup of the country would be regrettable "we would not purchase Union at the expense of justice." He continued: "Better that the instrument of confederation be rent in pieces and scattered to the winds than it should become a cloak for malice or a bond of iniquity."[26] The message was clear to his fellow countrymen that secession was a just response to northern aggression.

Quinlan's position is remarkable considering he had served in the South for less than a year. He perhaps came under the influence of the long-serving Irish priest there, Father James McGarahan. McGarahan had attacked Daniel O'Connell in the 1840s over the Irish "Liberator's" stance on slavery and had established himself as pro-southern since then.[27] Whatever the influences on him, after secession, Quinlan quickly endorsed the Confederacy. In the spring of 1861 he wrote that the new nation "must cut adrift from the North in many things of intimate social conditions and interests. We of the South," he continued, "have been too long on 'leading strings.'"[28]

Quinlan saw himself as a Confederate and was willing to break "the intimate social conditions" he had enjoyed with his former compatriots in the North. To instill this sense of nationalism in practical ways, he blessed the flag of P. N. Loughrey's Emerald Guards, before they departed for Virginia. He recognized all Confederate fast days and preached to troops stationed at forts protecting the city. He also facilitated Confederate recruitment by taking care of the money of Irish substitutes replacing draftees in the Confederate army. Quinlan held the money, sometimes in Confederate currency, other times in gold, for the substitutes and promised to pay beneficiaries if the soldier died in action. The Church was usually included as a beneficiary as well. In October 1862, for example, just days after the Confederate government had increased the conscription age from thirty-five to forty-five, Patrick Matthews, was paid $1,000 to replace one James Caldwell and joined the Fortieth Alabama Infantry. Quinlan was to disburse money to Matthews, with Caldwell's permission, over the period of enlistment. On the event of his death Matthews requested that any remaining money be given to his wife, or "in the event of her death to be equally divided" between his brothers and sisters "in Kings County (County Offaly) Ireland." The same month James Wall willed his bounty to his brother John in Mobile and if he had died or could not be found then to "the Catholic orphans." This role as banker gave confidence to the draftee too because if the substitute failed to sign up or deserted, he could claim back his money to try to hire a different substitute. Bernard Hughes, for example, deserted after only a few months and Quinlan returned the $1,750 remaining of the substitution fee to the original draftee. Overall, the Catholic cleric managed more than forty Irish substitution contracts thus increasing Irish participation in the Confederate war effort and helping make this element of conscription system run more smoothly.[29]

Even a confrontation with a Confederate official gave him a chance to display publicly his national spirit. Asked to bless the new St. Patrick's Church in Augusta, Georgia, in the spring of 1863, he undertook the journey by train traveling along the Mobile and Ohio Railroad to Meridian, Mississippi. A sentry there, however, refused to accept Quinlan's pass through the lines (signed by the commander in Mobile) as it was not on official stationary. Quinlan had to spend a very uncomfortable night in jail until the matter was sorted out and he was allowed to continue his journey. One of the Mobile newspapers, however, complained of the "abominable treatment" doled out to Quinlan.[30] The provost marshal in Columbus, J. M. White, quickly sent a letter of apology to the bishop. Representing, as he put it, "a Government office," he did not want the incident to escalate into a confrontation between southern Catholics and the Confederacy. He hoped that the misunderstanding over the pass would not be construed as a deliberate insult "to you as an individual or through you a denomination of Christians, *whose patriotism and loyalty have been forcibly evinced in the present struggle for national rights*" [my emphasis]. Reflecting an awareness of the importance of religion to the motivations of Catholic soldiers, many of whom were Irish, this Confederate officer did not want in any way to antagonize one of their spiritual leaders. Indeed, in similar fashion to the secessionists of Savannah who had welcomed the local Irish pastor onto their platform, he was displaying a considerable ethnic sensibility in apologizing not just to the Irish bishop for a real "indignity" but also to the wider community for any perceived one. In light of this larger motive, the officer concluded: "Should it be regarded expedient that this communication be published, you have my hearty concurrence."[31]

Quinlan replied in patriotic fashion, introducing himself as "[a] hearty supporter of our Government." He recognized the need for vigilance with passports but hoped for a more "'regular and definite form'" to avoid the hassle he had endured in Columbus. Undoubtedly easing Captain White's larger fear of an ethnic incident, he added: "I never entertained a thought that hostility to my creed prompted this annoyance, and I am exceedingly sorry that any such impression should be made." He then explained why: "During my three years experience in the South, I have, unexceptionally, been treated by my Protestant brethren everywhere with that warm hospitality and refined courtesy which constitute the peculiar and ennobling trait of Southern manners." He concluded that he would abide by the "olive-branch motto, 'forgive and forget.'" To make sure that the Irish and other Catholics of Mobile and elsewhere understood his sentiments, he had both White's and his letters published in a local newspaper.[32] A potential anti-Confederate incident had been turned into an opportunity to praise the "peculiar and ennobling manners" of the South with an Irish community leader clearly indicating the compatibility of Irish Catholics with Confederate citizenship.

Quinlan and Lynch were not alone in their episcopal support for the Confederacy. There was close to unanimity among Catholic bishops in the Confederacy toward the new state, and Irish Confederate soldiers and civilians throughout the country could be confident that their cause was a just and moral one. In the Confederate capital, Bishop John McGill was a very visible supporter of the new state and the war effort. His churches said prayers for the civil government and on one occasion he contemplated denying Union army chaplains the right to hear confessions while they served in Virginia because they were "officials of an invading army." Father John Teeling of St. Patrick's Church aided McGill in instilling Confederate patriotism in the city among the Irish. One Union chaplain imprisoned in the city in late 1862 described Teeling as a "rabid Secessionist." The Irish-born and educated Teeling had been pastor of St. Patrick's only since May 1861, but he had served as a chaplain to the Montgomery Guards. He told Richmond's Catholics to "stand firm in the assertion of their rights." Teeling's efforts had some success with his flock, as another Union chaplain on a visit to a Catholic Richmond family while on furlough from a Confederate prison remarked that when he stated that only Confederate "submission" would end the war, he caused "great offense" to his hosts. He had to admit that "the Catholics of Richmond, if we except the Germans, and a few Irish, were strongly for the South."[33]

In Wheeling, which became part of West Virginia in 1863, Irish American Richard Whelan was one of the most prominent supporters of secession in this Unionist section of Virginia. In western Virginia, thanks to Whelan, it appeared that Irish Catholics were more Confederate than many native Virginians. He argued against the creation of the new pro-Union state of West Virginia because his congregants' "allegiance [was] due to [their] state [i.e., Virginia], as the child is bound to the parent." Making a nuanced argument based on the Tenth Amendment to the United States Constitution, which reserved rights not explicitly granted to the Federal government to the "states," he failed to recognize the irony of his opposing West Virginia's secession from Virginia but supporting Virginia's secession from the Union.[34] He also felt betrayed by those Catholics in the North who joined the Union war effort. They were only aiding "New England fanatics, who have ever shown themselves ready to oppress—and against the very people whose general sense of right and honor prompted them to stand up for Catholic and foreigner, tho' Catholics and foreigners were so few among them." He saved particular ire for those Catholics in Ohio who, as they supported the Lincoln administration, because they were "fattening upon the soil which Virginia generously gave [to the United States in the Northwest Ordinance of 1787] for the commonweal."[35] Again, any Irish Catholic in Virginia who felt uncomfortable about secession could find Whelan's comments comforting.

The attitude of New Orleans clerics, who ministered to the largest Irish population in the South, was very important, especially in terms of Confederate recruitment. The Crescent City too provided its clerical Confederate partisans. The Abbé Napoleon J. Perché, later archbishop of the diocese of New Orleans, took it upon himself to reply to the questions of "Several Catholics" on the justice of seceding from the Union. Perché began: "I see no reasons why my opinions . . . should not be made public. I declare, therefore, that I make them known, not only as a citizen and the editor of a public newspaper, but as a minister of the Christian religion, who has been called upon to aid in dissipating the clouds which now hang over the American people." He continued: "I believe that the sacred office of Priesthood does not incapacitate its servants from speaking on vital social questions. The very station which we hold not only gives us the right, but makes it our duty to elucidate . . . whatever is obscure either in the moral or political world." The Abbé went on to provide a justification for secession with which any southern fire-eater would have been proud. This letter, published not only in his Catholic newspaper but also in a secular one, appeared about three weeks before Louisiana seceded: "I hesitate not to declare that the moment that the South can no longer uphold herself with the honor in the Union, it is her right—nay it is her duty—to secede." Perché concluded by blessing future Confederates: "To uphold one's country is not merely a right which one can exercise or neglect at one's pleasure; it is an obligation of conscience, a moral and religious duty."[36]

With many Irish, this clerical support for secession trumped John Maginnis's call to rally around the Union. Thousands of Catholic Louisianians, Irish, German, and Creole took Perché's advice and left to defend their new country with the blessing of their Catholic leaders. Thus, as in Charleston and Mobile, Irish Confederate units in New Orleans celebrated the Christian nature of their upcoming conflict. After celebration of High Mass at St. Alphonsus in the heart of the "Irish Channel," for example, Michael Nolan's Montgomery Guards heard their Irish pastors tell them that "their allegiance was first due to God, and next to their adopted states of Louisiana and the states allied with her." Blessing their flag then was appropriate because "the banner consecrated" represented these Irishmen's commitment to, if need be, participate in the "din of battle for the honor and rights of the nation"; in this case, the southern and not the Irish nation.[37]

Of course dissent in these early days of the Confederacy was difficult. Any Catholic cleric out of step with his pro-Confederate flock and the pro-Confederate non-Catholic majority became ineffective, ignored by his congregants, and disliked by natives. The only pro-Union bishop in the South, the northern-trained Irish American James Whelan of Nashville, resigned and returned North because of the opposition he generated among Catholic and Protestant Tennesseans. Even though the city fell to Union forces in early 1862, he himself recognized that he was not wanted in Nashville and made the calculated decision to move out of the Confederacy.[38] Apparently, the family members of those Irish still serving in Randall McGavock's "Bloody Tenth" Tennessee Infantry did not like their overtly pro-Union bishop.

The other Catholic Confederate bishops remained paragons of Confederate patriotism even as the euphoria of 1861 subsided. They tried to sustain Catholics even in the most difficult of circumstances. Bishop Quinlan, for example, lobbied hard to leave Confederate Mobile for occupied Pensacola to minister to the Catholics in the naval yard there without having to take an oath. Bishop Martin Spalding of Louisville's attempt to minister to Confederate camps in Kentucky got him labeled "a rebel and a spy" by one Union officer. One Irish American priest, a Father McDonough, who rode the circuit in north Alabama, "was in danger of being taken up as a spy, as he had to run the blockade often."[39] As prominent leaders of the Irish Confederate community they could not be seen to be taking any oath to the United States authorities.

Most southern clerics also saw this oath obligation as a serious interference by the State in Church affairs. This was the official response, but privately many, as white southerners, native or adopted, did not want to take the oath under any circumstances. Even if they took it for practical reasons, as Martin Spalding eventually did, some feared that such a move would alienate their congregations. Similar attempts by Union authorities forcing clerics to acknowledge publicly the United States' control of a region also proved contentious. Bishop Elder of Natchez provided the most notorious case. An adamant opponent of the oath, Elder constantly sought exemptions from it for himself and his clergy when leaving or entering his cathedral town. Tension reached a crescendo, however, when Elder refused to obey Special Order No. 31 ordering "public prayer . . . in behalf of the President of the United States and the Union." For his disobedience he was placed under house arrest across the Mississippi River in Vidalia, Louisiana. Elder defended his actions on classic separation of Church and State grounds: "Once make the Church a subject of the State in Her spiritual functions, and she is no longer a living Church of the Holy Ghost, infusing into her children the life of Catholic charity; she becomes a kind of *pious branch of police*" (emphasis in the original). He went on, disingenuously, to declare that "we, the Catholic Clergy of the diocese of Natchez, have done nothing to merit the molestation of the Government of the United States. We have never lent our public advocacy nor our private influence to its injury, neither before nor since the war began."[40] On the contrary, Elder and the other Catholic bishops in the South had supported the Irish and other Catholics fighting for the Confederacy and now, it seemed, supported continued opposition to the Union cause.

Elder's defiance must have made an impression on Irish Catholics serving in the army and would prove valuable propaganda for the Confederacy among the Irish in the South and back in Ireland. It certainly made an impression among Catholics in the North. With the intervention of Catholic clerics in the North, Secretary of War Edwin Stanton ordered Elder's release. The Federal government did not want to rile up even more Catholic opposition to the war. This episode also highlights that despite the bitterness generated by sectional divisions, Catholics North and South did try to maintain a relationship. This was particularly true as the war dragged on and northern Catholics, particularly Irish ones, began to become disillusioned with it. The devastating casualties and the metamorphosis of the war from one for Union to one to liberate the slaves turned northern Catholics into the most active opponents of Republican war policy. While many still remained pro-Union and supported War Democrat and former general George McClellan in the 1864 presidential election campaign, their calls for a ceasefire and peace talks in reality meant that there would be no need for the "reconstruction" already taking place under President Abraham Lincoln's guidance in states such as Louisiana. Even as partisan a Catholic and almost as much a Union man as Orestes Brownson had to admit most Catholics had sympathized with the South or were at best "neutral."[41]

This change in attitude by a majority of their northern brethren encouraged many southern Irish Catholics to believe that only through their church could their new country gain de facto recognition. Irish Catholics could save the Confederacy. Men such as James McMaster, editor of the Catholic *Freeman's Journal* in New York City, fed this belief. McMaster was a convert to Catholicism and had been born "MacMaster" but dropped the "a" to make his name more Irish; a direct appeal to his largely Irish readership. His newspaper had been owned by Bishop Hughes but McMaster bought it in 1848, and although very pro-Catholic, this proprietorship gave McMaster the leeway to pursue his own editorial line. Always a strong critic of Lincoln and the Republicans, McMaster had reluctantly supported the war but changed his tune as casualties mounted, and in particular, after the Emancipation Proclamation. By late 1862 his newspaper had become very hostile to the administration, earning it a ban from the U.S. mail and eventually McMaster an eleven-month spell in prison. Virulently racist, McMaster advocated that Catholics should not serve and fight for emancipation.[42]

McMaster became a hero to many Irish American Catholics in the North and the South, and from non-Catholic Confederates too. Both during and after the war, letters came from the South praising him for his service in their cause of "liberty." From occupied New Orleans, Irish priest Richard Kane, the pastor of Saint Patrick's, the main Irish church in the city, wrote to tell McMaster that Catholic and Protestant alike "appreciated" him. McMaster's opinions would do much more for reconciliation than any "proclamation" by General Benjamin Butler. "You are entitled to the undying thankfulness of every friend of liberty," the Irish priest told him. In Norfolk, Virginia, a woman outlined the story of a local man who had to admit that "'Although [he was] Protestant clergyman, I must confess that the Freeman's (Catholic) Journal is the only paper in the whole North that dares to speak out boldly against the vile acts of the despot in Washington.'" McMaster's female correspondent continued with her own take: "Of course as an Irish Catholic I was proud of this tribute of praise . . . and I think you will appreciate the compliment all the more that it was paid to you by a heretic and a rebel." Father James Corcoran of the diocese of Charleston also thanked the northern editor for his "kind sentiments." Confederate chaplain and later "poet-priest of the Confederacy" (see chapter 6) Father Abram Ryan wrote him as well to say, "There is not a one in the South today who has ever read the dear old Freeman's Journal, that does not claim, respect, honor and love the noble Editor as one of the truest and best of friends." The ultimate southern praise came after the war, when ex-president Jefferson Davis thanked McMaster for his "journal" which gave Davis "the great comfort . . . that justice and constitutional right can be so boldly vindicated as it now is in your periodical."[43]

Confederate authorities thus quickly realized the loyalty of the Catholic Church and its importance to Irish Catholic soldiers. Confederate military officers also recognized that the important influence of Catholic clergy on Irish military performance. Irish Catholics were considered to be "faithful soldiers" especially when a chaplain was present.[44] The Confederacy did not have an official chaplaincy service, but officers recognizing its value to soldiers' morale and performance often commissioned chaplains, or accepted unofficial ones.[45] The latter practice suited the Catholic Church in the South, because of its hierarchical and diocesan structure, ultimate supervision and control of priests lay with bishops. The bishops, however, were keen to cater to the spiritual needs of their soldiers.[46] Catholic soldiers in particular needed clergy to fulfill their Christian duties of receiving the sacraments.

Louisiana, with its large number of Catholic soldiers, provided many chaplains to the Confederate army. Most were of Creole origin, but Irishman Father James Sheeran was the exception. A Redemptorist (an order that specializes in missionary activity to those already Catholic), he had come from Ireland to Canada at age twelve with his family and moved eventually with them to Michigan. Educated there, he was ordained in 1855 and, in 1858, moved to New Orleans to work in the Redemptorist parish in the city, which catered mostly to poor Irish immigrants. Although he had grown up in the North and had spent only three years in the South, he volunteered to minister to a regiment in the 2nd Louisiana Brigade in the Army of Northern Virginia. He was happy to fulfill the spiritual needs of his Catholic flock, searching battlefields and hospitals for the wounded and the dead and also preparing his men for battle. In the latter he saw himself performing a military as well as a religious task. He wrote that he did "all in [his] power to keep them [Catholic soldiers] in the friendship of their God, for I had learned that no men fight more bravely than Catholics who approach the sacraments before battle." He had particular praise for the bravery of Irish units such as Michael Nolan's Montgomery Guards.[47]

Sheeran saw himself not just as a priest but as a member of the Confederate army officer corps. When captured in late 1864 he refused to take the oath of allegiance to the United States, rejecting this offer of parole by stating: "I am no citizen of the United States and am a chaplain in the Confederate army. . . . My home is in the South and there I demand to be sent." Later he even challenged General Phil Sheridan in person, demanding a pass through his lines to the South.[48] The experience of war had solidified rather than weakened his Confederate nationalism. He had slept on the "gravelly beds," as he put it, with fence rails "for pillows." He had endured the long marches and the joy of being able to wash in clean water ("Oh! that happy moment" he exclaimed when a shopkeeper in Frederick allowed him to wash in the back of his store during the brigade's march into Maryland in September 1862).[49]

Sheeran took it upon himself to lecture all on the benefits of the Confederacy, especially Irish Catholic Union prisoners to whom he ministered. He told one group of Union officers captured at the Second Battle of Manassas that they did not deserve to be paroled because they had "served under a commander [John Pope] who disregarded all the laws of civilized warfare and divested himself of every feeling of humanity." When the prisoners complained about the quality and quantity of the rations given them by the Confederates, Sheeran stated directly that "they had not legitimate cause of complaint, for their government did all they could to starve the people of the South by blockading our ports, ravaging the country, plundering the inhabitants, burning our towns, leaving thousands of our people homeless and hungry; and if they now suffered it was all their own fault."[50] When entering Maryland with the Army of Northern Virginia, he came upon a female "Unionist" chastising one of "his boys" for stealing food. Sheeran decided to investigate the matter and discovered that the woman was mistaken. He, tongue in cheek, asked her to give "three cheers for Jeff Davis" by way of apology, which she declined to do. He was more melancholy, however, when he saw the Stars and Stripes that had been flying over a Maryland public building torn up by Confederate troops. He remarked: "A few short years ago that very flag was the emblem of our national greatness and to defend it every Southern citizen would have sacrificed his life." Now it had become the "emblem of tyranny" and was understandably now being "torn into shreds" by those very same southerners.[51] As his prison experience highlights, this Irish Confederate remained devoted to the cause. He saw himself as a role model for his soldiers. After his release from prison he came on another parolee and was delighted to hear that his "boys had behaved themselves in prison after my departure." They had refrained from gambling and more importantly stayed in the army.[52] Sheeran was pleased to have had such a strong patriotic influence on his soldier flock.

Father Peter Whelan of Savannah held the same opinions as Sheeran on the justice of the Confederate cause and the importance of clerical support to Catholic Confederate soldiers. He had been an avid secessionist. Unlike Sheeran, though, he had lived in the South over thirty years when the war began. Born in County Wexford and educated in Kilkenny City, he heard the missionary call of Bishop John England and left Ireland in the early 1820s to become a priest for the diocese of Charleston. Ordained in 1830 he spent a large part of his career catering to the largely Irish Catholic settlement at Locust Grove, near Crawfordville, Georgia. This was a farming community in a cotton-growing area of east Georgia where many Irish immigrants had come to buy land and slaves. By the mid-1850s he was stationed in Savannah (which had become a diocese in 1850), where he assumed an administrative role because of the premature deaths of the first two bishops appointed there. This service in the increasingly secessionist Georgia city by the coast and his life in the cotton belt turned him into an ardent Confederate nationalist. Administration of the now Confederate diocese was not his passion and he gladly handed over the reins of the diocese to the new bishop (Augustin Verot) in the summer of 1861. Whelan did remain vicar general (the head priest and administrative assistant to the bishop), but it seems that he wanted more pastoral duties. When Verot asked for a volunteer to minister to Catholic troops, particularly the Irish Montgomery Guards, down the Savannah River at Fort Pulaski in late 1861, he jumped at the opportunity of sharing military life with his compatriots.[53]

Whelan was embodying the idea of not just Christian but also Confederate sacrifice. At Pulaski he came under severe Federal bombardment and was captured with the Montgomery Guards and other Confederate defenders when the fort fell to Union forces in April 1862. Transported north to prison, he suffered the deprivations of life at "Castle William" on Governors Island near New York City. Overcrowded with poor ventilation and sanitation, the prison became rampant with disease. Despite his incarceration, Whelan still saw himself as a military pastor and was pleased when the camp commandant allowed him to say Mass to Irish troops. He could have used his clerical status and Catholic connections to get a parole but he used his contacts instead to get supplies from Catholics in New York for his soldiers. Nonetheless, northern Catholic pressure eventually gained him a parole offer. Despite the fact that he was about sixty years of age, he refused release, preferring to stay with the other prisoners. The commander of his regiment, Colonel Charles Olmstead, told one story of Whelan's generosity toward Confederate troops. Olmstead and his fellow officers considered Whelan a member of the regimental staff and felt that he should have better attire as his only suit had become "shabby" through the incarceration at the "Castle." They managed to purchase a new coat for him and left it for him by his bunk while he was asleep. Soon afterward, however, Olmstead and the other officers noticed that Whelan was wearing his old coat again. Olmstead asked Whelan what had happened to the new coat and the priest replied that he had given to a soldier who had none. Olmstead complained why had he not given the destitute soldier the old coat instead? Whelan replied: "When I give for Christ's sake, I give the best."[54]

When all the Montgomery Guards were released and exchanged in August 1862, Whelan returned to Savannah and his post of vicar general. Because of his military experience, Verot put him in charge of the spiritual needs of the various Confederate posts in Georgia. As part of this duty, the French bishop asked Whelan to visit the Confederate prisoner of war camp at Andersonville in the southwestern part of the state. Andersonville became one of the most notorious military prisons, so much so that its commandant, Swiss-born Henry Wirz, was the only official Confederate officer to be tried and executed after the war.[55]

Whelan had already heard of the poor situation in the camp and had lobbied local Confederate General Howell Cobb to organize a quick exchange of the Union prisoners there. When he arrived at Andersonville in June 1864, conditions were dreadful. Overcrowded, sick, starving, and without proper shelter, many prisoners had dug holes in the ground to avoid the burning Georgia sun. Every day Whelan ministered to the sick, depressed, and dying from 9:00 A.M. to sundown, which left him "full of sorrow." He borrowed and collected money to buy bread in Savannah for the prisoners. When the prison population reached 33,000 the camp reverted to a "state of nature" with groups of "raiders" stealing from and often killing other prisoners. Confederate authorities eventually allowed the prisoners to organize self-defense groups and a judicial system that arrested, tried, convicted, and, on some occasions, executed "criminals." Whelan lobbied for clemency and consoled the convicted and those sentenced to death. Eventually, he picked up a bronchial infection and returned to Savannah, which was in chaos expecting the arrival of William T. Sherman on his "march to the sea" and he remained in the city when it fell at Christmas 1864. In 1861 Whelan had warned Father James Hasson that he might be tarred and feathered for his pro-Union views, but the experience of the ugly side of war had increased his sympathy for those who supported the Union. The reality of southern independence had taken the edge off his Confederate nationalism. Some Union prisoners commented on his care for the sick and dying and named the ardent secessionist the "angel of Andersonville." The Confederate lectures to Union prisoners of Father Sheeran were not for him. Also not for him was the bitterness toward northerners shown by fire-eaters, such as Edmund Ruffin, who committed suicide rather than submit to "hated Yankee rule." Whelan was sick of death and destruction.[56] As with many of his Irish congregants, the war had made him "less" Confederate and more conciliatory toward the North.

For other Irish priests, the war experience could also be disheartening. Father Patrick Ryan of Charleston felt his duties were getting on top of him. While expressing obedience to Bishop Lynch's wishes, he felt that he was not "qualified" to be an official military chaplain. He was already very busy running services at St. Patrick's, the only active Catholic church in the city. He did offer to visit the Catholic, mostly Irish, troops of the Charleston

Battalion stationed around the city to fulfill their "religious obligations" for their "spiritual good," but he could not "exercise any influence over the men in re-enlisting" in the service. Unlike Sheeran, he did not believe it was his duty to work for the Confederacy as well as the Church. Indeed, he continued, he "would feel a very great repugnance at such an undertaking." He told Lynch that the bishop needed to appoint a proper military chaplain to this position. Lynch was about to leave his diocese for a time, and there is no evidence of a reply, but Ryan highlights that for personal and political reasons the war could affect Irish Confederate morale. He would obey his superior's orders, but the conflict had disillusioned him of the cause itself, and he would not go out of his way to further it.[57]

In contrast to this reluctant chaplain, another Ryan (not related) did not lose faith in the Confederacy. On the contrary, it increased. Father Abram Ryan was not in the Confederacy when the war began but was stationed in Peoria, Illinois. Born in Hagerstown, Maryland, to recent Irish immigrants, Ryan grew up in Missouri. Here he became a strong advocate of southern rights. He even changed his name from Abraham to Abram to remove any connection to Abraham Lincoln. Spending the early part of the war stationed in "Union occupied" Missouri, upstate New York, and eventually Illinois, along with his brother's service and eventual death in the Confederate army radicalized him even more. As early as 1861 he was writing odes to Jefferson Davis and Alexander Stephens in church record books. He also, perhaps, began freelancing as a Confederate chaplain. Records indicate that he took long periods of sick leave from his official church duties for his neuralgia and these breaks coincided with reports of his appearances in various parts of the South ministering to Confederate Catholic soldiers. By 1864 it is certain that he was serving at the front with the Army of Tennessee. The bloody campaigns he witnessed and the death of his brother in April 1863 made him go beyond his ministerial duties to the soldiers into publicly commemorating and eulogizing their efforts on behalf of the new country. Through the war, Ryan emerged as a Confederate propagandist and would carry on in this role long after the Confederacy itself had disappeared. He became a classic example of what one historian has described as "the endurance of Confederates' attachment to their nation, even when their state ceased to exist."[58] Ryan's efforts for Confederate nationalism came too late to have much impact on the fate of the Confederacy itself, and it was in the memory of the former Confederacy that Ryan's effectiveness would be recognized (see chapter 6).

Catholic chaplain Father John Bannon, born in County Roscommon and reared in Dublin, had a more direct impact on the Confederate war effort.

A priest in St. Louis since 1853, he followed the Irishmen of that city's militias who joined the Confederate army in late 1861. While still in St. Louis he had been arrested with other pro-Confederates but continued to work under "parole." In December 1861, however, he escaped to join the Irish Confederates in southwestern Missouri. He had become a de facto military chaplain.[59] With the Missouri brigade he traveled through the southern part of the state and into Arkansas and eventually eastward to Mississippi. On his travels he suffered through bad weather and road conditions, as well as military bombardments. At the siege of Vicksburg, he visited the trenches every day to hear confessions and perform the last rites, even though he had been assigned to a hospital in the rear. Although he was not on a Confederate salary and was dependent on the charity of Catholics he met on his travels, his clerical status often won him special treatment. He lived as a member of staff and quartered with the officers. He thus became the chaplain of the entire brigade as well as other units in the Confederate armies he served in. He said Mass for Catholic troops from all states and administered the sacraments to them. On one occasion, for example, he was called to give extreme unction to a soldier from the predominantly Irish 2nd Tennessee Infantry who had been condemned to death. Bannon anointed the man's "shaved head" and was relieved when the death sentence was commuted at the last minute. Despite this activity on behalf of all Catholic soldiers, he paid special attention to the Irish Missourians. The back of his war diary, which bears the marks of having been written in the field, is full of accounts of money that he looked after for his soldiers. He was their banker. They trusted him with their pay, which he gave out to them when they requested it. Occasionally he borrowed from them as well and finally was able to repay all his debts when he was appointed an official chaplain with pay in February 1863, backdated to February 1, 1862.[60]

By the middle of 1863, Bannon and his Irish Missourians were involved in the campaign to save Vicksburg from Union capture. The Irish priest lived through the siege of that city but had a close call on one occasion when a Union shell from a "parrot rifle" shattered through the church where he was about to say Mass, severely wounding an Irish congregant. Bannon regretted the surrender of the city to the Federal forces on the Fourth of July, but after his parole he was able to grab some rest and recuperation with Bishop Quinlan in Mobile.[61] Rather than a return to chaplain service, however, the Confederate government had another task for him. They wanted him to go to Ireland to try to hinder reported Union recruitment there as well as general Irish emigration to the northern states. His service in the military had gained him a reputation as a dedicated Confederate. Indeed, when some of his fellow clergy thought of him as a potential appointment to the vacant see at Little Rock, Archbishop Francis Kenrick vetoed his candidacy because large parts of Arkansas were occupied by Union forces and Bannon has become known as a notorious rebel.[62]

His dedication had helped him make connections with prominent Confederates. Secretary of the navy and prominent Florida Catholic Stephen Mallory had helped Bannon, at the behest of Bishop Quinlan, to receive his official commission. It was to Mallory that Bannon went after his parole from the Vicksburg defeat, and it was through the Floridian that Bannon met Secretary of State Judah P. Benjamin. Benjamin, on behalf of the government, commissioned the priest as a Confederate agent in Ireland. The Confederacy, as part of its mission to the United Kingdom, had originally appointed a Trinity College Dublin graduate, Captain J. L. Capston, to represent it there. Capston was a competent officer but did not have enough contacts to sustain a serious effort against Union recruitment and general Irish emigration to the United States. Through pressure on the U.S. State Department, the British government tried to stop the former and had some success. Halting the latter would be a much tougher, perhaps impossible, task. Nonetheless, Bannon was well-suited to the job. He had been ordained in Maynooth, the national seminary of Irish Catholicism, giving him connections to hundreds of priests around the country. He had also been ordained by the most powerful cleric in nineteenth-century Ireland, the archbishop and later Ireland's first cardinal, Paul Cullen. Bannon knew Cullen well. Thus, the combination of his Confederate zeal, the fact that since the fall of Vicksburg and the capture of the Missouri brigade, he was without an official position, and his Irish connections meant that President Davis endorsed the idea and the Confederate government funded Bannon's new assignment. In October 1863 he ran the blockade and traveled across the Atlantic to his "secret mission" in Ireland.[63]

Upon arrival, Bannon immediately made contact with the Confederate diplomatic authorities in London and reported on his activities to them as well as to Benjamin back in Richmond. With Archbishop Cullen's blessing he began his mission to halt Irish emigrants' entry into the Union army. A handbill he had printed to be displayed in churches throughout Ireland indicates clearly the angle he was going to take in persuading the Irish against emigration to the northern states. He was going to use the controversial relationship the Catholic Church in the Confederacy had with Federal authorities. The flyer went into some detail on the "desecrations" made against

Catholicism and the motives behind these moves. The headlines ran "CAU-
TION to EMIGRANTS: Persecution of Catholics in America: The Taberna-
cle Overthrown! The Blessed Host scattered on the ground! Benediction Veil
made a Horse Cover of! All the Sacred Vessels carried off! The Monument
of the Dead defaced! The Priest imprisoned and afterwards exposed on an
Island to Alligators and Snakes! His house robbed of everything!" Bannon
continued: "Those and similar outrages, unparalleled in history, have been
committed on Catholics by Massachusetts Soldiers in the State of Louisiana, and published in the *Freeman's Journal*, New York." It was the remnants
of the "Know-Nothing Party" born of "Orangeism" which dominated the
Federal cause. Bannon's linking of the anti-Catholic Orange Order to the
Federal government was useful propaganda. Riots around Orange parades
had exploded again in Ireland during the 1850s and 1860s and religious tensions were high.[64]

The other tack he took to discourage emigration was self-preservation.
The United States was no longer the land of opportunity for Irish emigrants:
"The right of Habeas Corpus is now suspended—the home of liberty is now
the head quarters of a military despotism—the great Republic of the West,
now no longer exists—life and liberty is at stake." Any male emigrant's life
was "at stake" because upon landing in the United States he came "under
the CONSCRIPTION LAW." Bannon emphasized that the immigrant faced
"no alternative" but to "[become] a SOLDIER. In forty-eight hours he is
landed in the Swamps of the Carolinas, or on the Sand Bars of Charleston."
Bannon reminded potential emigrants what happened to Irish in the Union
army: "Let Irishmen remember the fate of MEAGHER'S BRIGADE, on the
bloody field of Fredericksburg, 5,000 strong! Now no more; and were refused permission to reorganize; some of the New York Papers stating that
they could afford to lose a few thousand of the scum of the Irish." While
Bannon's description of the casualties of the Irish brigade had some basis
in fact, his description of the brigade's failure to reorganize was not. That
reality had more to do with the Lincoln administration's general frustration
with politically appointed officers and Meagher's inability to recruit, than
anti-Irish bias. Nonetheless, Bannon felt free to use any misinformation to
aid his cause. The likelihood of direct confrontation with fellow Irishmen in
the Confederate army was never very high, but even less so in 1864. He still
warned, however, that any Irishman, who joined the Union army, by fair or
foul means, would "imbrue his hands in THE BLOOD OF HIS COUNTRY-
MEN" to "fight for a People that has the greatest antipathy to his birth and
creed."[65]

Bannon had two thousand copies of the circular printed for distribution. He also sent clippings from newspapers in the Confederacy to Irish nationalists such as William Smith O'Brien and John Martin. (Smith O'Brien was a former colleague of John Mitchel in the Young Ireland movement, and Martin was Mitchel's editorial colleague and his brother-in-law. Both had been imprisoned with him in Tasmania.) O'Brien and Martin were ardent supporters of the Confederacy in Ireland and expressed their opinions openly in the Irish press.[66] Bannon also cultured a relationship with A. M. Sullivan, editor of the prominent nationalist newspaper *The Nation*, feeding the editor information for his pro-Confederate articles. He encouraged the government in Richmond to have John Mitchel write more letters to the Irish newspapers, because Mitchel was considered "honest" by all shades of Irish political opinion, even the people who disagreed with him. On one occasion he wrote to the *Freeman's Journal* in Dublin, a paper with a large circulation, but also because "it is the morning paper mostly circulated amongst the priests of this city." He was disappointed, however, when a section of his letter in which he "identified the Puritans with the *Cromwellians* [Bannon's emphasis], a race yet hated by the Irish," was edited out. He regretted that he did not get to use the Cromwell image, which had worked so well in recruiting the Irish in the South into the Confederate army. He put this failure down to the fact that the paper was "liberal Whig" in orientation with a sizeable Protestant readership. The editor, Bannon surmised, did not want to offend their religious sensibilities with the connection of modern U.S. Protestantism to the hated Cromwell.[67]

The Confederate priest thus felt that his best efforts would be beyond the newspapers.[68] He believed that to get to the "young able-bodied emigrants" his circular and correspondence with clergy throughout Ireland would be far more effective than any press articles. He worried that "the effects of a newspaper correspondence are limited to the subscribers of the paper, who are mostly well to do people, and never much the class which supplies the emigration." Ultimately, he concluded: "There is no paper of sufficient circulation amongst the poor which could . . . aid our cause [no matter] how friendly . . . they might be to us." The better tactic was to put a "publication [his circular] immediately under the eyes of the peasantry, and place the article in their hands by free circulation." To fulfill this task, he sent circulars to his clerical friends. For example, he mailed a thousand posters to Queenstown, County Cork, and five hundred to Galway City, two major emigrant embarkation ports. In each place he encouraged priest friends to pin the posters up in all "the boarding houses usually occupied by expectant emigrants." In January 1864 he had another circular printed for distribution to "every parish priest" in Ireland.[69]

How effective was Bannon's campaign on behalf of the Confederacy? The *Times* of London apparently gave him some credit for stopping Union recruitment in Ireland, but it had always dismissed the extent of the phenomenon anyway.[70] The early 1860s had been difficult in Ireland with a number of failed harvests. Ironically, 1863 saw an improved harvest, but also almost a tripling of Irish emigration from 33,000 to 94,000. The relative economic upturn had given some the means to go to America. The per year statistics show that 94,000 Irish people left Ireland for America in 1863 and the same number in 1864, up from 33,000 in 1862 and 28,000 in 1861. More remarkable, though, is that of the overall Irish emigration in 1861 and 1862 about 45 percent went to the United States, but in 1863 and 1864 that percentage jumped to 85. Despite the increased casualty rates and the "destruction" of Meagher's Irish Brigade, Irish emigrants, it seems, were not discouraged from going to the United States. Quite the contrary it seems. The fact that post-Famine emigration had seen a rise in the number of women emigrating does not account for all of this shift toward the United States. The increases in emigration to America in 1863 and 1864 were not just because more women decided to go. Indeed, the percentage of men among Irish people leaving between 1861 and 1864 grew from just over 50 to 53 percent.[71]

It seems then that Bannon's efforts had very little, if any, effect on the Irish decision to emigrate to the United States. Secretary of State William Henry Seward's 1862 circular to American consulates and embassies promoting the "enhanced price of labour" seems to have countered any fears of the Irish becoming immediate "cannon fodder" and provided an economic incentive that trumped any fears about the war, which was fought mostly in the South anyway.[72]

Nonetheless, those young Irishmen who did emigrate in 1864 may not have joined the army because of Bannon's warnings. Opposition to Federal recruitment in Ireland had been widespread and very public, even before Bannon had arrived in Ireland. The most infamous case was that of the USS *Kearsarge*, which had recruited Irish sailors in Ireland in November 1863 but had neglected, according to the Irishmen, to tell them that they had enlisted in the military. Outcry in the newspapers and from the British government forced the return of the *Kearsarge* to Ireland and the release of sixteen Irish men among the crew in December 1863. Similarly, in early 1864 Irishmen recruited for mechanical work in Massachusetts by one Patrick Finney, complained bitterly when discovering upon arriving in the United States that there was no work for them except in the army. The local Boston Irish community rallied to many caught up in the "Finney case" providing relief to them. Five of the six (one had been killed in Virginia) who claimed to have been forced into the army were eventually discharged on orders, issued under direct pressure from the British Foreign Office, by Secretary of State William Henry Seward. Cardinal Cullen, who had allowed Bannon to distribute his anti-Union propaganda through the Church in Dublin, openly decried Irish volunteering in the Union army in May 1864.[73]

Irish emigrants seem then to have been aware of the dangers of U.S. military recruiters and were not afraid to express their opposition to involuntary enlistment. Bannon perhaps did play a role in the molding of Irish opinions toward the Union army. The Irish remained the most "under-represented in proportion to population" of any ethnic group in the Union army. From 1863 onward Irish recruitment to the Union army, declined precipitously.[74] Bannon's exact role in this decline is unclear, but what is more important from an Irish Confederate perspective is that the Confederate government was very pleased with his efforts. Secretary of State Judah P. Benjamin declared himself "gratified with the zeal, and discretion and ability shown by the Revd. Mr. Bannon in the service undertaken by him and [we] desire . . . to provide him with the necessary means for continuing his labours as long as he remains satisfied that his efforts are useful to our cause." Benjamin trusted Bannon's loyalty so much he gave him free rein in his mission, and the priest remained a Confederate zealot to the end.[75] After the war Bishop McGill of Richmond reportedly told Bannon that the Confederate Congress had awarded him $2,000 in absentia for his good work. (Bannon does not appear in the *Journal of the Confederate Congress*, but a lot of its business was conducted in camera.)[76] There is no doubt, however, that Bannon had displayed a strong Confederate patriotism to leading Confederates and left them with the impression that most Irish were sympathetic to the South.

Beyond Congress and commanding officers, Bannon and other Irish chaplains left an impression of patriotism among the lower echelons of the Confederacy too. Protestant native-born soldiers often commented favorably on the performance of priests in the army. Nuns too left positive impressions of Confederate patriotism. At war's outbreak, many Catholic orders of sisters had already gained a reputation for public outreach, especially in education. The various epidemics of the antebellum South, especially yellow fever, had extended their work into nursing. In Savannah, for example, the local Sisters of Our Lady of Mercy (an order originally founded by Bishop John England in Charleston in 1829 with mostly Irish members) had provided outstanding care in the city's 1854 yellow fever epidemic. When most of the wealthy natives fled the city, the Sisters stayed behind to help those too poor to leave. Bishop England had modeled this American order of his on the first one established in the United States, the Sisters of Charity of St. Joseph, which had been founded in 1809 in Emmitsburg by Mother (now Saint) Elizabeth Ann Seton. The Sisters of Charity and England's Sisters of Mercy had two roles, to help educate the Catholic poor and to be role models of Catholic charity in the community.[77]

Thus, nuns in the Confederacy sent religious articles to Irish soldiers to remind them of their faith and also took care of soldiers' young relatives. Peter Reilly of the Irish Jasper Greens in Savannah, for example, could take comfort from the fact that while he served in the Confederate army his young sister was in the care of the nuns, the Reilly parents having passed away. Nuns supervised the creation of Irish company flags and instilled in the young the values of being Catholic Confederates, the "Secession Pageants" of St. Vincent's Academy being a classic example of this. The good Catholic sisters reinforced the views of bishops and priests to Irish Confederates that their cause was a righteous one, but they also showed themselves models of Confederate nationalism. The local newspaper that publicized the first pageant, for example, commented on how "Southern" the event was. The sisters of St. Vincent's, with the support of their pastor, Jeremiah O'Neill, had demonstrated "a victory of *our* [educational institutions, which we have been taught hitherto to regard as inferior to those of Northern States" (my emphasis). Ultimately, these Irish Catholics had helped "the promotion of Southern education."[78] They had become seamless Confederates.

In a physical sense Irish nuns' greatest contribution to the Confederate cause was their work in military hospitals, but it also had an ideological impact. Throughout the Confederacy nuns were at the forefront of military nursing. Those sisters closest to the areas of battle were the first called into service. Virginia was the first state to see major conflict, and the Sisters of Charity in Richmond and Norfolk were the first to take in Confederate sick and wounded. Some of the sisters in Richmond went to the army near Manassas, in early 1862, to help in field hospitals, where they took care of over 500 patients. They evacuated with the Confederates in March and reestablished themselves at Gordonsville and eventually at Danville. Here they settled permanently, as this important railroad junction, close to North Carolina, became a center for Confederate medical care. They usually dealt with 1,500 to 2,000 patients at a time. The need for Catholic nurses became so great that the mother house in Emmitsburg had to send some south through the lines, thus drawing the ire of some Federal authorities who suspected them of being spies.[79] Bishop McGill with responsibility for Catholic Virginia also asked Bishop Lynch of Charleston for help and Lynch sent a number of his Sisters of Mercy. Led by a feisty County Kilkenny woman, Mother De Sales Brennan, who often challenged doctors about levels of care, the sisters operated the Montgomery hospital at White Sulphur Springs, without any pay from Confederate officials until May 1865. The Charleston sisters also worked in local city hospitals when their home town came under siege in 1863.[80]

Sisters also responded to calls for help in the western theater. Upon arriving in Mississippi with the Missouri Brigade in early 1862, Father Bannon met Sisters of Charity from Mobile operating a hospital in Corinth dealing with the mass of casualties from the war's bloodiest battle to that point, Shiloh. Nuns from New Orleans also served in Holly Springs. The Sisters of Mercy from Vicksburg left that city in 1862 to tend to wounded in Oxford. When Oxford fell to Union forces they went to Jackson and eventually back to Vicksburg in May 1863 and finally Mississippi Springs near Raymond. Although they had all been teachers before the war, they performed vital nursing duties during the Vicksburg campaign and after the surrender removed to Jackson, where they continued to care for wounded and sick soldiers.[81] After the Battle of Chickamauga in North Georgia in September 1863 the sisters from St. Vincent's in Savannah moved north to help with hospitals. The Sisters of Charity had been operating a hospital in Chattanooga, Tennessee, but evacuated with the Army of Tennessee that September, relocating to Dalton and eventually LaGrange, Georgia. Many casualties from the Confederate attempts to retake the city (initiated with the Battle of Chickamauga on September 17) began to flood major cities to the rear, especially Atlanta and Augusta. The latter was already a center of Confederate medical care because it had excellent railroad connections and was well away from the Federal armies operating in the South. The influx of the Chickamauga casualties, however, created the need for a new, third Confederate hospital. The Sisters of Mercy went there to nurse, earning the praise of local doctors.[82]

In general nuns had a great reputation among those who operated and/ or worked in Confederate hospitals. Lay Protestant nurse and native of Scotland Kate Cumming admired their quiet patriotism and described them as "perfect nurses." They worked extremely hard without complaining and she tried to model her own Confederate service on their dedication and professionalism. She eventually hoped that her own Episcopal Church would form religious orders akin to the ones she saw performing in Confederate hospitals. As late as 1865 she remarked on one hospital in Mobile that had nuns: "The Sisters of Charity are its Matrons, and we all know what they are in hospitals. And by the way why can we not imitate them in this respect, in these war times? Here one of them is a druggist; another acts part of a steward, and in fact, they take charge of the whole hospital, with the exception of the medical department."[83]

The sisters were Confederate paragons. Cumming hoped that their example would inspire other women in the Confederacy. She felt frustrated that any southern woman who worked in a hospital often had her "honor" questioned, but the sisters' status exempted them from some of the strictures of white womanhood. She was angry at one potential nurse she tried to recruit, a "Methodist," who told her that she would only "go into the hospital if she had in it a brother a surgeon." Cumming commented rhetorically: "I wonder if the Sisters of Charity have brothers, surgeons, in the hospitals where they go? It seems strange that they can do with honor what other Christian women cannot. Well, I [cannot] but pity those people who have such false notions of propriety." Cumming was angry that lay women were not willing to follow the example of these, mostly immigrant, nuns, and risk all for the cause.[84]

The sisters' good work for the Confederacy had a more direct impact on the soldiers they took care of. There are numerous stories from Catholic priests and nuns telling how the sisters changed many hearts and minds on Protestant views of the immigrant Catholic Church.[85] The most remarkable story, however, is that of Private Bill Fletcher, a Texas soldier who was wounded at Chickamauga. Transferred to the Third Georgia Hospital in Augusta, he initially displayed some hostility toward the mostly Irish nurses because he had been warned of the dangers of Catholicism at home in rural Texas. He quickly changed his mind, however, with the care he received from the sisters. In particular he credited them with saving his wounded foot, which doctors had initially wanted to amputate. The Sisters of Mercy intervened and persuaded the surgeon that with proper care and attention they could save the Texan's foot without jeopardizing his life. Fletcher and his foot survived for him to reminisce after the war: "I was in love with the women and the uniform at once, and I have not gotten over it yet." In the postwar period, Fletcher returned to Texas and made a fortune in the lumber business. He never forgot the Irish nuns and in 1897 worked with a Mother House in Galveston to open a hospital to be run by the Sisters of Charity. He himself never converted to Catholicism but he did overcome local opposition from some Protestant preachers to build a Catholic hospital in the city.[86]

These efforts of Irish bishops, priests, and sisters to make Catholicism an integral part of the Confederacy still lacked coordination. The demise of the *Charleston Catholic Miscellany* in late 1861(because of a fire) and the fall of New Orleans in April 1862 to Federal forces meant that there was no single prominent Catholic publication in the Confederate states. That writer of the "Confederate catechism," Bishop Verot of Savannah, sought to remedy the situation. He recruited a young Irish, former Confederate soldier, who had experience in printing and writing, to run a new newspaper in Augusta. Patrick Walsh had emigrated from County Limerick to Charleston with his parents in the early 1850s. He became a printer for a Charleston newspaper and earned enough money to go to Georgetown University in Washington, D.C., but he returned during the secession crisis to volunteer in a Confederate unit. Mustered out after twelve months, Walsh, it seems, did not reenlist for permanent service. As the youngest of three sons serving in the Confederate army, he supposedly received an exemption to look after his sick and decrepit parents who had moved to Augusta, Georgia.[87] Trained as a printer, he found work at the *Augusta Constitutionalist*, a strongly pro-Confederate newspaper, eventually becoming a writer and editor there. He was a prominent parishioner at the new St. Patrick's Church and this factor as well as his newspaper experience led him and a rich Catholic benefactor, Leopold T. Blome, at the behest of Bishop Verot, to open the *Pacificator* in late 1864.[88]

Edited by Walsh, it was an expressly Catholic newspaper. Under its masthead it described itself as a paper "devoted to the interests of the Roman Catholic Church in the Confederacy." Thanks to the vagaries of the war, this Church was "without a representative organ, without means of communication between the Bishops, the Pastors, and the people." The paper was also needed to highlight the Catholic participation in the "energy and activity" in the creation of the "young nation." Finally, the Confederate Catholic Church needed some journal "for the promulgation of [its] religious documents— to furnish Catholic readers with a pure Catholic literature and intelligence from the Catholic Church in other parts of the world." Its title, however, hinted at another motive for this venture. At first glance it might seem that Walsh and his sponsors had become disillusioned with the Confederacy and joined the explicitly anti-Confederate "Peace" movement. Walsh dismissed this opinion quickly by stating: "The separation of the Southern States from the Northern portion of the American Union and their organization of into an independent Confederacy has brought upon us the vengeance of those from whom we separated; and we now find ourselves, not only involved in a bloody struggle to maintain the rights of freemen, which we exercised, but, also, thrown upon our own resources in everything that concerns our existence—our spiritual and moral, as well as out temporal welfare." Thus the "peace" Walsh advocated was one in which the United States officially recognized the Confederacy and called off the war. *The Pacificator* first appeared in October 1864 when the only hope for the Confederate states was peace with recognition. Its last chance was George McClellan, the Democratic candidate for president in 1864. He was officially a "War" Democrat but supported negotiations with Confederate authorities and would seek a truce if elected.[89]

Walsh saw the Catholic Church, with its connections in the North, as a key player in any negotiations for a ceasefire. The front page of his paper contained for a number of weeks a long letter from a "Catholic Divine" entitled "An Address to the People of the United States in Behalf of Peace." Despite its olive-branch title, it was pretty much a harangue against the northern states, and especially the abolitionists. Thanks to northern extremists who controlled the Republican Party, secession and war had occurred because "the North has actually dissolved the Union by the Acts of their Legislatures." Rehashing all the arguments of 1861, Walsh highlighted the northern nullification of the fugitive slave law, the support for John Brown, etc., and how they had driven the South to "[act] merely on the abstract right of secession" and form its own nation. The resulting conflict was one of "defense" for the South once the North "invaded" Virginia. The North had to recognize that any government had to rely on the "consent of the governed" and to force the South back to into the United States would be folly. The newspaper's arguments for peace and Confederate recognition were written for all northerners but particularly Irish Catholics. Irish immigrant Judge Osborne Lochrane of Macon, Georgia, recognized as much when he stated that although he was a Protestant, he welcomed that the paper would cover "the interests of the Irish people." This coverage would help get the paper read in the United States and increase "the change of sentiment . . . spreading like a wave a light over the Northern mind" toward "Peace" and away "from the crimson tide of battle."[90]

The *Pacificator* was definitely targeted at Irish Americans, both in and outside the Confederacy. It carried a lot of Irish news and one Irish American from Augusta gave $100 to send it to Irish and other Catholic soldiers at the front. It particularly highlighted the support for the Confederacy in Ireland and tried to show how anti-Catholic the strongest advocates of the northern cause were. Some of the Catholic press in the North was indeed in favor of immediate peace leading to de facto recognition of the Confederacy, but the *Pacificator* probably had little effect on increasing that opinion. The paper seems to have been exclusively distributed in the Confederacy and, because of Union occupation, just in the parts of the country from Alabama eastward. Despite its pretensions of "international" influence, it remained then a southern paper that sought to increase patriotism and continue hope of success for Confederate Catholics. It carried news of Confederate successes in the Shenandoah Valley and the continued resistance of Wilmington against the Union blockade. It was probably read by soldiers as it published official general military orders only relevant to enlistees. Ultimately, like Bannon's efforts, the *Pacificator* failed to ensure Confederate victory. Walsh and his paper stayed loyal to the end and remained a very public example of Irish loyalty to the Confederacy even as it faced its ultimate destruction.[91]

Bishop Lynch of Charleston decided to do more than just advocate for Confederate recognition and peace in print. He hoped that his connections with the Vatican and other Catholic institutions in Europe might rescue the Confederacy from defeat. Communication with Rome was the first difficulty to overcome. The Union blockade of southern ports made official correspondence very difficult. The Vatican thus appointed Father J. W. Cumming of New York as the contact for southern clergy wishing to send correspondence to Rome and as the conduit for "private" correspondence. Father Cumming included a clipping from a northern newspaper warning him that his letters could be opened and examined by Union officials and any "treasonous" correspondence would not be forwarded.[92] Lynch had needed to stay in touch with Europe because of his desperate need for financial support. In December 1861 a fire in Charleston destroyed his cathedral church, his residence, a 17,000 volume library, a boys' orphanage, a school, and a former seminary as well as damaging the Sisters of Mercy convent. The offices of the new *Charleston Catholic Miscellany* were also destroyed and it ceased publication.[93] The various bombardments of Charleston later in the war increased damage to Catholic churches but also, it seems, Lynch's Confederate ardor. The three remaining churches south of Calhoun Street were all hit by shells and closed by the diocese. Only St. Patrick's further up the peninsula, just at the limit of the range of the Union guns, remained open for services.[94] Along with the infrastructural needs of his congregants, Lynch also had to deal with physical and financial needs of his clergy, religious, and laity. Lynch was also called upon by laity to take care of their monies as the war moved them from place to place. The state of South Carolina too appointed him to a board to help destitute families of Confederate servicemen.[95] He paid particular attention to Catholic soldiers. As early as January 1861 he visited an Irish company stationed as part of the Confederate forces besieging Fort Sumter at Castle Pinckney in Charleston Harbor. There, Lynch "celebrated Mass and preached a sermon suitable to the occasion," undoubtedly something to steel these defenders of the republic of South Carolina. Beyond the collective Lynch also aided individual Irish soldiers, never tiring in his support for the boys in the army.[96]

The extra work and the hardships inflicted by war made Lynch more committed to the Confederacy than he had been in April 1861. He, for example, refused to grow cotton on his diocesan land, instead insisting on foodstuffs only to help the war effort. Of course with a large investment in slaves he and his diocese had a large financial interest in the survival of the Confederacy. Along with the large correspondence that he received from priests and lay Catholics, his family and agents, especially his brother John, also kept him informed of the production on his land around the mid-sections of South Carolina. Lynch saw himself as a good Confederate paternalistic slaveholder and was interested in the lives and conduct of his slaves. He was also, however, willing to sell slaves through the Irish American slave trader Thomas Ryan and others, both those he owned personally and those bequeathed to him from pious Catholics. In 1862, for example, his brother wrote him to tell of a dilemma he had with one of their overseers and "John's family," a group of slaves working on one of the Lynch properties. Apparently, John's son was "idling" and the overseer "gave him a strapping." The young man's mother, however, intervened in the punishment and struck the overseer with a hoe telling him that he "was not put there to whip them." This defiance by this woman infuriated the overseer and he wanted to give her "a whipping," but "wanted to check with him [i.e., Lynch] first." John Lynch reminded the overseer that if the Patrick "intended selling her, a whipping such as she would be obliged to receive, would not increase her value." The overseer insisted then that the woman be sold because if she was left unpunished his ability "to correct any of them ['the young negroes'] the mothers will take this as a precedent. The bishop did apparently sell the woman, but also, keeping with his belief in not breaking up slave families, with all of her children. Of course after the sale it is unknown what happened to this slave family.[97]

Lynch believed in "Christian" slave ownership and that this type of proprietorship was a key element of Confederate identity. He thought that slaves should be Christians, Catholics specifically, and that slave families should not be broken up. As the Confederacy's prospects darkened in late 1863, he did not see slavery as the issue causing God to turn against the South.[98] He trusted that God was still on their side. In a statement to his flock in late November 1863 he called for "a novena" (nine consecutive days of prayer and special devotion), a special Mass "Pro Pace," and the praying of the "Litany of Loreto" for "Peace." By peace he, like Walsh, meant Confederate victory: "While our rulers and our armies in their respective spheres are making every effort and shrinking from no sacrifice to bring this struggle to a happy termination, it is fitting beloved brethren, that in the spirit of religion we should have recourse to Him in whose power are all things; and there is none that can resist His Majesty." Along with prayer and devotion, Lynch, as had many other southern preachers, called on Confederates to turn away from their sinful ways. These sins specifically were "the pernicious effects of camp life on habits, morals, and character" along with, on the home front, "greed, extortion, and injustice."[99]

Unlike many other Confederate clerics, Lynch could not bring himself to blame southern slaveholders' failure to live up to the responsibility of being Christian slaveholders for Confederate defeats. Lynch did not agree with the likes of Baptist preacher Isaac Taylor Tichman, who told the General Assembly of Alabama that military defeats happened because: "We have failed to discharge our duties to our slaves."[100] That was a criticism he did not adhere to in his explanations of the Confederacy's increasingly precarious position.

Still confident in the righteousness of the cause, Lynch believed that he personally needed to do something extraordinary to ensure Confederate survival. His status as a Confederate patriot and a Catholic bishop could perhaps save the day. Despite the sectional tensions and blockade, southern Catholics still had connections both in the North and in Europe, and, as early as 1862, some clergy believed that their Church could exploit these to end the war. Bishop Verot had hoped that a "committee of bishops going to Washington under a flag of truce might perhaps induce Lincoln and his cabinet from the ruinous course which they pursue." Bishop Martin Spalding wrote a "Dissertation" on the Civil War, which he had sent to inform Rome of the situation in the United States in 1863. Written in Italian, Spalding's piece was put in Pope Pius IX's hands and later published anonymously as from "a Kentucky priest" in the Vatican newspaper, L'Osservatore Romano. Spalding argued that the Catholic Church had to call for an end to the war. He outlined its causes, laying the blame squarely on the Lincoln administration and abolitionists who "hate the Catholic religion with an almost Satanic hate." Including a strong attack on emancipation and how this would destroy the "negro," the "Dissertation" can be easily read as Confederate propaganda.[101]

The importance of this tract can be seen in that pro-Union and Republican sympathizer Archbishop Purcell of Cincinnati, for example, did receive letters from the Vatican encouraging him to seek an end to the conflict, something that made him very nervous about Rome's views of the Union cause. The choice of Spalding, who initially was not front runner, in 1864 to become the new Archbishop of Baltimore, the symbolic head of the Church in America, was also telling. His diatribe against the Republicans and emancipation had not hindered his promotion chances.[102]

Some in the Confederate state department therefore came to agree with the view that the Catholic Church could perhaps change the Confederacy's fortunes. As a result, in February 1864 the department approached Bishop Lynch of Charleston, as the leading Catholic Confederate, with a request to go to Rome to represent their cause to Pope Pius IX. They hoped that papal recognition of the Confederacy might encourage other Catholic countries, especially France, to follow the pope's lead. Many Confederates had come to believe that Emperor Napoleon III of France wanted to support the Confederacy but was reluctant to do so without Great Britain. Perhaps Vatican approval would help move Napoleon. On March 3 Lynch replied to Secretary of State Benjamin: "The proposition which you made to me, that I should go to Rome as the Commissioner of the Confederate States to the Holy See, has demanded my most serious consideration. After mature reflection, I believe it my duty to accede to the desire of the Government, and to accept the position." His duty as a Confederate had trumped his "personal feelings" to stay in charge of his diocese. He did, however, he said, need three weeks "to arrange my ecclesiastical and personal affairs in view of an absence which may possibly be very protracted." Once his affairs had been put in order, he would go to Richmond to arrange his trip through the blockade and, while there, he would also "do myself the honor of paying my respects in person."[103] It took Lynch a little longer than three weeks to get organized, as he needed a secretary "who could write in Italian, and," in light of the ultimate goal, "French well." He duly received his commission from Jefferson Davis and left Richmond for Wilmington on April 6. He eventually got out of Wilmington on the 10th on board a blockade runner to Bermuda. From there he completed his journey to Europe.[104]

In Europe, having been granted an audience, Lynch first paid a visit to Emperor Napoleon before going to Rome. When he met Pius IX he made it plain that he was there to achieve recognition for the Confederacy.[105] Pius told the Irish Confederate that it was "clear that you are two nations" and offered to be a mediator in the conflict. This admission in a private audience, however, was not an official recognition, and Church officials later assured the United States ambassador in Rome that the Vatican had not done so.[106] Lynch realized this too and also became aware that a major sticking point in his negotiations for recognition was slavery. Pius had told him that "something must be done . . . to [bring about] a gradual preparation for their freedom at a future opportune time."[107]

This statement brought home to Lynch that he had to deal openly with the slavery issue. To try to change European opinion he wrote a rather lengthy pamphlet defending slavery and had it published in Italian, French, and German. He hoped it would persuade continental Europeans that slavery in the Confederacy was benign. Indeed, Lynch outlined that the institution was necessary to the benefit of blacks and whites alike. In his essay, "A Few Words on the Domestic Slavery in the Confederate States of America," Lynch did not defend slavery on religious or biblical grounds, but specifically on "social scientific" ones. The bishop saw himself as an enlightened man and even something of a scientist. His pamphlet gave a very negative view of black culture. Blacks could not take care of themselves, he wrote. They were lazy, promiscuous, and without firm control, a potential danger to themselves and others. "The negroes are, as a race, very prone to excesses, and unless restrained, plunge madly on the lowest depths of licentiousness." They had "very little regard for the sanctity of marriage." Despite his apparent belief in baptism for enslaved people, "the character of the negro race," Lynch believed, found it tough to obey "the strict requirements of Christian morality." The southern black "preserves much of his original character suited to the tropics, and not suited to other regions which demand from man a more active enduring and intelligent industry." Thus the "negro" needed to be "under a special authority."[108] Lynch's defense appeared in late 1864 in Italy and early 1865 in France and the German states, and he toured to promote it. It seems, though, to have had little effect in changing opinions. After Abraham Lincoln's reelection in November 1864 and his continuation of the total war policy initiated by his star Generals Grant and Sherman, Confederate defeat was inevitable. Lynch was fighting a lost cause.[109]

Nonetheless, his time in Europe reinforced his image as the most prominent Confederate Catholic. He was a role model of Confederate patriotism and improved the image of Irish Confederates. The war experience seemed to entrench his support for the cause to the point of risking life and limb to run the tight Federal blockade highlighting the case that as the actual and perceived harshness of Union war policy increased, so too could feelings of Confederate nationalism.[110] Unlike most Irish Confederate civilians, Lynch was a classic example of this phenomenon. He had become more unbridled in his defense of the Confederacy as the war progressed. His actions and rhetoric also indicated that racial slavery remained at the core of a lot of Confederate patriotism.[111]

The efforts of leading Irish Catholics did play a critical role in giving support to Irish troops, both in a spiritual and ideological sense, at the beginning of the war and as it progressed. Irish soldiers could fight with the confidence that their Confederate cause was a just and Christian one. Indeed, as with the Confederacy as a whole, religious inspiration remained the strongest element of their patriotism. More importantly though, for their own integration into the South, the very public Catholic actions and speeches helped to counter negative views of their religion and their efforts for the Confederacy. To the end, Confederate officials still believed that Irish Catholic soldiers under the influence of a patriotic priest could be good Confederates. The reality was, however, that most Irish civilians and many Irish soldiers did not retain their belief in the Confederacy or its potential for success, as Lynch, Bannon, and Walsh did. Also, their overtly Catholic efforts, while valuable in terms of displays of Irish loyalty, were all for naught, as the Confederacy lost the Civil War and disappeared.

The Church's strong support for the war would, however, help the Irish and other white southerners remember the conflict in a Confederate way. Enthusiastic secessionist chaplain Peter Whelan, for example, had become less Confederate as the conflict progressed and he witnessed some of its worst horrors. At war's end, the Angel of Andersonville to the Union soldiers who had been captured while conquering the South, spent the rest of his life pastoring to the mostly Irish congregation of St. Patrick's Church on the west side of Savannah. His death in 1871, however, transformed him back into the unambiguous Confederate patriot he had been in 1861. His funeral was apparently the largest seen in the city's history, with over "eighty-six carriages and buggies" making their way with the cortege to the Catholic cemetery. "A wreath of laurel, emblematic of his devotion to the South," adorned his coffin, and a large number of Confederate veterans, led by his former commander Colonel Olmstead, escorted his coffin.[112] Whelan was no longer just an Irish priest who had served with the Confederate army, whose views of war had changed over time, and who had lost most of his Confederate ardor. He had now become a major symbol of the former

Confederacy, the "Lost Cause" as it had been coined, a cause whose soldiers had fought loyally and valiantly until the bitter end. This cause, lost though it was, was something the Irish would understand and come to embrace. In the process, they could create an opportunity to bury the ambiguities of their experience and, instead, enshrine their "glorious" role in it.

CHAPTER 6

Another "Lost Cause"

The Irish after the Confederacy

In the commemoration of the Confederacy after the Civil War, the Irish in the South rediscovered a Confederate spirit they had lost during the conflict. After the surrender of the major Confederate armies in April and May 1865, all, including the most patriotic of them, accepted defeat and a return to the United States. The decision made by prominent Confederates such as Judah Benjamin, who chose foreign exile rather than face the reality of "Yankee rule," was not one for the Irish.[1] But would they accept the "reconstruction" that came with defeat? Initially they did, especially the lenient version implemented by Abraham Lincoln's successor, Andrew Johnson. A few were willing to give Radical Reconstruction a chance. Ultimately though, the Irish became implacable opponents of the Radicals and efforts to integrate African Americans into southern politics. In this opposition and through active participation in the "Lost Cause," the Irish helped seal their position as full members of the "Solid South." Familiar with the lost cause of Ireland's independence, they quickly learned the rituals of the new one developing in the former Confederacy. By embracing this important "civil religion" of the New South, the Irish could claim to be just as much "true southerners" as native white citizens. In the long run then, for the Irish Confederates and their descendants, their commemoration of the war was more important than their actual participation in it.

In May 1865, Confederate "ambassador" Patrick Lynch suddenly found himself a citizen without a country. Stationed in Rome when his diocesan seat fell to Union forces, he learned of the Confederacy's collapse there. With his country now defunct, and his task for its recognition moot, he believed he could just return to the United States to set about rebuilding his diocese. Proportionally, in terms of physical destruction, it was the worst hit diocese in the Confederacy. He knew he faced a desperate situation when he got home, because he even had to replace his "episcopal wardrobe, which General Sherman [had] kindly reduced to ashes." In one letter to a Catholic group in Vienna, Austria, he listed his tragic circumstances: "The diocese of Charleston is now truly desolate. During the cruel civil war . . . I have seen almost everything that my two predecessors had accomplished or that I had undertaken gradually perish." Overall, Lynch estimated the cost of the war to his diocese at $252,000, but, with prewar debts added in, he reckoned it was $316,500 in the red.[2]

The reality was, however, because of his prominence as the South's most public Irish Confederate, he would not be allowed to just pick up with American citizenship where he had left off in 1860. Although an official Confederate commissioner, Lynch did not feel he could be classified as "among the 'heads of Secession,'" those most likely to face the scrutiny of the victorious northerners. He had hoped that the lobbying of Archbishop Spalding, along with President Andrew Johnson's general amnesty of May 29, 1865, would get him back to the United States with no restrictions. He was mistaken. The Johnson administration denied him the general amnesty and stated that he had to make a "Special Application." In this application to Secretary of State Seward, Lynch seriously downplayed his role in the "rebellion," although he never used the word. He began by saying, in a very disingenuous manner, that he had been privately opposed to secession but that "standing aloof from politics . . . I did not feel called on to judge these political questions. . . . In the pulpit, I have always scrupulously avoided all political questions." He seemed to have forgotten his blessing of the Irish Volunteers and their Confederate service. After South Carolina seceded, he had done everything he could to stop the war and, once it began, "to mitigate its evils." He neglected to mention, however, his stout public defense of secession to Archbishop Hughes in 1861, the strongly pro-Confederate articles published in his diocesan newspaper, and the Te Deum performed in his cathedral on the fall of Fort Sumter. The very public debate with Hughes was severely embarrassing to him and something that in 1865 he did not attempt to justify. To aid Archbishop Spalding's efforts, Lynch wrote to tell him that this correspondence with Hughes had been "a *private letter*" and that "I was completely surprised at finding the letter published entire in the northern papers under my name. Had I been consulted I would not have consented. I never wrote politics in the Miscellany except against the Know Nothings."[3]

To counter any continued Federal qualms about his role in the Confederacy, he then listed his and his sisters' work among Union prisoners and wounded. "As opportunity arose I endeavored to do the same in Salisbury [North Carolina] and Richmond." Lynch named some Union officers who could testify to his good work. Halfway into the letter Lynch then dealt with "the elephant in the room": his diplomatic service of behalf of the Confederacy. According to Lynch his mission to the Vatican was purely one of peace. He just wished to end the carnage. "In common with many I could not help entertaining the [idea] that a friendly disinterested voice from abroad, spoken on some fitting occasion during the war, might be listened to by both parties, as it counseled peace and reconciliation." The mission apparently had nothing to do with recognition of the Confederacy. Lynch made no apology or mea culpa. He did conclude, however, with a recognition of the new reality he would face in the re-United States: "In the discharge of [ecclesiastical duties] I will feel bound in conscience to accept in good faith, the altered social state of the country, and to act in a manner . . . to promote the peace and good order of the community in which I labour."[4] Efforts on his behalf by northern clergy helped him eventually receive a pardon. He took the Oath of Allegiance in Paris and returned to Charleston to try to rebuild his diocese.[5] He was willing to accept the Federal victory and the reconstruction of the Union. Indeed, he offered "to promote the peace and good order" of South Carolina.[6]

More so than Lynch, Irish soldiers accepted defeat. Those who had deserted or, like Dominick Spellman, sought to take the oath of allegiance even before the various Confederate surrenders, had already done so. Those who had stayed (and survived) to the end took the oath willingly in the late spring and early summer of 1865. Hugh Gwynn, who served as an adjutant in the 23rd Tennessee Infantry, for example, started describing himself as a "loyal citizen" and said that he could "call for Andy Johnson [President Andrew Johnson] as lustily as any person."[7] Even die-hard Confederates such as A. G. Magrath sought reconciliation. Imprisoned at the end of the war near Savannah, he sought desperately for his release. He wrote Bishop Lynch looking for any aid that northern Irish Americans might provide to intercede with the new president in Washington for his release.[8] Under the General Amnesty issued in May 1865, Magrath, as a former Federal official and a leading Confederate, had to make the personal appeal to the president for pardon. In his fourteen-page letter directly to Johnson, he outlined his prewar career, disingenuously declaring that he had not been involved in politics "whatsoever," apart from 1850, when he opposed "the effort then made, for the secession of the state." In 1860, he had merely been an attorney and Federal judge carrying out his legal duties. He was, of course, interested in the presidential election and had come to the conclusion that "W[illiam Henry] Seward was right in his opinion that an irrepressible conflict was impending between capital and labor; or as it was considered by me, between the modes of labor in the states where negroes were held in servitude and such as prevailed where free labor only was known." Thus, he felt that South Carolina had a case in seceding and that there was no legal opinion countering it at the time. He believed that he had not done anything illegal or contrary to this oath to the Constitution.

Despite admitting the errors of his opinion, he still faced the awkward facts of his distinguished Confederate service. Again, skirting some of the facts, he justified his actions. He resigned from the bench before secession because he wanted to give President Lincoln plenty of time to find a replacement. How this Federal replacement was supposed to function in the "Republic of South Carolina," Magrath did not explain. He had been a Confederate judge, because he believed in "stability" and became governor reluctantly when the state legislature chose him. While governor he was not interested in military affairs, a complete lie, and concentrated on protecting civilians in a destitute state. He only pointed to mitigating circumstances, such as intervening against the placement of Federal prisoners of war in harm's way in the bombardment of Charleston and advocating the recognition of the prisoner of war rights of "Negro soldiers." He concluded that whatever the debates had been about secession and slavery, these questions were now "settled" by the Federal victory and all he wanted was to be released and allowed to display again his loyalty to the United States.[9] President Johnson was skeptical of Magrath's contrition. Although he was, by early 1866, out of prison and back home in Charleston, his full pardon was still not forthcoming. Magrath still wanted it though. He did not desire to remain a Confederate martyr. His appeal for amnesty was not just to be released from prison, but to become a United States citizen again. He again wrote to Johnson in 1866 pleading for a restoration of his political rights and had Benjamin Perry, the man Johnson had appointed provisional governor of South Carolina, write on his behalf.

Magrath was certainly a reconciliation role model for his former Confederate constituents, native and Irish alike. The Irish of Charleston had, however, already embraced Johnson's new order in the former Confederacy. It was some of these early oath-takers, as well as a large number of natives, who signed a petition, reaching over one thousand signatures, on Magrath's behalf. McCabes, O'Briens, and Bannons mingled with Balls, Pringles, and Pinckneys on the appeal. It seemed to work, and Magrath received his full and free pardon in January 1867.[10]

For other prominent Irish Confederates there was less grief in regaining citizenship. One of Magrath's Irish American appointees to a clerkship in the Confederate courts in South Carolina, John J. Maher of Barnwell, swore that he had only been an attorney and that he was "a poor man—never owned a slave—has no property except an office lot, the office itself having been destroyed by Federal troops in February last [1865]." All he wanted was a pardon to "practice his profession" and support his wife and four young children. He swore to be a "loyal and law-abiding citizen" of the United States and to "abide in and support all laws and proclamations which have been made in the existing rebellion with reference to the emancipation of slaves. So help me God." Governor Perry endorsed Maher's application and he received his pardon in about a month. Maher's neighbor, merchant J. J. Ryan, also sought a pardon because he had acted as a "receiver" for the Confederacy, collecting bills payable, etc., for the government. He obtained his pardon the same day he applied, even though he had owned more than twenty slaves in 1860.[11] Merchant James McCloskey of New Orleans was not a slaveholder but he had been an immediate secessionist at the Louisiana secession convention. He too received a quick pardon.[12]

Maher and McCloskey (and Ryan too, as he had not made known his substantial slaveholding, merely his merchandising), fit well into President Johnson's vision for reconstruction in the South, solid middle class white men who were not slaveholders. The United States government was more forgiving of poor folk than those who were rich. Those who owned property worth more than $20,000 had to apply for presidential pardon. Here, though, too, Johnson began to issue pardons with relative abandon, and wealthy Irishmen who sought them benefited. Thomas Ryan of Ryan's slave mart had to apply for one under this property provision. He was age sixty-five and had only "engaged in agricultural pursuits . . . in the interior of the state throughout the War."[13] He also received a pardon the same day of his application. Major Louisiana planter and secession ordinance signer Edward Sparrow of Louisiana had to wait five months but also earned his without too much bother.[14]

General Joseph Finegan had more explaining to do as he had not only served conspicuously in the Confederate army, but he had also been a secessionist leader in Florida. He took Magrath's tack, explaining that at the time he believed secession to be legal and constitutional, and also that he had been kind to Federal prisoners during the war. He stated that all he wanted was a chance to make money since he had lost all of his slaves and his plantation at Fernandina on Amelia Island had been confiscated. He was "sincerely desirous of living quietly and peaceably as a loyal citizen of the United States" and securing a living for his family. He displayed his new loyalty through applying for an amnesty in early July 1865 and was restored to full rights in April 1866.[15]

Across the South then the Irish accepted the demise of the Confederacy with ease. This did not mean, however, that they had been closet unionists throughout the war. Very few were. Under the Southern Claims Commission established in 1871, loyal southern Unionists could apply for compensation for any losses incurred at the hands of Federal forces. Only minuscule numbers of Irish applied. In Savannah, for example, of the 225 applications for compensation, only four came from Irish people, and none of the four received any money.[16] In general though it was very tough to make a successful claim. Applicants had to answer over thirty questions to ascertain if they had established any Confederate affiliation or given any support to the Confederacy. In Natchez, for example, Catherine Culhane applied for funds for a horse taken by occupying Union forces even though she had three sons in Confederate service. She did admit that her sons had served and claimed that they had joined up "against her will." Her only witness was an Irish police officer who himself had served in the Confederate army from 1861 through the siege of Vicksburg. Her claim for $250 was turned down because "no loyal acts" had been "shown." There was no evidence, the commission believed, that she had ever, publicly or privately, committed any overt act of loyalty to the United States during the conflict.[17] Patrick McNamara of New Orleans had worked with General Butler as soon as Federal forces occupied the city and claimed to have prevented his stepson from joining the Confederate army, even facing down one hard Confederate recruiter, "Mick O'Connor" (probably of the Irish Brigade, Company F, 6th Louisiana). He had, however, attended a Confederate rally early in the war and thus was denied compensation for damage to his property in the Crescent City.[18]

There were a few genuine cases of active Irish Unionism such as Michael Lynch of Atlanta. He was an avowed Unionist and a bookseller who continued to sell northern newspapers in the summer of 1861. The Confederate authorities eventually tried to arrest him after he had collaborated with Sherman's army during the occupation of the city in the fall of 1864 (after Sherman and his army had left for their "march to the sea"). He hid in various places, eventually in a secret part of his own house. As a "loyal U.S. citizen" of the South who was owed money from the Federal government, he applied for compensation. He eventually received it in 1877 for supplies he had provided to the Federal forces.[19] Similarly, Michael McNamara, who rented a small farm outside of Charleston, claimed to have been a Union man through the war. Although he had served in an Irish militia unit up to April 1861, he swore that he had resigned because he did not want to take the Confederate oath. A few times he was almost conscripted but had a medical disqualification and good relationship with the provost marshal in Charleston and so never served in the "rebel army." He also told of helping Federal prisoners by giving them water at the train depot in Charleston, but also that he obtained three passes for Union soldiers who had escaped from the Confederate prison at the Race Course, very near to his farm. He was able to get there because he sometimes used drovers when he bought cattle in the interior of the state. The soldiers, apparently, used the passes to go to Savannah by rail in an attempt to connect with the Federal forces on the Sea Islands near there. Having provided his Unionist bona fides, he claimed compensation for food and crops taken from him without payment by occupying Federal forces after the city fell in February 1865. The commission believed him, despite his initial service in the militia for five months after South Carolina's secession, and, in 1875, paid him $599.[20]

McNamara's deposition hints at an Irish Unionist fifth column in Charleston akin to a very active one that had existed in Atlanta. He first claimed that most of his militia company resigned in April 1861 and voted to disband because, they, like he, believed that it "was the duty of foreigners to sympathize with the Union because the government gives them protection and makes free men of them, which they are not at home." Later, however, he claimed he could "not remember" why the Montgomery Guards had "disbanded." There are some signs of Irish dissent in the city as the war came close to Charleston. One Federal prisoner incarcerated in the Charleston city jail in the spring of 1862 told of Confederate prisoners, some of whom were Irish, that were "bitterly opposed to the Confederate government." Their prison status for indiscipline or absence without leave may have colored their opinions, but other "foreigners" he met in the city he thought were "governed by self interest entirely. There is no feeling with them: North and South are alike to them and would be far from trusting them were I a rebel officer."[21] These men were not of the same opinion as William Ryan and his Irish Volunteers. Indeed, one pro-Union Irishman in Charleston, who was an official supporter of McNamara's petition to the Claims Commission, admitted that, despite a number of Irish men having signed up to join the Union army after the fall of the city in 1865, the Unionists in Charleston during the secession and Confederate period one could "count on the fingers of one hand."[22] Many Irish may have been indifferent to the Confederacy, but it did not necessarily make them patriotic Unionists and fifth columnists.

There were a few Irish in the postwar South who were more than just accepting of northern victory. Some wanted, as the Radicals did, to reconstruct the former Confederacy in a serious way. One E. A. Dowling came to Richmond, Virginia, to work with the Federal authorities there. His work for the new Unionist administration drew the ire of the local Ku Klux Klan, who warned this "Irish carpetbagger" to leave the city or face their wrath.[23] One who did face their actual wrath was Charles Dennis O'Keefe, who moved to Fort Mills, South Carolina, in 1869 to join his uncle. This uncle had lived in the state since the 1850s and had been elected a local magistrate on the Republican ticket. O'Keefe took up positions as a state tax collector and as a Federal census marshal, but he also became the president and secretary of the local Union League, which had 196 members, only 4 of whom, including O'Keefe, were white. It was this political activity with African Americans that brought him to the local Klan's attention. Indeed, he believed that, before his political activism in the League, "no person, for a stranger, was better liked or admired as I was." As a result of his work with African Americans, however, he was assaulted at the local railroad station and barely escaped with life. His uncle, as the local magistrate, bound O'Keefe's assailants to the peace. The Klan, according to O'Keefe, then threatened to kill him and he was thus afraid to return to his uncle's home. He instead took to the woods of York County, where he wandered around with others also hiding from the terrorist group. He eventually found the rail line to Charlotte and walked to that town for shelter, checking into a local hotel. Meeting a Republican friend, O'Keefe was told that he could be killed "as easily" there as across the state line. So nervous was he that he checked out of the hotel and erased his name from the register. He left for New York and never returned to the South.[24] The message was clear to any Irish "carpetbaggers" seeking to help the freedpeople: stay away.

What of long-term Irish residents of the South? Along with O'Keefe's uncle in York County, South Carolina, there were other Irish southerners who joined the Radical cause. Even though he had supported the Confederacy with his foundry making weapons for the army, Thomas (T. J.) Coghlan of Sumter, South Carolina, embraced the realities of emancipation and citizenship for blacks and became an early leader of the nascent Republican Party. A prominent Irish American Catholic and a former slaveholder, he was elected sheriff of Sumter County on the votes of freedmen. The Irish-born G. W. Reardon worked with Coghlan as clerk of court. Both men were active in getting out the Republican vote for all elections.[25]

The most famous Irish Republican in the state, and perhaps the whole South, however, was P. J. Coogan of Charleston. Coogan had been a merchant in the city before the war who ignored the examples of Magrath, Lynch, and the Irish Volunteers etc., and remained a Unionist. His opposition to the Confederacy became so prominent that to avoid certain arrest he abandoned the city in 1864, escaping to the Bahamas. He returned after the war and his foresightedness on the folly of the Confederacy got him elected, undoubtedly with some Irish votes, to the 1865 constitutional convention. There were rumors that he had been elected with the support of former secessionists, which may have been true because of his support in the Irish community. Some of the same people who had voted for A. G. Magrath in 1860 voted for Coogan too. He quickly quashed any speculation of Confederate sympathies and earned a certain notoriety among whites in being the only member of the South Carolina legislature, which he was also elected to, to endorse the civil rights provisions of the Radical-proposed Fourteenth Amendment to the U.S. Constitution granting citizenship to the African Americans and "equal protection of the laws" to all those citizens. He would later be elected assessor of the city of Charleston.[26]

This support for African American rights could hurt Coogan's political career, but he had another thing going for him in his appeal to Irish voters. He was active in the Fenian Brotherhood, a movement dedicated to the violent overthrow of British rule in Ireland. Initially, there was some resentment against Fenianism in the South amongst former Irish Confederates, because of the predominance of U.S. Army veterans in the movement. But once Fenian organizers allowed potential southern Fenians to name units, or circles as they were called, in honor of southern Irish heroes such as John Mitchel and Pat Cleburne, many came around to the group.[27] The Irish cause had thus become a way for Irish Confederate and Union veterans to reunite rather than divide.

The classic public gesture of this reconciliation for Ireland occurred in New Orleans. At an initial meeting in November 1865, Fenian leaders had condemned Britain for its support of the Confederacy through its construction of the CSS *Alabama*, but at a later meeting in December they made sure to have former Confederate colonels James Nelligan of the 1st Louisiana and Joseph Hanlon of the "Irish Sixth," attend, both of whom had been appointed vice presidents of the Brotherhood in the city. Also present, however, was Hugh Kennedy, publisher of the *True Delta* and good friend of the late John Maginnis (who had died in 1863), and the Federally appointed mayor of the city in 1864, along with his police chief, Irishman John Burke.

Burke's efficient administration of the city had allowed Union forces to transfer men out of the city for combat duty in 1864. They also were appointed vice presidents and sat beside the former Confederate Irish officers at the meeting. The United States and Irish flags were also prominently displayed.[28] It seemed that Irish issues, which had been used to encourage Irish southerners to become Confederates, were now useful in reconciling them with the United States.

John Mitchel's release from Federal incarceration was also important. After the fall of Richmond in April 1865, the Irish and Confederate patriot had moved to New York, where he again became a journalist, working on this occasion for the *Daily News*. Unlike many of his Confederate compatriots, he was not so accepting of defeat and continued to be a major public critic of Federal policy in the former Confederacy. As a result, the government arrested him in June and put him in prison at Fortress Monroe in Virginia. He claimed that he was "the only person who has ever been a prisoner-of-state to the British and American Government one after the other." As a result, he continued, "I despise the civilization of the nineteenth century, and its two highest expressions and hopes."[29] He was also imprisoned with two other notorious Confederates at Monroe, Jefferson Davis and the former Confederate secretary of state, Clement Clay (who was a suspect in the Lincoln assassination). While in the damp and dank prison cell, Mitchel became ill, contracting TB, from which he would survive, but never fully recover. His state of health and imprisonment, when other leading Confederates, such as Robert E. Lee, remained free, became a serious issue for Irish Americans. Fenian sympathizer and prominent New York politician Richard O'Gorman organized a petition for his release, and it was a Fenian organizer, Bernard Doran Killian, from St. Louis, with strong connections to the Johnson administration, who eventually secured this outcome in October. On leaving the prison Mitchel got a chance to speak to his fellow prisoners (and bring information to their loved ones) and he reportedly wrote that "the thieves have bound the good men." Thus, with Mitchel free, thanks in large part to the Fenians, prominent former Confederates, such as Dick Dowling of Houston, could join the Fenian movement without any qualms and work alongside their former enemies in the Union army to prepare for a military confrontation with Great Britain.[30]

The disastrous Fenian "invasions" of Canada and the abortive rebellion in Ireland soon dampened Fenian enthusiasm in the South. The fact that the new Radical administration of former Union supreme commander U. S. Grant, which had replaced the Johnson administration in March 1869, began to cooperate with the British government in cracking down on Fenian activities in the United States, seriously hindered Republican appeals to the Irish in the South. When Irish American but Radical supporter General Phil Sheridan embraced this crackdown in New Orleans, it turned even more Irish away from the new administration and its reconstruction policies.[31]

The anti-Radical press in the South had already warned Irish voters that the Republicans would let them down on Irish issues and now had been proven correct. These "Conservatives," as they often called themselves, made a play for Irish votes, pointing out that Radical Republicans' treatment of the former Confederate States, through both Congress and the army, was similar to Britain's treatment of Ireland. The Radical governor of Louisiana they described as "Oliver Cromwell," and the trials of those accused of Klan activities as facing packed juries like "Daniel O'Connell" had faced in Ireland.[32] Former Confederate senator James Chesnut of South Carolina, explained that the growth of the Ku Klux Klan as what "naturally arise[s] under all despotic governments." He explicitly used Ireland as an historical example of secret societies forming against externally imposed governments. Conservative opponents of the Radicals also used John Mitchel's death in 1875 at home in Ireland as an occasion to celebrate the connections between defeated Ireland the defeated South. In Richmond the Conservative governor James Kemper, a former Confederate general, attended the commemoration of the Irish and Confederate patriot's death along with the former secessionist governor, Henry S. Wise. They undoubtedly saw the Mitchel as a Confederate patriot, but would have been aware of the numerous Irish voters and societies also at the memorial.[33]

More than these appeals to Irish struggles, it was claims of race and Confederate heritage that helped retain any wavering Irish tempted by the Republicans. Conservative newspapers praised Irish immigrants and pointed out that the Radicals were concerned only with the welfare of the freedpeople. They were also keen to highlight the comparisons many northern Radicals had made between slavery and the Catholic Church during the war.[34] Those, like Denis O'Keefe, who ignored these appeals to racial solidarity could be intimidated into keeping quiet or leaving. In New Orleans, for example, even moderates like former Irish police chief John Burke could face the violence of the mob. He was attacked while observing the "riot" of July 1866 when the city police, now filled with many ex-Confederate soldiers, attacked the new state constitutional convention meeting in the city attempting to extend voting rights to blacks. Irish delegate J. D. O'Connell had tried to calm matters before the conflict when he recognized some of the police surrounding the convention hall and negotiated with them for a peaceful solution. In the process, they guaranteed everyone's safety if admitted into the convention hall, which O'Connell accepted. But, upon entering, breaking the promise they had given, the policemen began firing indiscriminately. Those not killed or wounded were arrested and hauled before an anti-Reconstruction magistrate.[35] Eight years later some Irishmen serving in the "Metropolitan" police, the pro-Reconstruction force founded by Republicans to uphold the rule of law in New Orleans, were killed in the so-called "Battle of Liberty Place" when an armed anti-Reconstruction militia attempted to take over the city. In the rural Catahoula Parish in north Louisiana, Irish immigrant and former Confederate cavalry officer James Forsythe was almost assassinated for supporting the Republicans and for promoting black voters.[36]

The reality was, though, that men sympathetic to Radical Reconstruction such as O'Connell, O'Keefe, and Coogan, were a distinct minority among the Irish in the South. Although most Irish had accepted the restoration of the Union under President Johnson's plan, they eventually rejected Radical Reconstruction. Even where they accepted Radical rule as a fait accompli, such as in South Carolina, where some Irish supported Coogan as well as a German political machine in the city that cooperated with the Radical state government in Columbia, they too, eventually turned against links of any kind and became "straight-out" opponents of the Radicals.[37]

The crux issue was political rights for African Americans. Irish people in the South resented the power flexed by freedpeople seeking their full rights as American citizens. The Memphis police force, which was predominantly Irish, were at the center of the infamous riot there in early May 1866 when a fight between them and some black soldiers led to an all-out attack on the black community and the burning of a black school.[38] Some Radicals blamed the Irish, among others, for the riot in New Orleans too, describing the police force behind it as "the scum of every nation." (One of the wounded police officers in the affray was indeed Irish.) The racial tone for the policemen who attacked the convention had been set by political leaders such as Hugh Kennedy and John Sullivan. Even though he was the Unionist mayor, Kennedy would have no truck with African Americans, refusing to support their right to political participation. Sullivan, like Kennedy, was another Irishman willing to accept the demise of the Confederacy, but who described any proposals for black suffrage as "nigger resolutions." The Irish were not necessarily the instigators of political opposition to black rights (former planter and Unionist governor J. Madison

Wells had appointed Kennedy mayor of New Orleans), but many were eager participants.[39]

Some Irish endorsed any calumny against Radical Reconstruction. Bishop Patrick Lynch had been contrite at the end of the war but he disliked Radical Reconstruction immensely. As a former slaveholder, he resented having to negotiate through the Freedmen's Bureau with former slaves on his property. He also feared the influx of rural freedmen to Charleston, recommending instead that they be quarantined on Folly Island, where they could be taught skills appropriate to their station, that is, laboring.[40] Even with black suffrage well-established and racial democracy a fact in the state, he referred to South Carolina's situation in a letter to European donors as comparable to the Prussian treatment of the French in the Franco-Prussian War. He wrote: "But the South is still in the condition of a conquered province." South Carolina in his view "resemble[d] in many points, what I conceive to be the condition of Alsace and Lorraine." Lynch's analogy was that the South was under an occupying foreign power. This "occupation" was disastrous because "the older inhabitants broken in fortune and broken in heart, are struggling in poverty." Worse, in his opinion, was the fact that "the civil government is in the hands of the emancipated negroes, who are the vast a majority and who even when well intentioned, are ignorant and incapable, and who, in fact, are led by crafty and unscrupulous adventurers, mostly from Northern States, who have come to make their fortunes, out of the wreck of the South."[41]

Lynch had completely endorsed the analysis of the "Redeemers," as those implacably opposed to the Radicals described themselves, and this belief in the injustice of Radical Reconstruction passed on to his congregants. A Catholic visitor to the South sympathetic to the plight of African Americans was shocked at the racism of many Irish in the former Confederacy, including Lynch. Years after the war, Lynch was apparently still defending the morality of slavery. When the visiting cleric told the Irish bishop of a story he had heard from a black barber about the breakup of a slave family before the war, Lynch did acknowledge that the breakup of slave marriages was "a great evil." But in every other way, "public morality was better in the days of slavery than now."[42] He seemed nostalgic for the Old South.

While most Irish in the South did not want the return of slavery, they did come to see emancipation as contrary to their interests. The Charleston Fenians, for example, originally organized by P. J. Coogan, were, by the early 1870s, describing the Fifteenth Amendment to the Constitution, which prohibited discrimination in voting on the basis of "race, color or previous condition of servitude," as "a despotic infraction of the rights of the southern people." In Mobile a Fenian organizer, trying to establish his acceptability to his Irish southerner audience, reportedly gave "a severe [verbal] flaying to the carpetbaggers and scalawags."[43]

A study of Mobile's Reconstruction era explains why the Irish in the South were never enamored with the Radical version of reuniting the country. Like elsewhere in the former Confederacy, the Irish there had accepted the end of the Confederacy. Some openly welcomed it, as dozens of Irish women and men received much-needed rations from the occupying Federal soldiers.[44] Although the Irish were not among the avid Unionists in the city, the death of leading Irish Confederates in the war, and the U.S. Army's fine job restoring order in the city, made them loyal citizens. Nonetheless, "semi and unskilled white labor could not compete with influx of former slaves to the city from the Alabama countryside." The poorer whites thus turned to the one weapon they had over the freedpeople, the vote. During the Presidential Reconstruction period of Andrew Johnson, when blacks could not vote, they had forced the city to discriminate against black draymen and laborers on street contracts, two key areas of employment for Irish immigrants. Radical Republicans, led by Mobilians with New England roots and some of the German population, took control of the city, however, in 1867, with the overwhelming support of recently enfranchised African American voters. In return for these vital black votes, black community leaders demanded municipal jobs from the white Republicans now in charge of the city. The Republicans obliged and "replaced eighteen street laborers, mostly Irish, with African Americans." The Radicals also tackled the police force, long a bastion of Irish employment, appointing for the first time blacks to regular positions, as well as leadership ones.[45] One Irish policeman reacted by resigning at these latter appointments stating that "although necessity may compel me to acknowledge a negro my equal, I will never admit that his my superior.'"[46] In Mobile, therefore, "Reconstruction never secured a white popular constituency."[47]

Irish voters were thus ripe for Conservative/Democratic appeals to join them in the overthrow of Radical Reconstruction, and they did in large numbers. Anthony Keiley, for example, played a key role in winning back control of the former capital of the Confederacy from Republicans and eventually became one its Redeemer mayors. In Charleston, M. P. O'Connor was the Redeemer candidate for Congress in the First District of South Carolina on the 1876 "Straight-Out" Democratic ticket with gubernatorial candidate Confederate General Wade Hampton. O'Connor was with Hampton in

Cainhoy, in a rural part of the district, when a shoot-out with black Republicans almost cost him his life. Bishop Lynch was in Europe collecting money for his ruined cathedral during the tumultuous campaign but kept up with the news through his sister the Ursuline nun, Mother Baptiste (Ellen). She told him that "everyone is in perfect admiration of Genl. Hampton's masterly insistency and endurance. He is truly a noble man!" She was tired of the Radicals and blacks having some say in the running of the state: "this new element down here catch the names of property holders who were rich before the war, and determine to get money out of them by 'hook or crook.'" It reminded her and others of "Ireland when the Orangemen used to swear to anything against the Catholics." With Hampton's election secure after the Compromise of 1877 (which ended Radical Reconstruction for good), Mother Baptiste felt relieved. "How worthy of all praise is Gov Hampton! What beautiful self government and Christian fortitude. He ought to be a Catholic and may I pray." Hampton had risen in such stature by May 1877 that the Catholic children in her school were being taught "'Hampton's March' on piano, harp and guitar and also 'Ode to Pope Pius IX.'"[48] In Louisiana, in another disputed and violent election, the "victory" of the Redeemer candidate for governor, Francis T. Nicholls, was celebrated in New Orleans at St. Patrick's Hall. The Irish had campaigned hard for Nicholls and provided him with a large majority in the city. The (John) Mitchel Rifles militia company made sure to "protect" his election too against any Radical attempt to overturn it.[49]

These Irish "Redemption" stories had serious Confederate roots. Nicholls had been a Confederate general and commander of the 2nd Louisiana Brigade (which had included Michael Nolan and his Montgomery Guards), and Irish veterans had supported him. Mother Baptiste's view of military Reconstruction had been colored by the destruction of her convent in Columbia during the Civil War, for which she and her order had sued the U.S. government for compensation.[50] The connection between the Confederate experience and opposition to Reconstruction was best exemplified in Charleston in 1877 and 1878. To celebrate the coming victory over the Republicans in early 1877, a group of prominent Irish Charlestonians, including Edward McCrady Jr., congressional candidate M. P. O'Connor, and a man who had been in the political wilderness since his pardon, A. G. Magrath, felt it appropriate to commemorate in bronze and stone the two companies of Irish Volunteers who served the Confederate States of America. Magrath had, however, returned to leadership in the Irish community as president of the mostly plebeian St. Patrick's Benevolent Society. They and others had organized a fund-raising meeting and intended to, as soon as possible, build a permanent memorial to these Carolina Confederates in the local Catholic cemetery.[51]

There was another more significant and durable reason for this exercise beyond the raising of a Confederate memorial. It was to interpret the whole Irish Confederate experience in a positive light. From this first meeting through the erection of the monument, the organizers wanted to highlight that their memorial would combine both Irish and southern causes. In a pamphlet, published to promote the collection of funds, they reminded potential supporters of the parallel struggles of Irish and southern independence by including the description of the 1861 ceremony at the cathedral where Bishop Lynch had welcomed the Irish Volunteers into his church and blessed their new Confederate flag.[52] It's not surprising that the monument committee included this report in the commemorative bulletin. Those days in 1861 had indeed been heady and it seemed that the defeat of Radical Reconstruction would bring as much excitement as when the state seceded. That day back in 1861, when Irishmen and women had filled the cathedral to pay homage to their Confederate heroes, was one of pride and celebration, before the real horrors of war and siege visited the Irish of Charleston. It was the highpoint of Confederate patriotism among the Irish, and thus, something to be nostalgic about in 1877. Forgotten were the privations, exemptions, desertions, oaths to the Union sought and/or taken, and the flirting with Radical Republicans through votes for P. J. Coogan. The memorial, while solemn in recognizing the sacrifices of the dead, was also to be a celebration of Irish Charlestonians place in their city, state, and region. The Irish in Charleston and elsewhere in the South were used to "lost causes" in Ireland. They now had another one to celebrate with their native-born white neighbors.

This Irish commemorative effort was also a very southern one. Since the Civil War's end, all over the region, white southerners had sought to reinterpret the Civil War to their own advantage. Led by organizations such as Ladies' Memorial Associations dedicated to maintaining Confederate cemeteries, they wanted to preserve the memory of the dead, but also the cause, even if it had been a "lost" one. The dead soldier and the cemetery were the focus of these earliest commemorations, and the Irish Volunteer memorial fit perfectly into this southern model. This focus on the "Confederate dead" meant that from the beginning, the memory of the Confederacy had religious overtones that would develop much further into a type of civil religion, something that defined a society and its citizens. As with any religion, the Lost Cause developed its own elaborate ceremonies, parades and memorials, icons, statues of Confederate heroes, and "saints," especially its "blessed Trinity," Generals Robert E. Lee, Thomas "Stonewall" Jackson, and President Jefferson Davis. Confederate cemeteries became places of pilgrimage on the various "feast" days of the Confederacy, which included Robert E. Lee's birthday and the anniversary of Stonewall Jackson's death. Clergy played a central role in all the events and were key to transforming historical commemorations into quasi-religious events.[53] Most Irish Americans, as Catholics, were familiar with elaborate religious ceremonies, far more so than most southerners, who had been raised in a more sober and plain evangelical tradition.

There were, however, two major spurts of Confederate memorializing, and during the first one, 1865 to 1885, over 70 percent of memorials were placed in cemeteries. Reflecting these placements, over 75 percent "incorporated themes of ceremonial bereavement" rather than "the later ones which featured a Confederate soldier atop a tall shaft on the Courthouse lawn." These memorials, however, could still speak of the greatness of the buried soldiers in the cemetery. In 1869 the Ladies' Memorial Association of Richmond, Virginia, perhaps erected the most famous memorial in the Hollywood Cemetery of that city—a forty-five-foot granite replica of an Egyptian pyramid. Other memorial associations chose Victorian funerary statues, but the most common as Foster puts it, "was some form of a classical obelisk . . . that featured simplicity, even dignity."[54]

Thus it was not coincidental that the Irish of Charleston wanted their similar version of Confederate respectability. On March 18, 1878 (the day after St. Patrick's Day, the feast day having fallen on a Sunday that year), they unveiled their permanent memorial and it took the form of the typical early Confederate memorials. This obelisk to the Irish volunteers fit the traditional southern pattern of a funerary memorial placed in a cemetery. But, at the same time, the monument was also an expression of their Irishness. After their traditional St. Patrick's parade in the morning, they reassembled in the afternoon at the great symbol Irish Charleston, Hibernian Hall, and then proceeded through the city to the railroad station. From there they took the short train journey north to the Catholic cemetery of St. Lawrence.[55] A. G. Magrath was the keynote speaker. As with native Lost Cause ceremonies, clergy were central. The other honored guest was therefore Irish native, Father D. J. Quigley of St. Patrick's Church, a parish that had been established specifically for the first wave of poor Irish immigrants, and one which remained at the heart of the Irish community in the city.[56] The event

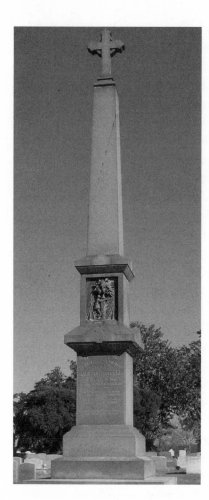

Irish Volunteer Memorial, Charleston, South Carolina (author's collection)

received copious coverage in the local newspaper, the *News and Courier*, one of the more prominent periodicals in the state and region. Its editor, Francis W. Dawson, English-born and a Confederate veteran, wrote of the ceremony and its cause that "the Irish Volunteers [were] true patriotism personified . . . fighting and dying for the Southern Confederacy with all the ardor and devotion of knights of fair renown, they stand before the people of Carolina the representatives of all that is great and brave and true."[57] The Irish it seemed had proved their Carolina patriotism again as they had at Gaines's Mill and Manassas.

They had intertwined very successfully their Irishness with their Confederate experience. It was explicit on the monument itself, where one can see the Palmetto tree, symbol of South Carolina, surrounded by shamrocks,

*Irish Volunteer Memorial Plate
(author's collection)*

with the muskets stacked to the side, and the harp of Erin hanging on this tree of Carolina. Ireland's symbols are entwined with the symbol of the lost cause of South Carolinian independence. But this plaque also reflects the lost cause of Ireland. The Irish were like, as Captain Edward Magrath had pointed out in 1861, the sons of Israel, a Diaspora. The symbolism is from Psalm 137:1–3: "By the Rivers of Babylon, there we sat down and wept when we remembered Zion. On the willows there we hung our lyres. For there our captors required of us songs, and our tormentors, mirth, saying 'Sing us one of the songs of Zion.' How can we sing the Lord's song in a foreign land?" The Irish Volunteers had stacked their muskets and hung their Irish harps in South Carolina, perhaps waiting to return to a free Ireland.

The Irish did express the rhetoric and aesthetic of exile, but rather than isolating them, feelings of banishment brought them closer to their new home. Magrath had recognized as much at the organizational meeting in 1877, finding again the voice he had during the Confederacy. Speaking there he first gave a history of the Volunteers, particularly their roots in the men of 1798, "who had been told that their love of country was treason." He listed the litany of Ireland's wrongs at the hands of England and then made this explicit connection: "We have lived to see how possible it is, that even in our own land, no bitterness excelled that felt by population locally intermingled but estranged politically." However, Magrath continued, the "United States chief magistrate" (the recently elected Rutherford Hayes under the Compromise of 1877) had come to his senses and restored "to the citizens of South Carolina the rights and privileges of the citizens of Massachusetts or Ohio."[58] Unlike in Ireland, reconciliation had been achieved in America.

The other message the Magrath conveyed was that the Irish Volunteers had played their role in this standing up for the "rights and privileges" of the white South. Irish Confederates, Magrath believed, had understood the importance of the southern cause better than any of because of their Irish experience. They "had fled from persecution at home" and knew "what oppression was—oppression for the sake of opinion—because of belief." Irishmen were always aware that Carolinians had allowed them the freedoms denied them in Ireland and had campaigned for Irish liberty: "With high and noble emotion, either deep-seated and heart inspiring sympathy, the distinguished sons of this state [South Carolina] have ever raised their voices in behalf of the rights and for the redress of the wrongs of the people of Ireland." The Confederate national project gave Irish immigrants an opportunity to pay the State back. "The day came when the exiles from Ireland testified how well [they] remembered the justice done to their native land. The Irish immigrant sealed with his life's blood the covenant between his people and the land in which he lived and for which he died."[59]

Omitting the complicated reality of the Irish Confederate experience, which as governor he had known only too well, Magrath highlighted instead, in very biblical imagery, that the Irish exile had spilled his blood for his new country, covenanting his relationship to it forever. The Lost Cause was "baptized in the blood" of the Confederate soldier, just as all Christians are baptized in the blood of Christ. He died on the Cross to save mankind, and the Confederate soldier had died to redeem the South. Magrath had stated unequivocally that the blood of the Irish Confederate soldier was also a part of the southern salvation story.[60]

Magrath and other speakers were reimagining, reinventing even, their Confederate experience in a more positive light. In his speech, he ignored, for example, the fact that he had had to make a judicial ruling from the Confederate bench to force all foreigners, including the Irish, to serve in the Confederate state's defense in its darkest hour.[61] The great memorializer of the Irish Volunteers and a scion of the Lost Cause, Edward McCrady Jr., loved to focus on his favorite soldier, Dominick Spellman, not knowing of course Spellman's change of heart toward the end of the war. He also, however, failed to mention what he did know, that thirty Irish Volunteers had deserted to the enemy or taken the oath when captured. Most of their names are listed in the commemorative program, taken from the original muster listed in the 1861 newspapers, but what happened to them is omitted. Only those killed in action had their sacrifice recorded by their name. Just death, or, as in Spellman's case, near death, were worthy of fulsome praise.[62] Selective amnesia combined with a permanent memorial incorporating the parallels of Irish and southern causes were the order of the day.

This use of the Lost Cause to reimagine the Irish Confederate story was not just a Charleston phenomenon. Irish in other parts of the South participated in this new civil religion. In Memphis, for example, the Irish embraced a great opportunity to participate in one of the South's first major Lost Cause commemorations in 1870. On April 28 of that year the body of General Pat Cleburne was moved from its original burial place in Spring Hill, Tennessee, to Helena, Arkansas, on the banks of the Mississippi River, where he had spent most of his American life. The reburial was at the instigation of the Ladies' Memorial Association in Helena, who saw Cleburne as their locality's greatest Confederate. For all ex-Confederates, this Irishman was the "Stonewall of the West," thus directly compared to one of the blessed Trinity of the Lost Cause. Cleburne's body would come through Memphis on its way to Arkansas. A number of Irish from Memphis, as well as Irish from Mississippi and Arkansas, had shared some of Cleburne's laurels as members of his "model" division, in the Army of Tennessee. Although an Anglican, Cleburne was seen by Irish Catholics throughout the South as one of their own. One Irish visitor noted that Cleburne's name had a "talismanic" effect on the Irish in the region. Some even named Fenian circles in his memory and the Fenian symbol of the sunburst was carved on the new memorial for his plot in Helena, even though he had never been a member of the organization.[63]

The Irish of Memphis were prominent in the procession of Cleburne's coffin through the city. When the body arrived at the train station it was met by sixteen pall-bearers, all veterans of Cleburne's division. But outside the station, the Irish militia unit, the Emmet Guard, formed a guard of honor. The procession then made its way to the Mississippi River, where the casket would be put on a steamboat to make the final leg down river to Helena. Led by a military band and a number of militia units, ex-Confederate president Jefferson Davis rode in an open carriage. Then came over one hundred veterans followed by the Cleburne Circle of Fenians from Memphis. Other Irish participants included the Hibernian Benevolent Relief Society and the Irish

Literary Association. When the cortege reached the wharf, an Irish veteran of Cleburne's division approached the coffin and kissed it. Then, crying, he knelt and prayed for the dead general. His personal tribute reportedly brought many others to tears. The Emmet Guards had the final honor of escorting the coffin to Helena.[64] Only eight years after Irish Memphians' full integration as white southerners had been challenged by their acceptance of Union occupation, the Lost Cause occasion of Cleburne's removal to Helena gave them an opportunity to emphasize again their integral place as citizens of the white South.[65]

One individual more than any other, however, proved to white southerners in Memphis and throughout the South that Irish American Catholics could be southerners in the aftermath of the Confederacy. Father Abram Ryan had served as a Confederate chaplain, but he would become famous for his commemoration of the Confederate cause. During the War, his brother's death in Confederate service seemed to awaken in him a more strident Confederate nationalism which he decided to commit to paper. In early 1865 he published the first of his "national" poetry and this fairly obscure chaplain was on his way to becoming the "Poet Priest of the Confederacy." His poems such as "The Sword of Robert E. Lee" and "The Conquered Banner" became standards for every white southerner. He still retained, however, a strong Irish sensibility. For example, he could with equal gusto condemn England's misrule in Ireland with poems such as "Erin's Flag," which began "Lift it up, lift it up, the Old Banner of Green, the Blood of its sons has but brightened its sheen, what though the tyrant has trampled it down, are its folds not emblazoned with deeds of renown?" Eventually, he also published his work in his newspaper, the *Banner of the South*, which he operated in Augusta, Georgia, with the aid of Patrick Walsh, as the voice of Catholics in that state, but also as the voice of unreconstructed white southerners. He reserved particular disdain for Radical Republicans and African Americans. His newspaper was on occasion virulently racist. Simultaneously, Ryan carried a lot of Irish and Catholic news. He was a strong supporter of the move to papal infallibility pushed by the ultramontane supporters of Pope Pius IX. But he and his southern supporters did not find it incongruous to be ultramontane Catholic, Irish American, and anti-Reconstruction southerner. His embrace of the Lost Cause even made Protestants in the South forgive and/or ignore his strident Catholicism.[66] When he died in 1886, his local newspaper the *Mobile Register* commented: "In that dark hour of lamentation, when the South was transformed into one vast cathedral, in which a whole people knelt in silence and in sorrow around the coffins of the slain, there came an unknown voice so strangely sweet, so deep, so clear, so grand, that every heart-felt thrilled by its pathos and power."[67] "Every heart" had "thrilled" to the voice of an Irish American priest.

As a leader of the cultural Lost Cause, Ryan received his due from the Confederate memorializers.[68] In 1913, however, he received two public memorials—one in Augusta, where he first achieved fame, and the other in Mobile, where he had died. In April of that year the city of Augusta unveiled a memorial to "four Georgia writers"—James R. Randall, Paul H. Hayne, Sidney Lanier, and Father Ryan—three of whom had connections to Augusta. All had connections to the Confederacy, serving in its cause directly and/or writing about it. Randall, a Catholic from Baltimore and Georgetown graduate, wrote the Confederate ode "Maryland, My Maryland" and had worked for Walsh at the Chronicle. He was buried in Augusta. Hayne, a South Carolinian, had moved to Augusta after Sherman's army had burned the family plantation, and was also buried there. He had written poems such as "The Battle of Charleston Harbor" commemorating Confederate heroism. Lanier, originally from Macon, Georgia, had served with distinction in Virginia and became a famous critic of Reconstruction. Ryan, the son of an Irish peddler, who had spent only a few years in Georgia, was in distinguished company. The mayor and city council turned out for the ceremony, as did local schoolchildren and clergy. One of Ryan's poems was sung by a local choir. His inscription read: "To the higher shrine of love divine—My lowly feet have trod—I want no fame, no other name—Than this a priest of God." This inscription would have pleased him but it was his Lost Cause fame, and not his priestly service, that had gotten him the recognition. The ceremony recognized the major Catholic element in the commemoration and concluded with a benediction from the priest from St. Patrick's Church.[69]

Just three months later the city of Mobile unveiled a statue to Ryan in a public park. Funds had been raised from "children all over the South" who had grown up reading and reciting Ryan's poetry. A Catholic priest from nearby Jesuit Spring Hill College made a speech recognizing Ryan's work as a priest, but the emphasis was on his service as a Confederate chaplain and poet. Local doctor Edward Craighead had been the driving force behind the memorial and described Ryan as a "Southern Hero" and "the poet of the South" whose "life and deeds" had "in the hearts of his people (i.e., white southerners) left a more enduring monument than can ever be erected by the hand of man." Ryan had become, with Admiral Raphael Semmes, the Confederate hero of Mobile. Nonetheless, the organizers recognized Ryan's Irish roots by including the "green flag of Ireland," which Ryan had extolled in his poetry, along with the "Stars and Bars" and "Stars and Stripes" on the speakers' platform. Ryan had, posthumously, continued to join the cause of Ireland with that of the Confederacy.[70]

This unifying nature of the Lost Cause for white southerners was one of its common features. It helped paper over the serious clefts within the white community during Reconstruction. With the victory of Redemption, however, divisions along class and geographical lines reemerged.[71] Certain proponents of a "New South" who embraced an industrial and urban future for the region within the growing United States upset some "unreconstructed" southerners as well as those, particularly farmers, who would have to suffer the transition from an agricultural to an industrial economy. In the 1880s these New South advocates turned again to the Lost Cause to achieve political unity. Henry Grady, editor of the *Atlanta Constitution*, was the New South's greatest exponent and he, for example, used former Confederate president Jefferson Davis to great effect in Georgia's 1886 gubernatorial election when the New South candidate, former general John B. Gordon, faced a tough campaign. Gordon had been a famous Civil War general but was now a leading attorney for northern-owned railroads. He needed to reestablish his southern authenticity. Grady invited Davis to visit Atlanta, ostensibly for the laying of the cornerstone of a monument to Confederate General Benjamin Hill, and gave the ex-Confederate president copious coverage in his newspaper. Of course, Gordon was constantly at Davis's side and this fact too was duly noted. The visit was a triumph attracting large crowds and helped Gordon win the election. The Lost Cause had become a valuable tool in promoting the New South and was now more about the present and the future than it had been about the past.[72]

Thus, a second great wave of Confederate memorializing occurred between 1885 and 1915. This time, the driving force came from the bottom up rather than the top down. Grady had definitely promoted this new interest in the Lost Cause, but large numbers of ordinary people embraced it and made it their own. The Cause was no longer the purview of grieving widows, former generals, and Irish American poet priests, but also of lawyers, merchants, and artisans, the men, in particular, who had been common Confederate soldiers. In a very Victorian fashion the movement was becoming bourgeois. Seeking to reassert their own southern authenticity among an increasingly "Yankified" South, the rising middle classes demanded recognition of their role in the war. The focus now would be on the living, rather than the dead, and would be more celebration than memorial. Veterans groups such as the Association of the Army of Northern Virginia (AANV) and the Association of the Army of Tennessee (AAT) emerged to replace in importance earlier memorial group such as the elitist, with its high annual dues, Southern Historical Society. Most of these veterans groups would unite under the banner of the United Confederate Veterans (UCV) in 1889. The UCV promoted camaraderie among and charity for veterans. They also sponsored a series of reunions around their annual meetings which by the mid-1890s attracted tens of thousands, and on a few occasions, over 100,000 visitors to the host cities. Southern towns and cities competed to attract the UCV reunions which by the early 1900s attracted far more nonveterans than actual Civil War participants. By then over 75 percent of southern counties had a UCV camp, usually based in the local town, and its magazine *The Confederate Veteran* was a major seller. This new popular Lost Cause endorsed reconciliation with the North, but as historian Edward Ayers observes, this "reconciliation helped to heighten the South's distinctiveness and to buttress the forces of reaction."[73]

The Irish in the postwar South actively participated in this new demotic phase of the Lost Cause. Living predominantly in urban areas, they were close to the events of this reinterpretation of Confederate memory. Also, there had been only two prominent Irish combat generals, and only one, Cleburne, had had a very distinguished record. The story the Irish Confederate was predominantly the story of the common soldier and Irish veterans joined the AANV, AAT, and UCV. New Orleans, in particular, which had provided the largest number of Irish soldiers for service, had active members of both organizations. Already linked to their former native-born officers during the struggle against Radical reconstruction, connections were maintained through these veterans' organizations.

To join the veterans' groups applicants had to fill out an application, describing briefly the unit they had served in and what their service had been. They also had to have a comrade vouch for their service. Once their application had been "proven to the satisfaction to any one of the officers, or members of the Executive Committee," and paid their initial dues of two dollars, or four if they wanted a badge as well as a membership certificate, they could become members. Dues, after that, were only one dollar a year. With such reasonable fees the associations attracted a lot of Irish applicants. On September 27, 1875, for example, both Dan Sullivan and Thomas Buckley, formerly of the 7th and 15th Louisiana Infantry regiments, applied to join the Louisiana division of the Association of the Army of Northern Virginia. Even though both had served in different Louisiana brigades, indeed in different divisions and corps, both had transferred to the Confederate navy after the Battle of Fredericksburg and felt comfortable in vouching for each other. The famous "Irish" 6th Louisiana naturally had a large number of applications. Captain Blayney T. Walshe of Company I, "Irish Brigade Company A," a twenty-two-year-old clerk from County Wexford, who had been elected second lieutenant by his Irish comrades, and later appointed captain, was among the first to join the AANV in January 1876. Indeed, his record was so distinguished the executive committee certified his membership without a co-signer. Once a member, Walshe vouched for numerous other Irish veterans including Bernard "Barney" Dunn, former sergeant of the Calhoun Guards in the Irish 6th. He had been wounded at Antietam and become the regimental wagon driver, but was just an illiterate fifty-six year old laborer in 1877. Walshe, "a dealer in gentlemen's fur goods," living in uptown New Orleans, had to fill out Dunn's application for him to which the laborer "made his mark." Even though Walshe had moved up in the world, he had remained friendly with his former comrade who still lived in the heart of an old Irish neighborhood near St. Theresa of Avila Church.[74]

It seems that just as combat experience had brought Irish classes together it was so again in the postwar veteran experience. Indeed, by joining the AANV both Walshe and Dunn were connected to their old division commander, Francis T. Nicholls, and the governor of Louisiana, who was also an active member of the association.[75]

Class or ethnicity, then, did not seem to be a barrier to entry into these Confederate veteran organizations. A discovered poor service record, however, could. If not known personally to the association executives, the organizations often did not just take an applicant's word on their service record. For example, the AAT in New Orleans wrote to a veteran they knew in Memphis to investigate the claim of one James Doyle, who claimed that he had served in the Irish-dominated 2nd Tennessee (5th Confederate) during the war. The contact got in touch with one Pat Kelly, a veteran of the regiment, who stated that Doyle had been arrested near Corinth, Mississippi, for refusing to fight and had been jailed in nearby Tupelo. This kind of incident was enough to be rejected. Even those who had fought bravely could be denied membership. One Patrick Murtha, for example, had served in the 1st Louisiana Infantry and had been wounded at the Battle of Malvern Hill in July 1862. Nonetheless, on the word of a former captain, he was denied membership because he took the "federal oath" while a prisoner. Patrick Healy of the 6th Louisiana did not get in to the AANV until nine years after he applied. He had been wounded at Gaines's Mill in June 1862, but had "deserted from hospital" the following December. But because he reentered service in a partisan Ranger unit in Mississippi, which was eventually confirmed, he was finally granted membership.[76]

Those Irish rejected from the veterans' groups lost not only fraternity with former comrades and contact with influential native southerners, but also, by the 1890s, more tangible benefits. Although Confederate veterans organizations did not focus as much on veterans benefits as did their Union counterpart, the Grand Army of the Republic (GAR), those UCV camps with larger memberships, usually in the cities, did provide pensions to those who had fallen on hard times, especially those handicapped by wounds received during the war. They also managed to persuade some ex-Confederate states to create and maintain "Confederate homes" for old veterans. The Association of Confederate Soldiers from Tennessee, for example, provided annual pensions of between $50 and $300 to disabled indigent veterans and secured places in a Confederate Veterans Home for those in need of shelter.[77]

Louisiana provided pensions too and depended on the veterans groups to help judge applicants for relief. Thus, the good word of former comrades and/or commanders was vital in receiving a stipend. One John Curley of New Orleans, for example, applied for a pension in 1897. By that stage the old veteran was almost destitute, reduced to selling pencils in the French Quarter. Curley had been wounded a number of times in battle and claimed "invalidity" on the rather rigorous application. Authorities sought a lot of detail from the veteran on his service and wounds, but also on his current status, including whether he partook of "intoxicants of any kind." Curley wisely replied that he did not. James McCann, also of New Orleans, was not as poor as Curley but had a large family to support. He had served in the Confederate marine corps in Mobile and wrote to his former commanding officer, one John Rapier, to gain support for his pension application. McCann was concerned that after almost forty years Rapier would not recall his service and sent a photograph to help refresh his commander's memory. Rapier did indeed remember McCann and endorsed wholeheartedly his application. About 25 percent of UCV camps helped provide financial support for veterans, but the Irish had the advantage of living in larger cities, whose veterans groups were far more likely to be part of this charitable 25 percent.[78]

For those who did not need and or seek financial aid or the contacts with leading former Confederates could still use the pages of the *Confederate Veteran* to tell their stories, seek out old comrades, or announce their passing.[79] There were no specific Irish veteran groups as there had been Irish units in the war. Thus, participation in these activities increased the southernness

James K. McCann (*Confederate Personnel Records, Louisiana Historical Association Collection, Louisiana Research Collection, Tulane University*)

of Irish veterans, and native soldiers often remembered their Irish comrades with fondness.[80] This integration of the Irish into native Confederate veteran organizations contrasts sharply with the experience of Irish Union veterans in the GAR. The GAR was by far the largest veterans' group in the United States and a very influential lobby in Washington, D.C. While there was no official anti-Irish policy in the GAR, its strong links to the Republican Party, along with its often militant Protestantism, often discouraged Irish vets from joining. When they did, they often formed their own distinctive Catholic camps.[81]

Thanks to the efforts of Father Ryan, Protestant boosters like Edward McCrady and A. G. Magrath, and prominent Irish American Catholic veterans such as Anthony Keiley, Irish ex-Confederates did not have the issues with the UCV that their compatriots in the North had with the GAR. The former Redeemer mayor of Richmond, Keiley had always seen himself as a representative of "middling sorts." After the war he was therefore keen to honor the experience of the common soldier and not just the generals. He republished a memoir of his time in Union prisons at Point Lookout, Maryland, and Elmira, New York, sending it to Robert E. Lee for approval. Passionate in his opposition to Radical Reconstruction and a virulent racist, Keiley eventually became a nationally prominent Democrat.[82] It was natural then that other veterans eager to erect a monument to the common soldier in Richmond, which after the placing of a massive statue to Robert E. Lee, marked the former Confederate capital as the place to memorialize the Lost Cause, turned to Keiley for support. He responded eagerly, making the first major speech on behalf of the monument to, as one correspondent put it, "one of the largest audiences ever gathered in Richmond." Keiley also helped pick a style for the monument, having seen many ancient columns while on government service in Europe and Egypt. He also endorsed the location on the prominent Libby Hill, which overlooked the James River on the city's eastside, close to the docks, and a working-class neighborhood that had boasted a sizeable Irish population. Lee's statue, raised in 1890, had been placed in a more salubrious and genteel suburb west of downtown. Libby Hill, he believed, would be the perfect spot for the "Confederate Infantry man whose face and form should tell that story of that immortal epoch." He ultimately described himself as "the monument's friend—whatever its form."[83]

Keiley's endorsement was important because the Soldiers' and Sailors' Monument, as it became known, had generated opposition from some elite Lost Cause practitioners. When the project had been first discussed in the late 1880s, former General Jubal Early, a major leader in the elite Southern Historical Society, and the keeper of the official Lee memory, objected that this new proposal would distract from the Lee statue, still a couple of years away from unveiling. In a reply to a solicitation for support, he wrote, "I think it is very unfortunate to start your scheme . . . at this time." He went on to impugn the motives of the organizers, stating that "Richmond seems to look on this [scheme] for monuments to Confederates as a means of bringing money into the pockets of her merchants and hotel keepers." He would not contribute until Lee was up. The organizers thus knew that they would have to solicit lots of small contributions from regular folk. In that effort they made sure to receive the blessing of Irish American Catholic Bishop John J. Keane of the Diocese of Richmond, who offered "best wishes for the success of the good cause." His endorsement, along with Keiley's heavy involvement, would be important for raising money in the Irish community.[84]

In May 1894 the memorial was unveiled on Libby Hill and over 100,000 turned out to see it. This special public event, and hundreds like it, if on a smaller scale, throughout the South, represented to southern whites what historian of the Lost Cause Gaines Foster describes as "a sense of community, that being outside the normal order of things, transcended the usual social and economic divisions of society." The fact that after 1885 these monuments, parades, and speeches were now held in the public square, and usually commemorated the common soldier by putting a likeness of him in his Confederate prime on the top of a classical column, it "reversed the order of society, as the common man became the focus of attention and praise." This new focus meant that "When the ceremony ended and people resumed their daily lives, when the ritual time closed, the order of society returned. But the temporary establishment of a special sense of community and the town's and its leaders' testimony of respect to the common man served to enhance the bonds of unity within society."[85] Through the Lost Cause, Irish and Irish Americans in the South felt that unity.

The classic case of this Irish inclusion occurred in Houston, Texas, in 1905. Here one can see all the elements of the new, more public and "booster" Lost Cause coming together with a strong and overt Irish influence. The city had never had a large Irish population in the antebellum era (the whole state of Texas had only about 3,500 Irish-born residents in 1860), but it did produce a very prominent Irish Confederate in Lieutenant Richard "Dick" Dowling and his Davis Guards, the heroes of Sabine Pass.[86]

Dowling died of yellow fever only a couple of years after the war, but he became Houston's most famous Confederate. It was natural for the local UCV camp to name their group in Dowling's honor. It was this group of veterans who first came up with the idea of a monument to Dowling in the early 1890s, which would be Houston's first public statue. The city was growing and would take off in the first decades of the twentieth century with the discovery of oil in East Texas and the construction of the Ship Canal in 1911, which made Houston accessible to ocean-going vessels. Every new city needs public memorials, and every southern city in the 1890s needed a Confederate memorial in a prominent place. The idea, however, was slow to take off until the veterans had the bright idea of exploiting Dowling's Irishness. By including the local Ancient Order of Hibernians Divisions, as well as other Irish groups such as the Emmet Council in 1901, the Dick Dowling Monument Committee raised the funds for a prominent memorial. The city responded with a prime location in the well traveled and central Market Square. There had been talk of unveiling the statue on September 8, the anniversary of the Battle of Sabine Pass, but such was the Irish involvement that the organizing committee chose, instead, St. Patrick's Day 1905 for the unveiling.[87]

When the big day arrived the *Houston Chronicle* stated that "'God Save Ireland' and 'Dixie' were blended in one harmony today." It began with a parade led by a carriage containing the four survivors of the battle. Groups of marching veterans and Irish association members followed. School

*Dick Dowling/Davis Guards Memorial,
Houston, Texas (author's collection)*

children sang and "a jam of humanity" observed the proceedings. Dowling's daughter brought huge cheers when she unveiled the statue. Made of Italian marble, Dowling in his artillery uniform was on top, but the pedestal had the names of Davis Guards inscribed on it. Both the governor of Texas and mayor of Houston made speeches praising the patriotism of the Irish as well hitting on the usual themes of Lost Cause speeches. Some locals felt strong enough to recognize the occasion with poetry. One Ellen R. Croom wrote in the *Chronicle*: "Remember that September Day—Just forty-one men with the Texas yell;—But they scattered the Yankee ships pell-mell—Oh But they fought right nobly and well—Those heroes with brave Dick Dowling—They were sons of Erin, and never were found—Grander knights of 'The Table Round.'" Dowling and his unit were "sons of Erin" but also Texans and upholders of the South's honor. In another newspaper poet J. M. Lewis remembered the past, but in keeping with the new Lost Cause, also recognized its importance for the present and the future in his poem "Dick Dowling." Lewis wrote: "'Now which of ye' he [Dowling] cried in sport 'would like to spoike a gun?'—'And where's the Irishman at all who ever learned to run?—I've a few words I'd loike to say To that Spalpeen this very day—Now who wid me will fight?' They stepped out everyone." "And" Lewis continued "we have builded a monument and told of it in stone—But, nay, Dick Dowling, not to you, but to ourselves alone—To show that the deed your heart dared dare, found echo in our own—For what availeth a stone to you whose fame shall outlast stone."[88]

Lewis expressed it well, even in his stage "Oirish" dialogue. The monument was not just about Irish bravery but was also one "to ourselves alone." The whole occasion told and tells us more about Houston in 1905 than the Battle of Sabine Pass in 1863. It speaks also to the place of the Irish in that city. Houston had finally arrived as a proper city, with its first major public Confederate memorial, and it was to an Irish immigrant and his Irish unit. There was nothing incongruous, it seemed, in this connection of Irish, Texan, and Confederate. The irony was that fifty-five years later the Democratic nominee for the presidency, Irish American Senator John F. Kennedy of Massachusetts, would have to prove the compatibility of being a Roman Catholic and an American to the Greater Houston Ministerial Association.[89] Apparently, nobody in 1905 Houston questioned the patriotism of Dick Dowling and his Davis Guards.

Like Ireland, white southerners examined the past to cope with a changing present (as the line in "Dixie" stated, "old times there are not forgotten").[90] Not every white southerner was totally enamored with the Lost Cause, often observing how conservative politicians exploited it to dissipate real class tensions.[91] Also, as the veterans began to die off, the torch of Confederate memory passed to groups like the United Daughters of the Confederacy. Formed in 1894 by a merger of some Ladies' Memorial Associations (LMAs), the UDC was far more exclusive than veterans groups and drew predominantly from the upper and middle classes. There do not seem to have been many Irish women involved in the earlier memorial efforts. Indeed, as Charleston highlights, it was Irish men who took the lead in organizing the cemetery memorials. Historians of southern women in general, however, have seen the Lost Cause as key to understanding white women's position in the postwar South. Women, more than the veterans even, needed to commemorate the cause. They, too, had sacrificed and needed to validate that sacrifice by memorializing their dead men. As a result, they could be more publicly active without challenging directly the dominant patriarchy. Evidence of Irish women participating in the LMAs and UDC is scant. Along with economic/class reasons for not participating (the UDC wanted only "refined" women as members), Irish women did not lament the passing of the Confederacy as much as upper class native women. Nonetheless, there is some evidence of "refined" native-born women of Irish heritage being active. The unmarried thirty-year old Nora Flanagan (sometimes Flannagan) of New Orleans, for example, was the daughter of a middle-class Irish father and Irish American mother. She worked as the recording secretary of New Orleans chapter no. 72. The most active of Irish American women in the UDC was Mattie McGrath of Baton Rouge. The granddaughter of Irish immigrants, she became a vice president of the Louisiana Division.[92] But, Flanagan and McGrath remained exceptions.

Nevertheless, whether exclusive or not, everybody in the region had to respect the tradition, and at some level it did help unite white southerners. Its rituals became part of what it meant to be southern in the New South. Through their engagement with it, Irish immigrants and their offspring overcame a mixed war record. The fact that they had known well a "lost cause" in Ireland and were familiar with the very Catholic trappings of the one in their new home, made it easy for them to participate.

And, many benefited directly from it, some in a great manner. Patrick Walsh, for example, personified this ease of Irish acceptance into the southern elite through the Lost Cause. He had been a strong Confederate supporter, but as the editor of the *Augusta Constitutionalist*, as well as the *Pacificator*, his military service was minuscule and had ended in early 1862. Nevertheless, in his strident opposition to Radical Reconstruction and his strong support of Father Ryan in the *Banner of the South*, he climbed the southern political ladder in spectacular fashion. After the end of Reconstruction he rejoiced in the "Redemption" of the South, and became, like his friend Henry Grady in Atlanta, a major propagator of the "New South," through the control of his new political vehicle, the *Augusta Chronicle*. As a New South believer he was a strong advocate of the Lost Cause, both in its early and later phases, as a strong believer in white supremacy. His personal, as well as public, connections to Confederate veterans through the UCV he exploited to his own advantage, as Grady had done in the 1886 election for John Gordon. Ostensibly a supporter of the "little guy," Walsh was really a booster of the "Bourbon" (Redeemer) cause in Georgia and an opponent of the "Populist revolt" led in Georgia by Tom Watson. Indeed, like Gordon, despite his Confederate rhetoric, he too was "retained" by a northern rail-road company and worked for northern economic interests in Georgia. Yet, he still held on to a lot of support among the working classes in Augusta and indeed helped "turn" Watson out of his congressional seat in 1892.

Walsh served on the city council of Augusta as well as in the state legislature and the Democratic National Executive Committee, and received the ultimate reward for his service to the Bourbon cause with his appointment to the United States Senate to fill the remainder of the term of the recently deceased former Confederate general Alfred H. Colquitt in 1893. Colquitt was one of the great "Bourbon Triumvirate" of Georgia Redeemers, and the Irish private had replaced the native general. Walsh failed in an attempt to gain a full new term in the Senate and instead became mayor of Augusta in 1897. Nonetheless, he had been for a few years the Irish-born actively Roman Catholic United States senator from Georgia. His somewhat untimely death in 1899 at the age of fifty-nine shortened his already distinguished political career. Walsh had made a remarkable journey from young immigrant, journeyman printer, and Confederate private to newspaper proprietor, mayor, and United States senator. He achieved this amazing rise not from his actual service in the Confederacy, but through his celebration of its memory.[93]

Walsh, in a spectacular way, exemplified the heights of the successful integration of the Irish into the New South.[94] His opposition to a radical restructuring of the South after the defeat of the Confederacy helped him gain major political office. His Confederate experience, both during and long after the war, had colored his opposition to Reconstruction, and this he parlayed into becoming the first and only Irish-born United States senator from the South, thereby becoming a vivid testament to the power of the Lost Cause in the lives of Irish southerners.

Ambiguous Confederates

The Irish experience of the Confederacy was indeed an ambiguous one. They had been reluctant secessionists, yet rallied in large numbers to the Confederacy when war began. Those who joined the armed forces were, in general, good fighters, but also more likely to desert than native Confederates. Irish civilians supported their "boys" in the service, but most tired of the Confederate cause as conditions worsened on the home front. So much so, that many welcomed the Union victory and occupation. Even their religious leaders, who remained loyal to the Confederacy, could not halt the loss of Confederate spirit. The Irish also accepted early Federal attempts to reconstruct the South, although they opposed Radical Republican efforts to ensure African American rights. Their use of the Lost Cause was a key element in their return to the Confederate fold and ensured them a place in the "New South." They did not become southern "under fire," but rather in the commemoration of the Confederacy.[1] As a result the real and complicated narrative of the Irish and the Confederacy disappeared.

In a military sense, both at home and at the front, Irish Confederates did not have a major impact on the overall war effort. Their early excitement and its dissipation did not affect the outcome of the conflict. They did, however, reflect clearly the problematic internal issues, military and domestic, of the Confederacy as whole. From examining the Irish we see crystallized the complexities of the Confederate armies in the field, great bravery under fire but also major disillusion with the war's direction. On the home front the Irish indicate the importance of the enthusiasm at the war's beginning with its parades, prayers, and ceremonies, but also the rapid decline in support for the cause as the reality of conflict hit home. Ultimately, the Irish Confederate story tells us of the weak nature of Confederate, and indeed American, nationalism in the mid-nineteenth century.

The Irish did, with some ease, drop their American identity, take up a Confederate one, and return quickly to the American version, whenever it suited. Those Irish Confederates who had fought bravely for the cause did so more to fulfill their own notions of Irish manliness or to support their comrades than because of any deep cultural connection to the Confederate States of America. Despite the best efforts of ardent Confederates, Confederate nationalism developed only in a civic way. When the state and army behind this civic nationalism collapsed, so too did loyalty to the nation. The Irish are an excellent example of this failure in Confederate ideology. It was only the maelstrom of Reconstruction and a coherent civil religion around the Lost Cause that created a cultural nationalism for the Confederacy. This postwar version, with its highly Catholic overtones, the Irish could embrace without reservation. They were, in fact, excellent postwar patriots. Ironically, in an ideological sense, the Confederacy was stronger after it had become defunct. The Irish stance on remembering the war clearly indicates this reality.[2]

To be fair to the creators of the new state, the Irish in the South had a cultural baggage that the Confederacy just could not replace. Their actual immigrant experience or, if born in America, the stories told them by their immigrant parents had left them with a strong sense of their own Irish ethnicity. It always played a role in their attitude to the Confederacy, which Confederate recruiters certainly acknowledged in their attempts to enlist Irish soldiers. In the tumultuous times of their American lives, the one thing the Irish were sure of was their Irishness and, for most of them, the Catholicism intertwined with it. They had a better definition of themselves than the natives they lived among. Even the manifest southern patriotism of the likes of T. W. MacMahon, John Mitchel, Bishop Patrick Lynch, and A. G. Magrath could not make the larger Irish population embrace the Confederacy wholeheartedly. All these leaders' labors did was assure the Irish of their place in the white racial hierarchy after the war. The Irish did not necessarily need a new republic preserving slavery to express that reality, especially one that brought death, destruction, and economic hardship. It was when racial supremacy was seriously challenged during Radical Reconstruction that the Irish could find a firmer common ground with native whites. This common ground was based in nostalgic "memories" of the Confederacy. In the commemoration of the "covenant" of "shared sacrifice," the Irish finally rallied to the Confederate cause unreservedly, lost though it was.

As a result, the distinct Irish story increasingly receded into the overall Confederate/white southern identity remembered on Lost Cause occasions. Father Ryan, for example, became the Poet Priest of the Confederacy but not part of the Irish American literary canon.[3] As the Irish integrated well into the white community and their account became subsumed into the general one, the "remembering" of the Confederacy would become less important to the Irish and their descendants' place in the region.

The Irish Confederate story, however, could be, when needed, revived to remind native southerners of Irish patriotism. In 1902, for example, Anthony Keiley's younger brother, Benjamin, was the Catholic bishop of Savannah. He claimed that, before becoming a priest, he had served, at age seventeen, in the Army of Northern Virginia toward the end of the war, although there seems to be no official record of it. Nonetheless, people accepted his Confederate status. At the time he became bishop, he faced increasing hostility toward Catholicism at the instigation of the embittered former Georgia Populist politician Tom Watson, who had blamed his electoral defeats in part on Patrick Walsh and the Catholic voters in Augusta.[4] In defending himself and his flock, Keiley was not afraid to play this Confederate card. In 1902 he created a regional stir when, in a Confederate Memorial Day speech in Savannah, he defended the late Jefferson Davis against the charges of treason brought against him by sitting U.S. president Teddy Roosevelt. Keiley began by proclaiming that "Slavery was not the cause of the war," a standard of Lost Cause rhetoric. He then moved on to Roosevelt's charge specifically, claiming that "Jefferson Davis was a statesman, a soldier, and a man of high character, a Senator, a Cabinet officer, a President not put in office by a bullet, but by ballot." In contrast: "Theodore Roosevelt's title to immortal fame will rest on shooting beasts, and profiting by the murderous act of a reprobate who shot a man." Letters of gratitude poured in from across the region in response to his attack on, as he described the sitting president (who had succeeded to the office after the assassination of President William McKinley), the "accidental occupant of the presidential chair." The Irish American Catholic bishop had defended southern honor, thus proving his loyalty to his community. On other occasions, Keiley labeled himself an "Unreconstructed Reb" and stated that he was still "a firm believer in the justice of the Cause of the South."[5] He genuinely believed in the Lost Cause, but he had also found it useful in opposing the anti-Catholicism of Watson and his ilk.

With his death in 1922, however, the utility of a Confederate heritage declined for Irish Americans, as indeed it did for most white southerners. Almost all of the Irish veterans were dead, and their successors were now southern-born. New immigrants arriving from Ireland in the late nineteenth and early twentieth centuries flocked to the industrial North, and not the cotton fields and plantation-like textile mills of the South. The "Irish" community was thus increasingly native, and not Irish, born. Indeed, Irish Catholic southerners became so confident of their place in the New South hierarchy, it became acceptable to break away from the dominant Lost Cause narrative. The Catholic and actively Irish nationalist mayor

John Patrick Grace of Charleston, who served in the office from 1911 to 1915 and again from 1919 to 1923, could, for example, be critical of those who idealized the past. "We must live with the living and not with the dead," he stated.[6] Grace had no time for Confederate memorializing. Similarly, in the 1930s, the descendant of Irish Catholic Georgians, Margaret Mitchell, could portray the folly of the Confederacy, which destroyed the Old South civilization she admired so much, now "gone with the wind."[7] As a result, the real Irish Confederate story became so intermingled in the southern one, it disappeared. Only in popular culture did it retain any kind of significance but just in the mythic sense of the eternal Irish rebel.[8]

While the descendants of Irish Confederates situated in centers of Irish settlement such as Charleston, Savannah, and New Orleans still expressed their ethnicity in very public ways, such as marching with their various societies on St. Patrick's Day and retaining their strong Roman Catholicism, they were now far more southern than Irish. Even though there were some notable exceptions, on the whole they endorsed the ugly realities of Jim Crow and black disfranchisement in the New South, reflecting the Lost Cause ideology of their Irish Confederate ancestors.[9] This reality meant that, along with their white Anglo-Saxon Protestant neighbors, they would have to go through the "Second Reconstruction" of the civil rights era, reflecting the long-term legacy of Irish involvement with the Confederate States of America.[10]

Irish Surnames in Mobile, Alabama, Units

To evaluate the "Irishness" of the names recorded for Mobile military units, I have followed the method developed by Malcolm Smith and Donald MacRaild. By comparing surnames listed in Griffith's Valuation, a survey of all Irish householders between 1853 and 1865, with surnames in the 1881 census of Suffolk, the English county with the least Irish immigration, they were able to generate a statistical estimate of how likely a given surname was to be of Irish origin, which they used to evaluate the "Irishness" of names in the database of Mobile units compiled by a local chapter of the United Daughters of the Confederacy. (Smith and MacRaild's research was supported in part by a grant from the Economic and Social Research Council of England and Wales). In my research, most of the names that I assessed as Irish had, by Smith and MacRaild's definition, a very high probability of being so. Beyond that, every name listed below appeared somewhere in Griffith's Valuation and thus could be Irish. Those names that had a high probability of being English as well, such as Griffin, I included only if the name appeared in an Irish unit. Some names that occurred in Irish units and Griffith's Valuation but that were also very common English names, such as Smith, were too uncertain to classify as Irish. The following names appeared in the collection of rosters that I assessed and counted as Irish. I also used this list in assessing names from other Confederate units in the Compiled Service Records.

Ahern	Cain (Keane)	Conners
Aherne	Callaghan	Conray (Conroy) (Irish unit)
Barry	Cannavin	Convy (Irish unit)
Birmingham (Irish unit)	Canny	Corcoran (Irish unit)
Bonner	Carey	Costello
Brady	Carr	Coughlin
Brannan	Casey (Irish Unit)	Courtney (Irish Unit)
Breen	Cassaday (Cassidy)	Cowley
Brennan	Cassidy	Coyne
Brophy	Cavanaugh (Kavanagh)	Cronin
Burke	Cochran	Croughan
Burns (Irish unit)	Collins (Irish unit)	Crowley
Byrnes	Conaly (Connelly)	Cullen
Caffey	Condon	Cummins
Cahall (Cahill)	Connelly	Curran

Curry (Irish unit)
Curtin
Cusic (Cusack)
Daily (Daly)
Dargan
Deely (Irish unit)
Denehey
Devine
Dohan
Dolan
Donley
Donnegan
Donnell
Donnelly
Donnivan
Donoho (Donoghue)
Donovan
Dorgan
Dougherty
Dowling
Doyle
Driscoll
Duane
Duff
Dugan
Duggan (Irish unit)
Dunn
Dwyre (Dwyer)
Eagan
Ellis
Elward (Irish unit)
Fagan
Fagin
Fanning
Farley
Farrell
Finnegan
Fitzgerald
Fitzpatrick
Flannery
Flood
Flynn
Foley
Fornan (Irish unit)
Foy (Irish unit)

Frawley
Gallagher
Galvin
Gannon
Garrity
Gaynor
Geary
Gildee
Given
Gleason (Gleeson)
Glenn (Irish unit)
Glennon
Gouldin
Griffin (Irish unit)
Hagan
Haggerty
Haley (Healy) (Irish unit)
Hall (Irish unit)
Hallisey (Irish unit)
Halpin
Hanley
Hanlin (Hanlon)
Hanlon
Harrington (Irish unit)
Hart (Irish unit)
Hays (Irish unit)
Healy
Hennessey
Hickey
Hogan
Holland
Horan
Horgan
Horrigan
Hough
Hughes
Hurley
Jennings (Irish unit)
Joyce
Kane (Keane)
Kean
Kearnes
Kearney
Kearns
Keating

Keefe
Kehoe
Kelly (Irish unit)
Kennedy (Irish Unit)
Kenny
Kent (Irish unit)
Keogh
Killon (Irish unit)
Kilroy (Irish unit)
Koyle
Lanahan
Langan
Leavy (Irish unit)
Loughrey
Lynch
Lyons
Mack
Mackey
Madden
Maguire
Maher
Mahoney
Malley
Mallon (Irish unit)
Malone
Maloney
Manning (Irish unit)
Martin (Irish unit)
McAdory (Irish unit)
McAfee (Irish unit)
McAuley
McAvoy
McBride
McCabe
McCarron (Irish unit)
McCarthy
McCready (Irish unit)
McDermott
McDevitt (Irish unit)
McDonell
McElroy
McFeely (Irish unit)
McGilvery
McGinnis
McGonigal

McGrath

McGraw

McGuin

McHugh

McInerney

McKenna

McKeon

McKibbin (Irish unit)

McKinney

McLaughlin

McMahon

McManus

McMullen

McNamara

McNiff (Irish unit)

McVoy

Meehan

Meenan

Mooney

Moore (Irish unit)

Moran

Moran

Morrison (Irish unit)

Morrissey

Muldon (Muldoon)

Mulligan

Murphy

Murray (Irish unit)

Nagles (Nagle)

Nash

Neely

Neill

Niolon (Nolan) (Irish unit)

Nonan (Nolan)

Noonan

Noonan (Irish unit)

Nugent

O'Brien

O'Connell

O'Connor

O'Donnell

O'Farrell

O'Keefe

O'Neal (Irish unit)

O'Neil

O'Rourke

Patterson

Patton

Phalen (Phelan)

Powers

Prendergast

Pursell (Purcell)

Quill

Quinn

Ray (Rea)

Reardon

Redmond

Regan (Irish unit)

Riley

Rogers

Rooney

Ryan

Ryley (Reilly)

Saggerty (Irish unit)

Scanlon

Scully

Shannon

Shea

Sheridan

Shields

Skehan

Skelly

Stafford (Irish unit)

Sullivan

Sweeney (Irish unit)

Tobin

Toomey

Trainor (Irish unit)

Troy

Walsh

Weelan (Whelan)

Welch

Notes

ABBREVIATIONS

AAB	Archives of the Archdiocese of Baltimore, Maryland
AAM	Archives of the Archdiocese of Mobile, Alabama
AANO	Archives of the Archdiocese of New Orleans, Louisiana
AANV	Association of the Army of Northern Virginia Papers, Louisiana Historical Association Collection, Tulane University, New Orleans
AAT	Association of the Army of Tennessee Papers, Louisiana Historical Association Collection, Tulane University, New Orleans
ACDC	Archives of the Catholic Diocese of Charleston, South Carolina
ACUA	Archives of the Catholic University of America, Washington, DC
CMS	Centre for Migration Studies, Ulster American Folk Park Omagh, Northern Ireland
CSRCS	Compiled Service Records of Confederate Soldiers, RG 109, National Archives and Records Administration, Washington, DC
DU	David M. Rubenstein Rare Books and Manuscripts Library, Duke University, Durham, North Carolina
EU	Special Collections, Robert Woodruff Library, Emory University, Atlanta, Georgia
FO	Foreign Office Records, National Archives of the United Kingdom, London
GDAH	Georgia Department of Archives and History, Morrow
HNOC	Williams Research Center, Historic New Orleans Collection, New Orleans, Louisiana
LC	Manuscripts Division, Library of Congress, Washington, DC
LHAC	Louisiana Historical Association Collection, Tulane University, New Orleans
LLMVC	Louisiana and Lower Mississippi Valley Collection, Louisiana State University, Baton Rouge
MC	Museum of the Confederacy, Richmond, Virginia
MDAH	Mississippi Department of Archives and History, Jackson
MDBMA	Monsignor Daniel J. Bourke Memorial Archives, Catholic Diocese of Savannah, Georgia
MHS	Missouri Historical Society, St. Louis
MPL	Mobile (Alabama) Public Library
MSCPL	Memphis and Shelby County (Tennessee) Library and Public Information Center
NARA	National Archives and Records Administration, Washington, DC
NAUK	National Archives of the United Kingdom, London
NYHS	New-York Historical Society, New York

OR   *War of the Rebellion: Official Records of the Union and Confederate Armies*
ORN   *Official Records of the Union and Confederate Navies in the War of the Rebellion*
PRONI   Public Record Office of Northern Ireland
RG   Record Group
SCDAH   South Carolina Department of Archives and History, Columbia
SCHS   South Carolina Historical Society, Charleston
SCL   South Caroliniana Library, University of South Carolina, Columbia
SHC   Southern Historical Collection, University of North Carolina, Chapel Hill
TU   Special Collections, Tulane University, New Orleans, Louisiana
UNDA   University of Notre Dame Archives, Notre Dame, Indiana
VHS   Virginia Historical Society, Richmond

INTRODUCTION

1. Sears, *To the Gates of Richmond*, 212, 222–25; OR, ser. 1, vol. 16, 681–83; CSRCS, 1st South Carolina Infantry (Gregg's) Regiment, NARA.

2. *The Irish Volunteers Memorial Meeting*, 16; *Southern Historical Society Papers* 22 (1894): 238.

3. Cauthen, *South Carolina Goes to War, 1860–1865*, 65–66.

4. CSRCS, 1st South Carolina Infantry (Gregg's) Regiment, NARA. For Elmira and its notoriety, see Gray, *The Business of Captivity*; and Horigan, *Elmira: Death Camp of the North*.

5. Kinsella, *The Táin*; Bartlett and Jeffrey, "An Irish Military Tradition?," 1–6; Turpin, "Cúchulainn Lives On," 26–31.

6. Bartlett and Jeffrey, "An Irish Military Tradition?," 7; Simms, "Gaelic Warfare in the Middle Ages," 99–115; Murtagh, "Irish Soldiers Abroad," 294–314.

7. Quoted in Bartlett and Jeffrey, "An Irish Military Tradition?," 13.

8. Foster, *Ghosts of the Confederacy*, 104–26. See also chapter 6.

9. Kennedy, *Population of the United States in 1860*, xxix; W. I. Burton, *Melting Pot Soldiers*, 112–60.

10. Tucker, *"God Help the Irish!,"* 11–48; Bruce, *The Harp and the Eagle*, 88, 104–12, 117–18, 123–33.

11. *Gods and Generals*, DVD; Gallagher, *Causes Won, Lost, and Forgotten*, 203–5.

12. Lonn, *Foreigners in the Confederacy*, 477–78; Wiley, review of *Foreigners in the Confederacy*, 561–63; Meneely, review of *Foreigners in the Confederacy*, 173–74.

13. Owsley, *Plain Folk of the Old South* (1982; repr. 2008). John Boles has written a new introduction to this new edition by LSU Press, which first published the book in 1982 with an introduction by Grady McWhiney. Two interesting diaries focusing on a couple of prominent Irish Catholic Confederates are Curran, *John Dooley's Civil War*; and Durkin, *Confederate Chaplain*.

14. Silver, "A New Look at Old South Urbanization"; Sigel, "Artisans and Immigrants," 21–30; Berlin and Guttman, "Natives and Immigrants"; Clark, "The South's Irish Catholics"; R. M. Miller, "The Enemy Within"; Brady, "The Irish Community in Antebellum Memphis"; Rousey, "Aliens in the WASP."

15. Burns, *The Civil War*; "Symbol of the New Ireland"; Robinson, "Cherishing the Irish Diaspora."

16. T. L. Jones, *Lee's Tigers*, 6–7, 233–54; Daniel, *Soldiering in the Army of Tennessee*, 128; Durkin, *Confederate Chaplain*; Curran, *John Dooley's Civil War*; Symonds, *Stonewall of the West*; Joslyn, *A Meteor Shining Brightly*; Tucker, *The Confederacy's Fighting Chaplain*; E. Gleeson, *Rebel Sons of Erin and Erin Go Gray!*; Gannon, *Irish Rebels, Confederate Tigers*.

17. O'Grady, *Clear the Confederate Way!*; O'Brien, *Irish Americans in the Confederate Army*; Tucker, *Irish Confederates*.

18. See, for example, O'Brien, *Irish Americans in the Confederate Army*, 4–5.

19. See chapters 2, 3, and 6.

20. Although not in complete agreement with their work, I find the ideas of Benedict Anderson and Eric Hobsbawm useful in understanding "Irishness" in the South. I much prefer the term "reimagine" rather than "invent" for the Irish in America. There is a major difference between reimagining cultural baggage in a new and foreign context and inventing an ethnicity as Sir Walter Scott and the Ossian Sagas did in Scotland. Anderson, *Imagined Communities*; Hobsbawm, Introduction; Trevor-Roper, "The Invention of Tradition." For ethnicity in an American context, see Schultz, *Ethnicity on Parade*. For Ireland and Irish Americans, see Kiberd, *Inventing Ireland*; and Meagher, *Inventing Irish America*.

21. See chapters 1 and 4.

22. Trent, *William Gilmore Simms*, 1; For more on Simms and his southern milieu, see Faust, *The Sacred Circle*; Dye, "A Sociology of the Civil War." For "man at the center," see Cash, *The Mind of the South*, 29–58.

23. I will, however, use the technique of isonymy (name analysis) on a small scale in an attempt to assess the number of Irish soldiers in the Confederate army. See chapter 2 and the appendix.

24. D. T. Gleeson, *Irish in the South*, 36.

25. Quigley, *Shifting Ground*, 216.

26. Ibid., 217.

27. Nor was it just a part of the Celtic South, "Attack and Die" thesis. Irish and native Confederates saw themselves as different. They may have had compatible political positions but in general they did not see each other as long-lost Celtic cousins subconsciously re-creating the various Celtic defeats over the centuries. See McWhiney and Jamieson, *Attack and Die*, 170–91. For critiques, see Robertson, review of *Attack and Die*, 128–29; and Berthoff, "Celtic Mist over the South," 523–46. While Berthoff's critique came out before the publication of his major work on the "Celtic South," *Cracker Culture*, McWhiney failed to deal with the criticisms in it. See also M. P. Johnson, review of *Cracker Culture*.

CHAPTER 1

1. W. C. Davis, *Rhett*, 87–107, 194–232, 396–97.

2. Magrath, *An Address Delivered in the Cathedral of St. Finbar*; Freehling, *Road to Disunion*, 2:399; *Seventh and Eighth Censuses of the United States, 1850 and 1860: Slave Schedule, Charleston County, South Carolina*, NARA; W. C. Davis, *Rhett*,

349–50; *Charleston Mercury*, Sept. 24, 30, Oct. 1, 1856; *Columbia Daily South Carolinian*, Oct. 2, 1856.

3. "A. G. Magrath," "John Magrath," Magrath Family Papers SCHS; Minutes of the Hibernian Society, Apr. 18, 1842, SCHS; Takaki, *A Pro-Slavery Crusade*, 201–16; Sinha, *The Counter-Revolution of Slavery*, 168–70; *The United States vs. William C. Corrie*, 6–7, 26–27.

4. *The United States vs. William C. Corrie*, 14–18.

5. Sinha, *Counter-Revolution of Slavery*, 153–86; [Magrath] *Three Letters on the Order of the Know-Nothings*.

6. D. A. Wilson, *United Irishmen, United States*, 23, 38–40, 46, 103–11, 135–37, 178; K. L. Brown, "United Irishmen in the South."

7. In particular, the campaigns for Catholic Emancipation and Repeal of the Union. See MacDonagh, *The Hereditary Bondsman* and *The Emancipist*; McCaffrey, *Daniel O'Connell and the Repeal Year*. For the famine, see Scally, *The End of Hidden Ireland*, 73–74, 88.

8. Quoted in Shoemaker, "Strangers and Citizens," 344; D. T. Gleeson, *Irish in the South*, 94–106.

9. Stephenson, *Alexander Porter*; Niehaus, *The Irish in New Orleans*, 81–83, 139–40; Howe, *The Political Culture of American Whigs*, 108–9. For Irish and Whigs, see Holt, *The Rise and Fall of the American Whig Party*, 185, 188, 203–4. For the importance of culture in Jacksonian politics, see Kohl, *The Politics of Individualism*.

10. John C. Calhoun to [Gilbert C. Rice] "Secretary of the Irish Emigrant Society," Sept. 13, 1841, in John C. Calhoun, *The Papers of John C. Calhoun*, 15:774; Niehaus, *Irish in New Orleans*, 84–85.

11. W. C. Davis, *Jefferson Davis*, 120–21; D. T. Gleeson, *Irish in the South*, 101–2.

12. D. T. Gleeson, *Irish in the South*, 107–20; Overdyke, *The Know-Nothing Party in the South*; Duesner, "The Know-Nothing Riots in Louisville"; Baker, "The Joyce Family Murders"; Towers, "Violence as a Tool of Party Dominance"; Soule, *The Know-Nothing Party in New Orleans*.

13. D. T. Gleeson, *Irish in the South*, 118–19; Crowson, "Southern Port City Politics," 232–42.

14. D. T. Gleeson, *Irish in the South*, 111; C. M. Simpson, *A Good Southerner*, 106–18; Freehling, *Road to Disunion*, 1:513–15; Varon, *Disunion*, 262.

15. *Vicksburg Daily Sentinel*, Nov. 13, 1840; *Vicksburg Tri-Weekly Sentinel*, June 5, 1841; *Natchez Mississippi Free Trader*, Feb. 12 and 27, 1851; *Charleston United States Catholic Miscellany*, Aug. 15, 1835; P. Kennedy to Vere Foster, Foster of Glyde Papers, Mar. 15, 1855, D6318/D/8/9, PRONI.

16. Kemble, *Journal of a Residence on a Georgia Plantation*, 105. For more on the remarkable Fanny Kemble, see Clinton, *Fanny Kemble's Civil Wars*; R. M. Miller "The Enemy Within," 34–40, 46–51; Fox-Genovese and Genovese, *The Mind of the Master Class*, 51–55, 146; Memminger, quoted in Jordan, "Schemes of Usefulness," 225.

17. Sigel, "Artisans and Immigrants"; M. P. Johnson, *Toward a Patriarchal Republic*.

18. Ignatiev, *How the Irish Became White*. See Roediger, *The Wages of Whiteness*, especially chapter 7. For good critiques of whiteness studies, see Kolchin,

"Whiteness Studies"; and particularly Arnesen, "Whiteness and the Historians' Imagination."

19. J. R. Lynch, *Reminiscences of an Active Life*, 9–15.

20. O'Toole, *Passing for White*. Patrick Francis became president of Georgetown University in 1874, while James Augustine became the United States' first (unacknowledged) African American bishop one year later when the pope appointed him bishop of Portland, Maine.

21. Wade, *Slavery in the Cities*, 80–87; Haunton "Law and Order in Savannah," 10–11; *Mobile Daily Register*, Apr. 13, 1859; Lockley, "Trading Encounters."

22. Forret, *Race Relations at the Margin*, 76.

23. Waldrep, *Roots of Disorder*, 33–34.

24. Seventh Census of the United States, 1850: Slave Schedule, Charleston Co., S.C., Plaquemines Parish, La., Adams Co., Miss., Taliaferro Co., Ga.; Eighth Census of the United States, 1860: Slave Schedule, Madison Co., Miss., Charleston Co., S.C., Plaquemines Parish, La., Taliaferro Co., Ga.; James Francis Tracy to Richard M. Scott, Mar. 29, Apr. 2, 1823, James Francis Tracy Papers, DU; "Deer Range Memorandums," "Plantation Journals," Maunsel White Collection, SHC; James, *Antebellum Natchez*, 156–57.

25. Seventh Census of the United States, 1850: Slave Schedule, City of New Orleans, La.; Eighth Census of the United States, 1860: Slave Schedule, City of New Orleans, La.

26. Eighth Census of the United States, 1860 Slave Schedule, Madison Co., Miss.; Slave Sale Broadside, 1852, SCHS; "Catalogue of Negro Slaves of the Estate of the Hon. William McKenna Deceased," Jan. 21, 1861, ACDC; Wakelyn, "Catholic Elites in the Slaveholding South," 224.

27. Patrick Murphy Diary, Patrick Murphy Collection, LLMVC.

28. Wells, *The Origins of the Southern Middle Class*, 152.

29. Rousey, "Friends and Foes of Slavery," 376–77. The cities are Savannah, Natchez, Montgomery, Baton Rouge, and Columbia.

30. McGovern, *John Mitchel*, 1–9, 57–86. For famine rhetoric, see Mitchel, *The Last Great Conquest of Ireland (Perhaps)*; and G. Davis, "Making History," 98–115.

31. McGovern, *John Mitchel*, 209–29. For Mitchel's continued importance beyond his time, see Ramon, *A Provisional Dictator*, 152–53; Maume, "Young Ireland, Arthur Griffith, and Republican Ideology," 155–74; Hart, *The IRA and Its Enemies*, 207.

32. For his first encounter with slavery, see Mitchel, *Jail Journal*, 153–54.

33. Quoted in *Savannah Morning News*, Jan. 19, 1854. For Mitchel and Carlyle, see Mitchel, *Jail Journal*, 204; Thomas Carlyle to Lord Clarendon, May 26, 1848, in *The Carlyle Letters Online*, vol. 23; Lynch, "Defining Irish Nationalism and Anti-Imperialism," 82–107. For Carlyle and slavery, see *The Commercial Review of the South and West* 2 (Apr. 1850): 527–38.

34. *Jackson Mississippian and State Gazette*, Apr. 11, 1854; *Boston Liberator*, Apr. 28, 1854, July 16, 1858; *Savannah Daily Morning News*, Dec. 31, 1856; John Mitchel to "Matilda," Aug. 6, 1855, D.107/M/1, Pinkerton Papers, PRONI.

35. *Knoxville Southern Citizen*, Jan. 21, Mar. 18, 1858.

36. Sinha, *Counterrevolution of Slavery*, 134–35; Takaki, *Pro-Slavery Crusade*, 146–59. The commercial conventions began in 1845 but became an annual event after 1852. V. V. Johnson, *The Men and the Vision of the Southern Commercial Conventions*, 1–15.

37. *De Bow's Review* 24 (June 1858): 580–87; *Washington National Intelligencer*, June 23, 1860; *Knoxville Southern Citizen*, June 3, 1858. Yancey's biographer considers his speech to this convention as a major element in the fire-eater's rise to notoriety. Walther, *William Lowndes Yancey*, 216–21. For comparison of Irish and southern struggles during the period, see D. T. Gleeson, "Parallel Struggles."

38. Fox-Genovese and Genovese, *The Mind of the Master Class*, 216–17. For more on Nott, see Horsman, *Josiah Nott of Mobile*. See also Fredrickson, *The Black Image in the White Mind*, 71–96; and *Boston Liberator*, Feb. 17, 1854.

39. Dwan, *The Great Community*, 31–41.

40. *Knoxville Southern Citizen*, Feb. 4, 1858.

41. Quoted in *Jackson Mississippian and State Gazette*, Mar. 10, 1858.

42. *Knoxville Southern Citizen*, Mar. 11, 1858. For Fitzhugh, see Wish, *Antebellum Writings of George Fitzhugh*.

43. *Vicksburg Tri-Weekly Sentinel*, June 5, 1841; P. Kennedy to Vere Foster, Mar. 19, 1855, Foster of Glyde Papers, D3618/D/8/9, PRONI; Robert McElderry to Thomas McElderry, 11 Mar. 1852, to David McElderry, Dec. 12, 1853, T2414/12; William McElderry to [Thomas McElderry], Dec. [1854], Robert McElderry Collection, T2414/8; Moses Paul to John Graham [copy], Dec. 29, 1840, Moses Paul Letter, T1568, PRONI.

44. The Journal of James Hamilton [typescript], Migration Database, CMS.

45. Campbell, *Slavery on Trial*, 134–35; Kemble, *Journal of a Residence*, 105, 124–25.

46. "Petition of Working Men and Mechanics of Charleston," 1858, General Assembly Petitions, SCDAH; Johnson and Roark, *Black Masters*, 178–85. See also Campbell, *Slavery on Trial*, 51.

47. Forret, *Race Relations at the Margins*, especially 184–22; Johnson and Roark, *Black Masters*, 175–76.

48. Johnson and Roark, *Black Masters*, 199–200; D. T. Gleeson, *Irish in the South*, 35–36, 51–53; De Bow, *Seventh Census*, 339; Kennedy, *Population of the United States in 1860*, 452. Between 1850 and 1860 the slave population in the city declined from 19,532 to 13,509.

49. Johnson and Roark, *Black Masters*, 266–69, 276–81; West, "'She is dissatisfied with her present condition.'"

50. John [Maginnis] to John McKowen, July 18, 1849, John McKowen Papers, LLMVC.

51. Sullivan, "Charleston, the Vesey Conspiracy," 68.

52. De Bow, quoted in Meyers, "Come Let Us Fly to Freedom's Sky," 33.

53. Quoted in A. Carey, *Parties, Slavery, and the Union*, 193–94.

54. William Conner to Annie Conner, Mar. 11, 1855, Annie Conner Collection, MSCPL.

55. Fitzhugh, *Sociology for the South*, 51, 58–59, 194, (quote on 206), and *Cannibals All!*, vi–vii, 38–39, 290–91.

56. Genovese, *A Consuming Fire*. For sources on the Catholic Church and slavery, see Zanca, *American Catholics and Slavery*.

57. Memminger, quoted in Jordan, "Schemes of Usefulness," 225.

58. Bishop John England to John Forsyth; *United States (Charleston SC) Catholic Miscellany*, Mar. 25, 1843; Buttimer, "'By Their Deeds, You Shall Know Them,'" 121.

59. For Vesey, see Egerton, *He Shall Go Out Free*. There has been controversy over how real the Vesey plot was. See M. P. Johnson, "Denmark Vesey and his Co-Conspirators," 915–76 ; Paquette and Egerton, "Of Fact and Fables," 8–48.

60. *Charleston United States Catholic Miscellany*, Aug. 1, 15, 1835; Freehling, *Prelude to Civil War*, 340–48.

61. O'Neill quoted in O'Connell, *Catholicity in the Carolinas and Georgia*, 514. See also Nelson, "'Come Out of Such a Land, You Irishmen,'" 58–81, and Nelson, *Irish Nationalists*, 57–85.

62. The best coverage of Repeal in the South is Murphy, *American Slavery, Irish Freedom*.

63. *Tribute of Respect to the Memory*, 10, 15.

64. *Charleston Irishman and Southern Democrat*, Sept. 5, 1829, July 19, 1830; Freehling, *Prelude to Civil War*, 181–82, 235–38, 365–69; D. T. Gleeson, *Irish in the South*.

65. Freehling, *Prelude to Civil War*, 260–300.

66. McPherson, *Battle Cry of Freedom*, 55–58; Freehling, *Road to Disunion*, 1:481–86, 519; *Mississippi Free Trader*, May 15, June 1, 2, 3, 11, 12, 1850, June 29. *Mississippi Free Trader* Subscription Book, Richard Elward Papers, DU; Olsen, *Political Culture and Secession in Mississippi*, 45–48;

67. D. T. Gleeson, *Irish in the South*, 136–37; A. Carey, *Parties, Slavery, and the Union*, 156–83; W. C. Davis, *Rhett*, 349, 358, 350; *Charleston Mercury*, Oct. 16, 1851.

68. W. C. Davis, *Rhett*, 348–51.

69. Freehling, *Road to Disunion*, 2:296–97, 309–22.

70. Johannsen, *Stephen A. Douglas*, 703–10, 741–43, 798–800.

71. Johannsen, *Stephen A. Douglas*, 457, 470, 482; Jacqueline Jones, *Saving Savannah*, 108–9 (quote on 120).

72. Dubin, *United States Presidential Elections*, 159. There are no totals for Charleston because voters in South Carolina did not vote directly for president before the Civil War because the legislature assigned presidential electors. In 1860 it awarded all eight to Breckinridge. Outside of New Orleans, breaking down the Irish vote by ward is difficult because ward totals were not always published in the newspapers.

73. Gower and Allen, *Pen and Sword*, 390, 429, 487, 543; Towers, *The Urban South*, 170–71, 206–7; Cooper, *Jefferson Davis*, 336–39.

74. Dubin, *United States Presidential Elections*, 162, 183, 186; Bland, *Life of Benjamin Butler*, 30–32.

75. Dubin, *United States Presidential Elections*, 159, 182; D. T. Gleeson, *Irish in the South*, 35; Brady, "The Irish Community in Antebellum Memphis," 30.

76. *New Orleans Daily True Delta*, June 14, Oct. 7, 9, 12, 17, 21, Nov. 3, 1860; Tarver, "The Political Clubs of New Orleans," 19.

77. Quoted in Niehaus, *Irish in New Orleans*, 157.

78. Tarver, "Political Clubs of New Orleans," 26–27; D. T. Gleeson, *Irish in the South*, 115; *New Orleans Daily True Delta*, Nov. 6, 1860.

79. *New Orleans Daily True Delta*, Nov. 13, 14, 18, 24, 1860.

80. Ibid., Dec. 19, 1860.

81. Ibid., Dec. 20, 21, 23, 27, 1860, Jan. 6, 12, 13, 1861.

82. Towers, *The Urban South*, 142–92. Michael Johnson believes that immediate secession in Georgia was driven by this fear; see *Toward a Patriarchal Republic*. For a critique, see Freehling, *Road to Disunion*, 2:581, n.11.

83. *Charleston Mercury*, Nov. 9, 17, Dec. 29, 1860, Jan. 5, 1861 (quote). For non-Irish, see McCurry, *Masters of Small Worlds*, 277–304.

84. Ellis, *The Moving Appeal*, 85–87, 112–14; *Memphis Daily Appeal*, Mar. 26, 28, Apr. 2, 1861; *De Bow's Review*, Jan. 1861, 67–77.

85. *Memphis Daily Appeal*, Mar. 26, 1861.

86. Ibid., Apr. 5, 1861.

87. Andrew Jackson to Maunsel White, Feb. 28, 1842, Correspondence, Maunsel White to Andrew Jackson, Jan. 26, Mar. 12, 1845, Letterbook, "Deer Range Memorandum, May 7, 1860–June 17, 1861," Maunsel White Collection, SHC. For the culture of Louisiana sugar planting, see Follett, *The Sugar Masters*.

88. M. D. O'Connor, *The Life and Letters of M. P. O'Connor*, 18–20, 140–41; Freehling, *Road to Disunion*, 2:396–406.

89. Quoted in D. T. Gleeson, *Irish in the South*, 140. See also D. T. Gleeson, "Parallel Struggles," 97–116; and McGovern, *John Mitchel*, 165–67.

90. Freehling, *Road to Disunion*, 396–97; *Charleston Mercury*, Nov. 17, 1860; C. C. Jones to Mary Mallard, Dec. 13, 1860 in Myers, *The Children of Pride*, 634; M. P. Johnson, "A New Look at the Popular Vote," 261–62.

91. Crofts, "Late Antebellum Richmond Reconsidered," 274–75; Lankford, *Cry Havoc!*, 115–25; Towers, *Urban South*, 28–29, 170–71, 210; *Memphis Daily Appeal*, Jan. 17, 1861; Subject File-Paulding, MDAH.

92. Wooster, *The Secession Conventions of the South*, 199–200; "The Florida Secession Convention," 384; Cornish, "An Irish Confederate," 3:186; Seventh Census of the United States, 1850: Slave Schedule, Lincoln County, NC; Eighth Census of the United States, 1860: Population Schedule and Slave Schedule, Lincoln County, NC, NARA.

93. Eighth Census of the United States, 1860: City of New Orleans; Wooster, "The Louisiana Secession Convention," 126–33; Dew, "The Long Lost Returns," 364–65.

94. Thomas, *The Confederate Nation*, 37–97; Dew, *Apostles of Disunion*.

95. One Republican saw the American Party as "simply a stepping stone" from being a free-soil Democrat or Whig on the road to becoming a Republican. Quoted in Gienapp, *The Origins of the Republican Party*, 418. Gienapp himself believes that the demise of the Know-Nothings after 1856 in states such as New York, Massachusetts, Connecticut, Pennsylvania, and Ohio "demonstrate the fundamental importance of the Know Nothings in the Republican coalition." 419. From the middle of 1855 "The spilt within the national [American] party was

repeated in state after northern state, as anti-slavery nativists abandoned Know-Nothingism for Republicanism and the Know-Nothing party came under the control of Silver Grey Whigs *more interested in Unionism than nativism*" [my emphasis]. Foner, *Free Soil, Free Labor, Free Men*, 226–60, quote on 240. In light of the explicit link between anti-slavery advocates and nativism, it is no wonder that Irish Catholic leaders in the North saw any Irish voting Republican as "voting for their own degradation." Quoted in Gienapp, *Origins*, 424. On the other hand Republican leaders such as Abraham Lincoln and William Henry Seward (of New York) had no time for nativism even if they accepted the votes and support of nativists. Oates, *With Malice toward None*, 107, 133; Van Deusen, *William Henry Seward*, 164–65.

CHAPTER 2

1. *New Orleans Daily True Delta*, Dec. 30, 1860, Jan. 9, 1861; Eighth Census of the United States, 1860, City of New Orleans; Eighth Census of the United States, 1860, Slave Schedule, City of New Orleans, NARA; Bearss, "The Seizure of Forts," 401–10.

2. *Charleston Mercury*, Jan. 17, 1856; *Charleston Tri-Weekly Courier*, Dec. 22, 1860; *Washington Daily National Intelligencer*, Nov. 13, 1860.

3. *Charleston Mercury*, Dec. 28, 1860; *Charleston Daily Courier*, Dec. 28, 1860. The "thrilling activities" are covered well in Detzer, *Allegiance*, 108–60; and Klein, *Days of Defiance*, 152–74.

4. *New Orleans Daily True Delta*, Nov. 3, 1860, Jan. 6, Feb. 1, 1861; Eighth Census of the United States, 1860, City of New Orleans, Louisiana, NARA; Rogers, *Irish-American Units*, 24.

5. *New Orleans Daily Picayune*, Apr. 2, 1861; *New Orleans True Delta*, Apr. 26, 1861.

6. Hayes-McCoy, "The Irish Pike," 98–128. The most iconic statue to the 1798 rebels is in Wexford town, site of their Wexford Republic and their greatest victory. It is of a young United Irishman "Croppy," so called for their republican cropped hair, carrying a pike in his right hand. "1798 Memorial—The Bullring Wexford."

7. John C. Calhoun to Chas. Jas. Faulkner, Aug. 1, 1847, Joseph W. Lesesne to John C. Calhoun, Sept. 12, 1847, in Calhoun, *The Papers of John C. Calhoun*, 24:481, 552–53.

8. Jefferson Davis to Malcolm D. Haynes, Aug. 18, 1849, in J. Davis, *The Papers of Jefferson Davis*, 4:31–32.

9. See chapter 1.

10. Quoted in Donald M. Williams, *Shamrocks and Pluff Mud*, 115.

11. There is a debate as to how terrible Cromwell was in Ireland, considering he was there for only nine weeks, and whether he was that much out of step with the standards of seventeenth-century warfare. Nonetheless, he and his minions' conquest of the island had profound negative effects on the political, economic, and social position of Catholics in Ireland. See Bottigheimer, "The Restoration Land Settlement in Ireland," 1–2; Lenihan, *Consolidating Conquest*, 127–35; Ó'Siochrú, *God's Executioner*; Tom Smith "The Image of Oliver Cromwell," 31–32. For

contrasting view on Cromwell in Ireland, see Tom Reilly, *Cromwell*. Reilly begins, however, by examining how hated Cromwell was/is in Ireland. For Irish hatred of Puritans, see Ó'Buachalla, "Irish Jacobitism and Irish Nationalism"; K. M. Miller, *Emigrants and Exiles*, 179.

12. Donald M. Williams, *Shamrocks and Pluff Mud*, 101–3.

13. Seigle, "Savannah's Own." For the case that Jasper's antecedents were in fact German, see G. F. Jones, "Sergeant Johann Wilhelm Jasper," 7–15. It is unclear, however, why the Irish, and not the Germans, would claim him as their national hero. In an era of growing ethnic pride, the fact that the German community, which had deeper roots in the South Carolina and Georgia lowcountry than the Irish, would not have known of their fellow "countryman's" service and exploited it to their own purposes is strange.

14. "Confederate States of America—Inaugural Address of the President of the Provisional Government"; Thomas, *The Confederate Nation*, 61–62; Cooper, *Jefferson Davis*, 330–31.

15. *Houston Tri-Weekly Telegraph*, Sept. 11, 1863.

16. Gannon, *Irish Rebels, Confederate Tigers*, 335–41; Eighth Census of the United States, 1860, City of New Orleans, Eighth Census of the United States, 1860, Slave Schedule, City of New Orleans, NARA; *New Orleans Daily True Delta*, June 7, 1861. CSRCS, 6th Louisiana Infantry Regiment, NARA. Confederate records list Strong as a clerk but neither of the two Henry Strongs in the Census for New Orleans is a clerk. One is listed as a barkeeper, but the Calhoun Guards provided uniforms and equipment to its recruits suggesting an organizer with more substantial wealth. Strong, the coffeehouse owner, had a personal estate of $5,000 recorded in the Census, a substantial amount in the early 1860s. Strong was married, which is also noted in his military record.

17. John C. Calhoun to "Secretary of the Irish Emigrant Society" [Gilbert C. Rice], Sept. 13, 1841, in Calhoun, *The Papers of John Calhoun*, 15:774. For the frustration of Whigs with Irish susceptibility to Democratic appeals to ethnicity, see D. T. Gleeson, *Irish in the South*, 95–100 and Holt, *Rise and Fall of the American Whig Party*, 117–18.

18. *Charleston Mercury*, July 23, 1861; *Natchez Weekly Courier*, Nov. 13, 1861.

19. Fanning, "Robert Emmet and Nineteenth-Century America," 53–83; Aldous, *Great Irish Speeches*, 22–25.

20. Quoted in *Washington Daily National Intelligencer*, Oct. 25, 1860.

21. *Fayetteville Observer*, June 9, 1862; V. A. J. Davis, *An Irish Knight of the 19th Century*; Cashin, *First Lady of the Confederacy*, 252.

22. Childs, "The Williamite War, 1689–1691," 190–92, 198–203; Bartlett and Jeffrey, "An Irish Military Tradition?," 15; Murtagh, "Irish Soldiers Abroad," 299–300, 305. For more on Sarsfield, see Wauchope, *Patrick Sarsfield and the Williamite War*.

23. Bruce, *Harp and Eagle*, 1, 63, 69, 83, 23, 153; Kennedy, *Population of the United States in 1860*, 346.

24. Gannon, *Irish Rebels, Confederate Tigers*, 362, 380; CSRCS, 2nd Tennessee (Walker's) Infantry, NARA; E. Gleeson, *Rebel Sons of Erin*, 343–56.

25. Drennan, *Fugitive Pieces in Verse and Prose*, 1–4; Whelan, *Tree of Liberty*, 61. For the Sarsfield Southron flag, see portrait of Captain Felix Hughes in the Old Courthouse Museum in Vicksburg. For the Irish Volunteers, see chapter 5.

26. *New Orleans Daily True Delta*, June 21, Aug. 13, Sept. 7, 1861; D. T. Gleeson, *Irish in the South*, 114.

27. For O'Connell and his troubles with Irish Americans, see Murphy, *American Slavery, Irish Freedom*; and D. T. Gleeson, *Irish in the South*, 129–31.

28. The Irish numbers in the St. Patrick's "Papal Brigade" were about 1,400, more a large regiment than a brigade. Spiers, "Army Organization," 352; *New York Times*, Oct. 6, 1860. See also Crean, "The Irish Battalion of St. Patrick," 52–60.

29. For more on the San Patricios, which also included a lot of non-Irish members, see Stevens, *The Rogue's March*; Hogan, *The Irish Soldiers of Mexico*; R. R. Miller, *Shamrock and Sword*.

30. Quoted in *Washington Daily National Intelligencer*, Sept. 17, 1847.

31. *Mississippi Free Trader and Natchez Gazette*, Apr. 3, Oct. 21, 23, 1847; *Cleveland Herald*, Oct. 12, 1847; *Greenville Mountaineer*, Oct. 15, 1847. The *Free Trader*, which would eventually be owned by Irish Catholic Richard Elward, covered the San Patricios' execution without once mentioning the name of their battalion or their ethnicity. It headlined the news "Executions of Deserters," Oct. 21, 1847.

32. O'Brien, *Irish Americans in the Confederate Army*, 221, 223; *Charleston Mercury*, Oct. 21, 1856; *Savannah Daily Morning News*, May 14, 1858; *Macon Daily Telegraph*, Mar. 5, 18, 1862; Coppock, *Memphis Sketches*, 224; Faherty, *The St. Louis Irish*, 79–80.

33. Gannon, *Irish Rebels, Confederate Tigers*, 357, 360; CSRCS, 6th Louisiana Infantry, NARA; T. L. Jones, *Lee's Tigers*, 41, 244–45, 249–50; O'Brien, *Irish Americans in the Confederate Army*, 218–20; Brooks and Jones, *Lee's Foreign Legion*.

34. CSRCS, 1st Georgia Volunteers (Olmstead's), 1st South Carolina (Charleston) Battalion, NARA.

35. CSRCS, 12th, 16th Mississippi Infantry, NARA; *Natchez Daily Courier*, May 3, 4, 14, 31, 1861; WPA, Source Material on Mississippi History—Jasper County, MSU; G. Davis, *Land!*, 184, 188, 213.

36. O'Brien, *Irish Americans in the Confederate Army*, 218–19; T. L. Jones, *Lee's Tigers*, 240–41.

37. William L. Nugent to [Governor] John J. Pettus, Apr. 18, 1861, quoted in Bettersworth, *Mississippi in the Confederacy*, 49.

38. Donnelly, *The Confederate Marine Corps*, 1–15; John de Courcy Ireland, "The Confederate states at sea in the American Civil War," 75–76. I am grateful to Lieutenant Colonel William Bell, United States Marine Corps, for information on the Confederate marines.

39. Wiecek, "Slavery and Abolition," 38–39; H. Johnson, "The Constitutional Thought of William Johnson," 136–38; John Hope Franklin and Loren Schweninger, *Runaway Slaves*, 279, 290. See also Cecelski, *The Waterman's Song*.

40. Ireland, *Ireland and the Irish in Maritime History*, Ireland did a lot to restore knowledge of that tradition, especially from the seventeenth and eighteenth centuries. Many Irish worked in transatlantic trade and in the Royal Navy too.

Linebaugh and Rediker, *Many Headed Hydra*: 278–81; Truxes, *Irish-American Trade*. For an island nation, however, it did not have the maritime tradition of, say, Iceland, another island in the North Atlantic. Its moderate climate and fertile soil made agriculture far more important than aquaculture, cattle much more so than fish. Irish boats, for example, were not conducive to deep sea fishing and thus many in the west of Ireland went hungry after the failure of the potato crop even though the sea was full of fish. Even those involved in the great colonial trade with North America usually had their ships constructed and registered in American ports. Kinealy, *This Great Calamity*, 205–6; Truxes, *Irish-American Trade*, 70, 75, 82.

41. Ireland, "Confederate States at Sea," 73–75; Roster of CSS *Tennessee*, MC; Still, *The Confederate Navy*, 7. For more on early organization of the Confederate navy, see Luriaghi, *History of the Confederate Navy*, 1–31; CSRCS, 1st South Carolina (Gregg's) Infantry, NARA.

42. D. T. Gleeson, *Irish in the South*, 27, 35, 40. The First Confederate Enlistment Act of April 1862 established the initial age and later extended it to forty-five in September of that year. The last extension occurred in February 1864. Shaw, "The Confederate Conscription and Exemption Acts," 364–405.

43. Kennedy, *Population of the United States in 1860*. Frank Towers highlights how Irish immigrants allied with large eastern shore planters and businessmen in Maryland's Democratic Party, forming a "patron-client alliance." It seems a strange alliance between a slave-owning elite and immigrant workers, but it grew in the malevolently nativist politics of the state's largest city. See Towers, *The Urban South and the Coming of the Civil War* (quote on 169). Baltimore's Know-Nothings were very strong and included violent gangs such as the "Blood Tubs" and the "Plug Uglies." See Baker, *Ambivalent Americans*, 38–39, 54, 124–34.

44. *Baltimore Sun*, Apr. 20, 22, 1861; Towers, *Urban South*, 170–71. For full description and analysis of riot, see Towers, "'A Vociferous Army of Howling Wolves,'" 1–27.

45. CSRCS, Who Served from the State of Maryland, NARA; Goldsborough, *The Maryland Line in the Confederate Army*, 275–95, 319–28; Ruffner, *Maryland's Blue and Gray*, 11–12. For more on name analysis, see the Appendix.

46. Matthews, "Beleaguered Loyalties," 9–24; and Mackey, "Not a Pariah, but a Keystone," 25–45. Both Matthews and Mackey are trying to counteract the influence of Coulter, *The Civil War and Readjustment in Kentucky*. For importance of Lost Cause in reinterpreting Kentucky's Civil War, see Marshall, *Creating a Confederate Kentucky*.

47. Kennedy, *Population of the United States in 1860*, xxxi; Owsley, "The Irish in Louisville," 14–21; Mittelbeeler, "The Aftermath of Louisville's Bloody Monday Election Riot," 197–219.

48. Kennedy, *Population of the United States in 1860*, xxxi–xxxii, 183–85; McDowell, "City in Conflict," 33, 58–67.

49. McDowell, "City in Conflict," 77–106.

50. O'Brien, *Irish Americans*, 218; CSRCS, Who Served from the State of Kentucky, NARA; Jenkins, *The Battle Rages Higher*, 368–78.

51. Freehling, *The South vs. the South*, 69. The number of a potential fighting population of 10,000 is gained by applying the 46 percent statistic to the Irish population of 22,000 in Kentucky.

52. Kennedy, *Population of the United States in 1860*, xxxii, 301.

53. Ibid., xxxii; Roed, "Secession Strength in Missouri," 412–23; Christopher Phillips, "Calculated Confederate," 389–414.

54. Phillip, *Damned Yankee*, 179–205; Winter, *The Civil War in St. Louis*, 42–55.

55. McGhee, *Guide to Missouri Confederate Units*, 148, 177–78, 238–39; Faherty, *The St. Louis Irish*, 77–80.

56. Faherty, *Exile in Erin*, 3–6, 37–51; Tucker, *The Confederacy's Fighting Chaplain*, 2–4, 21–23; Faherty, *St. Louis Irish*, 78. The total number of Missouri Confederates is disputed but with over thirty-five regiments, seven battalions, and twenty artillery batteries organized, 40,000 seems like a reasonable number; McGhee, *Guide*, xiii.

57. Patrick Ahearn to "Whom it may concern," Jan. 16, 1905, Patrick Ahearn Papers, MHS; CSRCS, 13th Arkansas Infantry, NARA.

58. Tucker, *Confederacy's Fighting Chaplain*, 13.

59. CSRCS, 8th Alabama Infantry, NARA; Gannon, *Irish Rebels, Confederate Tigers*, 327–92.

60. For use of Irish name analysis, see Doyle, *Ireland, Irishmen and Revolutionary America*, 51–76. See also Smith and MacRaild, "The Origins of the Irish in Northern England, 152–77. See also the Appendix for full explanation of this analysis.

61. See the Appendix.

62. "Partial List of Mobile Companies," MPL; Kennedy, *Population of the United States in 1860*, 1–3; D. T. Gleeson, *Irish in the South*, 40.

63. Lonn, *Foreigners in the Confederacy*, 496–98. See also CSRCS, 6th Virginia (Tredegar) Infantry Battalion, Local Defense, NARA; and CSRCS, 1st Louisiana Militia, NARA.

64. Noe, *Reluctant Rebels*, 2. The one factor that would have lessened enforced Irish enlistment, however, is the fall of New Orleans to Federal forces before the enactment of Confederate conscription. Indeed, Confederate records indicate that only *eighty-one conscripts total* were drafted in the parishes of East Louisiana between 1862 and early 1865. If the New Orleans Irish joined up at a rate of 35 percent in 1861, as in Mobile, the Confederacy lost the chance to conscript the 6,500 Irishmen left in the city when the Union army took over. OR, ser. 4, vol. 3, 1101–3.

65. McPherson, *Battle Cry of Freedom*, 606; Kennedy, *Population of the United States in 1860*, xxix–xxxii. K. M. Miller, *Emigrants and Exiles*, 581–82. There were over 1.6 million Irish immigrants listed in the 1860 U.S. census, of which only 84,000 lived in what would become the Confederate States. Even though the ratio of males to females for Irish emigrants between 1851 and 1910 was 1.08:1, if one accepted a lower 1:1 ratio, that would put over 800,000 Irish males in the United States in 1860. The age distribution for Irish male emigrants from 1852 to 1854 (the only years available before 1861) shows that 64 percent of Irish male emigrants were between the ages of fifteen and thirty-five with another 12 percent aged between thirty-five and fifty four. There were potentially then over 500,000 available recruits between fifteen and thirty-five. At 50 percent recruitment ratio that would

have provided over 250,000 soldiers for the Union cause. Another 96,000 would have been available by recruiting among the over thirty-fives, with a 50 percent recruitment ratio providing another 48,000 for service for a potential total of close to 300,000.

66. H. Jones, *Blue and Gray Diplomacy*, 44. For British attitude toward naturalization, see Samito, *Becoming American Under Fire*, 172–216.

67. Thomas Hagan to A. Fullerton, July 22, 1863; Joseph E. Brown to A. Fullerton, Aug. 8, 1863; Judah P. Benjamin to A. Fullerton, Oct. 8, 1863, Great Britain Consulate Collection, EU.

68. John Mangan Consular Certificate, Sept. 18, 1862, Great Britain Consulate Collection, EU.

69. Lonn, *Foreigners in the Confederacy*, 386–91; Berwanger, *The British Foreign Service*, 95–100.

70. Lonn, *Foreigners in the Confederacy*, 390; OR, ser. 4, vol. 3, 1101–3; Rable, *Confederate Republic*, 161–65; Bragg, *Joe Brown's Army*, 131–60; Berwanger, *British Foreign Service*, 97–98. North Carolina was an exception, with its large number of exemptions, despite the very small size of its foreign-born population, because state authorities there were more lenient in giving exemptions, granting more than 16,000, particularly for "disability." Georgia actually provided over 15,000 exemptions, nearly twice its number of draftees, but here the largest category was "state officials" again reflecting Governor Brown's attempts to thwart the central draft by putting men into service under his direct control.

71. William Mure to Earl [John] Russell, May 3, 1861, to Governor [Thomas] Moore, July 5, 1861, Foreign Office Records, FO5/788, NAUK.

72. Berwanger, *British Foreign Service*, 95–97; James Magee to Earl [John] Russell, Nov. 17, 1862, FO5/848, NAUK.

73. Noe, *Reluctant Rebels*, 114.

74. *Daily Richmond Examiner*, Oct. 10, 1862.

75. *Savannah Republican*, July 2, 1863.

76. Receipt Book of Bishop John Quinlan, Bishop Quinlan Papers, AAM.

77. Radley, *Rebel Watchdog*, 20; Massey, *Ersatz in the Confederacy*, 26, 125–34.

78. Thomas Hagan to A. Fullerton, July 22, 1863; Joseph E. Brown to A. Fullerton, Aug. 8, 1863; Judah P. Benjamin to A. Fullerton, Oct. 8, 1863, Great Britain Consulate Collection, EU.

79. Whitwell, *The Heritage of Longwood*, 4.

80. Majewski, *Modernizing the Slave Economy*, 137; Pierson, *Mutiny at Fort Jackson*, 38–39.

81. William Mure to Earl [John] Russell, July 9, 1861, FO5/788, NAUK;

82. Bettersworth, *Mississippi in the Confederacy*, 49.

83. For 1860 statistics, see D. T. Gleeson, *Irish in the South*, 40.

84. Gannon, *Irish Rebels, Confederate Tigers*, 24–25; Eighth Census of the United States, 1860, City of New Orleans.

85. Seventh Census of the United States, 1850, Mobile Co., AL, micro., NARA; Seventh Census of the United States, 1850, Mobile Co., AL, Slave Schedule, micro., NARA; Lonn, *Foreigners in the Confederacy*, 96.

86. Sheehan-Dean, *Why Confederates Fought*, 21; T. L. Jones, *Lee's Tigers*, 111, 240–41; Eighth Census of the United States, 1860, City of New Orleans, micro., NARA; CSRCS, 7th Louisiana Infantry Regiment, NARA.

87. CSRCS, 1st South Carolina (Gregg's) Infantry Regiment, NARA.

88. Quoted in Durkin, *John Dooley, Confederate Soldier*, 148; Curran, *John Dooley's Civil War*, xxii–xxv.

89. Thomas Smyth to Augustine Smythe, Apr. 12, 1861, in Smyth, *Autobiographical Notes*, 618–19.

90. Smyth, *Autobiographical Notes*, 3–4.

91. Quoted in Jennifer R. Gree, "'Stout Chaps Who Can Bear the Distress,'" 174–75. See also Franklin, *The Militant South*, 146–92.

92. *Charleston Courier*, quoted in File-Irish Volunteers, SCL. Minutes of the Hibernian Society, 1837, SCHS; *Charleston Mercury*, Dec. 28, 1860.

93. Quoted in McCurry, *Confederate Reckoning*, 336.

94. Sheehan-Dean, *Why Confederates Fought*, 21–23; Glatthaar, *General Lee's Army*, 17; *New Orleans True Delta*, Apr. 26, 1861; *Charleston Mercury*, Dec. 28, 1860.

95. Durrill, "Ritual, Community and War, 1109–10.

96. Manning, *What This Cruel War Was Over*, 6.

97. Glatthaar, *General Lee's Army*, 30; Sheehan-Dean, *Why Confederates Fought*, 36.

98. Seventh Census of the United States, 1850, Slave Schedule, Mobile Co., AL; Eighth Census of the United States, 1860, Slave Schedule, City of New Orleans, LA, Davidson Co., TN, Mobile Co., AL, Charleston Co., SC, micro., NARA.

99. Quoted in Glatthaar, *General Lee's Army*, 30.

100. Sheehan-Dean, *Why Confederates Fought*, 111–40, 166–75.

101. Curran, *John Dooley's Civil War*, xxi, 17.

102. John O. Farrell Diary [typescript], MC.

103. John McFarland to "Emma" Oct. 9, 1860, to "Mother" Apr. 20, 1861, to [Major E. Barksdale] Oct. 25, 1861, John Patten to Lizzie McFarland, June 10, 1864, Blackmore (Lizzie McFarland) Collection, MDAH; Eighth Census of the United States, 1860, Yazoo County, Mississippi, micro., NARA; CSRCS, First Mississippi Light Artillery, NARA.

104. D. T. Gleeson, *Irish in the South*, 97, 141; *Jackson Weekly Mississippian*, Nov. 21, 1860; John Logan Power "Siege of Vicksburg" Diary [micro.], J. L. Power Collection, MDAH; CSRCS, 1st Mississippi Light Artillery, NARA; John Patten to Lizzie McFarland, Mar. 19, 1865, Blackmore (Lizzie McFarland) Collection, MDAH.

105. Patrick Murphy Diary, Patrick Murphy Collection, LLMVC; CSRCS, Watson's Louisiana Artillery, NARA.

106. Lonn, *Foreigners in the Confederacy*, 391; *The Irish Volunteers Memorial Meeting*, 7–10; *Charleston Weekly Courier*, May 8, 1862.

CHAPTER 3

1. R. Taylor, *Destruction and Reconstruction*, 46.

2. Schott, *Alexander H. Stephens of Georgia*, 334–35.

3. Fogarty, *Commonwealth Catholicism*, 140–46; O'Grady, *Clear the Confederate Way*, 48–49; Eighth Census of the United States, 1860, Henrico Co., VA, micro., NARA; Eighth Census of the United States: Slave Schedule, 1860, Henrico Co., VA., micro., NARA.

4. W. C. Davis, *Battle at Bull Run*, 126.

5. Potts's diary in the Virginia Historical Society is listed as the "Isaac" Potts Memoir. The compiled service records however, show no Isaac Potts in the Confederate army. Francis Potts is listed as a 26-year-old clerk. Isaac Potts Memoir, VHS; CSRCS, 1st Virginia Infantry Regiment, NARA; Eighth Census of the United States, 1860, City of Portsmouth, VA, micro., NARA.

6. OR, ser. 1, vol. 2, 445, 461–62, 464.

7. Potts Memoir, VHS.

8. W. C. Davis, *Battle at Bull Run*, 129; CSRCS, 1st Virginia Infantry Regiment, NARA;

9. Colonel M. D. Corse, quoted in OR, ser. 1, vol. 2, 545; CSRCS, 1st Virginia Infantry Regiment, NARA.

10. OR, ser. 1, vol. 2, 481–82, 559–61, 570, 841; Gottfried, *The Maps of First Bull Run*, 18–19, 46–47; CSRCS, 27th Virginia Infantry Regiment, NARA.

11. CSRCS, 1st Virginia Infantry Regiment, NARA; Kenny, *The American Irish*, 141.

12. CSRCS, 15th Virginia Infantry Regiment, NARA.

13. Gannon, *Irish Rebels, Confederate Tigers*, 326–96.

14. Ibid., 22; Parrish, *Richard Taylor*, 71–73 (quote on 73), 100–103.

15. R. Taylor, *Destruction and Reconstruction*, 46.

16. Gannon, *Irish Rebels, Confederate Tigers*, 23–32.

17. Samuel M. Zulich and Alpheus Williams, quoted in OR, ser. 1, vol. 12, pt. 1, 570, 624.

18. T. L. Jones, *Lee's Tigers*, 79–80; OR, ser. 1, vol. 12, pt. 1, 780.

19. T. L. Jones, *Lee's Tigers*, 80. Quoted in Oates, *The War between the Union and the Confederacy*, 98. For O'Connor, see 756. CSRCS, 15th Alabama Infantry Regiment, NARA; Parrish, *Richard Taylor*, 186.

20. Quoted in R. Taylor, *Destruction and Reconstruction*, 73; Gannon, *Irish Rebels, Confederate Tigers*, 67–141;

21. William J. Seymour, quoted in T. L. Jones, *Civil War Memoirs of Captain William J. Seymour*, 65–66; T. L. Jones, *Lee's Tigers*, 198.

22. Pierson, *Mutiny at Fort Jackson*, 5.

23. Ibid., 17–21, 80–85, 104–12; OR, ser. 1, vol. 6, 521–32. With Union ships threatening to shell the city and no sign of a willingness on behalf of the city's authorities and citizens to resist, the supreme commander of New Orleans, General Mansfield Lovell, decided to evacuate his remaining forces up the Mississippi River. OR, ser. 1, vol. 6, 565–67.

24. OR, ser. 1, vol. 6, 531–32, 535, 544.

25. Henry Lawrence, quoted in Pierson, *Mutiny at Fort Jackson*, 68.

26. *New Orleans Daily Picayune*, Apr. 22, 1862.

27. The table examines the percentage rates for killed in action immediately or later from wounds, wounded but survived, counting only first wounds, desertions

(excluding those who rejoined another part of the Confederate service), desertions to the enemy where the Oath of Allegiance to the United States was sought and/or taken, and those captured on at least one occasion. Some prisoners of war were imprisoned on more than one occasion, having been exchanged and then captured again later. Finally, those incarcerated who sought and/or took the oath in a Union prison camp are included in the next-to-last category. The final category counts those who received discharges for non-domicile. Not included in this table are those who died from disease or those discharged for ill health and age. I have counted only those members of each unit who were Irish, including those who joined after the spring of 1861, draftees, and transfers in and out of the respective unit.

28. Glatthaar, *Soldiering in the Army of Northern Virginia*, 30.

29. Artillerymen had killed-in-action rates of about 5 percent vs. 14 percent for infantrymen in the Army of Northern Virginia. Glatthaar, *Soldiering in the Army of Northern Virginia*, 30, 54; Brooksher, *War along the Bayous*, 92.

30. CSRCS, 8th Alabama Infantry Regiment, NARA.

31. Robertson, *General A. P. Hill*, 59–66; Rhea, *Carrying the Flag*, 84–85, 91–98.

32. Sheehan-Dean, *Why Confederates Fought*, 36; Glatthaar, *General Lee's Army*, 30, 468.

33. Glatthaar, *Soldiering in the Army of Northern Virginia*, 30.

34. D. Brown, *The Galvanized Yankees*, 2; CSRCS, 3rd Confederate Infantry and 20th Louisiana Regiment, NARA.

35. CSRCS, 24th Alabama Infantry, NARA.

36. CSRCS, 5th Missouri Infantry, NARA.

37. CSRCS, 1st Louisiana (Nelligan's) Infantry, NARA.

38. CSRCS, 27th Virginia Infantry, NARA; Glatthaar, *General Lee's Army*, 468.

39. T. L. Jones, *Lee's Tigers*, 234. The exception here would be Nolan's Montgomery Guards. Glatthaar, *Soldiering in the Army of Northern Virginia*, 13.

40. CSRCS, 5th Missouri Infantry, 1st Louisiana (Nelligan's) Infantry, NARA.

41. CSRCS, 1st Louisiana (Nelligan's) Infantry, NARA.

42. D. Brown, *The Galvanized Yankees*, 1–11; CSRCS, 3rd Confederate Infantry, 13th/20th Louisiana Infantry, NARA.

43. CSRCS, 5th Missouri Infantry, 1st Louisiana (Nelligan's) Infantry, NARA.

44. William J. Seymour, quoted in T. L. Jones, *Lee's Tigers*, 189–90. Confusion reigns over the identity of the condemned man. Seymour apparently described him as John Connolly, but the compiled service records for the 6th show three men of that name in the regiment, in companies B, H, and K (with various spellings of the last name). Jones found evidence that it was one Cain Comfort, but when the records are disentangled, it seems probable that the man was John Conely of Company B who "deserted to the Yanks" in 1862. The other Connellys and Comfort seem to have lived beyond 1863, while Conely's record ends with his desertion to the enemy. The fact that he did not show up in other Confederate or Union records is not too surprising, as Confederate records on executions are, according to one expert, "understated," and Federal authorities did not keep organized records of those taking the oath until after the Battle of Gettysburg. Weitz, *More Damning than Slaughter*, 130, 188.

45. Weitz, *More Damning than Slaughter*, 130–32.

46. Ibid., 130; Pierson, *Mutiny at Fort Jackson*, 2–3, 39–40, 45–51. 91–92.

47. CSRCS, 1st Louisiana (Nelligan's) Infantry, NARA; Brownlee, *Gray Ghosts of the Confederacy*, 217–21.

48. CSRCS, 1st Louisiana (Nelligan's) Infantry, NARA.

49. Krick, *Stonewall Jackson at Cedar Mountain*, 248, 364; Robertson, *Stonewall Jackson*, 668, 907; O'Grady, *Clear the Confederate Way*, 82–83.

50. Glatthaar, *Soldiering in the Army of Northern Virginia*, 30; Quigley, *Shifting Ground*, 217.

51. Glatthaar, *General Lee's Army*, 316.

52. Sheehan-Dean, *Why Confederates Fought*, 5.

53. O'Grady, "Anthony M. Keiley"; "History of the Petersburg Riflemen" [manuscript], Keiley Family Papers, VHS.

54. CSRCS, 12th Virginia Infantry, NARA.

55. "History of the Petersburg Riflemen" [manuscript], Keiley Family Papers, VHS. Keiley never received an administrative position, but the voters of Petersburg did elect him to the Virginia state legislature in May 1863. He resigned his commission and became a politician. The war had embittered him. In this history of his company, which he seems to have written during the war (the handwritten history goes only to the Battle of Chancellorsville and is written in the back of the Company Record Book of a company in the 116th Ohio Infantry that served at the siege of Petersburg in later 1864), he wrote his views of the slaveholder's lack of support for the cause.

56. A. M. Keiley, *In Vinculis* 3–4, 25, 36, 47, 80, 96. For the Bermuda Hundred campaign, see Robertson, *Backdoor to Richmond*.

57. Joslyn, "Irish Beginnings, "1–17; Ruisi, "Helena, Arkansas: Cleburne's Early Years in the South," 18–33; Symonds, *Stonewall of the West*, 53–59, 63, 86–98, 101–3, 183–91. For the proposal, see OR, ser. 1, vol. 52, 586–92.

58. Quoted in Perdue and Perdue, *Pat Cleburne, Confederate General*, 289.

59. Symonds, *Stonewall of the West*, 185; Cobb quote in OR, ser. 4, vol. 3, 1009.

60. Quoted in OR, ser. 1, vol. 52, pt. 2, 591. See also Levine, *Confederate Emancipation*, 102–3.

61. Quoted in Levine, *Confederate Emancipation*, 103.

62. OR, ser. 1, vol. 52, pt. 2, 587, 592, ser. 4, vol. 3, 1009.

63. Connelly, *Autumn of Glory*, 31; McDonough and Connelly, *Five Tragic Hours*, 160–61.

64. Cozzens, *The Shipwreck of Their Hopes*, 370–84, Symonds, *Stonewall of the West*, 171–76; Joslyn, "'Open Stand Up Affair,'" 92–93.

65. Pierson, *Mutiny at Fort Jackson*, 71; CSRCS, 1st Louisiana (Nelligan's) Infantry, NARA.

66. Quoted in Hennessy, *Return to Bull Run*, 356, 357.

67. T. L. Jones, *Lee's Tigers*, 124.

68. Ibid., 170; CSRCS, 1st Louisiana (Nelligan's) Infantry, NARA.

69. *New Orleans Daily True Delta*, Mar. 19, 1861.

70. CSRCS, 1st Louisiana (Nelligan's) Infantry, NARA.

71. Barr, "Texas Coastal Defenses, 24–27.

72. OR, ser. 1, vol. 26, pt. 1, 311–12.

73. Phelps, *Charlestonians at War*, 84, 89, 136.

74. T. L. Jones, *Lee's Tigers*, 206–8; Gannon, *Irish Rebels, Confederate Tigers*, 328; CSRCS, 6th Louisiana Infantry, NARA; Eighth Census of the United States, 1860 (City of New Orleans), micro., NARA; Eighth Census of the United States: Slave Schedule, 1860 (City of New Orleans), micro., NARA.

75. Cornish, "An Irish Confederate," 179–220; E. Gleeson, *Erin Go Gray!*, 3–50; OR, ser. 1, vol. 36, pt. 1, 1032; T. L. Jones, ed., *Civil War Memoirs of Captain William J. Seymour*, 133.

76. Gower and Allen, *Pen and Sword*, 5–11, 188.

77. Ibid., 204–6.

78. Ibid., 206–11.

79. Ibid., 390, 429, 487, 543.

80. Ibid., 384, 427, 488–89, 512–13.

81. E. Gleeson, *Rebel Sons of Erin*, 19.

82. Ibid., 122–23, Gower and Allen, *Pen and Sword*, 672, 674.

83. E. Gleeson, *Rebel Sons of Erin*, 180–85; Ballard, *Vicksburg*, 261–71.

84. "The Famous Tenth Tennessee," *Confederate Veteran*, 13 (Dec. 1905): 553–60.

85. Fremantle, *Three Months in the Southern States*, 232.

86. Noe, *Perryville*, 227; Jenkins, *The Battle Rages Higher*, 289–406.

87. Quoted in T. L. Jones, *Lee's Tigers*, 110.

88. Bruce, *Harp and Eagle*, 122–34.

89. See, for example, O'Grady, *Clear the Confederate Way*, 250, 283; and McCarthy, *Green, Blue, and Grey*, 128. Eighth Census of the United States: Slave 1860, Habersham Co., GA., micro., NARA; Eighth Census of the United States: Slave Schedule, 1860, Habersham Co., GA., micro., NARA; *Washington Daily National Intelligencer*, Oct. 5, 1851; CSRCS, 24th Georgia Infantry, NARA; Thomas, "Irishmen outside Phillip's Legion." I am grateful to Mr. Sam Thomas of the Thomas R. R. Cobb house in Athens, Georgia, for allowing me access to his unpublished research on Cobb's Brigade.

90. Reily, *The Fredericksburg Campaign*, 296–97; 304–5, 308, 323, 336; Rable, *Fredericksburg! Fredericksburg!*, 230, quote on 233.

91. Coffman and Graham, *To Honor These Men*, 120–22, 364–70.

92. O'Grady, *Clear the Confederate Way*, 154–55, quote on 155.

93. Linderman, *Embattled Courage*, 80. Aaron Sheehan-Dean sees a hardening of Confederate attitudes as the war became harder but Gerald Linderman sees the combat experience causing a falling away of ideology if it ever existed for most soldiers at all. James McPherson finds that a combination of ideology, concepts of honor, and peer-pressure helped Civil War soldiers perform well in battle. Sheehan-Dean, *Why Confederates Fought*, 5, 180–81; McPherson, *For Cause and Comrades*.

94. Eighth Census of the United States: Slave Schedule, 1860, City of New Orleans, LA, micro., NARA; OR, Ser. 1, vol. 12, pt. 2, 671, quote on 715.

95. OR, ser. 1, vol. 19, pt. 1, 965, 974; Gannon, *Irish Rebels, Confederate Tigers*, 135–38; George Ring Diary, TU.

96. *Chattanooga Daily Rebel*, Oct. 1, 1862; *New Orleans Daily Picayune*, Oct. 10, 1862.

97. *Charleston Mercury*, June 4, 1862, July 23, 1863; *Charleston Tri-Weekly Courier*, Aug. 29, 1862.

98. See, for example, *Savannah Daily Morning News*, Dec. 30, 1862 and *Jackson Daily Southern Crisis*, Jan. 8, 1863.

99. Oates, *The War between the Union and the Confederacy*, 219, 755–56; CSRCS, 15th Alabama Infantry, NARA; *Gettysburg*, DVD.

100. Quoted in Donald M. Williams, *Shamrocks and Pluff Mud*, 106–7.

101. Quoted in ibid., 107.

102. *Charleston Tri-Weekly Courier*, July 10, 1862.

103. Gary Gallagher highlights the importance of the right personnel, or rather the lack of them, in Confederate defeat. Gallagher, *The Confederate War*, 151–53.

104. *Mobile Daily Advertiser and Register*, Oct. 7, 1863.

105. A. M. Keiley to [Bishop P. N. Lynch], Nov. 10, 1863, Bishop Lynch Papers, ACDC.

106. T. L. Jones, *Civil War Memoirs of Captain William J. Seymour*, 32–33, 48–49; Pierson, *Mutiny at Fort Jackson*, 17–19; T. L. Jones, *Lee's Tigers*, 101, 159, 166.

107. Quoted in Pierson, *Mutiny at Fort Jackson*, 113.

CHAPTER 4

1. Buttimer, "'By Their Deeds, You Shall Know Them,'" 63–66.

2. *Charleston Daily Courier*, Sept. 17, 1861; John Lynch to Bishop Patrick Lynch, Apr. 12, 1861, Lynch Family Papers, ACDC; *New Orleans Daily True Delta*, Mar. 19, 1861.

3. See, for example, Sterba, *Good Americans*; Muller, *Free to Die for their Country*.

4. Linderman, *Embattled Courage*, 7–60. See also McPherson, *For Cause and Comrades*, 46–61.

5. Thomas, *The Confederate Nation: 1861–1865* and *The Confederacy as a Revolutionary Experience*; and Faust, *The Creation of Confederate Nationalism*. Its roots of course lay in the antebellum era; see Quigley, *Shifting Ground*, and McCardell, *The Idea of a Southern Nation*. For the nation without a nationalism argument, see Escott, *After Secession*.

6. Beringer and others, *Why the South Lost the Civil War* and *The Elements of Confederate Defeat*, 23–31 (quote on 23); Whites, "The Civil War as a Crisis in Gender," 3–21; Faust, "Altars of Sacrifice," 1200–28.

7. Gallagher, *The Confederate War*; Sheehan-Dean, *Why Confederates Fought*; Rubin, *A Shattered Nation*, quotes on 6.

8. Drago, *Confederate Phoenix*, 5, 50.

9. *Savannah Daily Morning News*, Mar. 20, 1861.

10. Minutes of the Hibernian Society of Charleston, 1861, SCHS. *Charleston Mercury*, May 8, 23, 1861; John McFarland to "Emma", Oct. 9, 1860, to Messrs Rankin and Gilmour, Feb. 23, 1861, to Walter Scott, Feb. 3, 1861, to his mother, Aug. 21, 1861, to [Captain Yazoo Rifles], Apr. 22, 1861, to Captain N. Peake, Apr. 27, June 6, 1861, Blakemore (Lizzie McFarland) Collection, MDAH.

11. *New York Herald*, May 27, 1858, Oct. 16, 1860; MacMahon, *Cause and Contrast*, 81.

12. MacMahon, *Cause and Contrast*, vii, 1–22, 52–54, 62. For belief of miscegenation leading to debility, see Genovese, *Roll, Jordan, Roll*, 427–31.

13. Josiah Nott of Mobile was the classic antebellum purveyor of these theories, although he stated them as fact. See Horsman, *Josiah Nott of Mobile*. Nott's belief, that blacks and whites were separate species, was unacceptable to most white southerners because it contradicted the Genesis story in the Bible of all peoples being descended from Adam and Eve. See Genovese, *A Consuming Fire*, 81–84.

14. Quoted in Fox-Genovese and Genovese, *Slavery in Black and White*, 214.

15. MacMahon, *Cause and Contrast*, 32–33.

16. Ibid., 65; W. R. Taylor, *Cavalier and Yankee*, especially 177–202, 325–42. For the contradictory nature of the Cavalier myth, see Bonner, "Roundheaded Cavaliers?," 34–59. See also Watson, *Normans and Saxons*.

17. MacMahon, *Cause and Contrast*, 75, 168–70, 179.

18. Ibid., 179–92. Quote on 192.

19. Quoted in *Charleston Tri-Weekly Courier*, Jan. 16, 1862. See also *Fayetteville Observer*, Aug. 11, 1862.

20. J. D. B. De Bow quoted in Genovese and Genovese, *Slavery in Black and White*, 117; McGovern, *John Mitchel*, 168–74.

21. McGovern, *John Mitchel*, 175–77; Rable, *The Confederate Republic*, 1–5, 44–49, 85–87, 100–101, 174–77.

22. Quoted in Rable, *Confederate Republic*, 74–75.

23. Rable, *Confederate Republic*, 209; D. T. Gleeson, *Irish in the South*, 69; McGovern, *John Mitchel*, 176.

24. McGovern, *John Mitchel*, 180–82, quote on 180; Rable, *Confederate Republic*, 81, 206.

25. Osterhaus, *Partisans of the Southern Press*, 110–14 (quote on 113).

26. Osterhaus, *Partisans of the Southern Press*, 105.

27. Rable, *The Confederate Republic*, 129, 248.

28. *Milwaukee Daily Sentinel*, Dec. 3, 1864; *Richmond Daily Dispatch*, Nov. 23, 24, Jan. 25, Feb. 28, Mar. 24, 1865; Rable, *Confederate Republic*, 129–30, 360–61.

29. *Daily Richmond Examiner*, Jan. 7, 1864.

30. McCurry, *Masters of Small Worlds*, 5–36; Sheehan-Dean, *Why Confederates Fought*, 111–37.

31. *Daily Richmond Examiner*, Apr. 5, May 30, 1864. The Beaufort situation Mitchel was referring to was the famous "Port Royal Experiment" on the islands off Beaufort, South Carolina, which had fallen to Union forces early in the War. Plantations abandoned by pro-Confederate masters were confiscated, broken up, and given to slaves to operate. Rose, *Rehearsal for Reconstruction*.

32. McGovern, *John Mitchel*, 180–83; O'Connor, *Jenny Mitchel, Young Irelander*, 279–82; *Richmond Daily Dispatch*, Jan. 20, 1864.

33. *Daily Richmond Enquirer*, Dec. 27, 1862.

34. Ibid., May 29, 1863; Bruce, *The Harp and The Eagle*, 134–41.

35. *Daily Richmond Examiner*, Mar. 16, 19, June 1, Oct. 29, 1864.

36. D. T. Gleeson, *Irish in the South*, 154; McGovern, *John Mitchel*, 185–86, quote on 186.

37. Magrath, *Executive Documents*; *Fayetteville Observer*, Apr. 24, 1862; *Charleston Tri-Weekly Courier*, Aug. 2, 14, 1862; Hamilton, "The Confederate Sequestration Act," 373–408.

38. *Camden Confederate*, July 3, 1863; *Savannah Morning News*, July 14, 1863.

39. *Columbia Daily South Carolinian*, Dec. 20, 1864.

40. A. G. Magrath to Jefferson Davis, Dec. 20, 25, 1864, to [P. G. T.] Beauregard, Dec. 21, 28, 1864, to R. W. Barnwell, Dec. 30, 1864, to [W. J.] Hardee, Jan. 11, 21, 22, 1865, to R. E. Lee, Jan. 16, 1865, to A. H. Stephens, Jan. 25, 1865, to Joseph E. Brown, Jan. 26, 1865, Governor Magrath Letterbook, micro., Governor A. G. Magrath Papers, SCDAH.

41. "The Governor of the State, To the People of South Carolina," broadside, n.d. [Jan. 1865], Governor Magrath Letterbook, micro, Governor A. G. Magrath Papers, SCDAH.

42. Ibid.; Barrat, *Sherman's March*, 44–46.

43. A. G. Magrath to R. W. Barnwell, Dec. 30, 1864, to R. E. Lee, Jan. 16, 1865, to William N. Trescott, Jan. 9, 1865, Governor Magrath Letterbook, Governor A. G. Magrath Papers, SCDAH; Barrat, *Sherman's March*, 42.

44. Barrat, *Sherman's March*, 64–71; Fraser, *Charleston! Charleston!*, 267–69.

45. A. G. Magrath to W. J. Hardee, Mar. 17, 1865, to Col. Fair, May 14, 1865, Governor Magrath Letterbook, micro., Governor A. G. Magrath Papers, SCDAH; A. G. Magrath to Bishop P. N. Lynch, June 1865, Bishop Lynch Papers, ACDC.

46. Rable, *Confederate Republic*, 128–29, 154, 169–70, 327–28, 336; Cooper, *Jefferson Davis*, 394–95; Escott, *Military Necessity*, 18; H. S. Wilson, *Confederate Industry*, 89–91.

47. J. D. Lynch, *The Bench and Bar of Mississippi*, 455–61; P. G. T. Beauregard to J. L. Orr, Apr. 24, 1863, in OR, ser. 1, vol. 14, 909–10.

48. [James] Phelan to Jefferson Davis, Oct. 27, 1862, J[efferson] D[avis] to S. R. Mallory, Oct. 27, 1862, S. R. Mallory to [Jefferson Davis] in ORN, ser. 1, vol. 8, 842–43; McPherson, *Battle Cry of Freedom*, 612; *Daily Richmond Examiner*, Dec. 31, 1863; James Phelan to Jefferson Davis, Jan. 17, 1865, in J. Davis, *The Papers of Jefferson Davis*, 11:332–33.

49. Rable, *Confederate Republic*, 228, 233.

50. *Journal of the House of Representatives*, 67–68.

51. Ibid., 130–33, 152–53, 168–71, 314–15; *Charleston Tri-Weekly Courier*, May 8, Oct. 18, 25, Dec. 6, 1862.

52. *New Orleans Daily True Delta*, Feb. 16, 21, Mar. 7, 14, Apr. 9, 1861.

53. Ibid., Apr. 3, 21, 1861.

54. Ibid., June 1, 11, 1861. Roland, *The Confederacy*, 100–102; Marler, "'An Abiding Faith in Cotton,'" 247–76. For fears of military dictatorship in the Confederacy, see Rable, *Confederate Republic*, 147, 175, 209–10.

55. *New Orleans Daily True Delta*, May 31, June 7, 1861.

56. Ibid., May 2, 7, 8, June 7, 18, 1861. Quote on June 7.

57. *Journal of the House of Representatives*, 114; M. P. O'Connor to Bishop P. N. Lynch, Dec. 1, 1863, Bishop Lynch Papers, ACDC.

58. A. M. Keiley to [Bishop P. N. Lynch], Nov. 10, 1863, Bishop Lynch Papers, ACDC.

59. T. L. Jones, *Civil War Memoirs of Captain William J. Seymour*, 151; CSRCS, 12th Mississippi Infantry Regiment, NARA.

60. Buttimer, "'By Their Deeds, You Shall Know Them,'" 64–66;

61. Macarthy, *The Bonnie Blue Flag*; *New Orleans Daily Picayune*, Aug. 23, 1861, Obituary, Nov. 18, 1888; *Daily Richmond Examiner*, Nov. 12, 1863, Apr. 1, 1864; *Petersburg Daily Express*, Nov. 23, 1863. See also Abel, *Singing the New Nation*, 52–66; Emmet, *I Wish I Was in Dixie's Land*; For Emmet and Irish minstrelsy in America, see Nathan, "Dixie," 60–84; and Lott, *Love and Theft*, 47–51, 95–96, 136–43, 148–49.

62. *Little Rock Arkansas State Democrat*, Sept. 8, 1848; *Jackson Mississippian*, Apr. 20, 1849; *Natchez Mississippi Free Trader*, Feb. 16, Apr. 6, 1850; *New York Herald*, May 13, 1857; *Frank Leslie's Illustrated News*, June 13, 1857; *Charleston Mercury*, June 2, July 2, 1857.

63. I found Brenan's ballad reprinted from his former newspaper the *New Orleans Delta* (not Maginnis's *True Delta*), in the *Charleston Mercury*, July 23, 1856, and *Savannah Morning News*, July 25, 1856 and reprinted from the *New York Tribune* in the *Boston Liberator*, Aug. 8, 1856. Keiley probably got it from his brother's paper, the *Petersburg Express*. John D. Keiley Letterbook, [John D. "Jack" Keiley] to "Mother" [Margaret Cullen Keiley], July 23, 1861, Keiley Family Papers, VHS. For war in Kansas, see Etheson, *Bleeding Kansas*.

64. Kincaid, "The Story Behind the Song;" Kincaid, *The Irish American's Song*, CD. For the importance of song sheets in antebellum Irish American culture, see W. H. Williams, *'Twas Only an Irishman's Dream*, 32–50.

65. Bruce, *Harp and Eagle*, 20–21.

66. "Recollections of a Confederate Soldier" [typescript], William Robert Greer Papers, DU; Donald M. Williams, *Shamrocks and Pluff Mud*, 99–100.

67. William McBurney to Edward McCrady [Jr.], Edward McCrady Jr., Military Papers, SCHS, Sept. 16, 1861; *New Orleans True Delta*, Mar. 9, 1862.

68. William Ahern to Governor J. E. Brown, Feb. 22, 1862, M. J. Doyle to Governor Joseph E. Brown, Feb. 4, 1862, John H. Flynn to Governor Joseph E. Brown, Feb. 21, 25, 1862, Governor Brown Correspondence, RG 1–1–5, GDAH.

69. Lonn, *Foreigners in the Confederacy*, 341; Bagby, "The Great Railroad Raid," 36–44.

70. Lonn, *Foreigners in the Confederacy*, 323, 330, 332–33, 341, 375, 378; Wakelyn, "Catholic Elites," 224; "Necrology of Virginia Historical Society," 435–36.

71. Palmetto Importing and Exporting Company Share Certificates, John Knox Series, Wilson Family Papers, SHC. For importance of Charleston blockade running to the Confederate war effort, see Wise, *Lifeline of the Confederacy*, 163–66.

72. H. Pinckney Walker to Lord (John) Russell, July 13, 1863, FO, 5/907, NAUK.

73. Dew, *Ironmaker to the Confederacy*, 28, 234–39; P. Davis, *C.S. Armory Richmond*, 25, 31, 82, 88; Time Book, Confederate Arsenal Richmond, RG 109, NARA.

74. Thomas, *The Confederate Nation*, 205–6; Rubin, *A Shattered Nation*, 53–64.

75. For antebellum southern charity, see Lockley, *Welfare and Charity in the Antebellum South*. For contradictions between southern rhetoric on and practice of free-market economics, see Genovese and Genovese, *Slavery in Black and White*,

176–77. For other shifts in attitudes toward state interference in the Confederate economy, see Majewski, *Modernizing a Slave Economy*, 140–61.

76. *Daily Richmond Examiner*, Oct. 20, 1863; McCurry, *Confederate Reckoning*, 162–68, 201–9, quote on 209.

77. Lockley, *Welfare and Charity*, 147, 170–74; Governor F. W. Pickens to Bishop P. N. Lynch, Apr. 18, 1861, Bishop Lynch Papers, ACDC.

78. *Savannah Daily Morning News*, July 9, 1861.

79. *New Orleans Daily Picayune*, Aug. 8, 10, 14, 17, 1861; *New Orleans Daily Delta* quoted in *Fayetteville Observer*, Jan. 13, 1862.

80. *Savannah Daily Morning News*, Nov. 4, 1861; *Charleston Daily Courier*, Feb. 21, 1862; *Natchez Evening Gazette*, Mar. 1, 1862; *Natchez Weekly Courier*, Mar. 5, 1862; *Memphis Appeal* quoted in *Charleston Tri-Weekly Courier*, Apr. 26, 1862.

81. *Charleston Tri-Weekly Courier*, Mar. 13, 22, Apr. 10, May 22, Nov. 25, 1862.

82. Alfred A. Barbot to Bishop P. N. Lynch, Dec. 3, 1862, Bishop Lynch Papers, ACDC; *Charleston Tri-Weekly Courier*, Dec. 6, 1862, Jan. 20, Feb. 16, May 16, July 4, *Camden Confederate* Oct. 16, 1863.

83. Mrs. M. C. Barry to Bishop [P. N.] Lynch, Dec. 1, 1862, Bishop Lynch Papers, ACDC. For more on "refugee" life, see Massey, *Refugee Life in the Confederacy*.

84. P. N. Lynch to Francis Lynch, Nov. 13, 1861, Lynch Family Papers, ACDC; Patrick Ryan to Bishop P. N. Lynch, Aug. 26, 1863, Bishop Lynch Papers, ACDC; Moore, *The Juhl Letters*, 52.

85. Faust, *Mothers of Invention*, 40–45.

86. J. A. Corcoran to Bishop P. N. Lynch, May 29, 1862, Bishop Lynch Papers, ACDC.

87. *Savannah Daily Morning News*, Aug. 22, Nov. 20, Dec. 28, 1863; *Richmond Daily Examiner*, Sept. 3, 1863; E. M. Burton, *The Siege of Charleston*, 251–60.

88. Ballard, *Vicksburg*, 381–88, quote on 384. For Irish casualties, see *Vicksburg American Citizen*, June 30, 1863.

89. George Coppell to Lord [John] Russell, Jan. 3, 1862, FO5/848, NAUK.

90. F. J. Cridland to Earl [John] Russell, Aug. 31, 1863, Mar. 12, 1864, FO5/908/970, NAUK.

91. *Charleston Tri-Weekly Courier*, July 4, 1863; *Camden Confederate*, Sept. 18, Oct. 2, 16, 23, Nov. 27, Dec. 4, 11, 1863; *Charleston Mercury*, Jan. 29, 1864.

92. CSRCS, 1st Virginia Infantry Regiment, NARA; Kenny, *The American Irish*, 141.

93. Dew, *Ironmaker to the Confederacy*, 22–28, 236–37, 243–49, 262–64; Davies, *C.S. Armory Richmond*, 133. Some did serve in the battalion, see CSRCS, 6th (Tredegar) Infantry Battalion, Local Defense, NARA.

94. H. Pinckney Walker to Lord [John] Russell, Apr. 9, 1863, H. Pinckney Walker to Brig. Gen. [Thomas] Jordan, Apr. 6, 1863, FO5/906, NAUK. Many civilian war suppliers saw the personal and corporate economic benefits of Confederate patriotism. See De Credico, *Patriotism for Profit*, 21–109.

95. H. Pinckney Walker to Lord (John) Russell, July 13, 1863, 19 July 1864, FO 5/907, 5/909, NAUK; Lonn, *Foreigners in the Confederacy*, 391–95.

96. George Moore to Lord Lyons, June 6, 1863, FO 5/909, NAUK; Albert Brown, quoted in Lonn, *Foreigners in the Confederacy*, 393.

97. *Daily Richmond Examiner* Sept. 28, Oct. 19, 22, Nov. 19, 24, 1863, Jan. 26, July 8, 1864.

98. Ibid., Sept. 24, 1864.

99. Lonn, *Foreigners in the Confederacy*, 421; Rosen, *The Jewish Confederates*, 267–73.

100. Kimball, "The Bread Riot in Richmond," 152–53; Chesson, "Harlots or Heroines?," 131–75.

101. McCurry, *Confederate Reckoning*, 165–77, 180–9; St. Louis *Daily Missouri Democrat*, Oct. 6, 1863; [Rix], *Incidents of Life in a Southern City during the War*, n.p.

102. *Daily Richmond Examiner*, June 10, 1864.

103. Register of Arrests, Provost Marshall General's Office, Richmond, Virginia, Record Group 109, ch.9, vol. 244, NARA; Driver and Ruffner, *1st Battalion Virginia Infantry*, 105.

104. Neely, *Southern Rights*, 149–50.

105. Lonn, *Foreigners in the Confederacy*, 390–94, 406–10; *Charleston Tri-Weekly Courier*, Feb. 15, Apr. 15, 1862; Andrews, *Footprints of a Regiment*, 99.

106. Stephanie McCurry highlights the fleeting nature of patriotic ceremonies as symbols of civilian support for the cause. McCurry, *Confederate Reckoning*, 92–93.

107. Wetherington, *Plain Folk's Fight*, 178; Massey, *Ersatz in the Confederacy*, 161–69.

108. Edwards, *Scarlett Doesn't Live Here Anymore*, 85–99; Faust, *Mothers of Invention*. For active opposition, see Bynum, *The Free State of Jones*, 93–130 and Dyer, *Secret Yankees*.

109. Lonn, *Foreigners in the Confederacy*, 417–38; Bailey, "Defiant Unionists," 208–28; Bynum, *The Free State of Jones*, 93–130, *The Long Shadow of the Civil War*, 19–58; Williams, Williams, and Carlson, *Plain Folk in a Rich Man's War*; David Williams, *A People's History of the Civil War*, 310–14; Fowler "'We can never live in a southern confederacy,'" 97–121; Current, *Lincoln's Loyalists*.

110. Neely, *Southern Rights*, 146–47.

111. *New Orleans Daily True Delta*, Sept. 12, 22, 1862. The best work on Union occupation in the Confederacy is Ash, *When the Yankees Came*. For Butler and New Orleans, see Hearn, *When the Devil Came Down to Dixie*; Dawson, *Army Generals and Reconstruction*, 7–8; Trefousse, *Ben Butler*, 107–34; Nash, *Stormy Petrel*, 136–77; Nolan, *Benjamin Franklin Butler*, 150–225.

112. Edward Murphy to W. H. Renaud, June 1, Aug. 16, 1861, Murphy Family Papers, HNOC. Confederate troops who were being transported through Raleigh, North Carolina took it upon themselves to attack the offices of W. W. Holden's "peace" newspaper, *The Standard*. Clark, *Railroads in the Civil War*, 110–12.

113. John Hughes to Benjamin Butler, May 13, 1862, Joseph P. Murphy to Benjamin Butler, May 12, 1862, Jeremiah Hurly to Benjamin Butler, Aug. 1, 1862, Francis McDermott to [Benjamin] Butler, Dec. 2, 1862, Benjamin Butler to Henry Halleck, Aug. 27, 1862, Benjamin F. Butler Papers, LC.

114. Pay Roll of the U.S. Commission of Relief, Oct. 1, 1862, J. W. Shafer to Benjamin Butler, Oct. [?] 1862, Charles J. Paine to George C. Strong, Oct. 22, 1862, Benjamin F. Butler Papers, LC.

115. Annie Grace to [Benjamin] Butler, Sept. 1, 1862, Benjamin F. Butler Papers, LC.

116. Capers, *The Biography of a River Town*, 148–49, 157–59; Marszalek, *Sherman*, 191–93; Parks, "Memphis under Military Rule," 50–58; *Savannah Daily Herald*, Mar. 18, 1865.

117. *Daily Richmond Examiner*, June 11, 1863; *Memphis Daily Appeal*, Mar. 11, 1863; *Daily Richmond Enquirer*, Jan. 4, 1865. John Maginnis's death in 1863 absolved him of most of the blame for his paper's stance, outside of New Orleans anyway.

118. Ash, *When the Yankees Came*, 44. For the importance of community to honor in the South, see Wyatt-Brown, *Southern Honor*, 4, 9–14, 32–35, 47–48. For the loss of honor that defeat brought, see Wyatt-Brown, *The Shaping of Southern Culture*, 230–35.

119. Ash, *When the Yankees Came*, 176, 197–98, quote on 176; Hearn, *When the Devil Came Down to Dixie*, 90–109.

120. Irish civilians in the North, for example, could also undermine the "patriotic" efforts of Irish soldiers at the front. See Bernstein, *The New York City Draft Riots*; Spann, "Union Green," 193–209; Samito, *Becoming American Under Fire*, 128–29.

121. A. O. Abbott, *Prison Life in the South* (New York: Harper Brothers, 1866), 89–90; Frank Bennett Journal, DU.

122. Genovese, *A Consuming Fire*, 44–46; Stout, *Upon the Altar of the Nation*, 47–52; Berends, "'Wholesome Reading Purifies and Elevates the Man,'" 142–48; Mitchell, "Christian Soldiers?," 306–7.

CHAPTER 5

1. *Charleston Daily Courier*, Sept. 17, 1861.

2. Many Americans, northern and southern, saw the whole sectional crisis as a religious one. It is not surprising then how religion played a prominent role in soldiers' lives. See Noll, *The Civil War as a Theological Crisis*; Wiley, *The Life of Johnny Reb*, 180; C. R. Wilson, *Baptized in Blood*, 6–7; Faust, "Christian Soldiers" 63–90; Berends, "'Wholesome Reading Purifies and Elevates the Man,'" 142–48. For importance of Catholicism to Irish Union soldiers, see R. M. Miller, "Catholic Religion," 261–96.

3. For the dominance of the Irish in the antebellum Catholic Church, see Hennesey, *American Catholics*, 4–5; Morris, *American Catholic*, 50–76; Dolan, *In Search of American Catholicism*, 55–64.

4. For the revival of political Catholicism, see Donnelly, *Captain Rock*, 42–44, 12–33, 144–46; MacDonagh, *Hereditary Bondsman*, 228–29, 239–43, *The Emancipist*, 40–41, 153–54; Connolly, *Priests and People in Pre-Famine Ireland*, 40–42, 77; McCaffrey, "Irish Textures in American Catholicism," 4–5; Larkin, "The Devotional Revolution in Ireland," 625–52.

5. Schmidt, "An Overview of Institutional Establishments," 53–76.

6. R. M. Miller, "Some Speculations on Catholic Identity," 26–35, 44–48; D. T. Gleeson, *Irish in the South*, 90–91; Madden, *Catholics in South Carolina*, 75–80. For the importance of the Catholic Church in immigrant lives, see Jay P. Dolan, *The Immigrant Church*.

7. D. T. Gleeson, *Irish in the South*, 117–19.

8. Rev. C. C. Jones to Mary S. Mallard, Dec. 13, 1860 in Myers, *The Children of Pride*, 634. "Christ Church Savannah." O'Neill was often known as "Sr." because he had a nephew of the same name who was also a priest in the diocese of Savannah.

9. *Savannah Morning News*, July 9, 1861.

10. Father James Hasson to Bishop [P. N] Lynch, Mar. 9, 1861, Bishop Lynch Papers, ACDC.

11. Verot also earned the title "rebel" for his vocal opposition to papal infallibility at the First Vatican Council in 1870, see Gannon, *Rebel Bishop*, 31–32, 203–14; Bishop Augustin Verot to [Archbishop Francis Patrick Kenrick], 18 Jan. 1861, copy, Bishop Verot Collection, MDBMA; Verot, *A Tract for the Times* and, *A General Catechism*, 20.

12. John F. Quinn, "'Three Cheers for the Abolitionist Pope!,'" 67–93; C. Davis, *A History of Black Catholics in the United States*, 46–57. See also Curran, "'Splendid Poverty,'" 125–46; Murphy, *Jesuit Slaveholding in Maryland*; England "Letters to the Hon. John Forsyth," 3:106–91; Brokage, *Francis Patrick Kenrick's Opinion on Slavery*.

13. "Record of the Episcopal Acts of Rt. Rev. Augustin Verot, Bishop of Savannah and Administrator Apostolic of Florida," copy, Richard Reid Collection, MDBMA; *Savannah Morning News*, 9 July 1861; Wight, "Letters of the Bishop of Savannah, 99.

14. For the Confederate constitution, see Thomas, *The Confederate Nation*, 307–22.

15. *United States Catholic Miscellany*, Dec. 22, 1860; *Charleston Catholic Miscellany*, Dec. 29, 1860.

16. *United States Catholic Miscellany*, Dec. 15, 1860.

17. *United States Catholic Miscellany*, Aug. 7, 1822. For England's politics, see P. Carey, *Immigrant Bishop*; and Saunders and Rogers "Bishop John England of Charleston," 311–22. For England and slavery, see J. Kelly, "Charleston's Bishop England and American Slavery," 48–56.

18. *Charleston Catholic Miscellany*, Dec. 29, 1860.

19. M. C. Kelly, "A 'Sentinel of Our Liberties,'" 156–63; Meenagh, "Archbishop John Hughes and the New York Schools Controversy," 34–65; For more on Hughes, see Shaw, *Dagger John*.

20. M. C. Kelly, "A 'Sentinel of Our Liberties,'" 161; Sharrow, "John Hughes," 254–69.

21. Quoted in M. C. Kelly, "A 'Sentinel of Our Liberties,'" 163.

22. "History of the Catholic Diocese of Charleston," 81–82 [unpublished], Wolfe Collection, ACDC; *New York Times*, Sept. 4, 1861.

23. Robert Tyler to Bishop [Patrick] Lynch, Sept. 9, 1861, Rev. C. J. Croghan to Bishop [Patrick Lynch] Sept. 10, 1861, Bishop J. M. McGill to Bishop [Patrick Lynch], Sept. 2, 1862, T. C. Sullivan to Bishop [Patrick Lynch], Oct. 29, 1862, Bishop Lynch Papers, ACDC.

24. Heisser, "Bishop Lynch's People"; Bishop William Henry [Elder] to Archbishop J. M. Odin, Mar. 24, 1862, Archdiocese of New Orleans Collection, UNDA; D. T. Gleeson, *Irish in the South*, 142; Gerow, *Civil War Diary*.

25. Lipscomb, "The Administration of John Quinlan," 13–19 31–34.

26. Quoted in Lipscomb, "Administration of John Quinlan," 34. For Purcell and pro-Union stance, see Hennesey, *American Catholics*, 152–53; D. Spalding, "Martin John Spalding's 'Dissertation,'" 69.

27. Lipscomb, "Administration of John Quinlan," 31; D. T. Gleeson, *Irish in the South*, 130.

28. Quoted in Lipscomb, "Administration of John Quinlan," 37.

29. Ibid., 42, 54; Receipt Book, Bishop Quinlan Papers, AAM.

30. Lipscomb, "Administration of John Quinlan," 54–55.

31. Quoted in ibid., 55–56.

32. Quoted in ibid., 56–57.

33. Fogarty, *Commonwealth Catholicism*, 147–57 (quotes on 148), 156–57. See also Woods, *History of the Catholic Church*, 289–95.

34. Bishop R. Whelan to James McMaster, June 23, 1862, Jan. 29, 1863, James McMaster Collection, UNDA.

35. Quoted in Fogarty, *Commonwealth Catholicism*, 145–46.

36. *New Orleans Catholic Standard*, 9 Jan. 1861, in Society for Propagation of the Faith Collection, UNDA; T. L. Jones, *Lee's Tigers*, 6–7, 238–39; Daniel *Soldiering in the Army of Tennessee*, 122. See also Durkin, *Confederate Chaplain*.

37. *New Orleans Daily True Delta*, Mar. 19, 1861.

38. Hennesey, *American Catholics*, 154.

39. Bishop William Henry [Elder] to Archbishop J. M. Odin, May 21, 1863, Bishop John Quinlan to Archbishop J. M. Odin, Archdiocese of New Orleans Collection, UNDA; Archbishop J. M. Odin to [Propagation of the Faith], 20 July 1863, Society for the Propagation of the Faith Collection, UNDA; Bishop M. J. Spalding to Archbishop [J. B.] Purcell, Apr. 25, 1862, Archdiocese of Cincinnati Collection, UNDA.

40. Bishop William Henry [Elder] to Archbishop J. M. Odin, May 21, 1863, June 11, 1864, Archdiocese of New Orleans Collection, UNDA; *Vicksburg Daily Herald*, Aug. 23, 1864, in Society for the Propagation of the Faith Collection, UNDA; Pillar, *The Catholic Church in Mississippi*, 304–11; Hennesey, *American Catholics*, 152.

41. Hennesey, *American Catholics*, 158; R. M. Miller, "Catholic Religion," 276–79; Morris, *American Catholics*, 79; W. I. Burton, *Melting Pot Soldiers*, 37; O. A. Brownson to Count Charles De Montalembert, June 25, 1865, O. A. Brownson Collection, UNDA. For the ultimate disillusion, see Bernstein, *The New York City Draft Riots*.

42. Hennesey, *American Catholics*, 147–48; "James Alphonsus McMaster"; *New York Times*, Oct. 7, 1861; Dec. 30, 1886; McGreevy, *Catholicism and American Freedom*, 68–71; Spann, "Union Green," 194; "B. E. B" to [James McMaster], May 31, 1864, James McMaster Collection, UNDA.

43. Father R. Kane to James A. McMaster, Oct. 15, 1862, Mrs. M. McCarrick to [James] McMaster, Mar. 5, 1864, Father James A. Corcoran to [James McMaster] June 21, 1865, Father Abram J. Ryan to [James] McMaster, Feb. 5, 1866, Jefferson Davis to James A. McMaster, Sept. 18, 1867, James McMaster Collection, UNDA;

Bishop P. N. Lynch to Archbishop [Francis P. Kenrick], Feb. 9, 1861, Archbishop Kenrick Papers, AAB.

44. Blair Hoge to Dabney Maury 10 Jan. 1865, Confederate States of America Archives, War Department, Adjutant and Inspector General's Office, Letters and Papers, DU.

45. See, for example, Nicols-Belt, "Chaplains in the Army of Tennessee."

46. See, for example, Laurence O'Connell to Bishop [Patrick] Lynch, May 22, Aug. 16, 1863; C. J. Croghan to Bishop [Patrick] Lynch, May 6, 1863, Bishop Lynch Papers, ACDC.

47. Durkin, *Confederate Chaplain*, 6 (quote), 16–17.

48. Ibid., 67, 142 (quote), 147–48.

49. Quoted in ibid., 6, 26.

50. Quoted in ibid., 20.

51. Quoted in ibid., 26, 27.

52. Quoted in ibid., 142. For Sheeran's views on gambling, see ibid., 34–35.

53. Peter J. Meaney, "The Prison Ministry of Father Peter Whelan," 1–7.

54. Ibid., 8–9.

55. Ibid., 15–16; Marvel, *Andersonville*, 243–46. Wirz's execution has remained controversial. See Rutman, "The War Crimes and Trial of Henry Wirz," 117–33.

56. Meaney, "Prison Ministry of Father Peter Whelan," 17–23; Marvel, *Andersonville*, 141–44, 218. For Ruffin, see Walther, *The Fire-eaters*, 228–30 (quote on 229).

57. Father Ryan to Bishop [Patrick] Lynch, 1863, Bishop Lynch Papers, ACDC.

58. Beagle and Giemza, *Poet of the Lost Cause*, 30–32, 39, 67–103; Rubin, A *Shattered Nation*, 6.

59. Faherty, *Exile in Erin*, 3–6, 15, 38–41; Tucker, *The Confederacy's Fighting Chaplain*, 2–4, 22–25.

60. Tucker, *Confederacy's Fighting Chaplain*, 22–23, 138–43; John Bannon Diary, Yates-Snowdon Collection, SCL. I am grateful to Dr. Jeremiah Hackett of the University of South Carolina for deciphering the accounts in the back of the diary.

61. John Bannon Diary, Yates-Snowdon Collection, SCL.

62. Archbishop Francis Patrick [Kenrick] to Archbishop J. M. Odin, June 14, 1863, University of Notre Dame Collection, AANO.

63. Tucker, *Confederacy's Fighting Chaplain*, 99–100, 158–66, 181; Faherty, *Exile in Erin*, 6. For Cullen's massive importance, see Larkin, "Devotional Revolution in Ireland," Bowen, *Paul Cardinal Cullen* and O'Carroll, *Paul Cardinal Cullen*.

64. John Bannon to [J. P.] Benjamin, Nov. 9, 1863, and Enclosure, "Caution to Emigrants," Pickett Papers, LC. For the increase in the prominence of the Orange Order in mid-nineteenth-century Ireland, see Farrell, *Ritual and Riots*, 125–53. For the attack on the Charlestown, Massachusetts, convent, see Billington, *The Protestant Crusade*, 83–110.

65. John Bannon to [J. P.] Benjamin, Nov. 17, 1863, and Enclosure, "Caution to Emigrants," Pickett Papers, LC. For the demise of the Irish Brigade, see Bruce, *Harp of Erin*, 154–58.

66. John Bannon to [J. P.] Benjamin, Nov. 17, Dec. 15, 1863, Pickett Papers, LC. For the relationship of Mitchel with Smith O'Brien and Martin, see Keneally, *The Great Shame*, 98, 111, 144–50, 160, 239–40, 314, 329 and McGovern, *John Mitchel*, 63, 70–723, 83–84, 91–93, 101–3.

67. John Bannon to [J. P.] Benjamin, Nov. 23, Dec. 15, 1863, Jan. 19, [1864], Pickett Papers, LC; Hernon, *Celts, Catholics, and Copperheads*, 92–97.

68. They even founded their own newspaper, the *Index*. H. Jones, *Blue and Gray Diplomacy*, 68, 152–53.

69. John Bannon to [J. P.] Benjamin, Dec. 15, 1863, Jan. 19 [1864], Feb. 15, 1864, Pickett Papers, LC.

70. Faherty, *Exile in Erin*, 134; *The Times*, Jan. 6, June 10, 11, 1864.

71. Hernon, *Celts, Catholics, and Copperheads*, 22–24; Vaughan and Fitzpatrick, *Irish Historical Statistics*, 261; Schrier, *Ireland and the American Emigration*, 157.

72. Quoted in Hernon, *Celts, Catholics, and Copperheads*, 24.

73. Hernon, *Celts, Catholics, and Copperheads*, 30–35; Bruce, *Harp and Eagle*, 198–207. See also Rerucha, "Recruiting in Ireland."

74. For an example of a new Irish immigrant volunteering for the Union army and its lucrative bounty, see story of Thomas McManus in K. M. Miller, *Emigrants and Exiles*, 360–61. For the lack of Irish participation in the Union army, see McPherson, *Battle Cry of Freedom*, 606–7; and Bruce, *Harp and Eagle*, 194–96.

75. Judah P. Benjamin to Henry Hotze, Apr. 22, 1864, Henry Hotze to Father [John] Bannon, Aug. 16, 1864, Pickett Papers, LC.

76. Bannon mentioned the meeting with McGill and his secret award in a letter written fifty years after the War. Both of his biographers accept its veracity although Bannon does not appear in the index of the Confederate Congressional Journal. See Bannon, *The Confederacy's Fighting Chaplain*, 181; Faherty, *Exile in Erin*, 148; "General Index," *Journal of the Congress of the Confederate States of America, 1861–1865*.

77. Buttimer, "'By Their Deeds, You Shall Know Them,'" 11, 54–60; Campbell, "Bishop England's Sisterhood," 1–15. For the significance of Irish women to American orders, see Hoy, "The Journey Out," 65–98. For priests, see Meaney, "Prison Ministry."

78. Buttimer, "'By Their Deeds, You Shall Know Them,'" 64–66 (quotes on 64–65).

79. Fogarty, *Commonwealth Catholicism*, 164–69; Maher, *To Bind up the Wounds*, 70–72.

80. Fogarty, *Commonwealth Catholicism*, 172–75; C. Lining to Bishop [Patrick] Lynch, Aug. 15, 1863. Bishop Lynch Papers, ACDC; E. Moore Quinn, "'I have been trying *very* hard,'" 213–33.

81. Tucker, *Confederacy's Fighting Chaplain*, 6; Faherty, *Exile in Erin*, 77–80; Maher, *To Bind Up These Wounds*, 76; Isbell, *Vicksburg*, 97.

82. Buttimer, "'By Their Deeds, You Shall Know Them,'" 72–75.

83. Cumming, *A Journal of Hospital Life*, 17, 62, 74, 115 (quote on 164).

84. Quoted in ibid., 115.

85. See, for example, Fogarty, *Commonwealth Catholicism*, 165–66; Faherty, *Exile in Erin*, 112–13.

86. Buttimer, "'By Their Deeds, You Shall Know Them,'" 75–76. For the overall importance of Catholic nuns to Civil War nursing, see Maher, *To Bind Up These Wounds*.

87. Walsh seems to have provided this explanation of his discharge after the war. The Confederate compiled service records show two Patrick Walshs from Charleston. One (sometimes listed as "P. A. Walsh") served in the South Carolina militia for six months in 1861 and then disappears from the record. The other, more likely to be Patrick because his age was listed as twenty-two (Walsh was reportedly born in 1840), served for twelve months in the Palmetto regiment (Co. K. Second South Carolina Infantry) which was mustered "into State service about April 3, 1861, for twelve months." In late 1861 he was on "detached service" from the unit. The company then reenlisted "for the War" in May 1862, but the records indicate that Walsh did not do this. Confusing matters is the last mention of him notes that he "re-enlisted for Capt. Rhett's artillery Co." Walsh was, however, in plain view in Augusta and could have easily been arrested by Confederate conscription officials if he had deserted or shirked from re-enlisting. Callahan, "Patrick Walsh," 14–15, 27; CSRCS, 2nd South Carolina Infantry (Palmetto) Regiment, South Carolina Militia (Charleston Reserves), NARA.

88. Callahan, "Patrick Walsh," 15.

89. *Augusta Pacificator*, Oct. 8, 1864; Sears, *George McClellan*, 371–86. For the antiwar peace movement, which was particularly strong in North Carolina, see Rable, *The Confederate Republic*, 265–74, 292–84.

90. *Augusta Pacificator*, Oct. 8, 15, 22, 1864.

91. Ibid., Oct. 15, 22, 1864, Mar. 11, 1865.

92. J. W. Cumming to Bishop [Patrick] Lynch, Nov. 10, 1861, Jan. 17, 1862, June 30, 1863, Bishop Lynch Papers, ACDC.

93. [Bishop Patrick N. Lynch] to [Charles G. Schwarz] Sept. [?], 1865, [copy] Bishop Lynch Papers, ACDC; Bishop P. N. Lynch to Archbishop [M. J.] Spalding, Oct. 7, 1865, Archbishop Spalding Papers, AAB; Bishop Patrick Lynch to [Society for the Propagation of the Faith], 1865, Society for the Propagation of the Faith Collection, micro., UNDA.

94. Phelps, *Bombardment of Charleston*, 142–46.

95. Father James Corcoran to Bishop [Patrick] Lynch, Nov. 19, Dec. 5, 8, 1863, Father Patrick Ryan to Bishop [Patrick] Lynch, Mar. 20, 1862; Father Thomas Quigley to Bishop P. N. Lynch, Nov. 27, 1863, Jan. 30, 1864, Bishop Lynch Papers, ACDC; Heisser, "Bishop Lynch's People, 251.

96. John Daly to Bishop Patrick Lynch, Oct. 16, 1864; Father James Corcoran to Bishop [Patrick] Lynch Nov. 19, Dec. 5, 8, 1863, Bishop Lynch Papers, ACDC. Heisser, "Bishop Lynch's People," 251.

97. John Lynch to Bishop [Patrick] Lynch, Mar. 17, 1862, Lynch Family Papers, ACDC; Heisser, "Bishop Lynch's People," 243–48, 253, 258.

98. For Confederate clerics' critique of southern slaveholders, see Genovese, *A Consuming Fire*, 53–62.

99. "Pastoral Prayers for Peace," Nov. 26, 1863, Bishop Lynch Papers, ACDC.

100. Quoted in Genovese, *A Consuming Fire*, 58.

101. Hennesey, *American Catholics*, 152–53; D. Spalding, "Martin John Spalding's 'Dissertation,'" 66–85; T. W. Spalding, *Martin John Spalding*, 141; Bishop M. J. Spalding to Archbishop [J. B. Purcell], Mar. 22, 1864, Archdiocese of Cincinnati Collection, UNDA.

102. Wright, "Letters of the Bishop of Savannah," 99; D. Spalding, "Martin John Spalding's 'Dissertation,'" 66–68; Spalding, *The Premier See*, 179–81; Lalli and O'Connor, "Roman Views on the American Civil War," 21–41.

103. J. B. Jones, *A Rebel War Clerk's Diary*, 1:199–200, 217, 243; Bishop P. N. Lynch to J. P. Benjamin, Mar. 3, 1864 [typescript], Bishop Lynch Papers, ACDC.

104. Bishop P. N. Lynch to J. P. Benjamin, Mar. 25, Apr. 15, 1864 [typescript], Jefferson Davis to Bishop P. N. Lynch, Apr. 4, 1864 [typescript], Bishop Lynch Papers, ACDC.

105. Heisser, "Bishop Lynch's Civil War Pamphlet," 682.

106. Quoted in ibid., 683; Alvarez, "The Papacy in the Diplomacy of the Civil War," 246–47.

107. Quoted in Heisser, "Bishop Lynch's Civil War Pamphlet," 683.

108. Heisser, "A Few Words on the Domestic Slavery in the Confederate States by Patrick N. Lynch, Part I," 64–103, "A Few Words on the Domestic Slavery in the Confederate States by Patrick N. Lynch, Part II," 93–123 (quotes on 97–99, 109).

109. Heisser, "Bishop Lynch's Civil War Pamphlet," 684–86; Donald, *Lincoln*, 490–501, 540–41, 547; Smith, *Grant*, 284–91; Marszalek, *Sherman*, 259–317.

110. Sheehan-Dean, *Why Confederates Fought*, 191.

111. See, for example, Schott, *Alexander H. Stephens*, 334–35.

112. Meaney, "Prison Ministry of Father Peter Whelan," 23–24.

CHAPTER 6

1. Meade, *Judah P. Benjamin*, 6, 319–28; W. C. Davis, *The Union that Shaped the Confederacy*, 229–32. Edmund Ruffin committed suicide rather than live, as he put it, under "Yankee rule." Scarborough, *The Diary of Edmund Ruffin*, 875.

2. C. Davis, *A History of Black Catholics*, 119; [Bishop Patrick N. Lynch] to [Charles G. Schwarz], Sept. 1865, copy, Bishop Lynch Papers, ACDC; Bishop P. N. Lynch to Archbishop M. J. Spalding, Oct. 7, 1865, Archbishop Spalding Papers, AAB; Bishop P. N. Lynch to [Propagation of the Faith], Society for the Propagation of the Faith Collection, UNDA.

3. *New York Times*, Sept. 4, 1861; Hennesey, *American Catholics*, 152; Bishop P. N. Lynch to Archbishop M. J. Spalding, July 1, 1865, Archbishop Spalding Papers, AAB. In the same letter, Lynch, conscious of the controversial nature of his mission, mentioned that "When I first came abroad, I thought it might be more prudent considering my position not to write." For politics, see *Charleston Catholic Miscellany*, Dec. 29, 1860, May 25, June 1, 1861. For financial reasons the *Miscellany* ceased publication in late 1861. For Lynch's prosecession stance, see also Madden, *Catholics in South Carolina*, 76–77.

4. Bishop P. N. Lynch to Archbishop M. J. Spalding, May [?], 1865, Bishop P. N. Lynch to William Seward, June 24, 1865 [copy sent to Archbishop M. J. Spalding], Archbishop Spalding Papers, AAB.

5. Copy of President Johnson's Pardon, Aug. 4, 1865, Copy of Bishop Lynch's "Oath of Allegiance," Oct. 14, 1865, Bishop Lynch Papers, ACDC.

6. Bishop P. N. Lynch to William Seward, June 24, 1865 [copy sent to Archbishop M. J. Spalding], Archbishop Spalding Papers, Archives of the Catholic Archdiocese of Baltimore.

7. Hugh S. Gwynn to "Francis", Aug. 7, 1865, Hugh S. Gwynn to "Mrs. Johnson" Aug. 7, 1865, Hugh Gwynn Letters, MC; McKitrick, *Andrew Johnson and Reconstruction*, 156.

8. A. G. Magrath to Bishop [Patrick] Lynch, Nov. 8, 1865, Bishop Lynch Papers, ACDC.

9. A. G. Magrath to Andrew Johnson, June 14, 1865, Magrath, A. G. file, Confederate Amnesty Papers, South Carolina, 1865–1867, RG 94, NARA.

10. B. F. Perry to Andrew Johnson, July 30, 1865; Petition on behalf of A. G. Magrath; A. G. Magrath to Andrew Johnson, July 6, 1866; Presidential Pardon for A. G. Magrath, Jan. 19, 1867, Magrath, A. G. file, Confederate Amnesty Papers, South Carolina, 1865–1867, RG 94, NARA.

11. John J. Maher to Andrew Johnson, Aug. 7, 1865 [Endorsed as pardoned, Sept. 6, 1865], Maher, John J. File; J. J. Ryan to Andrew Johnson, Aug. 8, 1865 Ryan, J. J. file; Thomas Ryan to James Speed (attorney general of the United States), Aug. 18, 1865, Confederate Amnesty Papers, South Carolina, 1865–1867, RG 94, NARA; Eighth Census of the United States, 1860, Slave Schedule, Barnwell County, South Carolina, micro., NARA.

12. McCloskey did not even write a letter of explanation; he merely applied for the pardon under the property clause and received it. James McCloskey to [Andrew Johnson] July 7, 1866 [Endorsed as pardoned July 26, 1866], Confederate Amnesty Papers, Louisiana, 1865–1867, RG 94, NARA.

13. Eighth Census of the United States, 1860, Slave Schedule, Charleston County, South Carolina, micro., NARA; Thomas Ryan to James Speed (attorneys general of the United States), Aug. 18, 1865, Ryan, Thomas file, Confederate Amnesty Papers, South Carolina, 1865–1867, RG 94, NARA.

14. Edward Sparrow to Andrew Johnson, July 21, 1865 [Endorsed as pardoned Dec. 27, 1865], Sparrow, Edward file, Confederate Amnesty Papers, Louisiana, 1865–1867, RG 94, NARA.

15. Joseph Finegan to Andrew Johnson] July 5, 1865 [Endorsed as pardoned Apr. 5, 1866], Finnegan [sic], Joseph file, Confederate Amnesty Papers, Florida, 1865–1867, RG 94, NARA.

16. Chatham County, Barred and Disallowed Claims, Approved Claims, Georgia, Southern Claims Commission Records, RG 217, NARA.

17. Culhane, Catherine file, Adams County, Barred and Disallowed Claims, Mississippi, Southern Claims Commission Records, RG 217, NARA.

18. McNamara, Patrick file, Orleans, Barred and Disallowed Claims, Louisiana, Southern Claims Commission Records, RG 217, NARA.

19. Lynch, Michael file, Fulton County, Approved Claims Georgia, Southern Claims Commission Records, RG 217, NARA; Dyer, *Secret Yankees*, 58, 216.

20. McNamara, Michael file, Charleston County, Approved Claims South Carolina, Southern Claims Commission Records, RG 217, NARA.

21. Frank Bennett Journal, DU.

22. P. J. Coogan, quoted in McNamara, Michael, file, Charleston County, Approved Claims South Carolina, Southern Claims Commission Records, RG 217, NARA.

23. "K.K.K." to E. A. Dowling, June 27, 1870, Gosman Family Papers, NYHS.

24. *Testimony taken by the Joint Committee to Inquire into the Conditions in the Late Insurrectionary State*, House Report, No. 22, 1:36–39 (quote on 38).

25. Moore, *The Juhl Letters*, 175, 225, 245; Seventh Census of the United States, 1850, Slave Schedule, Sumter County, South Carolina, NARA; Ninth Census of the United States, 1870, Sumter County, South Carolina, NARA.

26. Foner, *Reconstruction*, 299. For Coogan testimony on his life in Confederate Charleston, see McNamara, Michael, file, Charleston County, Approved Claims South Carolina, Southern Claims Commission Records, RG 217, NARA; *New York Herald*, Sept. 13, 1865; *New York World*, Jan. 9, 1867; *Charleston Tri-Weekly Courier*, Oct. 14, 1869.

27. H. Jones, *Blue and Gray Diplomacy*, 196–200; J. Daly [James Stephens] to "Brother" [John O'Mahony], May 20, 1864, Patrick Condon to P. J. Downing, Mar. 31, 1866, Fenian Brotherhood Records, ACUA.

28. Brennan, "Fever and Fists," 290, 295–98.

29. Quoted in McGovern, *John Mitchel*, 185.

30. McGovern, *John Mitchel*, 185–93; R. W. Dowling to Col. [James Kelly], Aug. 25, 1866, Fenian Brotherhood Records, ACUA.

31. General Phil Sheridan to War Department, June 4, 1866, in Grant, *The Papers of Ulysses S. Grant*, 16:217.

32. *New Orleans Daily Picayune*, Aug. 1, 1866; *Atlanta Daily Constitution*, July 28, 1868; One Mr. McMaster quoted in *Testimony taken by the Joint Committee to Inquire into the Conditions in the Late Insurrectionary State*, Senate Report No. 44, 3:1963.

33. Quoted in Snay, *Fenians, Freedmen and Southern Whites*, 13; *New Orleans Daily Picayune*, Apr. 23, 1875.

34. See, for example, *New Orleans Daily Picayune*, July 7, 1870, Nov. 24, 1872, Mar. 18, 1873, and *Memphis Avalanche*, May 11, 1866. For the connection between anti-Catholicism and abolitionism, see Emmons, *Beyond the American Pale*, 70–72, 80–84.

35. Hollandsworth, *An Absolute Massacre*, 109, 120, 125.

36. Hogue, *Uncivil Wars*, 122; Nystrom, *New Orleans after the Civil War*, 76, 183–84.

37. Foner, *Reconstruction*, 571–72. For the rise of the German political machine in Charleston, see Jeffrey G. Strickland, "Ethnicity and Race in the Urban South."

38. D. T. Gleeson, *Irish in the South*, 176–78.

39. Hollandsworth, *An Absolute Massacre*, 25, 30, quote on 25.

40. Bishop P. N. Lynch to General [Ralph] Ely, Dec. 27, 1865, Bishop P. N. Lynch to General O. O. Howard, Feb. 1, 1866, draft, Bishop Lynch Papers, ACDC.

41. Bishop P. N. Lynch to [Propagation of the Faith?] 1873, Society for Propagation of the Faith Collection, micro., UNDA.

42. Peter Benoit Diary [typescript], 138, 215, 238, UNDA.

43. "Interesting Transcriptions and Cataloging Notes from the Nationalist of 1868–1869" [typescript], MPL.

44. See Relief Receipts and [Director of Catholic Male Orphan Asylum] to Colonel George A. Robinson, Sept. 23, 1865, Records of the Bureau of Refugees, Freedmen, and Abandoned Lands, RG 105, micro., Mobile County, Alabama. NARA.

45. Fitzgerald, *Urban Emancipation*, 69–70, 103.

46. Quoted in ibid., 103.

47. Fitzgerald, *Urban Emancipation*, 40.

48. O'Connor, *The Life and Letters of M. P. O'Connor*, 146–50, 159–60; Williamson, *After Slavery*, 406–12; M. B. Lynch to P. N. Lynch, Dec. 1, 1876, Feb. 22, 1877, May 1, 1877, typescript, Richard Madden Papers, ACDC.

49. *New Orleans Daily Picayune*, Mar. 16, 17, Nov. 10, 13, 1876; Burns, "St. Patrick's Hall," 77.

50. T. L. Jones, *Lee's Tigers*, 133; Bishop P. N. Lynch to Archbishop M. J. Spalding, Oct. 7, 1865, Archbishop Spalding Papers, AAB. Fire was actually started by retreating Confederates. For controversy on "burning of Columbia," see Marszalek, *Sherman*, 322–25.

51. *The Irish Volunteers Memorial Meeting*; Phelps *Charlestonians in War*; CSRCS, 1st South Carolina Infantry (Gregg's) Regiment, NARA.

52. *Charleston Daily Courier*, Sept. 17, 1861.

53. Cox, *Dixie's Daughters*; Foster, *Ghosts of the Confederacy*; C. R. Wilson, *Baptized in Blood*; Janney, *Burying the Dead*.

54. Foster, *Ghosts of the Confederacy*, 40–41.

55. *The Irish Volunteers Memorial Meeting*, 9–10.

56. Ibid, 11–12.

57. *Charleston News and Courier*, Mar. 18, 19, 1878.

58. *The Irish Volunteers Memorial Meeting*, 7.

59. Ibid., 11.

60. C. R. Wilson, *Baptized in Blood*.

61. Bruce, *The Harp and The Eagle*, 257–64.

62. William McBurney to Edward McCrady Jr., Sept. 16, 1861, Edward McCrady Jr., to Thomas Ryan, Feb. 13, 1862, Edward McCrady Jr. Military Papers, SCHS; *The Irish Volunteers Memorial Meeting*, 16; CSRCS, 1st South Carolina Infantry (Gregg's) Regiment, NARA. For McCrady's overall Lost Cause efforts, see Holden, *In the Great Maelstrom*, 48–66.

63. Symonds, *Stonewall of the West*, 171–76; Connelly, *Autumn of Glory*, 273–75; Joslyn, "'An Open, Stand Up Affair,'" 113–42; Patrick Condon to P. J. Downing, Mar. 31, 1866, Fenian Brotherhood Records, ACUA; Joslyn, "Epilogue," 198.

64. Joslyn "Epilogue," 283, 288–90; Perdue and Perdue, *Pat Cleburne*, 434–37.

65. D. T. Gleeson, *Irish in the South*, 176–78; Foner, *Reconstruction*, 361–62.

66. C. R. Wilson, *Baptized in Blood*, 58–59; Hubbell, *The South in American Literature*, 477–79; Augusta *Banner of the South*, Mar. 20, Apr. 24, 1869; Weaver, *Selected Poems of*

Father Ryan, 5; O'Connell, *Furl That Banner*, 211–12. The best and newest biography of Ryan is Beagle and Giemza, *Poet of the Lost Cause*.

67. *Mobile Register*, Apr. 28, 1886, quoted in O'Connell, *Furl That Banner*, 204.

68. Bishop John O'Sullivan to Father [Abram Ryan], Mar. 5, 1886, Bishop O'Sullivan Papers, AAM.

69. Knight, *Georgia's Markers*, 2:955–56; Worthington, *Literary Charleston*, xxiii–xiv; Price, *Stories with a Moral*, 199–202; 231–39, 247–48.

70. *Mobile Daily Register*, July 12, 1913; *Mobile Sunday Register*, July 13, 1913. For Semmes, see *Mobile Daily Register*, June 18, 1900; Fox, *Wolf of the Deep*; and J. M. Taylor, *Confederate Raider*.

71. White opponents of Reconstruction disagreed on everything from party nomenclature to tactics, even as late as 1876. The Compromise of 1877 gave whites more room to oppose each other. Foner, *Reconstruction*, 412–25, 570–71; Perman, *The Road to Redemption*, 57–86, 237–63; Robert Zuczek, *State of Rebellion*, 161–63; Cooper, *The Conservative Regime*, 45–83.

72. Foster, *Ghosts of the Confederacy*, 95–98.

73. Ibid., 104–14, 133–41; Ayers, *The Promise of the New South*, 334–38.

74. AANV Applications Volume, 55-V, LHAC, TU; Gannon, *Irish Rebels, Confederate Tigers*, 337, 380; Tenth Census of the United States, 1880, Orleans Parish, Louisiana, micro. NARA; D. T. Gleeson, *Irish in the South*, 59.

75. AANV Certificates, 55-V, LHAC, TU.

76. Luke W. Finlay to Charles G. Johnson, May 15, 1875, Confederate Personnel Records–James Doyle, 55-P, LHAC, TU; AANV, Application Volumes, 55-V, LHAC, TU; Gannon, *Irish Rebels, Confederate Tigers*, 389.

77. D. T. Gleeson, *Irish in the South*, 32–36; Charter Articles of Organization, MC; Fourth Annual Reunion, MC; Minutes of the Sixth Annual Meeting, MC.

78. Confederate Personnel Records–John Curley, James McCann to John Rapier, Aug. 1, 1903, John Rapier to James McCann, Aug. 5, 1903, Confederate Personnel Records–James McCann, 55-P, LHAC, TU; Foster, *Ghosts of the Confederacy*, 131–32.

79. See for example, *Confederate Veteran* 7 (Apr. 1899): 177, 9 (Mar. 1901): 126, 10 (1902): 326, 13 (July 1905): 322, 15 (Sept. 1907), 422, 23 (June 1915): 274, 25 (Aug. 1917): 372, 37 (Mar. 1929): 188.

80. *Confederate Veteran* 1 (Oct. 1893): 307–9, 2 (June 1894): 181, 14 (Oct. 1906): 444, 27 (June 1919): 208, 30 (Oct. 1922): 377–79.

81. Bruce, *The Harp and The Eagle*, 234–36. For more on the GAR, see McConnell, *Glorious Contentment*.

82. O'Grady, "Anthony M. Keiley," 613–35; Keiley, *In Vinculis*; "History of the Petersburg Rifles," Keiley Family Papers, VHS; R. E. Lee to A. M. Keiley, May 5, 1866, R. E. Lee Papers, VHS. President Grover Cleveland would nominate Keiley as Ambassador to Italy and later the Hapsburg Empire in the mid-1880s.

83. *Souvenir Unveiling Soldiers' and Sailors' Monument*, 21; A. M. Keiley to [W. E. Cutshaw], 28 Oct. 1889, Confederate Soldiers' and Sailors' Monument Association Papers, MC.

84. Jubal Early to Carlton McCarthy, Dec. 7, 1888, Bishop John J. Keane to D. C. Richardson, Dec. 17, 1887, Soldiers' and Sailors' Monument Association Papers, MC.

85. *Souvenir Unveiling Soldiers' and Sailors' Monument*, 5–21; Foster, *Ghosts of the Confederacy*, 131.

86. D. T. Gleeson, *Irish in the South*, 27, 145–47 OR, ser. 1, vol. 16, pt. 1, 310–12; Alwyn Barr, "Texas Coastal Defenses, 1861–1865," *Southwestern Historical Quarterly* 65 (July 1961): 1–31.

87. *Houston Chronicle*, Mar. 16, 1905; *Houston Post*, Mar. 17, 1905.

88. *Houston Chronicle*, Mar. 17, 1905; *Houston Post*, Mar. 17, 1905.

89. Sorensen, *Kennedy*, 188–93.

90. For more on Ireland's and the South's similar obsession with the past, see Kieran Quinlan, *Strange Kin*, 217–46. For the South, see Woodward, *The Burden of Southern History*; Brundage, *The Southern Past*; Cobb, *Away Down South*.

91. "Pitchfork" Ben Tillman of South Carolina, who became governor and a U.S. senator in the 1890s, had to overcome an undistinguished Confederate past which his opponents were not afraid to use against him. He responded by threatening to turn the military college in Charleston, The Citadel, whose cadets had fought in the Civil War, into a women's college. He eventually backed off that idea. Kantrowitz, *Ben Tillman*, 118–21, 182.

92. Foster, *Ghosts of the Confederacy*, 171–72; Cox, *Dixie's Daughters*, 8–33; Whites, *Civil War as a Crisis in Gender*, 165–68; "Historical Souvenir: Ninth Annual Meeting of the United Daughters of the Confederacy," United Daughters of the Confederacy Collection, MC; *Confederate Veteran* 15 (July 1907): 329; Twelfth Census of the United States, 1900: City of New Orleans, Louisiana, micro., NARA.

93. *Confederate Veteran* 7 (Apr. 1899): 177; Werner, "The New South Creed," 573–600; Callahan, "Patrick Walsh," 14–29; Woodward, *Tom Watson*, 167–69, 188, 227, 241–43, and *Origins of the New South, 1877–1913*, 14–17. For more on the "New South," see Gaston's classic, *The New South Creed*.

94. Walsh, inevitably, received his own memorial with a statue of his likeness in downtown Augusta close to St. Patrick's Church. Knight, *Georgia's Markers*, 2:958–60.

CONCLUSION

1. Christian G. Samito in his study of the Union war effort sees military combat as the key element in gaining Irish and African American equality and full citizenship in the eyes of the law. See Samito, *Becoming American under Fire*.

2. Even though I disagree with some historians on the extent and depth of Confederate nationalism, I do acknowledge the importance of the postwar period in assessing it. See, for example, Rubin, *A Shattered Nation*, 141–200.

3. He has only recently been recognized as an Irish poet as well as a southern one. See Beagle and Giemza, *Poet of the Lost Cause*, 4, 94. The premier analysis of Irish American literature, however, does not mention him. He is thus not recognized as part of the "Irish Voice" in the United States. See Fanning, *The Irish Voice in America*.

4. Woodward, *Tom Watson*, 74, 418–25.

5. Buttimer, "New South, New Church," 66–70 (quotes on 66, 67, and 68). For Watson's anti-Catholic campaign, see Woodward, *Tom Watson*, 418–25.

6. Quoted in Yuhl, *A Golden Haze of Memory*, 42. For more on Grace's maverick politics in the Jim Crow South, see Boggs, "John Patrick Grace."

7. Mitchell, *Gone with the Wind*.

8. Hollywood movies such as *Run of the Arrow* (1957) and *Major Dundee* (1965), as well as *Gods and Generals* (2003), highlight this persistence. In the former, the Confederate Irish Virginian soldier "O'Meara" (played with a poor Irish accent by Rod Steiger) kills the last Union casualty at Appomattox. He is such a Rebel, from his Irish and southern experiences, he refuses to surrender and flees west, where he joins with the Indians on the Plains because he wants to kill "Yankees." Renouncing his Americanness he becomes a Sioux rather than accept the end of the war. In the latter, Captain Benjamin Tyreen (played by Richard Harris with a much better Irish accent) is an Irish Confederate officer prisoner of war, and a formerly court-martialed U.S. officer, who is forced to join with Union officer Major Dundee (Charlton Heston) to chase down a renegade Apache warrior in Mexico. Tyreen hates Dundee for having been the deciding vote in his prewar court-martial but, because he has promised to lead his men in this chase of the Apache, feels obliged to honor his commitment. After killing the Apache chief, Tyreen and Dundee are about to renew their old feud but are attacked by French forces in Mexico. Tyreen is mortally wounded and bravely saves the whole expedition by riding to his death and leading the French forces away from the main party. For scholarly analysis of *Major Dundee*, see Gilligan "'Fall in with the Major,'" 233–48.

9. A good example of the ambiguities of Irish southerners toward race is Flannery O'Connor. She was named for the wife of the last captain of the Irish Jasper Greens whose likeness is in the statue of the Irish Confederate memorial in Savannah. Edmunds, "Through a Glass Darkly," 559–85. For a critical view of O'Connor and race, see Kahane, "The Artificial Niggers," 183–98. See also Simpson, *Flannery O'Connor*, 90–102, for a more sympathetic look at O'Connor's racial views. For an exception to the general Irish story, see the attempts, ultimately unsuccessful, at biracial unionism on the Savannah waterfront in the 1880s. Hunt, "Savannah's Black and White Longshoremen."

10. See for example, the report of "Racial Incidents" around the 1961 St. Patrick's Day parade, where black and white gangs clashed in the streets of downtown Savannah, *Savannah Morning News*, Mar. 18, 1961. See also Manning and Rodgers "Desegregation of the New Orleans Public Schools," 31–42, and Gallagher, "The Catholic Church, Martin Luther King Jr., and the March in St. Augustine," 149–72.

Selected Bibliography

MANUSCRIPT COLLECTIONS

Atlanta, Georgia
 Special Collections, Robert Woodruff Library, Emory University
  Great Britain Consulate Collection

Baltimore, Maryland
 Archives of the Archdiocese of Baltimore
  Archbishop Kenrick Papers
  Archbishop Spalding Papers

Baton Rouge, Louisiana
 Louisiana and Lower Mississippi Valley Collection, Louisiana State University
  John McKown Papers
  Patrick Murphy Collection

Belfast, Northern Ireland
 Public Record Office of Northern Ireland
  Foster of Glyde Papers
  Moses Paul Letter
  Pinkerton Papers
  Robert McElderry Collection

Chapel Hill, North Carolina
 Southern Historical Collection, University of North Carolina
  Maunsel White Collection
  Wilson Family Papers

Charleston, South Carolina
 Archives of the Catholic Diocese of Charleston
  Bishop Lynch Papers
  "Catalogue of Negro Slaves of the Estate of the Hon. William McKenna
   Deceased"
  Lynch Family Papers
  Richard Madden Papers
  Wolfe Collection
 South Carolina Historical Society
  Edward McCrady Military Papers
  Hibernian Society Records
  Magrath Family Papers
  Slave Sale Broadside, 1852

Columbia, South Carolina
South Carolina Department of Archives and History
General Assembly Petitions (Microfilm)
Governor A. G. Magrath Papers (Microfilm)
South Caroliniana Library, University of South Carolina
Irish Volunteers File
Yates-Snowdon Collection

Durham, North Carolina
David M. Rubenstein Rare Books and Manuscripts Library, Duke University
Confederate States of America Archives
Frank Bennett Journal
Richard Elward Papers
William Robert Greer Papers
James Francis Tracy Papers

Jackson, Mississippi
Mississippi Department of Archives and History
Blackmore (Lizzie McFarland) Collection
Subject File: Paulding
J. L. Power Collection

London, England
National Archives of the United Kingdom
Foreign Office Records

Memphis, Tennessee
Memphis and Shelby County Library and Public Information Center
Annie Conner Collection

Mobile, Alabama
Archives of the Archdiocese of Mobile
Bishop Quinlan Papers
Bishop O'Sullivan Papers
Mobile Public Library
"Interesting Transcriptions and Cataloging Notes from the Nationalist of 1868–1869"
"Partial List of Mobile Companies with Partial Membership of Each Serving in the Confederate War"

Morrow, Georgia
Georgia Department of Archives and History
Governor Brown Correspondence

New Orleans, Louisiana
Archives of the Archdiocese of New Orleans
University of Notre Dame Collection
Howard-Tilton Memorial Library, Tulane University

George Ring Diary
Louisiana Historical Association Collection
Williams Research Center, Historic New Orleans Collection
Murphy Family Papers

New York City, New York
New-York Historical Society
Gosman Family Papers

Notre Dame, Indiana
University of Notre Dame Archives
Archdiocese of Cincinnati Collection
Archdiocese of New Orleans Collection
Father Peter Benoit Diary (typescript)
O. A. Brownson Collection
James McMaster Collection
Society for the Propagation of the Faith Collection (microfilm)

Omagh, Northern Ireland
Centre for Migration Studies, Ulster American Folk Park
James Hamilton Diary (typescript online)

Richmond, Virginia
Ellen S. Brockenbrough Library, Museum of the Confederacy
Charter Articles of Organization and Rules and Regulations of the Association of the
Army of Tennessee, Louisiana Division
Confederate Soldiers' and Sailors' Monument Association Papers
Fourth Annual Reunion, Benevolent Association, Army of Northern Virginia, Louisiana
Division
Hugh Gwynn Letters
John O. Farrell Diary (typescript)
Minutes of the Sixth Annual Meeting of the Association of Confederate
Soldiers, Tennessee Division.
Roster of the CSS Tennessee
United Daughters of the Confederacy Collection
Virginia Historical Society
Keiley Family Papers
Robert E. Lee Papers
Isaac (Frank) Potts Memoir

St. Louis, Missouri
Missouri Historical Society
Patrick Ahearn Papers

Savannah, Georgia
Monsignor Daniel J. Bourke Memorial Archives, Catholic Diocese of Savannah
Richard Reid Collection
Bishop Verot Collection

Washington, DC
    Archives of the Catholic University of America
        Fenian Brotherhood Records
    Library of Congress
        Benjamin F. Butler Papers
        Pickett Papers
    National Archives and Records Administration
        Record Group 94, Confederate Amnesty Papers
        Record Group 105, Records of the Bureau of Refugees, Freedmen, and
            Abandoned Lands
        Record Group 109
            Compiled Service Records of Confederate Soldiers (microfilm)
            Register of Arrests, Provost Marshall General's Office, Richmond
            Time Book, Confederate Arsenal, Richmond
        Record Group 217, Southern Claims Commission Records

PUBLIC DOCUMENTS AND PRINTED COLLECTIONS

Calhoun, John C. *The Papers of John C. Calhoun*. Vol. 15. Edited by Clyde N. Wilson.
    Columbia: University of South Carolina Press, 1984,
————. *The Papers of John C. Calhoun*. Vol. 24. Edited by Clyde N. Wilson. Columbia:
    University of South Carolina Press, 1998.
Davis, Jefferson. *The Papers of Jefferson Davis*. Vol. 4. Edited by Lynda Caswell Crist
    and others. Baton Rouge: Louisiana State University Press, 1983.
————. *The Papers of Jefferson Davis*. Vol. 11. Edited by Lynda Caswell Crist and
    others. Baton Rouge: Louisiana State University Press, 2004.
De Bow, J. D. B. *The Seventh Census of the United States: 1850*. Washington, DC: U.S.
    Government Printer, 1853.
Eighth Census of the United States, 1860. Washington, DC: National Archives and
    Records Administration. Microfilm.
Grant, U. S. *The Papers of Ulysses S. Grant*. Vol. 16. Edited by John Y. Simon.
    Carbondale: Southern Illinois University Press, 1988.
Journal of the House of Representatives of the State of South Carolina Being the Session of 1862
    (and extra session of 1863). Columbia: Charles P. Pelham, State Printer, 1862 [sic].
    Microfilm.
Kennedy, Joseph C. G. *Population of the United States in 1860: Compiled from the Original*
    Returns of the Eighth Census. Washington, DC: U.S. Government Printing Office, 1864.
Ninth Census of the United States, 1870. Washington, DC: National Archives and
    Records Administration. Microfilm.
O'Connor, Mary D. *The Life and Letters of M. P. O'Connor: Written and Edited by His*
    Daughter. New York: Dempsey and Carroll, 1893.
Official Records of the Union and Confederate Navies in the War of the Rebellion. 30 vols.
    Washington, DC: U.S. Government Printing Office, 1894–1922.
Seventh Census of the United States, 1850. Washington, DC: National Archives
    and Records Administration. Microfilm.

Testimony taken by the Joint Committee to Inquire into the Conditions in the Late
    Insurrectionary State, H.R.Rep. No. 22, pt. 3. 42nd Cong., 2nd sess. (1872).
Testimony taken by the Joint Committee to Inquire into the Conditions in the Late
    Insurrectionary State. S.Rep. No. 44, pt. 5. 42nd Cong., 2nd sess. (1872).
Twelfth Census of the United States, 1900. Washington, DC: National Archives
    and Records Administration. Microfilm.
War of the Rebellion: Official Records of the Union and Confederate Armies. 128 vols.
    Washington, DC: U.S. Government Printing Office, 1880–1902.

BOOKS

Abbott, A. O. Prison Life in the South. New York: Harper Brothers, 1866.
Abel, E. Lawrence. Singing the New Nation: How Music Shaped the Confederacy,
    1861–1865. Mechanicsburg, PA: Stackpole Books, 2000.
Aldous, Richard. Great Irish Speeches. Waltham, MA: Quercus Publishing, 2007.
Anderson, Benedict. Imagined Communities: Reflections on the Origin and Spread of
    Nationalism. 3rd ed. New York: Verso Press, 2006.
Andrews, W. H. Footprints of a Regiment: A Recollection of the 1st Georgia Regulars, 1861–
    1865. Reprint. Edited by Richard M. McMurry. Atlanta: Longstreet Press, 1992.
Ash, Stephen V. When the Yankees Came: Conflict and Chaos in the Occupied South,
    1861–1865. Chapel Hill: University of North Carolina Press, 1999.
Ayers, Edward L. The Promise of the New South: Life after Reconstruction. New York:
    Oxford University Press, 1992.
Baker, Jean H. Ambivalent Americans: The Know Nothing Party in Maryland. Baltimore:
    Johns Hopkins University Press, 1977.
Ballard, Michael B. Vicksburg: The Campaign That Opened the Mississippi. Chapel Hill:
    University of North Carolina Press, 2004.
Barrat, John G. Sherman's March through the Carolinas. Reprint. Chapel Hill: University
    of North Carolina Press, 1996.
Beagle, Donald Robert, and Bryan Albin Giemza. Poet of the Lost Cause: A Life of
    Father Ryan. Knoxville: University of Tennessee Press, 2008.
Beringer, Richard E., and others. The Elements of Confederate Defeat: Nationalism, War
    Aims, and Religion. Athens: University of Georgia Press, 1988.
———. Why the South Lost the Civil War. Athens: University of Georgia Press, 1986.
Bernstein, Iver. The New York City Draft Riots: Their Significance for American Society and
    Politics in the Age of the Civil War. New York: Oxford University Press, 1990.
Berwanger, Eugene H. The British Foreign Service and the American Civil War. Lexington:
    University Press of Kentucky, 1994.
Bettersworth, John K., ed., Mississippi in the Confederacy: As They Saw It. Baton Rouge:
    Louisiana State University Press, 1961.
Billington, Ray Allen. The Protestant Crusade, 1800–1860: A Study of the Origins of
    American Nativism. New York: Peter Smith, 1963.
Bland, T. A. Life of Benjamin Butler. New York: Charles T. Dillingham, 1879.
Bowen, Desmond. Paul Cardinal Cullen and the Shaping of Modern Irish Catholicism.
    Dublin: Gill and Macmillan, 1983.

Bragg, William Harris. *Joe Brown's Army: The Georgia State Line, 1862–1865*. Macon, GA: Mercer University Press, 1987.

Brokage, Joseph D. *Francis Patrick Kenrick's Opinion on Slavery*. Washington, DC.: Catholic University Press of America, 1955.

Brooks, Thomas Walter, and Michael Dan Jones. *Lee's Foreign Legion: A History of the 10th Louisiana Infantry*. Gravenhurst, Ontario: Published by author, 1995.

Brooksher, William Riley. *War along the Bayous: The 1864 Red River Campaign in Louisiana*. Washington, DC: Brassey's, 2000.

Brown, Dee. *The Galvanized Yankees*. Urbana: University of Illinois Press, 1963.

Brownlee, Richard S. *Gray Ghosts of the Confederacy: Guerilla Warfare in the West, 1861–1865*. Baton Rouge: Louisiana State University Press, 1984.

Bruce, Susannah Ural. *The Harp and the Eagle: Irish-American Volunteers and the Union Army, 1861–1865*. New York: New York University Press, 2006.

Brundage, W. Fitzhugh. *The Southern Past: A Clash of Race and Memory*. Cambridge, MA: Belknap Press, 2005.

Burton, E. Milby. *The Siege of Charleston, 1861–1865*. Columbia: University of South Carolina Press, 1970.

Burton, William I. *Melting Pot Soldiers: The Union's Ethnic Regiments*. 2nd ed. New York: Fordham University Press, 1998.

Bynum, Victoria E. *The Free State of Jones: Mississippi's Longest Civil War*. Chapel Hill: University of North Carolina Press, 2002.

———. *The Long Shadow of the Civil War: Southern Dissent and Its Legacies*. Chapel Hill: University of North Carolina Press, 2010.

Campbell, James M. *Slavery on Trial: Race, Class, and Criminal Justice in Antebellum Richmond, Virginia*. Gainesville: University Press of Florida, 2007.

Capers, Gerald M. *The Biography of a River Town, Memphis: Its Heroic Age*. Chapel Hill: University of North Carolina Press, 1939.

Carey, Anthony Gene. *Parties, Slavery, and the Union in Antebellum Georgia*. Athens: University of Georgia Press, 1997.

Carey, Patrick. *An Immigrant Bishop: John England's Adaptation of Irish Catholicism to American Republicanism*. Yonkers, NY: U.S. Catholic Historical Society, 1982.

Cash, W. J. *The Mind of the South*. Reprint. New York: Vintage Books, 1991.

Cauthen, Charles Edward. *South Carolina Goes to War, 1860–1865*. Chapel Hill: University of North Carolina Press, 1950.

Cecelski, David S. *The Waterman's Song: Slavery and Freedom in Maritime North Carolina*. Chapel Hill: University of North Carolina Press, 2000.

Clark, John Elwood. *Railroads in the Civil War: The Impact of Management on Victory and Defeat*. Baton Rouge: Louisiana State University Press, 2002.

Clinton, Catherine. *Fanny Kemble's Civil Wars*. New York: Oxford University Press, 2001.

Cobb, James C. *Away down South: A History of Southern Identity*. New York: Oxford University Press, 2006.

Coffman, Robert M., and Kurt D. Graham. *To Honor These Men: A History of the Phillips Georgia Legion Infantry Battalion*. Macon, GA: Mercer University Press 2007.

Connelly, Thomas Lawrence. *Autumn of Glory: The Army of Tennessee, 1862–1865.* Baton Rouge: Louisiana State University Press, 1971.

Connolly, S. J. *Priests and People in Pre-Famine Ireland, 1780–1845.* 2nd ed. Dublin: Four Courts Press, 2001.

Cooper, William J., Jr. *The Conservative Regime: South Carolina, 1877–1890.* Columbia: University of South Carolina Press, 2005.

———. *Jefferson Davis, American.* New York: Random House, 2001.

Coppock, Paul R. *Memphis Sketches.* Memphis: Memphis and Shelby County Library, 1976.

Coulter, E. Merton. *The Civil War and Readjustment in Kentucky.* Gloucester, MA: Peter Smith Publishing, 1926.

Cox, Karen L. *Dixie's Daughters: The United Daughters of the Confederacy and the Preservation of Confederate Culture.* Gainesville: University Press of Florida, 2003.

Cozzens, Peter. *The Shipwreck of Their Hopes: The Battles for Chattanooga.* Urbana: University of Illinois Press, 1996.

Cumming, Kate. *A Journal of Hospital Life in the Confederate Army of Tennessee from the Battle of Shiloh to the End of the War.* Louisville, KY: John P. Morton and Co., 1866.

Curran, Robert Emmet, ed. *John Dooley's Civil War: An Irish American's Journey in the First Virginia Infantry Regiment.* Knoxville: University of Tennessee Press, 2012.

Current, Richard Nelson. *Lincoln's Loyalists: Union Soldiers from the Confederacy.* New York: Oxford University Press, 1994.

Daniel, Larry J. *Soldiering in the Army of Tennessee: Portrait of Life in a Confederate Army.* Chapel Hill: University of North Carolina Press, 1991.

Davis, Cyprian. *A History of Black Catholics in the United States.* St. Louis: Crossroad Publishing, 1990.

Davis, Graham. *Land! Irish Pioneers in Mexican and Revolutionary Texas.* College Station: Texas A&M University Press, 2002.

Davis, Paul J. *C.S. Armory Richmond: A History of the Confederate States Armory, Richmond, Virginia and the Stock Shop at the C.S. Armory, Macon, Georgia.* Carlisle, PA: Published by author, 2000.

Davis, Varina Ann Jefferson "Winnie." *An Irish Knight of the Nineteenth Century: Sketch of the Life of Robert Emmet.* New York: J. W. Lovell, 1888.

Davis, William C. *Battle at Bull Run: A History of the First Major Campaign of the War.* Baton Rouge: Louisiana State University Press, 1981.

———. *Jefferson Davis: The Man and His Hour.* New York: Harper Collins, 1991.

———. *Rhett: The Turbulent Life and Times of a Fire-Eater.* Columbia: University of South Carolina Press, 2001.

———. *The Union That Shaped the Confederacy: Robert Toombs and Alexander H. Stephens.* Lawrence: University Press of Kansas, 2001.

Dawson, Joseph G. *Army Generals and Reconstruction, 1862–1877.* Baton Rouge: Louisiana State University Press, 1982.

De Credico, Mary A. *Patriotism for Profit: Georgia's Urban Entrepreneurs and the Confederate War Effort.* Chapel Hill: University of North Carolina Press, 1990.

Detzer, David. *Allegiance: Fort Sumter, Charleston, and the Beginning of the Civil War.* Boston: Mariner Books, 2002.

Dew, Charles B. *Apostles of Disunion: Southern Secession Commissioners and the Causes of the Civil War*. Charlottesville: University Press of Virginia, 2002.

———. *Ironmaker to the Confederacy: Joseph R. Anderson and the Tredegar Iron Works*. New Haven: Yale University Press, 1966.

Dolan, Jay P. *The Immigrant Church: New York's Irish and German Catholics, 1815–1865*. Notre Dame, IN: University of Notre Dame Press, 1992.

———. *In Search of American Catholicism: A History of Religion and Culture in Tension*. New York: Oxford University Press, 2003.

Donald, David Herbert. *Lincoln*. New York: Simon and Schuster, 1996.

Donnelly, James S., Jr., *Captain Rock: The Irish Agrarian Rebellion of 1821–1824*. Madison: University of Wisconsin Press, 2009.

Donnelly, Ralph W. *The Confederate Marine Corps: The Rebel Leathernecks*. Shippensburg, PA: White Mane Publishing, 1989.

Doyle, David N. *Ireland, Irishmen and Revolutionary America, 1760–1820*. Dublin: Mercier Press, 1981.

Drago, Edmund L. *Confederate Phoenix: Rebel Children and Their Families in South Carolina*. New York: Fordham University Press, 2008.

Drennan, William. *Fugitive Pieces in Verse and Prose*. Belfast, Ireland: F. D. Finlay, 1815.

Driver, Robert J., and Kevin Conley Ruffner. *1st Battalion Virginia Infantry, 39th Battalion Virginia Cavalry, 24th Battalion Virginia Partisan Rangers*. Lynchburg, VA: H. E. Howard, 1996.

Dubin, Michael. *United States Presidential Elections, 1788–1860: The Official Results by County and State*. Jefferson, NC: McFarland and Co., 2002.

Durkin, Joseph T., ed. *Confederate Chaplain: A War Journal by James B. Sheeran*. Milwaukee: Brice Publishing, 1960.

———. *John Dooley, Confederate Soldier: His War Journal*. Washington, DC: Georgetown University Press, 1945.

Dwan, David. *The Great Community: Culture and Nationalism in Ireland*. Dublin: Field Day, 2008.

Dyer, Thomas G. *Secret Yankees: The Union Circle in Confederate Atlanta*. Baltimore: Johns Hopkins University Press, 2001.

Edwards, Laura F. *Scarlett Doesn't Live Here Anymore: Southern Women in the Civil War Era*. Urbana: University of Illinois Press, 2000.

Egerton, Douglas R. *He Shall Go Out Free: The Lives of Denmark Vesey*. Lanham, MD: Rowman and Littlefield, 2004.

Ellis, Barbara G. *The Moving Appeal: Mr. McClanahan, Mrs. Dill, and the Civil War's Great Newspaper Run*. Macon, GA: Mercer University Press, 2003.

Emmet, Dan D. *I Wish I Was in Dixie's Land*. New York: Firth, Pond and Co., 1860.

Emmons, David M. *Beyond the American Pale: The Irish in the West, 1845–1920*. Norman: University of Oklahoma Press, 2010.

Escott, Paul D. *After Secession: Jefferson Davis and the Failure of Confederate Nationalism*. Baton Rouge: Louisiana State University Press, 1978.

———. *Military Necessity: Civil-Military Relations in the Confederacy*. Westport, CT: Greenwood Press, 2006.

Etheson, Nicole. *Bleeding Kansas: Contested Liberty in the Civil War Era*. Lawrence: University Press of Kansas, 2006.

Faherty, William Barnaby. *Exile in Erin: A Confederate Chaplain's Story; The Life of Father John B. Bannon*. St. Louis: Missouri Historical Society, 2002.

———. *The St. Louis Irish: An Unmatched Celtic Community*. St. Louis: Missouri Historical Society, 2001.

Fanning, Charles. *The Irish Voice in America: 250 Years of Irish-American Fiction*. 2nd ed. Lexington: University Press of Kentucky, 1999.

Farrell, Sean. *Ritual and Riots: Sectarian Violence in Ulster, 1798–1886*. Lexington: University Press of Kentucky, 2000.

Faust, Drew Gilpin. *The Creation of Confederate Nationalism: Ideology and Identity in the Civil War South*. Baton Rouge: Louisiana State University Press, 1989.

———. *Mothers of Invention: Women of the Slaveholding South in the American Civil War*. Chapel Hill: University of North Carolina Press, 1996.

———. *The Sacred Circle: The Dilemma of the Intellectual in the Old South*. Baltimore: Johns Hopkins University Press, 1977.

Fitzgerald, Michael W. *Urban Emancipation: Popular Politics in Reconstruction Mobile, 1860–1890*. Baton Rouge: Louisiana State University Press, 2002.

Fitzhugh, George. *Cannibals All!; or, Slaves without Masters*. Richmond, VA: A. Morris, 1857.

———. *Sociology for the South; or, The Failure of Free Society*. Richmond, VA: A. Morris, 1854.

Fogarty, Gerald P. *Commonwealth Catholicism: A History of the Catholic Church in Virginia*. Notre Dame, IN: University of Notre Dame Press, 2010.

Follett, Richard. *The Sugar Masters: Planters and Slaves in Louisiana's Cane World*. Baton Rouge: Louisiana State University Press, 2007.

Foner, Eric. *Free Soil, Free Labor, Free Men: The Ideology of the Republican Party before the Civil War*. New York: Oxford University Press, 1970.

———. *Reconstruction: America's Unfinished Revolution, 1863–1877*. New York: Harper and Row, 1988.

Forret, Jeff. *Race Relations at the Margins: Slaves and Poor Whites in the Antebellum Southern Countryside*. Baton Rouge: Louisiana State University Press, 2006.

Foster, Gaines M. *Ghosts of the Confederacy: Defeat, the Lost Cause and the Emergence of the New South, 1865–1913*. New York: Oxford University Press, 1988.

Fox, Stephen R. *Wolf of the Deep: Raphael Semmes and the Notorious Confederate Raider CSS Alabama*. New York: Alfred A. Knopf, 2004.

Fox-Genovese, Elizabeth, and Eugene D. Genovese. *The Mind of the Master Class: History and Faith in the Southern Slaveholders' Worldview*. Cambridge, MA: Harvard University Press, 2005.

———. *Slavery in Black and White: Class and Race in the Southern Slaveholders' New World Order*. New York: Cambridge University Press, 2008.

Franklin, John Hope. *The Militant South, 1800–1861*. Reprint. Urbana: University of Illinois Press, 2002.

Franklin, John Hope, and Loren Schweninger. *Runaway Slaves: Rebels on the Plantation*. New York: Oxford University Press, 2000.

Fraser, Walter J., Jr. *Charleston! Charleston!: The History of a Southern City*. Columbia: University of South Carolina Press, 1991.

Fredrickson, George M. *The Black Image in the White Mind: The Debate on Afro-American Character and Destiny, 1817–1914*. 2nd ed. Hanover, NH: University Press of New England, 1987.

Freehling, William W. *Prelude to Civil War: The Nullification Controversy in South Carolina, 1816–1836*. New York: Oxford University Press, 1992.

———. *The Road to Disunion*. 2 vols. New York: Oxford University Press, 1990, 2007.

———. *The South vs. the South: How Anti-Confederate Southerners Shaped the Course of the Civil War*. New York: Oxford University Press, 2001.

Fremantle, [Arthur Lyon]. *Three Months in the Southern States, April–June 1863*. New York: John Bradburn, 1864.

Gallagher, Gary W. *Causes Won, Lost, and Forgotten: How Hollywood and Popular Art Shape What We Know about the Civil War*. Chapel Hill: University of North Carolina Press, 2008.

———. *The Confederate War*. Cambridge, MA: Harvard University Press, 1997.

Gannon, James P. *Irish Rebels, Confederate Tigers: A History of the 6th Louisiana Volunteers*. Mason City, IA: Savas Publishing, 1998.

Gannon, Michael V. *Rebel Bishop: The Life and Era of Augustin Verot*. Milwaukee: Bruce Publishing, 1964.

Gaston, Paul M. *The New South Creed: A Study in Southern Mythmaking*. New York: Alfred A. Knopf. 1970.

Genovese, Eugene D. *A Consuming Fire: The Fall of the Confederacy in the Mind of the White Christian South*. Athens: University of Georgia Press, 1998.

———. *Roll, Jordan, Roll: The World the Slaves Made*. New York: Pantheon Books, 1974.

Gienapp, William E. *The Origins of the Republican Party, 1852–1856*. New York: Oxford University Press, 1987.

Glatthaar, Joseph T. *General Lee's Army: From Victory to Collapse*. New York: Free Press, 2008.

———. *Soldiering in the Army of Northern Virginia: A Statistical Portrait of the Troops Who Served under Robert E. Lee*. Chapel Hill: University of North Carolina Press, 2011.

Gleeson, David T. *The Irish in the South, 1815–1877*. Chapel Hill: University of North Carolina Press, 2001.

Gleeson, Ed. *Erin Go Gray!: An Irish Rebel Trilogy*. Indianapolis: Guild Press of Indiana, 1998.

———. *Rebel Sons of Erin: A Civil War Unit History of the Tenth Tennessee Infantry (Irish) Confederate States Volunteers*. Indianapolis: Emmis Publishing, 1993.

Goldsborough, W. W. *The Maryland Line in the Confederate Army, 1861–1865*. Baltimore: Guggenheimer, Weil and Co., 1900.

Gottfried, Bradley. *The Maps of First Bull Run: An Atlas of the First Bull Run (Manassas) Campaign, Including the Battle of Ball's Bluff*. New York: Savas Beatie, 2009.

Gower, Herschel, and Jack Allen, eds. *Pen and Sword: The Life and Journals of Randal W. McGavock*. Nashville: Tennessee Historical Commission, 1959.

Gray, Michael P. *The Business of Captivity: Elmira and Its Civil War Prison*. Kent, OH: Kent State University Press, 2001.

Hart, Peter. *The IRA and Its Enemies: The Revolution in Cork, 1916–1923.* New York: Oxford University Press, 1998.

Hearn, Chester G. *When the Devil Came Down to Dixie: Ben Butler in New Orleans.* Baton Rouge: Louisiana State University Press, 1997.

Hennesey, James. *American Catholics: A History of the Roman Catholic Community in the United States.* New York: Oxford University Press, 1983.

Hennessy, John J. *Return to Bull Run: The Campaign and Battle of Second Manassas.* Norman: University of Oklahoma Press, 1993.

Hernon, Joseph M., Jr. *Celts, Catholics, and Copperheads: Ireland Views the American Civil War.* Columbus: Ohio State University Press, 1968.

Hogan, Michael. *The Irish Soldiers of Mexico.* Guadalajara, Mexico: Fondo Editorial Universitado, 1997.

Hogue, James K. *Uncivil Wars: Five New Orleans Street Battles and the Rise and Fall of Reconstruction.* Baton Rouge: Louisiana State University Press, 2011.

Holden, Charles J. *In the Great Maelstrom: Conservatives in Post–Civil War South Carolina.* Columbia: University of South Carolina Press, 2002.

Hollandsworth, James G., Jr. *An Absolute Massacre: The New Orleans Riot of July 30, 1866.* Baton Rouge: Louisiana State University Press, 2001.

Holt, Michael F. *The Rise and Fall of the American Whig Party: Jacksonian Politics and the Onset of the Civil War.* New York: Oxford University Press, 2003.

Horigan, Michael. *Elmira: Death Camp of the North.* Mechanicsburg, PA: Stackpole Books, 2002.

Horsman, Reginald. *Josiah Nott of Mobile: Soldier, Physician, and Racial Theorist.* Baton Rouge: Louisiana State University Press, 1987.

Howe, Daniel Walker. *The Political Culture of American Whigs.* New York: Oxford University Press, 1984.

Hubbell, Jay B. *The South in American Literature, 1607–1900.* Durham: Duke University Press, 1959.

Ignatiev, Noel. *How the Irish Became White.* New York: Routledge, 1995.

Ireland, John de Courcy. *Ireland and the Irish in Maritime History.* Glendale, AZ: Glendale Publishing, 1985.

The Irish Volunteers Memorial Meeting and Military Hall Festival. October–November, 1877. Charleston, SC: The News and Courier Book and Job Presses, 1878.

Isbell, Timothy T. *Vicksburg: Sentinels in Stone.* Jackson: University Press of Mississippi, 2006.

James, D. Clayton. *Antebellum Natchez.* Baton Rouge: Louisiana State University Press, 1968.

Janney, Caroline E. *Burying the Dead but Not the Past: Ladies' Memorial Associations and the Lost Cause.* Chapel Hill: University of North Carolina Press, 2007.

Jenkins, Kirk C. *The Battle Rages Higher: The Union's Fifteenth Kentucky Infantry.* Lexington: University Press of Kentucky, 2003.

Johannsen, Robert. *Stephen A. Douglas.* Urbana: University of Illinois Press, 1997.

Johnson, Michael P. *Toward a Patriarchal Republic: The Secession of Georgia.* Baton Rouge: Louisiana State University Press, 1977.

Johnson, Michael P., and James L. Roark. *Black Masters: A Free Family of Color in the Old South*. New York: W. W. Norton, 1984.

Johnson, Vicki Vaughn. *The Men and the Vision of the Southern Commercial Conventions, 1845–1871*. Columbia: University of Missouri Press, 1992.

Jones, Howard. *Blue and Gray Diplomacy: A History of Union and Confederate Foreign Relations*. Chapel Hill: University of North Carolina Press, 2010.

Jones, Jacqueline. *Saving Savannah: The City and the Civil War*. New York: Alfred A. Knopf, 2008.

Jones, J. B. *A Rebel War Clerk's Diary at the Confederate States Capital*. Vol. 1. Philadelphia: J. B. Lippincott and Co., 1866.

Jones, Terry L. *Lee's Tigers: Louisiana Infantry in the Army of Northern Virginia*. Baton Rouge: Louisiana State University Press, 1987.

———, ed. *The Civil War Memoirs of Captain William J. Seymour: Reminiscences of a Louisiana Tiger*. Baton Rouge: Louisiana State University Press, 1997.

Joslyn, Mauriel Phillips, ed. *A Meteor Shining Brightly: Essays on Maj. Gen. Patrick R. Cleburne*. Milledgeville, GA: Terrell House Publishing, 1998.

Kantrowitz, Stephen. *Ben Tillman and the Reconstruction of White Supremacy*. Chapel Hill: University of North Carolina Press, 2000.

Keiley, A. M. *In Vinculis; or, The Prisoner of War: Being the Experience of a Rebel in Two Federal Pens Interspersed with Reminiscences of the Last War, Anecdotes of Southern Generals, etc.* Richmond, VA: West and Johnson, 1865.

Kemble, Fanny. *Journal of a Residence on a Georgia Plantation, 1838–39*. Edited by John A. Scott. Reprint. Athens: University of Georgia Press, 1984.

Keneally, Thomas. *The Great Shame and the Triumph of the Irish in the English-Speaking World*. New York: Doubleday, 1999.

Kenny, Kevin. *The American Irish: A History*. New York: Longman, 2000.

Kiberd, Declan. *Inventing Ireland: The Literature of the Modern Nation*. Cambridge, MA: Harvard University Press, 1997.

Kinealy, Christine. *This Great Calamity: The Irish Famine, 1845–1852*. Dublin: Gill and Macmillan, 1995.

Kinsella, Thomas, trans. *The "Táin": From the Irish Epic "Táin Bó Cúailnge."* New York: Oxford University Press, 1970.

Klein, Maury. *Days of Defiance: Sumter, Secession, and the Coming of the Civil War*. New York: Vintage Books, 1999.

Knight, Lucian Lamar. *Georgia's Markers, Memorials, and Legends*. Vol. 2. Atlanta: Byrd Printing, 1914.

Kohl, Lawrence F. *The Politics of Individualism: Party and the American Character in the Jacksonian Era*. New York: Oxford University Press, 1991.

Krick, Robert K. *Stonewall Jackson at Cedar Mountain*. Chapel Hill: University of North Carolina Press, 2001.

Lankford, Nelson D. *Cry Havoc!: The Crooked Road to Civil War, 1861*. New York: Penguin Viking, 2007.

Lenihan, Pádraig. *Consolidating Conquest: Ireland, 1603–1727*. New York: Longman, 2008.

Levine, Bruce. *Confederate Emancipation: Southern Plans to Free and Arm Slaves in the Civil War*. New York: Oxford University Press, 2007.

Linderman, Gerald F. *Embattled Courage: The Experience of Combat in the American Civil War*. New York: Free Press, 1987.

Linebaugh, Peter, and Marcus Rediker. *Many-Headed Hydra: Sailors, Slaves, Commoners and the Hidden History of the Revolutionary Atlantic*. Boston: Beacon Press, 2000.

Lockley, Timothy J. *Welfare and Charity in the Antebellum South*. Gainesville: University Press of Florida, 2007.

Lonn, Ella. *Foreigners in the Confederacy*. Chapel Hill: University of North Carolina Press, 1940.

Lott, Eric. *Love and Theft: Blackface, Minstrelsy, and the American Working Class*. New York: Oxford University Press, 1995.

Luriaghi, Raymond. *A History of the Confederate Navy*. Annapolis, MD: U.S. Naval Institute Press, 1996.

Lynch, James Daniel. *The Bench and Bar of Mississippi*. New York: E. J. Hale and Co., 1881.

Lynch, John Roy. *Reminiscences of an Active Life: The Autobiography of John Roy Lynch*. Edited by John Hope Franklin. Chicago: University of Chicago Press, 1970.

Macarthy, Harry. *The Bonnie Blue Flag: Composed, Arranged and Sung at Personation Concerts*. New Orleans: A. E. Blackmar and Bro., 1861.

MacDonagh, Oliver. *The Emancipist: Daniel O'Connell, 1830–1847*. New York: St. Martin's Press, 1991.

———. *The Hereditary Bondsman: Daniel O'Connell, 1775–1829*. New York: St. Martin's Press, 1987.

MacMahon, T. W. *Cause and Contrast: An Essay on the American Crisis*. Richmond, VA: West and Johnston, 1862.

Madden, Richard C. *Catholics in South Carolina: A Record*. Lanham, MD: University Press of America, 1985.

Magrath, A. G. *An Address Delivered in the Cathedral of St. Finbar before the Hibernian Society, St. Patrick's Benevolent Society, and Irish Volunteers on St. Patrick's Day, 1837*. Charleston, SC: Thomas J. Eccles, 1837.

———. *Executive Documents, Letter to the Collector, January 29, 1861*. Charleston, SC: Evans and Cogswell, 1861.

———. *Three Letters on the Order of the Know-Nothings Addressed to Hon. A. P. Butler*. Charleston, SC: A. J. Burke, 1855.

Maher, Mary Denis. *To Bind Up the Wounds: Catholic Sister Nurses in the U.S. Civil War*. Westport, CT: Greenwood Press, 1990.

Majewski, John. *Modernizing the Slave Economy: The Economic Vision of the Confederate Nation*. Chapel Hill: University of North Carolina Press, 2009.

Manning, Chandra. *What This Cruel War Was Over: Soldiers, Slavery, and the Civil War*. New York: Vintage Books, 2006.

Marshall, Anne E. *Creating a Confederate Kentucky: The Lost Cause and Civil War Memory in a Border State*. Chapel Hill: University of North Carolina Press, 2010.

Marszalek, John F. *Sherman: A Soldier's Passion for Order*. New York: Free Press, 1993.

Marvel, William. *Andersonville: The Last Depot*. Chapel Hill: University of North Carolina Press, 1994.

Massey, Mary Elizabeth. *Ersatz in the Confederacy: Shortages and Substitutes on the Southern Homefront*. Reprint. Columbia: University of South Carolina Press, 1993.

———. *Refugee Life in the Confederacy*. Reprint. Baton Rouge: Louisiana State University Press, 2001.

McCaffrey, Lawrence J. *Daniel O'Connell and the Repeal Year*. Lexington: University Press of Kentucky, 1982.

McCardell, John. *The Idea of a Southern Nation: Southern Nationalists and Southern Nationalism, 1830–1860*. New York: W. W. Norton, 1979.

McCarthy, Cal. *Green, Blue, and Grey: The Irish in the American Civil War*. Cork, Ireland: Collins Press, 2009.

McConnell, Stuart. *Glorious Contentment: The Grand Army of the Republic, 1865–1900*. Chapel Hill: University of North Carolina Press, 1992.

McCurry, Stephanie. *Confederate Reckoning: Power and Politics in the Civil War South*. Cambridge, MA: Harvard University Press, 2010.

———. *Masters of Small Worlds: Yeoman Households, Gender Relations, and the Political Culture of the Antebellum South Carolina Low Country*. New York: Oxford University Press, 1997.

McDonough, James Lee, and Thomas L. Connelly. *Five Tragic Hours: The Battle of Franklin*. Knoxville: University of Tennessee Press, 1983.

McGhee, James E. *Guide to Missouri Confederate Units, 1861–1865*. Fayetteville: University of Arkansas Press, 2008.

McGovern, Bryan P. *John Mitchel: Irish Nationalist, Southern Secessionist*. Knoxville: University of Tennessee Press, 2009.

McGreevy, John T. *Catholicism and American Freedom*. New York: W. W. Norton, 2003.

McKitrick, Eric L. *Andrew Johnson and Reconstruction*. Chicago: University of Chicago Press, 1960.

McPherson, James M. *Battle Cry of Freedom: The Civil War Era*. New York: Oxford University Press, 2003.

———. *For Cause and Comrades: Why Men Fought in the Civil War*. New York: Oxford University Press, 1997.

McWhiney, Grady. *Cracker Culture: Celtic Ways in the Old South*. Tuscaloosa: University of Alabama Press, 1989.

McWhiney, Grady, and Perry D. Jamieson, *Attack and Die: Civil War Military Tactics and Southern Heritage*. Tuscaloosa: University of Alabama Press, 1982.

Meade, Robert Douhat. *Judah P. Benjamin, Confederate Statesman*. Reprint. Baton Rouge: Louisiana State University Press, 2000.

Meagher, Timothy J. *Inventing Irish America: Generation, Class, and Ethnic Identity in a New England City, 1880–1928*. Notre Dame, IN: University of Notre Dame Press, 2000.

Miller, Kerby M. *Emigrants and Exiles: Ireland and the Irish Exodus to North America*. New York: Oxford University Press, 1985.

Miller, R. R. *Shamrock and Sword: The Saint Patrick's Battalion in the Mexican American War*. Norman: University of Oklahoma Press, 1989.

Mitchel, John. *Jail Journal*. Reprint. Dublin: M. H. Gill and Son, 1921.

———. *The Last Great Conquest of Ireland (Perhaps)*. Edited by Patrick Maume. Reprint. Dublin: University College Dublin Press, 2005.

Mitchell, Margaret. *Gone with the Wind*. New York: Macmillan, 1936.

Moore, John Hammond, ed. *The Juhl Letters to the "Charleston Courier": A View of the South, 1865–1871*. Athens: University of Georgia Press, 1974.

Morris, Charles. *American Catholic: The Saints and Sinners Who Built America's Most Powerful Church*. New York: Vintage Books, 1998.

Muller, Eric L. *Free to Die for Their Country: The Story of Japanese American Draft Resisters in World War II*. Chicago: University of Chicago Press, 2004.

Murphy, Angela. *American Slavery, Irish Freedom: Abolition, Immigrant Citizenship and the Transatlantic Movement for Irish Repeal*. Baton Rouge: Louisiana State University Press, 2010.

Murphy, Thomas. *Jesuit Slaveholding in Maryland, 1707–1838*. New York: Routledge, 2001.

Myers, Robert Manson, ed. *The Children of Pride: A True Story of Georgia and the Civil War*. New Haven, CT: Yale University Press.

Nash, Howard P. *Stormy Petrel: The Life and Times of General Benjamin F. Butler, 1818–1893*. Rutherford, NJ: Farleigh Dickinson University Press, 1969.

Nelson, Bruce. *Irish Nationalists and the Making of the Irish Race*. Princeton, NJ: Princeton University Press, 2012.

Neely, Mark E., Jr. *Southern Rights: Political Prisoners and the Myth of Confederate Constitutionalism*. Charlottesville: University Press of Virginia, 1999.

Niehaus, Earl F. *The Irish in New Orleans, 1800–1860*. Baton Rouge: Louisiana State University Press, 1956.

Noe, Kenneth W. *Perryville: This Grand Havoc of Battle*. Lexington: University Press of Kentucky, 2001.

———. *Reluctant Rebels: The Confederates Who Joined the Army after 1861*. Chapel Hill: University of North Carolina Press, 2010.

Nolan, Dick. *Benjamin Franklin Butler: The Damnedest Yankee*. Novato, CA: Presidio Press, 1991.

Noll, Mark A. *The Civil War as a Theological Crisis*. Chapel Hill: University of North Carolina Press, 2006.

Nystrom, Justin A. *New Orleans after the Civil War: Race, Politics and a New Birth of Freedom*. Baltimore: Johns Hopkins University Press, 2011.

Oates, Stephen B. *With Malice toward None: The Life of Abraham Lincoln*. New York: Penguin, 1977.

Oates, William Calvin. *The War between the Union and the Confederacy and Its Lost Opportunities*. Reprint. Dayton, OH: Morningside Books, 1985.

O'Brien, Sean Michael. *Irish Americans in the Confederate Army*. Jefferson, NC: McFarland and Co., 2007.

O'Carroll, Ciarán. *Paul Cardinal Cullen: Portrait of a Practical Nationalist*. Lancaster, PA: Veritas Press, 2009.

O'Connell, David. *Furl That Banner: The Life of Abram J. Ryan, Poet Priest of the South*. Macon, GA: Mercer University Press, 2006.

O'Connell, J. J. *Catholicity in the Carolinas and Georgia: Leaves of Its History*. Reprint. Spartanburg, SC: Reprint Co., 1972.

O'Connor, Rebecca. *Jenny Mitchel, Young Irelander: A Biography*. Tucson: O'Connor Trust, 1988.

O'Grady, Kelly J. *Clear the Confederate Way!: The Irish in the Army of Northern Virginia.* Mason City, IA: Savas, 2000.

Olsen, Christopher. *Political Culture and Secession in Mississippi: Masculinity, Honor, and the Antiparty Tradition, 1830–1860.* New York: Oxford University Press, 2002.

O'Reilly. Francis Augustin. *The Fredericksburg Campaign: Winter War on the Rappahannock.* Baton Rouge: Louisiana State University Press, 2003.

Ó'Siochrú, Micheál. *God's Executioner: Oliver Cromwell and the Conquest of Ireland.* New York: Faber and Faber, 2008.

Osterhaus, Carl R. *Partisans of the Southern Press, Editorial Spokesmen of the Nineteenth Century.* Lexington: University Press of Kentucky.

O'Toole, James M. *Passing for White: The Healy Family of Georgia, 1820–1920.* Amherst: University of Massachusetts Press, 2003.

Overdyke, W. Darrell. *The Know-Nothing Party in the South.* Baton Rouge: Louisiana State University Press, 1950.

Owsley, Frank. *Plain Folk of the Old South.* 1982. Reprint, with a new introduction by John Boles. Baton Rouge: Louisiana State University Press, 2008.

Parrish, T. Michael. *Richard Taylor: Soldier Prince of Dixie.* Chapel Hill: University of North Carolina Press, 1992.

Perdue, Howell, and Elizabeth Perdue. *Pat Cleburne, Confederate General.* Hillsboro, TX: Hill Junior College Press, 1973.

Perman, Michael. *The Road to Redemption: Southern Politics, 1869–1879.* Chapel Hill: University of North Carolina Press, 1984.

Phelps, W. Chris. *The Bombardment of Charleston, 1863–1865.* Gretna, LA: Pelican, 2002.

———. *Charlestonians at War: The Charleston Battalion.* Gretna, LA: Pelican, 2004.

Phillip, Christopher. *Damned Yankee: The Life of General Nathaniel Lyon.* Columbia: University of Missouri Press, 1990.

Pierson, Michael D. *Mutiny at Fort Jackson: The Untold Story of the Fall of New Orleans.* Chapel Hill: University of North Carolina Press, 2008.

Pillar, James J. *The Catholic Church in Mississippi, 1837–1865.* New Orleans: Hauser Press, 1964.

Price, Michael E. *Stories with a Moral: Literature and Society in Nineteenth-Century Georgia.* Athens: University of Georgia Press, 2000.

Quigley, Paul. *Shifting Ground: Nationalism and the American South, 1848–1865.* New York: Oxford University Press, 2012.

Quinlan, Kieran. *Strange Kin: Ireland and the American South.* Baton Rouge: Louisiana State University Press, 2005.

Rable, George C. *The Confederate Republic: A Revolution against Politics.* Chapel Hill: University of North Carolina Press, 1994.

———. *Fredericksburg! Fredericksburg!* Chapel Hill: University of North Carolina Press, 2002.

Radley, Kenneth. *Rebel Watchdog: The Confederate States Army Provost Guard.* Baton Rouge: Louisiana State University Press, 1989.

Ramon, Marta. *A Provisional Dictator: James Stephens and the Fenian Movement.* Dublin: University College Dublin Press, 2007.

Reilly, Tom. *Cromwell: An Honourable Enemy.* London: Weidenfeld and Nicolson, 2000.

Rhea, Gordon C. *Carrying the Flag: The Story of Private Charles Whilden, the Civil War's Most Unlikely Hero.* New York: Basic Books, 2005.

[Rix, William]. *Incidents of Life in a Southern City during the War: A Series of Sketches Written for the Rutland Herald by a Vermont Gentleman Who Was for Many Years a Prominent Merchant in Mobile.* Mobile: Privately published, 1880.

Robertson, James I., Jr. *General A. P. Hill: The Story of a Confederate Warrior.* New York: Vintage Books, 1992.

———. *Stonewall Jackson: The Man, the Soldier, the Legend.* New York: Macmillan 1997.

Robertson, William Glenn. *Backdoor to Richmond: The Bermuda Hundred Campaign, April–June 1864.* Baton Rouge: Louisiana State University Press, 1987.

Roediger, David R. *The Wages of Whiteness: Race and the Making of the American Working Class.* Reprint. New York: Verso Books, 2007.

Rogers, Thomas G. *Irish-American Units in the Civil War.* New York: Osprey, 2008.

Roland, Charles P. *The Confederacy.* Chicago: University of Chicago Press, 1960.

Rose, Willie Lee. *Rehearsal for Reconstruction: The Port Royal Experiment.* New York: Oxford University Press, 1964.

Rosen, Robert E. *The Jewish Confederates.* Columbia: University of South Carolina Press, 2000.

Rubin, Anne Sarah. *A Shattered Nation: The Rise and Fall of the Confederacy, 1861–1868.* Chapel Hill: University of North Carolina Press, 2005.

Ruffner, Kevin Conley. *Maryland's Blue and Gray: A Border State's Union and Confederate Junior Officer Corps.* Baton Rouge: Louisiana State University Press, 1997.

Samito, Christian G. *Becoming American under Fire: Irish Americans, African Americans, and the Politics of Citizenship during the Civil War Era.* Ithaca, NY: Cornell University Press, 2009.

Scally, Robert J. *The End of Hidden Ireland: Rebellion, Famine, and Emigration.* New York: Oxford University Press, 1995.

Scarborough, William Kauffman, ed. *The Diary of Edmund Ruffin: A Dream Shattered, June 1863–June 1865.* Baton Rouge: Louisiana State University Press, 1989.

Schott, Thomas E. *Alexander H. Stephens of Georgia: A Biography.* Baton Rouge: Louisiana State University Press, 1996.

Schrier, Arnold. *Ireland and the American Emigration, 1850–1900.* Reprint. Chester Springs, PA: Dufour Editions, 1997.

Schultz, April R. *Ethnicity on Parade: The Invention of the Norwegian American through Celebration.* Amherst: University of Massachusetts Press, 2009.

Sears, Stephen W. *George McClellan: The Young Napoleon.* New York: Da Capo, 1999.

———. *To the Gates of Richmond: The Peninsula Campaign.* New York: Houghton Mifflin, 2001.

Shaw, Richard. *Dagger John: The Unquiet Life and Times of Archbishop John Hughes of New York.* New York: Paulist Press, 1977.

Sheehan-Dean, Aaron. *Why Confederates Fought: Family and Nation in Civil War Virginia.* Chapel Hill: University of North Carolina Press, 2007.

Simpson, Craig M. *A Good Southerner: The Life of Henry A. Wise of Virginia.* Chapel Hill: University of North Carolina Press, 1985.

Simpson, Melissa. *Flannery O'Connor: A Biography*. Westport, CT: Greenwood Press, 2005.

Sinha, Manisha. *The Counter-Revolution of Slavery: Politics and Ideology in Antebellum South Carolina*. Chapel Hill: University of North Carolina Press, 2000.

Smith, Jean Edward. *Grant*. New York: Simon and Schuster, 2002.

Smyth, Thomas. *Autobiographical Notes, Letters and Reflections*. Edited by Louisa Cheves Stoney. Charleston, SC: Walker, Evans and Cogswell, 1914.

Snay, Mitchell. *Fenians, Freedmen and Southern Whites: Race and Nationality in the Era of Reconstruction*. Baton Rouge: Louisiana State University Press, 2007.

Sorensen, Ted. *Kennedy*. New York: Harper and Row, 1965.

Soule, Leon Cyprian. *The Know-Nothing Party in New Orleans: A Reappraisal*. Baton Rouge: Louisiana Historical Association, 1961.

Souvenir: Unveiling Soldiers' and Sailors' Monument. Richmond, VA: J. L. Hill Printing, 1894.

Spalding, Thomas W. *Martin John Spalding: American Churchman*. Washington, DC: Catholic University of America Press, 1973.

———. *The Premier See: A History of the Archdiocese of Baltimore, 1789–1994*. Baltimore: Johns Hopkins University Press, 1995.

Stephenson, Wendell Holmes. *Alexander Porter, Whig Planter of Old Louisiana*. Cambridge, MA: Da Capo Press, 1969.

Sterba, Christopher M. *Good Americans: Italian and Jewish Immigrants in the First World War*. New York: Oxford University Press, 2003.

Stevens, Patrick F. *The Rogue's March: John Riley and the St. Patrick's Battalion, 1846–1848*. Washington, DC: Potomac Books, 2005.

Still, William N. *The Confederate Navy: The Ships, Men, and Organization, 1861–65*. London: Conway Maritime Press, 1997.

Stout, Harry S. *Upon the Altar of the Nation: A Moral History of the Civil War*. New York: Penguin, 2007.

Symonds, Craig L. *Stonewall of the West: Patrick Cleburne and the Civil War*. Lawrence: University of Kansas Press, 1997.

Takaki, Ronald T. *A Pro-Slavery Crusade: The Agitation to Reopen the African Slave Trade*. New York: Free Press, 1971.

Taylor, John M. *Confederate Raider: Raphael Semmes of the Alabama*. Washington, DC: Brassey's, 1994.

Taylor, Richard. *Destruction and Reconstruction*. New York: D. Appleton and Co., 1879.

Taylor, William R. *Cavalier and Yankee: The Old South and American National Character*. Cambridge, MA: Harvard University Press, 1980.

Thomas, Emory M. *The Confederacy as a Revolutionary Experience*. Englewood Cliffs, NJ: Prentice Hall, 1971.

———. *The Confederate Nation, 1861–1865*. New York: Harper and Row, 1981.

Towers, Frank. *The Urban South and the Coming of the Civil War*. Charlottesville: University Press of Virginia, 2004.

Trefousse, Hans L. *Ben Butler: The South Called Him Beast*. New York: Twayne Publishers, 1957.

Trent, William Peterfield. *William Gilmore Simms*. Boston: Houghton Mifflin, 1892.

Tribute of Respect to the Memory of Their Late Distinguished Brother Member, the Right
Reverend Bishop England by the Hibernian Society of Charleston, South Carolina.
Charleston, SC: Hibernian Society, 1842.

Truxes, Thomas M. Irish-American Trade, 1660–1783. New York: Cambridge
University Press, 2004.

Tucker, Philip Thomas. The Confederacy's Fighting Chaplain: Father John B. Bannon.
Tuscaloosa: University of Alabama Press, 1992.

———. "God Help the Irish!": The History of the Irish Brigade. Abilene, TX: McWhiney
Foundation Press, 2007.

———. Irish Confederates: The Civil War's Forgotten Soldiers. Abilene, TX: McWhiney
Foundation Press, 2007.

The United States vs. William C. Corrie, Presentment for Piracy: Opinion of the Hon. A. G.
Magrath. Charleston, SC: S. G. Courtenay and Co., 1860.

Van Deusen, Glyndon G. William Henry Seward, Lincoln's Secretary of State: The
Negotiator of the Alaska Purchase. New York: Oxford University Press, 1967.

Varon, Elizabeth. Disunion: The Coming of the American Civil War, 1789–1859. Chapel
Hill: University of North Carolina Press, 2008.

Vaughan, W. E., and A. J. Fitzpatrick. Irish Historical Statistics: Population, 1821–1921.
Dublin: Royal Irish Academy, 1978.

Verot, Augustin. A Tract for the Times. Baltimore: John Murphy and Co., 1861.

———. A General Catechism on the Basis Adopted by the Plenary Council of Baltimore for the
Use of Catholics in the Confederate States of America. Augusta, GA: F. M. Singer, 1862.

Wade, Richard C. Slavery in the Cities: The South, 1820–1860. New York: Oxford
University Press, 1964.

Waldrep, Christopher. Roots of Disorder: Race and Criminal Justice in the American South,
1817–1880. Urbana: University of Illinois Press, 1998.

Walther, Eric H. The Fire-eaters. Baton Rouge: Louisiana State University Press,
1992.

———. William Lowndes Yancey and the Coming of the American Civil War. Chapel Hill:
University of North Carolina Press, 2006.

Watson, Ritchie Devon, Jr. Normans and Saxons: Southern Race Mythology and the
Intellectual History of the American Civil War. Baton Rouge: Louisiana State
University Press, 2008.

Wauchope, Piers. Patrick Sarsfield and the Williamite War. Dublin: Irish Academic
Press, 2009.

Weaver, Gordon, ed. Selected Poems of Father Ryan. Jackson: University Press of
Mississippi, 1973.

Wells, Jonathan Daniel. The Origins of the Southern Middle Class, 1800–1861. Chapel
Hill: University of North Carolina Press, 2004.

Wetherington, Mark. Plain Folk's Fight: The Civil War and Reconstruction in Piney Woods
Georgia. Chapel Hill: University of North Carolina Press, 2005.

Whelan, Kevin. The Tree of Liberty: Radicalism, Catholicism and the Construction of Irish
Identity, 1760–1830. Notre Dame, IN: University of Notre Dame Press, 1997.

Whites, LeeAnn. The Civil War as a Crisis in Gender: Augusta, Georgia, 1860–1890.
Athens: University of Georgia Press, 1995.

Whitwell, William. *The Heritage of Longwood*. Jackson: University Press of Mississippi, 1975.

Wiley, Bell I. *The Life of Johnny Reb: The Common Soldier of the Confederacy*. New York: Bobbs-Merill, 1951.

Williams, David. *A People's History of the Civil War: Struggles for the Meaning of Freedom*. New York: New Press, 2005.

Williams, David, Teresa Crisp Williams, and R. David Carlson. *Plain Folk in a Rich Man's War: Class and Dissent in Confederate Georgia*. Gainesville: University Press of Florida, 2002.

Williams, Donald M. *Shamrocks and Pluff Mud: A Glimpse of the Irish in the Southern City of Charleston, South Carolina*. Charleston, SC: Booksurge Publishing, 2005.

Williams, William H. A. *'Twas Only an Irishman's Dream: The Image of Ireland and the Irish in American Popular Song Lyrics, 1800–1920*. Urbana: University of Illinois Press, 1996.

Williamson, Joel. *After Slavery: The Negro in South Carolina during Reconstruction, 1861–1877*. Chapel Hill: University of North Carolina Press, 1965.

Wilson, Charles Reagan. *Baptized in Blood: The Religion of the Lost Cause, 1865–1920*. Athens: University of Georgia Press, 1980.

Wilson, David A. *United Irishmen, United States: Immigrant Radicals in the Early Republic*. Ithaca, NY: Cornell University Press, 1998.

Wilson, Harold S. *Confederate Industry: Manufacturers and Quartermasters in the Civil War*. Jackson: University Press of Mississippi, 2002.

Winter, William C. *The Civil War in St. Louis: A Guided Tour*. St. Louis: Missouri Historical Society Press, 1994.

Wise, Stephen R. *Lifeline of the Confederacy: Blockade Running during the Civil War*. Columbia: University of South Carolina Press, 1988.

Wish, Harvey, ed. *Antebellum Writings of George Fitzhugh and Hinton Rowan Helper on Slavery*. Cambridge, MA: Harvard University Press, 1960.

Woods, James M. *A History of the Catholic Church in the American South, 1513–1900*. Gainesville: University Press of Florida, 2011.

Woodward, C. Vann. *The Burden of Southern History*. 3rd ed. Baton Rouge: Louisiana State University Press, 1993.

———. *Origins of the New South, 1877–1913*. Baton Rouge: Louisiana State University Press, 1951.

———. *Tom Watson: Agrarian Rebel*. New York: Oxford University Press, 1963.

Wooster, Ralph A. *The Secession Conventions of the South*. Princeton, NJ: Princeton University Press, 1962.

Worthington, Curtis, ed. *Literary Charleston: A Lowcountry Reader*. Charleston, SC: Wyrick Publishing, 1996.

Wyatt-Brown, Bertram. *The Shaping of Southern Culture: Honor, Grace, and War, 1760s-1880s*. Chapel Hill: University of North Carolina Press, 2001.

———. *Southern Honor: Ethics and Behavior in the Old South*. New York: Oxford University Press, 1982.

Yuhl, Stephanie E. *A Golden Haze of Memory: The Making of Historic Charleston*. Chapel Hill: University of North Carolina Press, 2005.

Zanca, Kenneth J., ed. *American Catholics and Slavery, 1789–1866*. Lanham, MD: University Press of America, 1994.

Zuczek, Robert. *State of Rebellion: Reconstruction in South Carolina*. Columbia: University of South Carolina Press, 1996.

ARTICLES AND ESSAYS

Alvarez, David J. "The Papacy in the Diplomacy of the American Civil War." *Catholic Historical Review* 69 (April 1983): 227–48.

Arnesen, Eric. "Whiteness and the Historians' Imagination." *International Working Class and Labor History* 60 (2001): 3–32.

Bagby, Milton. "The Great Railroad Raid." *American History* 35 (August 2000): 36–44.

Bailey, Ann J. "Defiant Unionists: Militant Germans in Confederate Texas." In *Enemies of the Country: New Perspectives on Unionists in the Civil War South*, edited by John C. Inscoe and Robert C. Kenzer, 208–28. Athens: University of Georgia Press, 2001.

Baker, David L. "The Joyce Family Murders: Justice and Politics in Know-Nothing Louisville." *Register of the Kentucky Historical Society* 102 (Autumn 2004): 357–82.

Barr, Alwyn. "Texas Coastal Defenses, 1861–1865." *Southwestern Historical Quarterly* 65 (July 1961): 1–31.

Bartlett, Thomas, and Keith Jeffrey. "An Irish Military Tradition?" In *A Military History of Ireland*, edited by Thomas Bartlett and Keith Jeffrey, 1–6. New York: Cambridge University Press, 1996.

Bearss, Edwin C. "The Seizure of Forts and Federal Property in Louisiana." *Louisiana History* 2 (1961): 401–10.

Berends, Kurt O. "'Wholesome Reading Purifies and Elevates the Man': The Religious Military Press in the Confederacy." In *Religion and the American Civil War*, edited by Randall M. Miller, Harry S. Stout, and Charles Reagan Wilson, 131–66. New York: Oxford University Press, 1998.

Berlin, Ira, and Herbert Guttman. "Natives and Immigrants, Free Men and Slaves: Urban Workingmen in the Antebellum American South." *American Historical Review* 88 (December 1983): 1175–1200.

Berthoff, Rowland. "Celtic Mist over the South." *Journal of Southern History* 52 (November 1986): 523–46.

Bonner, Robert E. "Roundheaded Cavaliers?: The Context and Limits of the Confederate Racial Project." *Civil War History* 48 (March 2002): 34–59.

Bottigheimer, Karl S. "The Restoration Land Settlement in Ireland: A Structural View." *Irish Historical Studies* 18 (March 1972): 1–21.

Brady, Joe. "The Irish Community in Antebellum Memphis." *West Tennessee Historical Society Papers* 40 (December 1986): 24–44.

Brown, Katherine L. "United Irishmen in the South: A Reevaluation." In *Ulster Presbyterians in the Atlantic World*, edited by David A. Wilson and Mark G. Spencer, 87–103. Dublin: Four Courts Press, 2006.

Burns, Francis P. "St. Patrick's Hall and Its Predecessor, Odd Fellows Hall." *Louisiana History* 4 (Winter 1963): 73–83.

Callahan, Helen. "Patrick Walsh: Journalist, Politician, Statesman." *Richmond County History* 9 (Summer 1977): 14–29.

Chesson, Michael B. "Harlots or Heroines?: A New Look at the Richmond Bread Riot." *Virginia Magazine of History and Biography* 92 (April 1984): 131–75.

Childs, John. "The Williamite War, 1689–1691." In *A Military History of Ireland*, edited by Thomas Bartlett and Keith Jeffrey, 188–201. New York: Cambridge University Press, 1996.

Clark, Dennis. "The South's Irish Catholics: A Case of Cultural Confinement." In *Catholics in the Old South: Essays on Church and Culture*, edited by Randall M. Miller and Jon L. Wakelyn, 195–209. Macon, GA: Mercer University Press, 1983.

Cornish, Rory T. "An Irish Confederate: General Joseph Finegan of Florida." In *Confederate Generals of the Western Theater*, edited by Lawrence Lee Hewitt and Arthur W. Bergeron Jr., 3:179–220. Knoxville: University of Tennessee Press, 2011.

Crean, C. P. "The Irish Battalion of St. Patrick at the Defense of Spoleto, September 1860." *Irish Sword* 4 (1959–60): 52–60.

Crofts, Daniel W. "Late Antebellum Richmond Reconsidered." *Virginia Magazine of History of Biography* 107 (Summer 1999): 253–86.

Curran, R. Emmett. "'Splendid Poverty': Jesuit Slaveholding in Maryland, 1805–1838." In *Catholics in the Old South*, edited by Randall M. Miller and Jon L. Wakelyn, 125–46. Macon, GA: Mercer University Press, 1999.

Davis, Graham. "Making History: John Mitchel and the Great Famine." In *Irish Writing: Exile and Subversion*, edited by Pail Hyland and Neil Sammells, 98–115. London: Macmillan, 1991.

Dew, Charles B. "The Long Lost Returns: The Candidates and Their Totals in Louisiana's Secession Election." *Louisiana History* 10 (Autumn 1969): 353–69.

Duesner, Charles E. "The Know-Nothing Riots in Louisville." *Register of the Kentucky Historical Society* 61 (Summer 1963): 122–47.

Durrill, Wayne K. "Ritual, Community and War: Local Flag Presentations and Disunion in the Early Confederacy." *Journal of Social History* 39 (Summer 2006): 1105–22.

Dye, Renée. "A Sociology of the Civil War: Simms's *Paddy McGann*." *Southern Literary Journal* 28 (Spring 1996): 3–23.

Edmunds, Susan. "Through a Glass Darkly: Visions of Integrated Community in Flannery O'Connor's *Wise Blood*." *Contemporary Literature* 37 (Winter 1996): 559–85.

England, John. "Letters to the Hon. John Forsyth, on the Subject of Domestic Slavery." In *The Works of the Right Rev. John England, First Bishop of Charleston: Collected and Arranged under the Advice and Direction of His Immediate Successor, the Right Rev. Ignatius Aloysius Reynolds*. Volume 3, 106–91. Baltimore: John Murphy and Co., 1849.

Fanning, Charles. "Robert Emmet and Nineteenth-Century America." *New Hibernia Review* 8 (Dec. 2004): 53–83.

Faust, Drew Gilpin. "Christian Soldiers: The Meaning of Revival in the Confederate Army." *Journal of Southern History* 53 (Feb. 1987): 63–90.

———. "Altars of Sacrifice: Confederate Women and the Narrative of War." *Journal of American History* 76 (Mar. 1990): 1200–1228.

Fowler, John D. "'We can never live in a southern confederacy:' The Civil War in East Tennessee." In *Sister States, Enemy States: The Civil War in Kentucky and Tennessee*, edited by Kent T. Dollar, Larry Whiteaker, and W. Calvin Dickinson, 97–121. Lexington: University Press of Kentucky, 2009.

Gallagher, Charles R. "The Catholic Church, Martin Luther King Jr., and the March in St. Augustine." *Florida Historical Quarterly* 83 (Fall 2004): 149–72.

Gilligan, Paula. "'Fall in with the Major': Race, Nation, Class and the Confederate Irish." In *Screening Irish-America: Representing Irish Americans on Film and Television*, edited by Ruth Barton, 233–48. Dublin: Irish Academic Press, 2009.

Gleeson, David T. "Parallel Struggles: Irish Republicanism in the American South." *Éire-Ireland* 34 (Summer 1999): 97–116.

Gree, Jennifer R. "'Stout Chaps Who Can Bear the Distress': Young Men in Antebellum Military Academies." In *Southern Manhood: Perspectives on Masculinity in the Old South*, edited by Craig Thompson Friend and Lorri Glover, 174–95. Athens: University of Georgia Press, 2004.

Hamilton, Daniel W. "The Confederate Sequestration Act." *Civil War History* 52 (Dec. 2006): 373–408.

Haunton, Richard H. "Law and Order in Savannah, 1850–1860." *Georgia Historical Quarterly* 56 (Spring 1972): 1–24.

Hayes-McCoy, G. A. "The Irish Pike." *Journal of the Galway Archaeological and Historical Society* 20 (1943): 98–128.

Heisser, David C. R. "Bishop Lynch's Civil War Pamphlet on Slavery." *Catholic Historical Review* 84 (Oct. 1998): 681–96.

———. "Bishop Lynch's People: Slaveholding by a South Carolina Prelate." *South Carolina Historical Magazine* 103 (July 2001): 238–62.

Heisser, David C. R., ed. "A Few Words on the Domestic Slavery in the Confederate States by Patrick N. Lynch, Part I." *Avery Review* 2 (Spring 1999): 64–103.

———. "A Few Words on the Domestic Slavery in the Confederate States by Patrick N. Lynch, Part II." *Avery Review* 3 (Spring 2000): 93–123.

Hobsbawm, Eric. Introduction: "Inventing Traditions." In *The Invention of Tradition*, edited by Eric Hobsbawm and Terence Ranger, 1–14. New York: Cambridge University Press, 1992.

Hoy, Suellen. "The Journey Out: The Recruitment and Emigration of Irish Religious Women to the United States, 1812–1914." *Journal of Women's History* 6 (Winter–Spring 1995): 65–98.

Ireland, John de Courcy. "The Confederate states at sea in the American Civil War: the Irish Contribution." *The Irish Sword* 14 (Summer 1980): 73–94.

Johnson, Herbert. "The Constitutional Thought of William Johnson." *South Carolina Historical Magazine* 89 (July 1988): 132–44.

Johnson, Michael P. "A New Look at the Popular Vote for Delegates to the Georgia Secession Convention." *Georgia Historical Quarterly* 56 (Summer 1972): 259–76.

———. Review of *Cracker Culture: Celtic Ways in the Old South*, by Grady McWhiney. *Journal of Southern History* 55 (Aug. 1989): 488–90.

———. "Denmark Vesey and his Co-Conspirators." *William and Mary Quarterly* 58 (Oct. 2001): 915–76.

Jones, George Fenwick. "Sergeant Johann Wilhelm Jasper." *Georgia Historical Quarterly* 65 (Winter 1981): 7–15.

Jordan, Laylon P. "Schemes of Usefulness: Christopher Gustavus Memminger." In *Intellectual Life in Antebellum Charleston*, edited by Michael O'Brien and David Moltke Hansen, 211–29. Knoxville: University of Tennessee Press, 1986.

Joslyn, Mauriel Phillips. "'An Open Stand Up Affair': Cleburne's Defense at Ringgold Gap." In *A Meteor Shining Brightly: Essays on Maj. Gen. Patrick R. Cleburne*, edited by Mauriel Phillips Joslyn, 75–98. Milledgeville, GA: Terrell House Publishing, 1998.

———. "Epilogue." In *A Meteor Shining Brightly: Essays on Maj. Gen. Patrick R. Cleburne*, edited by Mauriel Phillips Joslyn, 183–98. Milledgeville, GA: Terrell House Publishing, 1998.

———. "Irish Beginnings." In *A Meteor Shining Brightly: Essays on Maj. Gen. Patrick R. Cleburne*, edited by Mauriel Phillips Joslyn, 1–17. Milledgeville, GA: Terrell House Publishing, 1998.

Kahane, Claire. "The Artificial Niggers." *Massachusetts Review* 19 (Spring 1978): 183–98.

Kelly, Joseph. "Charleston's Bishop England and American Slavery." *New Hibernia Review* 5 (Winter 2001): 48–56.

Kelly, Mary C. "A 'Sentinel of Our Liberties': Archbishop John Hughes and Irish Intellectual Negotiations on the Civil War Era." *Irish Studies Review* 18 (May 2010): 155–72.

Kimball, William J. "The Bread Riot in Richmond, 1863." *Civil War History* 7 (June 1961): 149–54.

Kolchin, Peter. "Whiteness Studies: The History of Race in America." *Journal of American History* 89 (June 2002): 154–73.

Lalli Anthony B. and Thomas H. O'Connor, "Roman Views on the American Civil War." *Catholic Historical Review* 57 (Apr. 1971): 21–41.

Larkin, Emmet. "The Devotional Revolution in Ireland, 1850–1875." *American Historical Review* 77 (June 1972): 625–52.

Lipscomb, Oscar Hugh. "The Administration of John Quinlan: Second Bishop of Mobile, 1859–1883." *Records of the American Catholic Historical Society of Philadelphia* 78 (Mar.–Dec. 1967): 1–163.

Lockley, Timothy J. "Trading Encounters between Non-Elite Whites and African Americans in Savannah, 1790–1860." *Journal of Southern History* 66 (Feb. 2000): 25–48.

Lynch, Niamh. "Defining Irish Nationalism and Anti-Imperialism, Thomas Davis and John Mitchel." *Éire-Ireland* 42 (Spring-Summer 2007): 82–107.

Mackey, Thomas C. "Not a Pariah, but a Keystone: Kentucky and Secession." In *Sister States, Enemy States: The Civil War in Kentucky and Tennessee*, edited by Kent T. Dollar, Larry Whiteaker, and W. Calvin Dickinson, 25–45. Lexington: University Press of Kentucky, 2009.

Manning, Diane T., and Perry Rodgers. "Desegregation of the New Orleans Public Schools." *Journal of Negro Education* 71 (Winter-Spring 2002): 31–42.

Marler, Scott P. "'An Abiding Faith in Cotton:' The Merchant Capitalist Community of New Orleans, 1860–1862." *Civil War History* 54 (Sept. 2008): 247–76.

Matthews, Gary R. "Beleaguered Loyalties: Kentucky Unionism." In *Sister States, Enemy States: The Civil War in Kentucky and Tennessee*, edited by Kent T. Dollar, Larry Whiteaker, and W. Calvin Dickinson, 9–24. Lexington: University Press of Kentucky, 2009.

Maume, Patrick. "Young Ireland, Arthur Griffith, and Republican Ideology: The Question of Continuity." *Éire-Ireland* 34 (Summer 1999): 155–74.

McCaffrey, Lawrence J. "Irish Textures in American Catholicism." *Catholic Historical Review* 78 (Jan. 1992): 1–18.

Meaney, Peter J. "The Prison Ministry of Father Peter Whelan, Georgia Priest and Confederate Chaplain." *Georgia Historical Quarterly* 71 (Spring 1987): 1–7.

Meenagh, Martin. "Archbishop John Hughes and the New York Schools Controversy of 1840–43. *American Nineteenth Century History* 5 (Spring 2004): 34–65.

Meneely, A. Howard. Review of *Foreigners in the Confederacy*, by Ella Lonn. *American Historical Review* 46 (Oct. 1940): 173–74.

Meyers, Arthur S. "Come Let Us Fly to Freedom's Sky: The Response of Irish Immigrants to Slavery in the Late Antebellum Period." *Journal of Southwest Georgia History* 7 (1989): 20–39.

Miller, Randall M. "Catholic Religion, Irish Ethnicity in the Civil War." In *Religion and the American Civil War*, edited by Randall M. Miller, Harry S. Stout and Charles Reagan Wilson, 261–96. New York: Oxford University Press, 1998.

———. "The Enemy Within: Some Effects of Foreign Immigrants on the Antebellum Southern Cities." *Southern Studies* 24 (Spring 1985): 30–53.

———. "Some Speculations on Catholic Identity in the Old South. In *Catholics in the Old South*, edited by Randall M. Miller and Jon L. Wakelyn, 11–52. Macon, Ga.: Mercer University Press, 1999.

Mitchell, Reid. "Christian Soldiers?: Perfecting the Confederacy." In *Religion and the American Civil War*, edited by Randall M. Miller, Harry S. Stout, and Charles Reagan Wilson, 297–311. New York: Oxford University Press, 1998.

Mittelbeeler, Emmet V. "The Aftermath of Louisville's Bloody Monday Election Riot of 1855." *Filson Historical Quarterly* 66 (Apr. 1992): 197–219.

Murtagh, Harman. "Irish Soldiers Abroad, 1600–1800." In *A Military History of Ireland*, edited by Thomas Bartlett and Keith Jeffrey, 294–314. New York: Cambridge University Press, 1996.

Nathan, Hans. "Dixie." *The Musical Quarterly* 35 (Jan. 1949): 60–84.

"Necrology of Virginia Historical Society." *Virginia Magazine of History and Biography* 2 (Apr. 1895): 435–36.

Nelson, Bruce. "'Come Out of Such a Land, You Irishmen': Daniel O'Connell, American Slavery, and the Making of the 'Irish Race.'" *Éire-Ireland* 42 (Spring/Summer 2007): 58–81.

Nicols-Belt, Tracy. "Chaplains in the Army of Tennessee: Warring Disciples Carrying the Gospel." *Tennessee Historical Quarterly* 63 (Dec. 2004): 232–49.

Ó'Buachalla, Breandán. "Irish Jacobitism and Irish Nationalism." In *Nations and Nationalism: France, Britain and Ireland in the Eighteenth Century Context*, edited by Michael O'Dea and Kevin Whelan, 103–18. Oxford, England: Voltaire Foundation, 1995.

O'Grady, Joseph P. "Anthony M. Keiley (1832–1905): Virginia's Catholic Politician." *Catholic Historical Review* 54 (Jan. 1969): 613–35.

Parks, Joseph H. "Memphis under Military Rule, 1862–1865." *East Tennessee Historical Society Publications* 14 (1942): 50–58.

Paquette, Robert L., and Douglas R. Egerton. "Of Fact and Fables: New Light on the Denmark Vesey Affair." *South Carolina Historical Magazine* 105 (Jan. 2004): 8–48.

Phillips, Christopher. "Calculated Confederate: Claiborne Fox Jackson and the Strategy of Secession in Missouri." *Missouri Historical Review* 94 (July 2000): 389–414.

Quinn, E. Moore. "'I have been trying *very hard* to be *powerful "nice"*': The Correspondence of Mother M. De Sales [Brennan] in the American Civil War." *Irish Studies Review* 18 (May 2010): 213–33.

Quinn, John F. "'Three Cheers for the Abolitionist Pope!': American Reaction to Gregory XVI's Condemnation of the Slave Trade, 1840–1860." *Catholic Historical Review* 90 (Jan. 2004): 67–93.

Robertson, James I., Jr. Review of *Attack and Die: Civil War Military Tactics and Southern Heritage*, by Grady McWhiney and Perry D. Jamieson. *Journal of Southern History* 49 (Feb. 1983): 128–29.

Roed, William. "Secession Strength in Missouri." *Missouri Historical Review* 72(July 1978): 412–23.

Rousey, Dennis C. "Aliens in the WASP Nest: Ethnocultural Diversity in the Antebellum Urban South." *Journal of American History* 79 (June 1992): 152–64.

———. "Friends and Foes of Slavery: Foreigners and Northerners in the Old South." *Journal of Social History* 35 (Winter 2001): 373–96.

Ruisi, Anne M. "Helena, Arkansas: Cleburne's Early Years in the South." In *A Meteor Shining Brightly: Essays on Maj. Gen. Patrick R. Cleburne*, edited by Mauriel Phillips Joslyn, 18–33. Milledgeville, Ga.: Terrell House Publishing, 1998.

Rutman, Darret B. "The War Crimes and Trial of Henry Wirz." *Civil War History* 6 (June 1960): 117–33.

Saunders, R. Frank Jr., and George Rogers. "Bishop John England of Charleston: Catholic Spokesman and Southern Intellectual, 1820–1842." *Journal of the Early Republic* 13 (Fall 1993): 311–22.

Schmidt, Raymond H. "An Overview of Institutional Establishments in the Antebellum Southern Church." In *Catholics in the Old South*, edited by Randall M. Miller and Jon L. Wakelyn, 53–76. Macon, Ga.,: Mercer University Press, 1999.

Sharrow, Walter G. "John Hughes and a Catholic Response to Slavery in Antebellum America." *Journal of Negro History* 57 (July 1972): 254–69.

Shaw, William L. "The Confederate Conscription and Exemption Acts." *American Journal of Legal History* 6 (Oct. 1962): 364–405.

Sigel, Fred. "Artisans and Immigrants in the Politics of Late Antebellum Georgia." *Civil War History* 27 (Sept. 1981): 21–30.

Silver, Christopher. "A New Look at Old South Urbanization: The Irish Worker in Charleston, South Carolina, 1840–1860." In *South Atlantic Urban Studies*, vol. 3, edited by Samuel M. Hines and others, 131–72. Columbia: University of South Carolina Press, 1977.

Simms, Kathleen. "Gaelic Warfare in the Middle Ages." In *A Military History of Ireland*, edited by Thomas Bartlett and Keith Jeffrey, 99–115. New York: Cambridge University Press, 1996.

Smith, Malcolm, and Donald M. MacRaild. "The Origins of the Irish in Northern England: An Isonymic Analysis of the 1881 Census." *Immigrants and Minorities* 27 (July–Nov. 2009): 152–77.

Smith, Tom. "The Image of Oliver Cromwell in Folklore and Tradition." *Folklore* 79 (Spring 1968): 17–39.

Spalding, David. "Martin John Spalding's 'Dissertation on the American Civil War.'" *Catholic Historical Review* 52 (1966–67): 66–85.

Spann, Edward K. "Union Green: The Irish Community in the Civil War." In *The New York Irish*, edited by Ronald H. Bayor and Timothy J. Meagher, 193–209. Baltimore: Johns Hopkins University Press, 1996.

Spiers, E. M. "Army Organization and Society in the Nineteenth Century." In *A Military History of Ireland*, edited by Thomas Bartlett and Keith Jeffrey, 335–57. New York: Cambridge University Press, 1996.

Sullivan, Kathleen. "Charleston, the Vesey conspiracy, and the Development of Police Power." In *Race and American Political Development*, edited by Joseph Lowndes, Julie Nokov, and Dorian T. Warren, 58–79. New York: Routledge, 2008.

Tarver, Jerry L. "The Political Clubs of New Orleans in the Presidential Election of 1860." *Louisiana Historical Quarterly* 4 (Spring 1963): 19–29.

Towers, Frank. "Violence as a Tool of Party Dominance: Election Riots and the Baltimore Know-Nothings, 1854–1860." *Maryland Historical Magazine* 93 (Spring 1998): 4–37.

———. "'A Vociferous Army of Howling Wolves': Baltimore's Civil War Riot of 1861." *Maryland Historian* 23 (Dec. 1992): 1–27.

Trevor-Roper, Hugh. "The Invention of Tradition: The Highland Tradition of Scotland." In *The Invention of Tradition*, edited by Eric Hobsbawm, 15–42. New York: Cambridge University Press, 1992.

Turpin, John. "Cúchulainn Lives On." *Circa* 69 (Autumn 1994): 26–31.

Wakelyn, Jon L. "Catholic Elites in the Slaveholding South." In *Catholics in the Old South*, edited by Randall M. Miller and Jon L. Wakelyn, 211–40. Macon, Ga.: Mercer University Press, 1999.

Werner, Randolph D. "The New South Creed and the Limits of Radicalism: Augusta, Georgia, before the 1890s." *Journal of Southern History* 67 (Aug. 2001): 573–600.

West, Emily. "'She is dissatisfied with her present condition': Requests for Voluntary Enslavement in the Antebellum American South." *Slavery and Abolition* 28 (Dec. 2007): 329–50.

Whites, LeeAnn "The Civil War as a Crisis in Gender." In *Divided Houses: Gender and the Civil War*, edited by Catherine Clinton and Nina Silber, 3–21. New York: Oxford University Press, 1992.

Wiecek, William W. "Slavery and Abolition before the United States Supreme Court." *Journal of American History* 65 (June 1978): 34–59.

Wight, Willard, ed. "Letters of the Bishop of Savannah, 1861–1865." *Georgia Historical Quarterly* 42 (Mar. 1952): 93–105.

Wiley, B. I. Review of *Foreigners in the Confederacy*, by Ella Lonn, *Journal of Southern History* 6 (Nov. 1940): 561–63.

Wooster, Ralph A. "The Florida Secession Convention." *Florida Historical Quarterly* 58 (Winter 1958): 373–85.

———. "The Louisiana Secession Convention." *Louisiana Historical Quarterly* 34 (Apr. 1951): 103–33.

NEWSPAPERS AND CONTEMPORARY PERIODICALS

Augusta (GA) Banner of the South

Augusta (GA) Pacificator

Baltimore Sun

Boston (MA)Liberator

Camden (SC) Confederate

Charleston (SC) Daily Courier

Charleston (SC) Irishman and Southern Democrat

Charleston (SC) Mercury

Charleston (SC) News and Courier

Charleston (SC) Tri-Weekly Courier

Charleston (SC) United States Catholic Miscellany

Charleston (SC) Weekly Courier

Chattanooga Daily Rebel

Cleveland (OH) Herald

Columbia Daily South Carolinian

The Commercial Review of the South and West

Confederate Veteran

Daily Richmond (VA) Enquirer

Daily Richmond (VA) Examiner

De Bow's Review

Fayetteville (NC) Observer

Frank Leslie's Illustrated News

Greenville (SC) Mountaineer

Houston (TX) Chronicle

Houston (TX) Post

Houston (TX) Tri-Weekly Telegraph

Jackson (MS) Daily Southern Crisis

Jackson Mississippian and State Gazette

Knoxville (TN) Southern Citizen

Little Rock Arkansas State Democrat

Macon (GA) Daily Telegraph

Memphis Daily Appeal

Milwaukee Daily Sentinel

Mobile Daily Advertiser and Register

Mobile Daily Register
Mobile Sunday Register
Natchez Evening Gazette
Natchez Mississippi Free Trader
Natchez Weekly Courier
New Orleans Daily Picayune
New Orleans Daily True Delta
New York Herald
New York Times
New York World
Petersburg (VA) Express
Richmond (VA) Daily Dispatch
Savannah (GA) Daily Herald
Savannah (GA) Daily Morning News
Savannah (GA) Republican
Southern Historical Society Papers
The Times (London)
Vicksburg American Citizen
Vicksburg Daily Herald
Vicksburg Daily Sentinel
Vicksburg Tri-Weekly Sentinel
Washington (DC) Daily National Intelligencer

INTERNET AND MEDIA RESOURCES

"1798 Memorial—The Bullring Wexford." Available at http:www.irishwarmemorials. iehtmlshowMemorial.php?show=101. Accessed Sept. 10, 2010.

Burns, Ken. The Civil War. DVD. PBS, 1990.

The Carlyle Letters Online, ed. Kenneth J. Fielding, vol. 23, available at http: carlyleletters. dukejournals.org cgi contentfull23. Accessed Jan. 21, 2008.

"Christ Church Savannah." Available at http:christchurchsavannah.orgHistory. htm. Accessed June 1, 2010.

"Confederate States of America—Inaugural Address of the President of the Provisional Government, Feb. 18, 1861." Available at http:avalon.law.yale. edu19th_centurycsa_csainau.asp. Accessed Sept. 10, 2010.

"General Index" Journal of the Congress of the Confederate States of America, 1861–1865. Available at http:memory.loc.govammemamlawlwcc.html. Accessed Aug. 21, 2010.

Gettysburg, DVD. Directed by Ronald F. Maxwell. Turner Home Entertainment, 1993.

Gods and Generals, DVD. Directed by Ronald F. Maxwell. Turner Pictures, 2003.

"James Alphonsus McMaster." Catholic Encyclopedia. Available http:www. newadvent.orgcathen09506a.htm. Accessed June 1 2010.

Kincaid, David The Irish American's Song: Songs of the Union and Confederate Irish Soldiers, 1861–1865, CD. Haunted Field Music, 2006.

———. "The Story Behind the Song: 'Kelly's Irish Brigade.'" Available at
   http:www.thewildgeese.compagesdkiram2.html. Accessed May 15, 2010.
Major Dundee, DVD. Directed by Sam Peckinpah. Sony Home Entertainment, 1965.
Robinson, Mary. "Cherishing the Irish Diaspora." Address to the Joint Sitting of
   the Houses of the Oireachtas, Feb. 2, 1995. Available at http:www.oireachtas.
   ieviewdoc.asp?fn=documentsaddresses2Feb1995.htm. Accessed Apr. 20, 2010.
Run of the Arrow, DVD. Directed by Samuel Fuller. Fox, 1957.
"Symbol of the New Ireland: Mary Robinson." *Time*, June 29, 1992. Available at
   http:www.time.comtimemagazinearticle0,9171,975888,00.html. Accessed Apr.
   20, 2010.

UNPUBLISHED MATERIALS

Boggs, Doyle W. "John Patrick Grace and the Politics of Reform in South Carolina,
   1900–1931." Ph.D. diss., University of South Carolina, 1977.
Brennan, Patrick. "Fever and Fists: Forging an Irish Legacy in New Orleans."
   Ph.D. diss., University of Missouri, 2003.
Buttimer, Brendan J. "New South, New Church: The Catholic Public Schools of
   Georgia, 1870–1917." M.A. thesis, Armstrong Atlantic State University, 2001.
Buttimer, James A. "'By Their Deeds, You Shall Know Them': Georgia's Sisters of
   Mercy." M.A. thesis, Armstrong Atlantic State University, 1999.
Campbell, Anne Francis. "Bishop England's Sisterhood, 1829–1929." Ph.D. diss.,
   St. Louis University, 1965.
Crowson, Brian Edward "Southern Port City Politics and the Know-Nothing Party
   in the 1850s." Ph.D. diss., University of Tennessee, 1994.
Hunt, Monica. "Savannah's Black and White Longshoremen, 1856–1897." M.A.
   thesis, Armstrong Atlantic State University, 1993.
McDowell, Robert E. "City in Conflict: A History of Louisville, 1860–1865." M.A.
   thesis, University of Kentucky, 1953.
Owsley, Stanley "The Irish in Louisville." M.A. thesis, University of Louisville,
   1974.
Rerucha, Caroline Margaret. "Recruiting in Ireland for the American Civil War."
   Ph.D. diss., Trinity College, Dublin University, 2000.
Seigle, Michael Damon. "Savannah's Own: The Irish Jasper Greens, 1842–1865."
   M.A. thesis, Armstrong Atlantic State University, 1994.
Shoemaker, Edward M. "Strangers and Citizens: The Irish Immigrant Community
   in Savannah, 1837–1861." Ph.D. diss., Emory University, 1990.
Strickland, Jeffrey G. "Ethnicity and Race in the Urban South: German Immigrants
   and African Americans in Charleston, South Carolina During Reconstruction."
   Ph.D. diss., Florida State University, 2003.
Thomas, Sam. "Irishmen Outside Phillip's Legion." Spreadsheet in possession of
   author.

Index

Ryan, J. J., 191
Ryan, Father Patrick, 167–68
Ryan, Thomas, 44–45, 66, 69–70
Ryan, William, 99–101, 207
Ryan's Slave Mart, 18

St. Louis, Mo., 152; Irish in/from, 35, 47, 52, 57–58, 63, 89, 92. *See also* Bannon, Father John
St. Patrick's Benevolent Society (Charleston), 6, 11, 38, 126, 201, 207
St. Vincent's Academy/Convent (Savannah), 112–13, 132, 175–78
San Patricio, Tex.: Irish in/from, 32
"San Patricios," 51–52
Sarsfield, Patrick, 42
Savannah, Ga., 13–14, 126–27, 189, 193; Irish in/from, 7, 12, 15, 28, 30–33, 39, 45, 47, 50–51, 52–53, 60, 112–14, 135, 138–39, 144–45, 147, 154, 166, 174–76, 191, 223–24. *See also* Hibernian Society: Savannah; O'Neill, Father Jeremiah, Sr.; St. Vincent's Academy/ Convent; Whelan, Father Peter
Scots-Irish, 5, 7, 17, 101, 103–4, 116
Secession: Irish and, 35–40, 152–53, 175; nonslaveholders and, 36–37
2nd Louisiana Infantry Regiment: Irish in, 47
2nd Maryland Light Artillery (CSA): Irish in, 55
2nd Tennessee (Walker's) Infantry Regiment: Irish in, 48, 104, 169, 212
Seminole War (1835–42), 6
Semmes, Raphael, 209
Seton, Saint Elizabeth Ann, 175
17th Virginia Infantry Regiment: Irish in, 48, 76
7th Louisiana Infantry Regiment: Irish in, 47, 52–53, 66, 109, 211
Seward, William Henry, 173–74, 188–89
Seymour, Isaac, 79
Seymour, William J., 110–11, 132
Shannon, J. J., 53
Shea, Michael, 90

Sheeran, Father James, 164–65, 167–68
Sheridan, Phil, 164, 197
Sherman, William T., 126–27, 147–48, 167, 184, 187, 192, 209
Shiloh, Battle of, 176
Simms, William Gilmore, 6–7
16th Mississippi Infantry Regiment: Irish in, 53
6th Louisiana Infantry Regiment: Irish in, 47, 49, 52, 59, 65–66, 69, 78–80, 84–85, 87, 88–90, 93, 100, 110, 192, 212. *See also* Monaghan, William; Strong, Henry
Skinner, Frank, 75
Slavery: Catholic Church in South and, 15, 25–26; Irish and, 10, 12, 16–19, 21–25, 69; Irish participation in, 17–18, 181–82; as motivation for Irish Confederate patriotism, 93–96, 115–17, 125–26
Slidell, John, 13, 33–35
Smyth, Thomas, 67, 150
Songs: Irish Confederate, 70, 133–34, 251 (n. 61)
Southern Claims Commission, 192–93
Spalding, Archbishop Martin, 161–62, 182–83, 188
Sparrow, Edward, 40, 127–28, 191
Spellman, Dominick, 1–3, 4, 6, 9, 85, 89, 97, 109, 189, 206–7
Spotsylvania, Battle of: Irish Confederates in, 100
Strong, Henry, 46, 66, 69, 78, 89, 106–7, 238 (n. 16)
Substitution. *See* Conscription
Sullivan, Dan, 211
Sullivan, Eugene, 135
Sullivan, John, 198
Swift, Jonathan, 116

Taylor, Richard, 78–80
Teeling, Father John, 159
Telfair, Edward, 52
10th Louisiana Infantry: Irish in, 49, 104

Confederates in, 78–79, 85

Wise, Henry S., 14

Women, Irish, 173, 200; and bread riots, 143–44; and Confederate industry, 136; and Confederate patriotism, 111, 112–14, 132, 139–40, 142, 146, 148, 201–2, 218–19. *See also* Free Markets; Nuns

Yancey, William Lowndes, 14, 46, 234 (n. 37)

Young Ireland, 19, 118, 133, 172

Yorktown, Battle of: Irish Confederates in, 76

Yulee, David, 40, 101